NAMIBIA OLD AND NEW

NAMIBIA
OLD AND NEW

*Traditional and Modern Leaders
in Ovamboland*

BY

GERHARD TÖTEMEYER

ST. MARTIN'S PRESS · NEW YORK

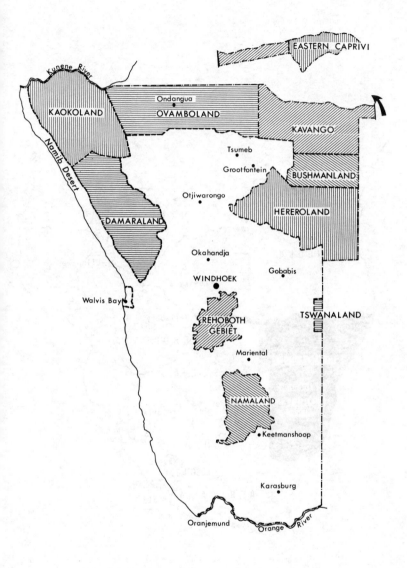

Namibia (South West Africa)

Institute of Cartography, University of Stellenbosch

Southern Africa

Institute of Cartography, University of Stellenbosch

ACKNOWLEDGEMENTS

In the preparation of this book the author has received significant help and co-operation from a very large number of sources, public and private. It is impossible to mention all these sources by name, but my thanks are due to all who, through their knowledge, encouragement and financial support, contributed to my research in Ovamboland and in writing this book. Grants were made by the Harry Crossley and Dirkie Uys Bursary Funds, the Council for Scientific Research and the Fund for Scientific Research of the University of Stellenbosch.

This book represents an updated elaboration of my thesis (in Afrikaans) presented for the degree of Doctor of Philosophy at the University of Stellenbosch in 1974, entitled "Die Rol van die Wambo-Elites in die Politieke Ontwikkeling van Owambo". The theoretical part of the thesis has been omitted in the book. Special thanks are due to the promoter of the thesis, Professor W. B. Vosloo, head of the Department of Political Science and Public Administration, University of Stellenbosch.

I am also greatly obliged to the South African Institute of International Affairs, with whose co-operation this book is published. Finally, I would like to thank my publisher, Mr Christopher Hurst, for his valuable assistance in preparing the manuscript for publication.

Stellenbosch, December 1977   G.T.

CONTENTS

Contents

MAPS

FOREWORD

Ovamboland, the most northerly part of Namibia, has become a focus of international political activity. Apart from containing the largest single population group—nearly half the total population of Namibia—it has recently become an active military zone following the decolonization of Angola and coming to power of the MPLA. These events have also influenced political developments in Ovamboland and the rest of Namibia.

The serenity which characterized the development of Ovamboland until the 1950s has become a thing of the past. Since it was chosen by the South African Government in the 1960s as a model of its Homelands policy in Namibia, new developments—and conflicts—have become apparent there.

One such conflict, which has never ceased to be intense, is that being waged between the supporters of the traditional system in Ovamboland, who see the area as a separate entity, and those who see the territory's future as an integral part of a united Namibia. This struggle is being waged especially between the traditional leaders and their supporters on the one hand, and the new, modernizing leaders and their supporters on the other. The conflict in Ovamboland reflects in microcosm the one that is occuring in Namibia on a larger scale.

Ovambos were among the first to provide leadership in the awakening of political consciousness in Ovamboland and the rest of Namibia. The South West Africa People's Organization (SWAPO) originated within the cadre of Ovambo workers who were employed outside Ovamboland and who accused the Whites of exploiting their labour, and it has become the most important national political organization in Namibia. As well as their contribution in the secular field, the Ovambos have given religious leadership as well: the Evangelical Lutheran Ovambokavango Church has become the first indigenous black independent church in Namibia and is the strongest single church in the territory, overshadowing the longer-established churches. This Church has an influence at all levels of society. The majority of the population of Ovamboland are members, and, next to SWAPO, it has become the principal channel for those who feel dissatisfied, exploited, oppressed or neglected. The trust and credibility which this church has built up within the community makes it an important instrument in the development process of Namibia. The growth of Black consciousness, the search for a Black identity, the awareness of the resourcefulness of Black power and the formation of their own Black theology has found substance within the Ovambokavango Church, with repercussions throughout Namibia.

ix

International pressure upon South Africa, especially following upon recent UN Resolutions, to abandon and relinquish her control of Namibia has led to the search for new forms of communal development and the establishment of a new political order. SWAPO's emphasis on communalism and a unitary state has been rejected by the South African Government and by the White authorities in Namibia. This standpoint has been fully endorsed by a Constitutional Conference in Namibia, composed on an ethnic basis, convened in 1975 to decide on the constitutional future of the country. This body accepted ethnicity as the basis of power sharing and power allocation; hence Ovamboland was assured of continuing as a Homeland, with its existing system of government. This led to a new crisis in Ovamboland and Namibia. The new "deal" proposed by the Constitutional Conference has intensified the critical attitude of Black modernizing and leadership groups. The deep desire for an ethnically undivided unitary state of Namibia has thus increased.

The dissatisfaction among the population has led to a renewed sense of the importance of Ovamboland's future. It is often asked what forces are going to play the most important role in the future Ovamboland, at what political cost South Africa can maintain its military presence and task force in Ovamboland, whether the traditional authority can maintain itself without White protection, and what will be the consequences for Ovamboland if SWAPO takes over Namibia?

This book will discuss these and other problems relating to the development process of Ovamboland and Namibia and attempt to provide a clearer understanding of them. It also indicates possible means of preventing a full confrontation between the traditional and the new modernizing forces, and between Black and White.

A final word should be said about the author's method of investigation. In common with most investigators of political and social phenomena, he devised a series of fundamental questions and submitted these to representatives of the various élite groups of Ovamboland—traditional, modern and in-between—and of Ovambos resident in Katutura, a township of Windhoek, Namibia's capital. At certain points in this book, from page 58 onwards, the answers to particular questions are presented, within the narrative, in a standard tabular form. The author is convinced that the reader will be helped by the sense of immediacy conveyed by these "raw" findings.

I

THE COUNTRY, THE PEOPLE
AND THE TRADITIONAL ORDER

1. *Geography*

Ovamboland is in the most northerly part of Namibia, being bounded on the north by Angola, in the east by Kavango, in the south by the Etosha Game Reserve and in the west by the Kaokoveld. The first provisional border with any sort of international character was decided on by a treaty between England and Portugal in 1815, confirmed by both governments two years later, whereby the 18th degree of latitude would form the southern boundary of Angola and the northern boundary of Ovamboland. This frontier passed through the middle of present-day Ovamboland.

The reason for the treaty was England's increasing interest in the area north of Namaqualand and in the hinterland of Walvis Bay. Her special commissioner, W. Coates Palgrave, attempted to annex portions of the present Namibia. Meanwhile Germany's interest in the territory was also growing, and she and Portugal entered into a convention on 30 December 1886, which laid down that the boundary separating the Portuguese and German possessions in Namibia would run from the mouth of the River Kunene up to the cataracts formed south of Humbe by the junction of the Serra Lana and Kunene Rivers. From this point the boundary would run parallel with the latitude (meridian) up to the Kubango River, now the Okavango. Then it would follow the course of this river as far as the town of Andara, and from there in a direct line to the rapids of Catima (Katima Mulilo) on the Zambesi.[1] However, that convention, which divided the Kwanyama tribal area into two, was not yet a final demarcation of frontiers, but rather a splitting up of German and Portuguese spheres of interest.[2]

The boundary line was open to various interpretations. The resultant uncertainty was further aggravated because, since neither power erected border posts, the border remained very fluid. The western, southern and eastern boundaries of Ovamboland were defined in a decree of the German Governor of South West Africa on 25 January 1906. The western boundary ran from Zwartbooi Drift on the Kunene to the junction with 18°30' latitude in the vicinity of Ongandura. The southern boundary began here and went straight to the junction with 17°30' longitude, which formed the eastern boundary.[3] These frontiers, too, were not final, and were altered in course of time.

The biggest bone of contention was the northern border, over which a difference of opinion later arose concerning which falls on the Kunene were specified in the 1886 agreement. In consequence there was a disputed strip from the Kunene to the Okavango.[4] In 1926 the Ruacana Falls were accepted as the border point, as the result of a joint commission between South Africa and Portugal. Then in 1928 the common northern frontier was moved seven miles southwards through international arbitration. In this way several tribal areas lost considerable stretches of land, and many Kwanyamas and Kwambis left their erstwhile residential and grazing areas and trekked southwards to areas under South African control. The last territorial adjustment was made in the form of an addition in the south resulting from the recommendations of the Odendaal Report in 1964.

The Ovamboland of today is situated between the fourteenth and eighteenth degrees of longitude east and between 17°20′ and 18°40′ of latitude south, the total area covering about 56,072 sq. km. or slightly less than one-sixteenth of the entire area of Namibia.[5] During the session of the Legislative Council in 1974, the Ovamboland Government was asked to do its utmost to have the northern border moved back to its original position, i.e. as it was before the partitioning between the German and Portuguese Governments in 1886, with the object of reuniting the Kwanyamas and Kwambis. In 1976 the Chief Minister of Ovamboland, the Rev. K. Ndjoba, pointed out "that the historical borders of the Ovambo nation include the Kaokoveld, the Etosha Pan and the surrounding area down to a southern line running from Kamanjab to Otavi and Grootfontein, including Tsumeb, which is seen as the traditional port to Ovamboland".[6a]

Except for the hilly and well-wooded country in the north-west and in the environs of Ruacana, the land of Ovamboland as a portion of the Central African plain is characterized by level Kalahari sand flats, situated at an average of 1,000 metres above sea level. The overall impression of Ovamboland is of an entirely even landscape with palm trees and baobabs. The ground descends gradually to the Etosha Pan.[6]

The climate is sub-tropical with annual rainfall varying from 400 to 600 mm., mainly between December and March.[7] Droughts occur periodically. Humidity averages 50 per cent, rising from 30 per cent in September to 70 per cent in March.[8] The mean annual temperature, which rarely falls below freezing-point, is 22.5° C.

Because of the flatness of the terrain, Ovamboland has no perennial rivers, though the whole area is covered with a network of *oshanas*, which can be described as pans (or depressions) filled with water that cannot flow away, partly through the absence of steep slopes.[9] Apart from rain, the *oshanas* are fed by rivers that rise in the highlands of Angola. In the north they are watered by tributaries of the Kavango, and in the north-west by those of the Kunene. The most important river, the Cuvelai, sometimes overflows from northern Ovamboland and covers the *oshanas*, whence it drains off gradually to the Etosha Pan.

2. *The Ovambos: Ethnic Origins and Composition*

There are conflicting opinions on the origin of the Ovambos and how long they have already been settled in their present territory. For example, it is disputed whether they or the Kavangos were the first Bantu groups to be established in Namibia. With the exception of Arden-Clarke and Tyrrell, most ethnologists agree that the Ovambos have lived in Ovamboland at least since the mid-sixteenth century.[10]

According to the ethnologist J. P. Bruwer, they originated in the matriarchal population belt of Central Africa, migrating to their present area in the fifteenth century. They lived on the banks of an unidentified lake in the Rift Valley of Central Africa, where there are still tribes north of the Zambezi that show ethnic resemblances to the Ovambos, and who have been found in those parts since the Middle Ages.[11]

The Ovambos themselves have three legends concerning their origins. According to one, they had three ancestors—Amangundu, Kantene and Omungandjera. Amangundu and his wife were created by God, who struck an ant-heap with a stick. A hole appeared and He commanded them to come forth. Two people emerged, a man and a woman, and the man's name was Amangundu. The woman became pregnant and gave birth to a son, who was named Kanzi by his father. Subsequently another son was born, whom his father called Nangombe and then the woman had a daughter.[12]

An obvious variation of this myth tells us that Kalunga, the supreme divine being of the Ovambo, brought forth a man and a woman out of the earth. In contrast to the previous story, the man was called Noni, the bearer of the spear, who had four children—three sons and a daughter. The eldest son's name was "the cattle-man", who had to breed the cattle and tend them. The second son was called "the man of the soil", and his task was to sow; while the third son was named "the man of the fire", as it was his job to watch the fire and the sheep. The daughter, known as "Janoni", was to become the ancestral mother.[13] This highly symbolic tale reflects the activities, the religion—Kalunga and the holy fire—and the matriarchal order of the Ovambos.

Another legend records that the Herero and Ovambo peoples had two ancestral fathers who were brothers, Nangombe and Kathu, whose common father was Nangombe Ya Mungundu. Together the brothers journeyed southwards from the upper reaches of the Zambezi[14] until they came to a large omomborombonga tree in the Ondonga district, where they went their separate ways. Kathu trekked further with his herds of cattle, first going westwards to the Kaokoveld. Some of his party, the Ovahimbas, stayed there, while he travelled on southwards with the remainder. In the meantime Nangombe and his followers remained behind as farmers on the plains of what is now Ovamboland.[15]

It has not yet been proved whether the third of these traditional tales can be accepted as valid. It is, however, worth noting that the founding father's name, Amangundu, also known by its variant, Ya Mungundu, is often referred to in narratives. It is noteworthy, too, that the son of Amangundu, Nangombe, is mentioned in two of the legends and regarded as the actual progenitor of the Ovambos.[16]

It can be assumed that the Kavangos and the Ovambos, coming as a joint group from the east, first migrated southwards and thereafter westwards past the headwaters of the Zambezi, to the bank of the Okavango River. They were evidently led by two sisters. The Kavangos stayed on the banks of the Okavango, while the Ovambos moved further west to the grassy plains with their *Oshanas*, where they were to establish themselves as tillers of the soil and cattle farmers.[17] The only inhabitants of this region were small bands of Bushmen.

Tradition has it that the Ovambos here split up into different groups. One, under the leadership of Paramount Chief Sitenue, settled on the Kunene near the place where the river turns in a westerly direction. Vedder estimates their arrival there in about 1550. He probably refers here to the tribes (with whom there is a close kinship), who would finally gravitate to present-day Angola.

The second group, led by Kambungo, trekked to a lake or pan in the interior called Hakafia. It divided a second time, half its members accompanying Kambungo to a place in the neighbourhood of the only rock in Ovamboland, where the main kraal was built. The other half of the group with one exception did not stay long at Hakafia. It had a number of leaders, who included Hamakuambi, Hamungandjera and Omundongo. Of the tribes existing today, the Kwambi, the Ngandjera and the Ndonga still bear the names of their leaders, of whom the first to depart with his following was Kanene. Because of the innumerable cattle they took with them, they were called Ovakwanyama (the meat-eaters). Another explanation for the origin of the name is that these Ovambo went to a tract of territory abounding in game, with the result that they abandoned their mainly meatless diet and became flesh-eaters.

A further body, headed by Hamungandjera, trekked from Hakafia and proceeded west to their present home. He was to become the first paramount chief of the Ngandjera tribe (=ironmongers). The Kwaluudhi broke away from this group and in course of time formed their own tribe with their own tribal area.

Hamakuambi and his people (=potters), who were to take up their abode in the present homeland of Kwambi, were the last group to leave Hakafia. The sole group that remained behind, known as the mother-group, was that of Omundongo and his followers; this was to form the Ndonga tribe, with Omundongo as its first paramount chief.[18] Bruwer regards the Ndonga as the nucleus of all Ovambo tribes, because all heads of the other Ovambo races traditionally received their power from the paramount chief of the Ndonga.[19] The Mbalantus (=people of the ruling house) and the Kolonkhadhi-Eunda (=those who live on the left) hived off from the Ndonga tribe.

Two schools of thought exist on the derivation of the name Ovambo. These maintain respectively that they originate from the Ovambo and the Herero languages. The first of these views (held by Hugo Hahn) was that it was derived from *Ova-mbo* or *Oyoambo* which means "they over there". Hahn later changed his opinion, asserting that the root of the word, *mbo*, is connected with *egumbo* meaning "fixed abode or dwelling", to distinguish them from the Bushmen who lived in primitive huts. Galton supported his theory,[20] but both opinions sound questionable.

The alternative view that the word originates from the Herero language is more convincing. Schinz believes that the word "Ovambo" was taken from the Ovaherero, of which the root was not *mbo* but *jamba*. The

Omuherero called the Ovambo *Ajamba, Ayamba* or *Ovajamba*. It means "the rich" as distinct from the *Aashimba* or *ovatjimba* (*Ovahimba*), which stands for "poverty". Ovambo gradually developed from *Ovajamba*.[21] Schinz's arguments are supported by Bruwer and by Himmelreich. Bruwer states that when the Ovambos settled in their present area, they were known as *Ajamba* (*Ayamba, Aayamba, Ovajamba*), a name later used by the Hereros to refer to them. Himmelreich also interprets this name as "the rich".[22]

That the word originates from the Herero tongue, is still the most acceptable explanation. This view is shared by Andersson, the first white traveller to Ovamboland, who evidently learnt the word from the Hereros. He uses it in the spelling *Ovambo* and/or *Ovampo* as a derivative of Ovambo (plural) or *omuambo* (singular).[23] The most authoritative backing comes from H. Tönjes, who identifies Ovambo as a creation of the Hereros, but does not give an explanation of the word.[24] The meaning thus remains obscure, although "the rich" seems to be the most likely interpretation.

Already in the nineteenth century Andersson described the Ovambos as handsome people, whose appearance was not really negroid.[26] His conclusion is borne out by Galloway's somatometric tests according to which the Ovambo on the average are big and strong. Six facial types are encountered—Negroid, Bushman, Mediterranean, Armenoid, Mongoloid and "Boskop". The torso is narrower and the skin colour darker than in the South African Bantu.[26]

Schinz points out that their facial features reveal every possible shape from "European" to Negro.[27] He is supported here by L. G. Green who says that their fine features are not usual in the natives of Southern Africa, but appear rather to be a feature of the Semitic nations, suggesting Egypt as the Ovambos' possible country of origin.[28] Loeb refers to the Ovambos (specifically the Kwanyama) as an "enclave of ancient Mediterranean survival".[29]

These hypotheses are speculative, but it is striking that the Ovambos do not have a typical or uniform appearance, but reveal the influence of non-Bantu groups, including Bushmen. Yet in every instance the predominant traits are those of the Bantu group.

The Ovambo consist of seven main tribes—the Ndonga, Kwanyama, Kwambi, Ngandjera, Mbalantu, Kwaluudhi and the Kolonkadhi-Eunda. Roughly 1,000 Khung—and Heikom-Bushmen are also to be found in Ovamboland,[30] mostly in the south-west. Groups of Herero descendants live in the Kolonkadhi-Eunda tribal area.

The Kolonkadhi-Eunda dwell in the westernmost region bordering on the Kaokoveld, and the Kwaluudhi live adjacent to them on the eastern side. To the north-east of the Kwaluudhi on the northern frontier lies the home of the Mbalantu, and south of them are the Ngandjara. The Kwambi are the most centrally situated group, the Ndonga the most easterly. Northwards of the Ndonga is the home of the most populous tribe, the Kwanyama, who are divided by the northern border with Angola. They are the only tribe who do not live exclusively in Ovamboland apart from five other related, mainly small, Ambo tribes established in Angola—the Ohashima, Ombandja, Ehanda, Kwamato, and Evale. According to

Redinha (1960), altogether 62,141 people belonging to the Ambo tribes live in Angola. Official Portuguese sources, however, quoted a total of 115,442 in 1960, which included the Evale, (Ohas) Hima, Kwamato and Kwanyama.[31] Since the outbreak of widespread fighting in Angola in 1974, large numbers of Angolan Ambos, among them members of the Kwanyama tribe, have fled to Ovambo.

Each tribe in Ovamboland functions as a separate entity in its own defined territory. The various dialects which are spoken all form part of the same tongue, the two related indigenous languages being Oshindonga and Oshikwanyama, which are also written languages.

Reliable statistics on the analysis of the Ovambo tribes have only been available since the population census in 1960. All the other numbers quoted in Table 1 are based on estimates that sometimes vary considerably, but the Table shows the growth of the Ovambo tribes over nearly 100 years.

Some of the tribal areas are more densely populated than others, the largest concentration being in the Ndonga and Kwanyama areas. As long ago as 1875 Andersson referred to a density of 100 people per square mile in the Ndonga tribal area,[44] since when it has increased considerably. Increases in the Kwanyama, and to some extent in the Mbalantu areas, can be ascribed to natural growth and to an influx from Angola since the 1920s. This influx continued until the 1950s and caused the government much concern.[45] Today the average density of the total population is computed at six persons per sq. km. Yet it should be remembered that some parts of Ovamboland are uninhabitable and that the population is therefore not evenly distributed. For instance, in 1960 in the Kwanyama district, 36.56 per cent of the total Ovambo population lived in 15 per cent of the area of Ovamboland. Apart from poor estimates, the fluctuation in numbers must be attributed to periodic droughts and resultant famines which, particularly during the depression of the 1920s and '30s and in 1946/7, were responsible for many deaths and a decrease in population growth. There was a large population increase from 1960 to 1970, and if the official figures are correct, the number of Ovambo inhabitants must have risen in ten years by more than 100,000, i.e. by more than 43 per cent. Similar sustained growth could bring the total Ovambo population up to more than 1,000,000 people by the year 2,000, which is equivalent to trebling the 1970 population. Of the entire Ovambo population in 1970 there were 290,421 living in Ovamboland, 50,245 (mostly temporarily) in the rest of Namibia, and the rest temporarily outside Namibia.

Whereas the population of Ovamboland represented 45.5 per cent of Namibia's total inhabitants in 1960, it had risen to 46.3 per cent by 1970, Namibia's total then being 762,184. The whites were the second largest group in Namibia with 90,583, or 11.9 per cent.[46] In 1974 the Ovambos represented 46.5 per cent of the total Namibian population.

3. *The Traditional Social Order*

Ovamboland has been shown to have seven related tribes, each forming a reasonably cohesive social and autonomous unit, and holding sway over a definable area of land, each with its own separate social and political

OVAMBOLAND POPULATION ANALYSIS

	1876[32]	±1887[33]	1898[34]	1915[35]	1927[36]	1932[37]	1938[38]	1951[39]	1960[40]	1970[42]	1974[43]
Ndonga	20,000	20,000	15,000	60,000	65,000	45,000	34,195	53,404	68,601 (28.66%)[41]	95,600 (27.94%)[41]	—
Kwanyama	30,000	20,000	70,000	50,000	55,000	45,000	41,215	81,451	87,511 (36.56%)	132,400 (38.65%)	—
Kwambi	5,000	15,000	5,000	20,000	8,000	7,000	11,405	22,239	28,341 (11.84%)	39,600 (11.55%)	—
Ngandjera	10,000	10,000	5,000	15,000	6,000	6,600	5,996	12,803	18,527 (7.74%)	24,500 (7.15%)	—
Mbalantu	4,000	?	3,000	?	7,000	5,200	6,349	12,958	17,665 (7.38%)	24,100 (7.03%)	—
Kwaluudhi	6,000	8,000	2,000	8,000	7,000	6,100	6,169	9,244	12,040 (5.03%)	16,600 (4.85%)	—
Kolonkadhi-Eunda	?	?	2,000	?	1,500	2,100	2,532	5,705	6,678 (2.79%)	9,700 (2.83%)	—
Bushmen	—	—	—	—	500	—	—	2,449	878	1,814	—
Total	75,000	73,000	102,000	153,000	150,000	117,000	107,861	200,253	240,241	344,314	396,000
Coloureds	—	—	—	—	—	—	—	—	1	235	—
Whites	—	—	—	—	—	—	—	—	195	1,012	—

organization, but till recently without a proper central authority that could unite the tribes within a single national state.[47]

The traditional social organization of the Ovambos is still predominantly matrilineal, although the Ovambos are increasingly engaged in a transitional process from matrilineality to patrilineal descent. The mother's brother (*tatakulu*) has always been an important personage as regards authority, succession and inheritance. Each tribe is subdivided into septs or "clans" (*emapata*, singular *epata*), in which membership is inherited through the mother, whose family name the children bear. The individual family is the most important socio-economic unit. Although monogamy is the usual practice, polygamy often occurs, and the more wives a man has, the higher is his standing in the community.

Each tribal area is subdivided into wards (*mikunda*), consisting of a number of native villages (kraals, *eumbo*). The kraals of the Kwanyama are distinguished by several rondavels or huts, mostly surrounded by stockades and often linked up by passageways. Cattle-kraals usually form part of the residential complex, and the higher the rank of the paterfamilias, the larger is the household in proportion and the greater the intricacy of the kraal.

Participation in public life is, in the traditional set-up, chiefly limited to the man, although the mother of a chief may exert influence. However, on the whole the woman is subservient to the man.[48] As a result of his journey to Ovamboland in the middle of the nineteenth century, Andersson remarked that women were regarded as merchandize and obtainable against payment of two or three oxen and one or two cows. This observation must be treated with some suspicion, because gifts to the father and mother of a bride are not comparable with the *lobola* custom practised by other Bantu races. A woman may not hold an official position; that is reserved for the man, whose status, authority and prestige are determined by his descent, age, wisdom and material possessions.

Religion is traditionally characterized by belief in a Supreme Being and ancestral spirits. All seven Ovambo tribes believe in Him, and He is known among the Kwanyama as Kalunga, who lives in the air but sometimes comes down to earth. He is not personified, but is omnipresent and omniscient; all good and evil emanate from Him. He represents, on the one hand, life, especially in the form of rain, and on the other hand death in the guise of famine and pestilence. The "good" and the "bad" originate with Him, and His favours cannot be obtained by means of offerings. He is exalted above human insults and disrespect: He is not seen, but sees everyone. Kalunga does not need human help and is not interested in the individual, but in the universe. Neither is He a law-giver, since moral obligations are rooted in tribal customs, not in Him.[49] Yet He expects good conduct and conformity with tribal ethics, such as adherence to tribal customs.[50] Violation of these is not a misdeed against Kalunga, but against the community, including the ancestral spirits and codes of behaviour. Kalunga "lives" in the holy fire, which may never go out, because the life and welfare of the tribe depend on it. Fire is emblematic of the life and death of the chief, who in turn symbolizes the life of his people. If the fire is extinguished, ill-luck is visited on the whole tribe.[51] Warneck, one of the early missionaries in Ovamboland, expressed the opinion that the ordinary Ovambo sees in the chief the personification of Kalunga. By contrast van Tonder has pointed out that Kalunga is not immanent in the chiefs, but that in fact a close bond exists between Him and them.[52] It seems clear that the homage paid to Kalunga and the awe in which He is held mirror the respect towards, and fear of, the chief.[53]

In the past a chief was regarded as the incarnation of the deity. Vedder considers that the Ovambo's philosophy of life is composed of three worlds. The first world, where Kalunga dwells, is "above" humanity. All the nobility of the land gather round Him, and the ordinary man has little chance of reaching this uppermost realm. The second world is that in which human beings live, while the third is under the earth, where the dead dwell in poverty and misery.[54] Vedder's description vividly illustrates the élitist thinking of the Ovambos, who make a clear distinction between the normal member of the tribe and the paramount head or chief, each belonging to a separate stratum. Some writers, therefore, differentiate between the aristocracy and the ordinary people. However, it has not been fully proved that a clearly demarcated class structure existed in Ovamboland. It seems more likely that instead of a class system there existed a system based on status, renown, power and eminence by virtue of descent and/or outstanding ability. Hence it would be more correct to talk of a classification based on status or rank.

Another significant remark of Vedder concerns the world of the departed. There is belief in a life after death. The veneration of ancestral spirits thus plays an extremely important part, and death in the life of the Ovambos assumes a more portentous role than birth. Dymond even avers that the Ovambo cult is not characterized by adoration of gods, but by ancestor worship.[55] Yet it is difficult to divorce the one from the other, and there is an interdependence between the two. Magic and the witch-doctor also occupy a significant position within the world of spirits, many social habits and codes of behaviour being fashioned by religion, such as the effect of good and evil spirits. The whole life of the Ovambos "is wrapped in a world of magico-religious influences. Not only are there numerous spirits constantly working for good or evil, but also various prohibitions to be observed and endless superstitions to disturb the equanimity of the people. The customary rites directed towards these influences are in many instances, especially amongst the Ukuanyama, still rigidly practised at the present time".[56]

Hence it appears that the traditional religious activities of the Ovambos constitute an important part of their social life and structure, determining the values and setting the standards of behaviour within this social framework.

4. *The Traditional Political Order*

In Ovamboland most tribes were individually subject to the autonomous authority of hereditary chieftainships. This is true of the Ndonga, the Ngandjera, the Kwaluudhi, the Kwambi before 1932 and the Kwanyama before 1917. In other tribes the authority rests in the headmen. The chiefs function together with the headmen as chiefs-in-council, and the headmen together as headmen-in-council. These headmen are elected separately by each tribe. Headmanship is not hereditary, although a nephew is frequently elected in place of his uncle, and a son in place of his father, but there is in fact a tendency to make the office of a senior-headman hereditary. Chiefs or headmen are the administrative heads in every tribe. These tribes are each subdivided into districts (*oshilonga*), in charge of which there are senior-headmen (*elenga*), with further subdivisions into wards (*omikunda*) under the authority of headmen. The boundaries of districts and wards are staked off primarily to tally with topographical and political considerations. The senior-headman is responsible for his district and is assisted in an advisory capacity by the headmen of the wards in his district. Each headman of a ward is in turn responsible for the native villages and kraals in his ward. When a tribe is headed by a chief, all the headmen are jointly answerable to him, but in other tribes the senior-headmen have collective responsibility.

It is necessary to note that the headmen and chiefs have specific liabilities not only towards their subjects, but also towards the dead. This applies above all to ruling chiefs. The luck and ill-luck of the tribe are in their hands, and they are accountable in person for all happenings, both good and bad. Both the chief-in-council and the headmen-in-council act in the traditional order as legislators and policy-makers. One of their important tasks within their political jurisdiction is the "sale" and allocation of land still held in tribal trust. The traditional feudal land-tenure system in Ovamboland stipulates that a man can own only for his lifetime a plot of ground sold to him, thereby stressing simultaneous control over the land and the individual. After this death, the land reverts to the chief or the senior-headmen as trustees, and it is then "resold". Only arable land is distributed, but sufficient pastureland is set aside for the communal use of the whole tribe. The headmen and chiefs also have the duty of defence against external enemies, the maintenance of peace and order, the co-ordination of agricultural activities, provision for the poor and the general progress of the tribe.

Because of the high status and rank held by chiefs and headmen, they wield the highest political authority, but tribal order demanded until quite recently that they should not cross the borders of their tribal areas. Formerly it was believed that if this regulation were broken, it could lead to the death of the visitor or of the person visited. Interference from outside in tribal matters is not tolerated, and when it occurs it is regarded as an act of aggression.

Almost all writers allude to the absolute authority over subjects not only of the chiefs but also of the headmen.[57] The extensive privileges and authority enjoyed by tribal heads have often given rise to arbitrary abuse; several of them in their day were notorious for their cruelty and autocratic behaviour. Their conduct and decisions could never be queried. It was only at a late stage that headmen within the Ovambo tribes were able to counterbalance the chief's power, and then only to the extent that authority within the traditional society became decentralized. This development first began late in the nineteenth century, since when it has been possible to speak of a well-developed structure of central authority or a traditional political structure within each tribe. The political organization of the Ovambo tribes has become characterized more and more by a delegated executive authority down to the smallest units in the tribe.

When determining policy, the chiefs and the senior-headmen have been making increasing use of advice from subordinates possessing special influence or wisdom. They became advisory tribal councils which were gradually to help in fixing and implementing policy, and in the administration of justice, have by degrees exerted firmer control over these matters, to ensure that headmen and chiefs act according to tribal customs and norms. Authority is still recognized, but emphasis is being laid on the duties and responsibilities of tribal leaders. Their claim to undivided power in all areas of life is being more and more curtailed and delegated.

As already indicated, the status of the senior-headmen and headmen, in contrast to that of the chiefs, plays no basic role in the right of succession. Should the chief die, he is usually succeeded by his brother or the eldest son of his eldest sister, but the chief-in-council may consider the recommendations of the headmen with due consideration to tribal tradition. While age is important in the appointment of senior-headmen, it is of no account in regard to the succession of chiefs. Senior-headmen often have successors from the same clan, and are appointed mainly on the strength of their influence, reputation, status, wisdom and material wellbeing. A further criterion is the initiative that a man may display in the interests of his tribe's advancement (women cannot be elected to this position). When a senior-headman dies in the Kwanyama tribal area, a successor is nominated to his area and seat on the Kwanyama tribal council by the remaining seven members of the council. The majority vote for his election is final. In other tribal areas, the inhabitants of the relevant district assemble and make their choice.

Elderly senior-headmen in the Kwanyama tribal area have recently begun the custom of withdrawing from public and other administrative matters and then appointing deputies (in every instance their close relatives).[58] The motive behind this is an attempt to establish the custom of ensuring that succession to the senior-headmanship flows from relationships; it is the wish of every senior-headman who is the owner of a district to prevent such a "property" from falling into "foreign" hands. This is reflected in the practice of endowing a person who shows the qualities of leadership with gifts of cattle from an early age, thus placing him in a position of power by virtue of material wealth.

Irrespective of his duties as a member of the tribal council, every senior-headman also has administrative duties towards his district, and he transmits the resolutions of the tribal council through his own headmen to the inhabitants. Moreover, he has a seat on the tribal appeal court and the district court (this will be dealt with later in detail).

A senior-headman in the district is assisted by (sub)headmen, who are heads of wards (*omikunda*) consisting of about fifteen kraals or native villages, and a (sub)headman is the liaison between the senior-headman and the inhabitants of his ward. A (sub)headman is usually appointed by one or more senior-headmen.

The framework of traditional government in Ovamboland at present is briefly as follows:

Kwanyama tribal area. At first the Kwanyama had a chief, who ran the area together with headmen, but the last chief, Mandume, died during a punitive expenditure by South African troops in 1917. The South African Government thereupon set up a tribal council of eight senior-headmen in lieu of the chieftainship and divided the tribal area into eight districts, with a senior-headman in charge of each. These districts were split up into wards controlled by (sub)headmen.

Ndonga tribal area. A chieftainship system with fifty-one wards (*omikunda*). At the head of every ward there is a headman directly responsible to the chief, who is assisted by nine senior-headmen. Some headmen also have sub-headmen. There was disagreement among the Ndonga over their former chief, Paulus Elifas and his successor Filemon Elifas because a portion of the tribe did not recognize them as the rightful successors to Chief Martin Ashikoto, who was deposed for criminal acts and banished from his area for a time.

Kwambi tribal area. The Kwambi had a chief until 1932 when he was relieved of his office. The South African Government replaced the chieftainship with a tribal council of four senior-headmen, allocating a district to each of them.

Ngandjera tribal area. A chieftainship system with thirty wards, each controlled by a headman, with the headmen under the authority of the chief. Munkundi, the present chief, who was elected in 1972 to succeed the dead chief Uushona Shiimi, does not enjoy the full support of the tribe. He is assisted by four senior-headmen.

Mbalantu tribal area. Has had no chief for the last 100 years. The tribe consists of fourteen clans, each with its own hereditary leader. The Mbalantu had no central government until the South African Government created a tribal council of four senior-headmen in 1915.

Kwaluudhi tribal area. Tribal government in this area consists of a chief, four senior-headmen and thirty-nine headmen, each in charge of a ward. Every headman is directly responsible to the chief.

Kolonkadhi-Eunda tribal area. This most sparsely populated tribal area has never had a chief. Political power was still in the hands of several hereditary heads of autonomous clan groups, all with equal status, when the South African Department of Bantu Administration and Development appointed five of them as headmen in Kolonkadhi and three in Eunda, of whom two are senior-headmen.

5. *The Traditional Juridical Order*

Besides the legislative body, the chief-in-council and headman-in-council constitute the highest juridical entity within the tribe. The law administered is customary law. Although it is gradually being influenced by Western legal norms (e.g. Roman–Dutch law), in general the accepted and authorized tribal practices hold good. The customary law is comprehensive, and is largely concerned with the protection of persons and property, the fulfilment of contractual obligations and the order and security of the tribe as a whole. Particular attention is paid to the right of heredity, land rights, chiefly succession rights and the law on liability, which are strictly implemented.

W. Louw, investigating the Ngandjera, found that legal concepts make no clear distinction between civil and criminal transgressions, but that certain types of offence may only be heard by the chief's court, which is itself a distinction. Compensation plays a significant role in the administration of justice, and in fact always forms part of the obligations imposed on an accused. In addition to the maintenance of law and order, the legal concept is concerned with restoring a disturbed situation to normality, and compelling a convicted offender to pay a fine into the court.[59] What Louw reports on the rule of law among the Ngandjera is also true with some variations of other tribes, but one important difference is that in the chieftainship system the chief is the main receiver of fines.

The administration of justice follows the same pattern of decentralization as the political authority. The lowest court is the local "ward" court with the (sub)headman as president. He hears matters affecting his ward, but cannot hear cases involving rape, murder or wounding. In this "ward" court, the judgment is submitted for approval to the senior-headman of the district, who has no seat in that court. Furthermore, the only cases heard in it are those concerning the inhabitants of the ward in question. The next highest authority is the district court, which does not differ essentially from the "ward" court, except that here the senior-headman of the particular district takes the chair and hears those cases specially relating to the different wards within the same district. The district court also serves as an appeal court for matters heard in the "ward" courts. The highest and final court in a tribal area is the chief's court, where a chieftainship system is still in existence, or a tribal court consisting of senior-headmen with councillors. This court tries cases referred to it by the lower courts, and serves as an appeal court for cases heard by these lower courts. The judgment of this court was formerly binding, but now an appeal can be made to a magistrate against the finding of the tribal court or the chief's court. Among the Kwanyamas the court with the highest jurisdiction consisted of the Bantu Commissioner together with three headmen in rotation. Any person was at liberty to appeal from the tribal court, which consisted of the eight senior-headmen, to this higher court.[60]

Since the advent of white control, the tribal courts have been deprived of specific legal powers. Nowadays these courts deal mainly with civil matters, but also with minor criminal offences. All serious offences are referred direct to the Supreme Court in Windhoek or to the Republic of South Africa depending on the circumstances. In some instances a preliminary examination can be conducted by a magistrate. Statutory wrongs such as road accidents and road offences are heard by the magistrate.

Ovamboland was declared a magisterial district in 1920. The local administration of justice was largely retained, although it had no statutory recognition. Roman–Dutch law is applicable to the whole of Namibia, but the traditional law of Ovamboland, i.e. the indigenous customary law, is also largely preserved. The procedure adopted in the traditional courts is generally informal, and all males (but no women and children) may attend the sessions of court. The prosecutor, now the secretary of the tribe, and the witnesses all have their turn in pleading their cases before the "judges". Punishments are usually severe, and the tribal police (tribal messengers) are employed to carry them out, also to apprehend the accused. The penalties meted out are in the form of corporal punishment and fines, which can be paid in kind or by means of labour. The death penalty may no longer be imposed by a traditional court.

Among the Ovambo population an increasing resistance to corporal punishment has been noted, particularly in the 1970s. After several political opponents of the traditional authority were given strokes with the *epoloko* (rib of a palm branch) in 1973, leaders of the Ovambokavango and Anglican Churches applied to the Supreme Court at Windhoek for an interdict to forbid the tribal authorities concerned to impose and administer corporal punishment, which they were accused of doing without a proper trial and without the accused having a chance to defend himself. Objections were also lodged against punishments of more than ten strokes and against corporal punishment being inflicted on women or on any victims in public. When the judgment of the Supreme Court did not satisfy the complainants, the matter was referred to the South African Appeal Court in Bloemfontein, and judgment was given on 24 January 1975: "The Appellate Division ordered that the Ovambo tribal authority be interdicted from arresting, detaining and inflicting punishment on any ground that [the accused] is, or is suspected of being, a member of DEMCOP or of SWAPO, or on the grounds that he has or is suspected of having carried out the lawful activities of these organizations." It was also laid down that no corporal punishment could in future exceed ten strokes or be administered in public, and that women could no longer be subjected to it. It was further decreed that any corporal punishment prescribed must first be reported to the magistrate for the territory in Ondangwa, who was bound to notify the Registrar of the Appeal Court. Moreover fourteen days had to elapse after the magistrate was first informed before the punishment could be administered.[61]

During the last few years a provisional legal code has been drawn up for the chief's courts and tribal courts in conjunction with white officials. It represents the first set of written legal rules for the Ovambo tribes. An example of this is the legal code now binding on the Ngandjera, which deals with the most serious offences and the fines that may be imposed. The worst offences mentioned are manslaughter (if not tried by the Supreme Court of South West Africa), assault, arson, malicious damage to property, theft, adultery, seduction of girls under eighteen, slander, trespassing on property (also with cattle), the holding of meetings without the consent of the chief, destruction of green trees, carrying weapons without permission, reckless driving of motor vehicles, neglect of children, the aged and the physically handicapped, omission to pay the tribal levy, failure to report stock diseases, bad language in public and rude, disrespectful conduct towards old people. Punishment is imposed in the form of fines, of either money or cattle, and varies with age. If the offender is over fifteen years old, he receives the "full" punishment, while there is remission for those between the ages of seven and fourteen, and no punishment for children under the age of seven. Legal concepts make provision for both individual and group liability, thus stressing the close connection between relatives.[62] This signifies *inter alia* that the mother's brother also has some say over her children in certain cases, and will pay their fines or even punish them himself.

A significant recent addition to the body of law in the territory is the "Ovamboland Civil and Criminal Jurisdiction of Chiefs, Headmen, Chiefs' Deputies and Headmen's Deputies Amendment Act. No. 3 of 1974", introduced mainly as a reaction against the interdict by the Supreme Court in Windhoek and the Appeal Court in Bloemfontein against corporal punishment, which was regarded by Ovamboland's traditional leaders as interference in the domestic affairs of their country. The Act provides for the establishment in Ovamboland of an Appeal Council superior to the highest tribal court.[63]

The influence of western legal concepts on traditional law is unmistakable, yet it often happens that a chief alters this legal code at will in order to conform with old tribal customs. Often, for example, the judgment of the white magistrate at Ondangwa is not considered binding. A person found not guilty of manslaughter by the magistrate can be indicted again in the traditional courts if there is dissatisfaction over this finding. The chief purpose of such action appears to be that of obtaining from him compensation which, in traditional law, he owes to the family which has suffered loss through the death of one of its members. Such occurrences cause discontent among the population and clearly reflect how the old legal institutions and rules are not keeping pace with the social *mores* of a modern society.

Chiefs and headmen are also no longer competent to decide in divorce or separation cases, and in all traditional courts only matters affecting members of their own tribe may be heard. Any case between an Ovambo and a white falls outside the jurisdiction of the traditional courts and is tried by the white magistrate in Ondangwa.

The land and succession laws still cause exceptional problems. It was already pointed out in the oldest sources on the Kwanyama and Ndonga legal systems that the right of succession is made complex because of maternal rights.[64] In general, a man's principal heirs are his sister's sons from the eldest to the youngest, and after them his mother's brother(s). A woman's children, sometimes only the daughters, are the chief and in fact sole heirs of her estate, with the reservation that assets which she has inherited from her mother's side shall become the inheritance of her matrilineal relatives.[65] A man during his lifetime can bequeath some of his personal possessions such as cattle to his children, provided that the cattle do not belong to any group related to his mother.

In 1952 the South African Act on Civil Marriages also became applicable to Ovamboland. In 1954 it was laid down that the belongings of a deceased person could be distributed according to traditional laws and practices, if the marriage were solemnised and no belongings and no agreements over the estate existed before the marriage. This type of marriage is observed mainly by the Roman Catholics, the Anglicans and a small group of Lutherans, whereas the vast majority of Lutherans follow the Ordinance on Marriages No. 33 of 1963 (S.W.A.), which corresponds to the South African Act on Civil Marriages. There is still a custom in the Ovambokavango Church whereby a married couple, after celebrating their marriage, have to sign a document (will) stipulating that the survivors, whether the husband, wife or children, are the chief heirs.

During an enquiry in 1970 by the Select Committee on Land Ownership and Utilisation, it transpired that the methods of land ownership are the same in all tribes. The chiefs or senior-headmen own the land in the name of the tribe, and everyone must still buy any land so that he can possess it temporarily until his death. Although the headmen and chiefs are free to give away land for nothing, the old traditional allotment of land for individual right of enjoyment still remains. The compensation for a plot of ground varied in 1972 from R20 to R200, and this money is received by the chief, the senior- and other headmen. Chiefs and senior-headmen as a rule obtain their land and wards gratis.[66] As a result of these land awards, numbers of problems occur over the right of succession, but more so when the temporary owner of the land dies. It is evident that this existing traditional hereditary right has long been the cause of conflicting opinions among the Ovambos; on the one hand, the Ovambo has traditional obligations towards his near relatives, but on the other he wants to decide himself who is to inherit his property. An Ovambo man's natural desire is to provide a sure future for his wife and children after his death, but within the matriarchal order this is only partly possible. A special problem experienced by a man is that the plot of ground which he has purchased from the chief or headman cannot remain the property of his family after his death, but must revert to the chief or headman. Among the Ngandjera, a man's younger brother has first claim to the land after his death. If he already owns land and does not wish to use that of his elder brother, he can nominate a claimant or leave the decision to the chief, but in every instance the land has to be paid for again.[67] Thus no one can inherit land, apart from the legally accepted successor to a headman.[68] Difficulties also often occur over the appointment of a chief, as the right of succession is founded on the matriarchal system, although the only existing chiefs are men. As a rule a chief is succeeded by one of his brothers, or by a son of his eldest sister, or by a son of the sister's daughters, but this is not necessarily the case. It is here that problems arise.

It will thus be clear that the population of Ovamboland still lives largely according to its own traditional legal system, in which any change must be gradual. Some modifications that have come about in the last two decades through the influence of white administration will be more fully discussed in a later chapter. With all its limitations, the traditional Ovambo legal system has satisfied the demands of a traditional way of life, but with growing social, economic and political modernization, it cannot remain untouched. The necessary steps to adapt it to modern life are now being taken.

6. The Traditional Economic Order

Within the traditional Ovambo community there is still a close connection between wealth and prestige on the one side and power on the other. Those in positions of power, like headmen and chiefs, were always well off in comparison with the rest, with larger and more complex native villages (kraals), more livestock, more extensive farmlands, generous hospitality and a large retinue. The structure of the kraal has always shown the pre-eminence of the individual family as a socio-economic unit among the Ovambos. Many blood relatives and near-relatives affect the complexity and size of a kraal, and no affluent Ovambo allows his kinsmen to live in poverty, which would be a blot on his name and a scandal for his clan.[69] The Ovambo's kraal has been compared to a miniature self-governing state.[70]

Before Ovamboland became Christianized, wealth was measured in terms of the number of a man's wives, since the more he had, the larger the farmlands that could be cultivated. The women's main task was to till the soil—which enabled them, to some extent, to regulate the output from the land. A rich Ovambo could also keep a large domestic staff, and so carry on widespread cultivation. However, larger crops and the resulting economic strength and status also entailed obligations. In times of economic adversity, such as droughts and famines, economic assistance was expected from the well-to-do for their fellow-tribesmen. It was the duty of the rich to build up stocks which could bridge periods of crisis, and by giving this aid they could acquire greater prestige and influence.

The traditional subsistence economy is characterized by agriculture and stock-breeding, but within the past century the emphasis has shifted, with stock-raising acquiring greater scope. The reasons for this lies in the nature of the land. Situated on a monotonous uniform plateau, consisting of a deep layer of Kalahari sand with a clay bed underneath, Ovamboland does not lend itself to intensive cultivation. Its has poor drainage capacity, inferior soil which requires large-scale fertilising, and lacks water. The only way the land can be worked is by the "heaps method". Small heaps of soil are scraped together and formed into a mound (90×60 cm. in area and 45 cm. high) in which the seed is planted. Because of floods in the rainy season this technique guarantees that the tops of the mounds remain above the water level. Planting time is just before the summer rains.

The most important kinds of grain cultivated by the Ovambo—it is now their staple food—is *mahangu*, with kaffir corn of less importance. Both types were named by Galton and Andersson,[71] who remarked that the inhabitants were largely dependent on these grains for their livelihood.[72] Other traditional crops are beans, pumpkins, water-melons, calabashes and ground-nuts. The grain was effectively stored in large sealed baskets, protected from ants and resting on short poles. It could be stored for as long as five years.[73]

Stock-breeding was next in importance to agriculture. Cattle accounted for 80 per cent or more of the livestock, the remainder consisting chiefly of goats, with small numbers of sheep and hoofed animals. The normal Ovambo cattle are notably small—about 1.22 m. high at the shoulder, and

weighing between 250 and 400 kg.; through their hardiness they adapt
easily to the generally meagre grazing conditions. This toughness also
affords them good resistance to the dreaded lung-disease, which sometimes
appears in Ovamboland.

As in most Bantu communities, it is the quantity rather than the quality
of cattle owned that confers social prestige, but this is especially so in
Ovamboland because livestock have become the most important and most
precious possession on account of the traditional land-tenure system and
inheritance laws.

Cattle were also considered the most valuable medium of exchange,
especially when dealing with neighbouring tribes. Later on the Ovambos
traded with whites and Portuguese coloureds, bartering cattle for weapons
and ammunition. The most important commodities obtained from nearby
tribes were copper and iron, Ovamboland being devoid of minerals.[74]
Another vital economic pursuit was, and still is, fishing. Flooding in the
rainy season from northerly rivers, especially the Cuvelai in Angola,
brought down great quantities of fish, which remained behind in the
oshanas. These fish would breed and then be caught by the Ovambo
women between June and August.

Thus the Ovambos were an economically active society, considering the
limited possibilities and resources at their disposal. Both the man and the
woman had vital roles: it was the woman's task to hoe the land, prepare
food and beer and provide for the general needs of the family, and the
man's to look after the cattle and see to the heavier physical work.

To summarize, the traditional Ovambo community has an agrarian
subsistence economy, tending to economic and technical backwardness.
Some of the implements in use pre-date in their origins the discovery of the
plough and the wheel; land is not worked effectively enough, and rotation
of crops is almost unknown. In general, production is for local short-term
consumption, and husbanding of large stocks is ruled out. Formerly, the
production of food in good years was barely sufficient, and today there is
still danger of famine in bad years. One reason for this may be that land
still remains tribal property and therefore under communal ownership—without providing the incentive which exists when land is owned by
an individual. Another problem is that in a society such as that of the
Ovambos, where a traditional élite holds power, and there is not a dynamic
middle class, efforts at modernizing are hampered and obstructed when
they do not accord with accepted traditional practices. Consequently
development in Ovambo is in a state of stagnation, with the geographical
isolation contributing an additional factor.

II

CONTACT WITH THE WHITES

1. The Christian Churches

Besides contact with the Portuguese in Angola, it was the visits of an Englishman, Sir Francis Galton, and a Swedish physician, Charles John Andersson, to the southern Ovambo tribes in 1851 that led to the initial contact between whites and the Ovambo peoples. The most significant result of Galton's and Andersson's journeys was that a Christian mission focussed its attention on Ovamboland. Hugo Hahn and Johannes Rath, members of the Rhenish Mission, a German Lutheran missionary society, which was already active in South West Africa, undertook a journey of reconnaissance to Ovamboland in 1857. Further expeditions and increasing contacts with heads of tribes there, who expressed a wish to receive missionaries, led to the beginning of missionary activities there. These inaugurated an entirely new phase in Ovamboland's history, viz. "the period of Christianisation and civilisation".[1]

From the viewpoint of Christianity the Ovambos were heathens who had to be converted. The resulting process of religious and ideological transformation within the traditional framework would necessarily lead to a reappraisal of values and to more flexible and varied activities and aims. It is a well-known phenomenon that modernization is often marked by the entry on the scene of religious movements, which apply effective methods of organization in order to bring long-standing traditional religious values into dispute as being inconsistent with new religious concepts. A synthesis may also be sought between traditional religious practices and forms, on the one hand, and the content and values of fresh religious views on the other.

(a) *The Lutheran Mission.* The Lutheran missionaries, mainly of the Finnish Lutheran Church, were the largest single instrumental factor in changing and modernizing Ovamboland. This institution, together with other Christian churches which were to enter the missionary field in Ovamboland later, was an extremely vital, innovative force in transforming the land economically, socially and politically from a closed traditional society to one moving towards modernization.

Owing to a shortage of money and manpower, the Rhenish Mission offered Ovamboland to the Finnish Missionary Society in Helsingfors (Helsinki) as a mission field. This offer was accepted, and on 9 July 1870 the first nine Finnish missionary workers started their activities there. The Ovambos in the early years evidently had the wrong idea about the work and motives of the missionaries, who neither succeeded in coming up to their expectations as magicians nor in bringing material benefits, to which they were accustomed in their dealings with Portuguese traders.[2]

The first mission success was scored only on 6 January 1883, when six Ovambo men were baptised, but since then the growth of the Finnish Mission Church has been as follows:[3]

	Members
1890	489
1910	2,018
1920	7,695
1930	23,126
1940	35,732
1950	63,451
1960	118,316
1970	194,884
1972	213,796
1974	230,000

From 1891 to 1916 the Rhenish Mission also worked in Ovamboland. Both the Finnish and the Rhenish Lutheran Churches considered it their task to preach the Gospel, to live up to it strictly and to act as advisers and educators in every sphere of Ovambo life. The Ovambos, accustomed to the idea of a chief deciding on all matters affecting their lives, expected the same from the white missionaries—who were placed in a dilemma whenever tribal chiefs asked for political advice. Both Lutheran Churches in Ovamboland were known for their strongly pietistic attitude concerning the rigid separation of religion and politics, not realizing that religion and politics were not separable in traditionalism. Often they were unaware too—unintentionally—that tribal chiefs felt a threat to their political power when their religious views were queried or censured. No real appreciation of the need for the separation of religion and politics was to dawn on the traditional leaders till much later, when political control in Ovamboland was assumed by a white government.

The Lutheran missionaries' almost complete lack of involvement in politics was a feature of both mission churches. On the other hand they made an exceptional contribution on a cultural level, especially the Finnish Mission, which exerted a modernizing influence. Apart from evolving Oshindonga and Oshikuanyama as written languages, translating the Bible and publishing religious literature and school books, attention was also given to training native teachers. Besides establishing many schools, they founded the first teachers' training college in 1913 at Oniipa, followed by a similar institution for girls in the 1920s.

With the development of Oshindonga and Oshikuanyama as written tongues, increasing efforts have been made to teach the Ovambos to read. When one of the two white official languages also became necessary in Ovamboland, the Finnish Mission introduced Afrikaans in 1925 as the official language.[4] An important occurrence was also the establishment in 1941 of a local church magazine *Omukwetu*, which is now circulated in a fortnightly edition of 10,000 copies.

In 1923 a start was made in training native ministers. The change-over fom the Finnish Mission Church to the autonomous and independent Ovambokavango Church took place in 1954. This church was the first in Ovamboland to become autonomous and is now led by Dr. L. Auala, its African bishop. The achievement of autonomy for the Ovambokavango Church, which has meant the withdrawal of more and more Finnish missionaries from mission work in the country, reflects the attitude of the Finnish Church right from the beginning—that an autonomous native church should be founded as soon as possible. Out of 97 ministers in 1972 only four were whites.

Another important contribution made by the Finnish Church is in the domain of medical care, where Finnish women doctors and nurses especially have distinguished themselves. Attention has been paid to the training of Ovambo medical staff and especially nurses, because from the beginning the Finns have had a tradition that medical work should be done mainly by women. In a matriarchal society like Ovamboland, in which many women no longer play the same inferior role as in other African communities, it was a fruitful policy, for the social position of women has been greatly strengthened through the Finnish woman's example in modernizing Ovamboland in medicine, religion and education. In 1971, out of a total of 102 Finnish Mission co-workers, 79 were women.[5]

The contribution of the Finnish Church has been less impressive in the economic sphere, but it has made great efforts to improve agricultural methods and to grow new crops. It has also trained artisans, though on a small scale, and has encouraged handicrafts. Palm-leaves are treated for use in basket-work, which has become one of Ovamboland's chief exports.

The aid and assistance from the Finnish Church have resulted in many changes, above all in Ovamboland's social structure, for the Ovambos have altered from bellicose tribesmen to a peaceful Christianized community, in which polygamy has given way to monogamy. At the same time the position of women has advanced from that of a subordinate helpmate to the man to one of equality, at least in principle. Girls and boys are equal beneficiaries of educational development.

The most radical political contribution of the Finnish Mission, next to stopping tribal wars, has been their victory over tribal particularism. They stimulated the political process of evolution towards unity and tribal community of interests, and thus a process of Ovamboland nation-building began. The Ovambo Christian convert identifies himself increasingly first as an Ovambo and secondly as a member of a specific tribe.

The missionaries wrought profound changes in the religious thinking and practices of the Ovambos. Smith asserts that even those who have not become Christians and adhere to an animistic faith have been influenced in their thoughts about God (*Kalunga*) by missionary doctrines.[6] In consequence, a centre group has arisen which desires to share in the advantages of both schools of thought and observance, Christian and animistic alike. Having allowed themselves to be guided by experience, they have taken their decisions on the basis of expected material benefit. On the other hand there have also been those who, as Smith puts it, have felt "that they must have *some* religion, indeed as much religion as possible. What form it shall finally take is decided empirically. Amongst this class of persons it is not unusual to find those who, while continuing to be heathen, teach their children to recite Christian hymns and prayers".[7]

Apart from Christians and this centre group with its religion based on utilitarianism, there is a third group, whose members have begun to doubt their old faith and even to renounce it, but have not been ready to accept Christian values in its place. While they have been convinced that ancestor worship and all its ancillary customs are false and futile, yet they have not been prepared to support a new faith in its place. "They are consequently devoid of any belief whatever concerning the unseen world and the purpose of life."[8]

In a fourth group are those Ovambos who have believed in traditional, animistic ideas and practices, but whose worship of ancestor spirits and their belief in *Kalunga* have continued to be the essence of their spiritual views. Smith calls them the orthodox ancestor worshippers, who are mostly to be found in the kraals of headmen and who, having been much more under the influence of fortune-tellers and witch-doctors, are convinced that to abandon old ways and customs would evoke the wrath of the spirits.[9]

Tuupainen agrees more or less with Smith's portrayal, but makes a further subdivision. She distinguishes between actual Christians, secularized Christians with strongly materialist attitudes, a third group consisting of those who stand aloof from religious matters (who "have broken themselves off from God") and a fourth group with a syncretistic outlook that blends elements of both Christianity and the old traditional religion.[10]

The Christian concepts of justice, guilt and sin have made drastic inroads into long-cherished notions on vendetta, the meting out and administering of punishment to settle any wrongs, and the approval of polygamy and pregnancy in unmarried girls after initiation, ideas diametrically opposed to the Christian moral code. It has been difficult for the Ovambos to accept that after payment of a fine for an offence against tribal customs, there is still a need for forgiveness from God, with whom, in his traditional form as Kalunga, Ovambos have had a somewhat impersonal relationship. According to tradition, punishable acts are never committed against Kalunga, but in a personal capacity against the community. In other words, any punishment imposed by the society on, and undergone by, an Ovambo directly connected to that society wipes out a crime for good.

As may be inferred from these individual examples, traditional religious views and habits made themselves felt in every sphere of daily life. This was a very practical faith, which was not fully understood by the white missionaries, with their immersion in western tradition. Hence the principal differences between the animistic and the Christian religion were either not recognized or ignored. Christianized Ovambos were expected to relinquish much of their traditional outlook on God and the world.

The replacement or adjustment of the concept of God in the spiritual life of the Ovambo presented fewer problems than the dilemma which missionaries created in the practical everyday existence. It was absurd to demand that traditional and tried social, economic and political customs should be summarily rejected with the acceptance of Christianity. Mere denunciation, without alternative substitutes, created a vacuum that often seriously endangered existential survival.

(b) *The Roman Catholic Mission.* After disastrous initial attempts in the late nineteenth and early twentieth centuries to start missionary work among the Ovambos in Ovamboland and Angola, the Catholics were given consent by the Kwanyamas in 1923 to found a mission station in their tribal area. The Administrator of South West Africa required from both the Roman Catholic and Anglican Missions an undertaking that they would (a) confine themselves to the area allocated to them; (b) conclude their own agreements with the headmen; and (c) promise in writing to (1) support and promote government policy, (2) encourage Ovambos to work in the South, (3) teach their members loyalty towards the administration, (4) confirm the authority of the headmen and leaders in their territory, and (5) emphasise practical education and only introduce new syllabuses into their schools after discussion with the Director of Education.[11] It was the first time that a white authority outside Ovamboland had set conditions on how mission work there was to be carried on. The political stipulations made were especially notable, as they did not specifically exclude the missions from politics.

The Roman Catholic Mission, with its predominantly white (mostly German), personnel, has specialized in spiritual and medical ministry. Schools and hospitals have been opened, but they have not established local education centres for teachers. Training of indigenous clergy has made slow progress and has been conducted outside Ovamboland. Not until 1967 was the first African priest installed, and only two Roman Catholic Ovambos were studying for the priesthood at Roma, Lesotho, in 1972. Only lay church-workers can be trained in Ovamboland, but the training of nurses is meeting with more success.

On the whole, there is less autonomy and independence in the Roman Catholic missionary activities than in the other churches of Ovamboland. A strong paternalistic attitude still persists among the white missionaries, who insist that any Ovambo joining the ministry must have the same training and qualifications as whites. These qualifications, which even now relatively few Ovambos are able to acquire, will hamper the development of a local independent Catholic Church for a long time.

The Catholics have tried harder than the other missionary societies to incorporate much of the traditional culture and its customs into their doctrines. Many animistic practices are not regarded *a priori* as incompatible with the Christian religion and value-system. In the economic sphere, there has been no notable contribution in education or vocational training. Where politics is concerned, it has always been a feature of the Catholic Mission in Ovamboland not to interfere in politics, but rather to keep aloof and even to be non-political. The younger and better qualified Ovambo Catholics resent the political neutrality of white Roman Catholic churchmen, and these white missionaries will be less able in future to keep outside politics because ever greater pressure is being applied by the younger Ovambos for a more definite attitude. This trend has recently been confirmed.

Among the Christian Ovambos in Ovamboland, the Roman Catholics are in a minority; in 1972 its membership numbered between 30,000 and 35,000.[12]

(c) *The Anglican Mission.* As early as 1860 Bishop Gray of Cape Town expressed a wish to begin mission work among the Ovambos.[13] In 1903 Bishop A. G. S. Gibson came back from a journey to Ovamboland with favourable impressions of the possibilities for mission work there. Shortage of money and misgivings as to whether the Germans would allow their missionaries in South West Africa prevented the Anglicans from starting their mission work at once.

They finally entered the missionary field in Ovambo in 1924, becoming active among the Kwanyama tribe. St. Mary Mission, founded at Odibo (Odimbo) in 1925, is still the chief station of this mission. An immediate decision was taken then to establish church and school buildings and a hospital, and since those early years the Anglican Mission in Ovamboland has been outstanding for its intense activity and dedication, which have found a ready response among the Kwanyamas. Considerable support came from the younger people particularly, and thus enabled the mission to expand its activities rapidly among the Kwanyama tribe. This work was later extended to the Kwambi tribe.

The Anglican Mission is largely autonomous, but still forms part of the Synod of the Anglican Church in South West Africa. Although the Mission Church has had a Ovambo archdeacon as head since 1969, the White bishop of the Synod of Damaraland remains the overall leader, with his headquarters in Windhoek. A clash between the traditional Kwanyama tribal council and the archdeacon, P. Shilongo, led to the latter being ordered to leave the tribal area in September 1973.

The membership of the Anglican Mission Church totalled 40,000 in 1972, with twenty-eight congregations. In the same year ten of its priests and many times that number of lay staff were Africans. The priests and lay assistants are being trained in Ovamboland, and advanced training is given in South Africa, but in 1972 the Mission in Ovamboland possessed no graduates among its local personnel.[14] All white church workers are now being replaced by Africans.

The Anglican Mission's contribution to modernization has remained mostly limited to the spiritual and medical care of the population. During recent years this church has become actively involved in politics, which has led to a split from the Anglican Church and the founding in 1971 of a local church, the Ovamboland Independent Church.

(d) *The Ovamboland Independent Church.* According to its founder, the Rev. Peter Kalangula, this church was established because of discord between members of the Anglican Mission in Ovamboland and the then officiating head of the Synod of Damaraland, Bishop Colin Winter, on the future status of the Anglican Mission in the territory. The disputes hinged mainly on the principle of whether it should be known any longer as a

Mission or whether it should acquire the semi-autonomous status of an archdeaconship. Another minor point at issue was the use of English as the medium for public worship. Kalangula and his followers advocated the use of Ovambo languages as the most convenient for members of the congregations, whereas the archdeacon in Ovamboland favoured English. Thus it was not on theological questions but merely on practical ones that there was dissent.[15] In 1974 this church claimed a membership total of 13,000 members, with eight congregations and fifteen ministers, which included several lay-preachers.

Among his adversaries in the other three church groupings in Ovamboland Kalangula, who since 1973 has been a member of the Ovamboland Legislative Council, has been regarded as an opportunist, making common cause with the South African Government. But his motives should be seen primarily in his acceptance of customs and patterns of ecclesiastical organization from the past under white leadership, and in his personal brush with Bishop Winter, whose changes in the organization and status of the Anglican Mission in Ovamboland he would not endorse. True to his convictions, Kalangula has accepted the aid of the whites, i.e. the South African Government, whose authority the Anglican archdeaconship and the majority of its followers in Ovamboland reject.

(e) *Other Faiths.* Besides 70,000–75,000 Ovambos who in 1972 belonged to no Christian Church (20%–22% of the whole population) and adhered to animistic views, there are a few other religious minority groups. At Oshakati in 1972 there was a group of Zionists headed by an Ovambo who had resided for many years in South Africa, where he had become a member of the Zionist faith. There were also about 300 Seventh Day Adventists in 1972, served by two Ovambo clergymen at Oshakati.

Kritzinger alludes to a claim made that the Apostolic Faith Mission in Ovamboland had 1,800 to 2,000 members in 1971. Three Ovambo preachers were doing church work among these members under the direction of a white missionary at Grootfontein.[16] Kritzinger also refers to the Full Evangelical Church of Christ, which in 1971 claimed 500 members in Ovamboland.[17] These groups do not exert any meaningful influence on the development of the country, and up to the present there have been no religious, syncretistic or other separatist and sectarian movements in Ovamboland.

The Dutch Reformed Church began missionary activities in Ovamboland in recent times, especially since the termination of the Tripartite ("Driehoek") Agreement.[18] Living in the Kwanyama tribal area there is a one-time member of the Ovambokavango Church, the Rev. N. S. Paulus, who had undergone training at a D.R. Church training institution for non-white ministers. He established the first D.R. mission congregation at Onuno in the Kwanyama tribal area on 19 May 1973; by 1974 it had eighty members. Three Ovambos received theological training in 1973 at the D.R. Mission School at Orumana in the Kaokoveld, and one of them, the Evangelist P. P. Hanunyela, began working among the Uukwaluudhi tribe in November 1974.

Chief J. S. Taapopi of the Kwaluudhi tribe, a member of the Ovam-

bokavango Church, was received into the D.R. Church owing to problems
with the local pastor of the Ovambokavango Church. In July 1975 the
Evangelical Reformed Church in Africa (D.R.) took shape, which was a
combination of the congregations of Ovamboland, Kavango and
Kaokoland, only Whites being elected to the first executive church council.
There were about 2,000 members belonging to this new "black" church in
Namibia in 1975.

The impression is prevalent in Ovamboland that the South African
Government is deliberately trying to advance the mission work of
Afrikaans Churches inside and outside the homelands in order to eliminate
missionaries "from abroad", or to replace them or to neutralize their
influence. In consequence there is some tension between the Lutheran,
Roman Catholic and Anglican Churches on one side and the Afrikaans
Churches on the other. Objections are being raised that the latter get
concessions and opportunities which are not offered to the older established
churches. It is also alleged that the reason for this is purely political, and
unconnected with concern for the welfare of the non-whites; the D.R.
Church is supposedly allowing itself to be used in these tactics, thus sowing
doubts among the other churches about its theological motives.[19]

Whatever the merits of the case, any acts of the D.R. Mission in
Ovamboland, especially by the white clergy, must meet with considerable
opposition from the Ovambos in the current political climate of the
country. Hence the question arises whether these acts further the *bona fide*
objectives of the Church.

(*f*) *Church and State.* From the 1920s onwards, South African government officials have been uneasy over the role and influence of the churches
in Ovamboland, particularly as they lead to the breakdown of tribal
customs. In a report of the Union Government to the League of Nations in
1928 on the administration of South West Africa, the official in charge of
Ovamboland commented as follows on the influence of the churches on the
local population:

As the Mission develops, so does the influence of the Churches in Ovamboland
become ever stronger and more marked. The Finnish Mission, which has been
working in Ovamboland for nearly sixty years, especially in Ondonga, is well
established. Under its influence, the old tribal life and discipline are gradually
breaking down and disappearing, and thus the power and influence of the headmen
and chiefs are being weakened.[20]

The anxiety evident in this report was to increase among Union
Government officials in Ovamboland. Since the 1920s estrangement and
conflict between the South African Government, represented by its
officials, and the Ovambo churches, has increased both in range and
intensity. The first clear indications of this are reflected in government
reports based on information and observations from the Bantu Commissioner in Ovamboland. These reports contradict publications of the
missionary societies on their work and success among the Ovambos.

A government report published in 1936 complained of a lack of
co-ordination between the missionaries and the civil administration. It saw

no reason why the Government should not intervene in mission activities. It was felt that the extent to which the African's daily existence was being influenced by the missionaries had become a matter for the state. It was further alleged that the curricula of the missionaries "showed a definite tendency to discard native laws and customs, and that, because Ovamboland was being ruled in accordance therewith, missionaries were therefore making the task of the civil administration more difficult".[21] In the same report the missionaries were advised to honour tribal custom as far as possible, since it was in the interests of the Africans themselves to interfere with it as little as possible.

The government report for 1938, quoting from a report by the Bantu Commissioner for Ovamboland, discussed in detail the government's objections to the political, economic and social activities of the missionary societies. It contended that law and order existed in Ovamboland thanks only to the presence there of government officials, which alone enabled the Finnish Mission to make such good progress. At the same time, the report said that during its seventy-year presence in Ovamboland the Mission had succeeded in breaking up the tribal system and achieved little besides.

According to Major Hahn, who drafted this very one-sided document, the missionary societies were paying too much attention to education, which was leading to an unchecked proliferation of uncontrolled "bush" schools. Hahn's observation was significant. His report stated that even during the 1920s on account of their real or supposed knowledge, the "teachers" in those schools were competing with the authority of the headmen in the wards. The more Christians there were in a particular ward, the greater the the stature and influence of the teacher. Hahn referred scornfully to this development as a "delightfully easy way of attaining power and prestige" which, he maintained, would enable more and more "Christians" (*his* quotation marks) with a defective knowledge of reading and writing to act as teachers.[22]

Another of Hahn's objections to the teachers was that the missionary societies deliberately supported this development. For example, they were empowering the teachers to conduct themselves as semi-judicial bodies to settle civil and criminal disputes, as long as both parties were Christians. This meant limiting the traditional dispensation of justice by tribal courts and chief's courts, which was contrary to Hahn's wishes. Here he quite rightly discerned growing alienation and tension between "Christians" and "heathens". Already at that time a trend was taking root in which Christians were beginning to heed the advice of a Christianized teacher rather than that of a headman. The traditional leaders complained to him that they were being deprived of their powers and were unable to stop it.

As a result the Government issued a proclamation to control the work of the missionary societies in Ovambo,[23] its main object being to check the rise of "bush" schools and the consequent undermining of the headmen's authority. Its effect was that no school could be founded without the consent of the Administrator of South West Africa and unless a missionary society was in a position to exercise sufficient control over its outlying stations. Hahn hoped that the result would be the disappearance of the dissension between Christians and heathens. [24]

Another of Hahn's complaints against missionary activity was that it was subverting the traditional economic order of the Ovambos. A similar objection was mentioned in the Government report quoted for 1935. The most significant charge in this paper, as in that of Hahn, concerned the missions' opposition to polygamy which, in Hahn's view, helped the owner of a kraal to build up a large domain and a strong economic unit, because the more women there were to cultivate the farm lands, the less was the danger of famine. The report for 1935 put the standpoint of the Government clearly: "As far as the Government is concerned, there is no need for objecting to well-ordered polygamy. Quite the reverse. Where it is closely bound up with the economic life of people, there are valid reasons for not disturbing it. Polygamy is the pattern on which the social and economic organization of Ovamboland is based, and any sudden change in this regard would tear the country's social order asunder."[25]

According to Hahn, the children of school-going age were hampering the economic life of the Ovambos. Instead of helping to tend the cattle and till the soil they were attending school. Hahn was opposed to Christians making contributions to the church in the form of wheat, and said that he had noticed how in times of famine the kraals of Christians were worse off than those of heathens. He had concluded that the Christian religion in Ovamboland was unfavourable to the inhabitants economically, and that traditional organization and tribal tradition were lacking in Christian wards.

Hahn had to acknowledge that the missionary societies also provided valuable services, particularly in medical care. He also recognized that the acquisition of reading and writing skills was beneficial, despite the criticism of the teachers. He also claimed that in a country of such vast distances, where many men were absent from home on contract labour in Southern South West Africa, the ability to read and write was an important factor in communication. He conceded, too that the missionary societies in general were promoting development and higher living standards among the Ovambos, but asserted their methods were wrong. He wrote: "It is thought to impose a European standard on a primitive people in a country where the opportunities for earning the necessary money to maintain such as standard are practically non-existent. As soon as a native is Christianized, he thinks he must wear European clothes, and being already limited to one wife and a small kraal, is unable to provide for them. ... If through mission influence the tie provided by the *epata* [clan] were broken because of different religious outlooks, it would mean the disruption of the greatest influence in the country for the unity of the people. On it are based the laws of succession and inheritance."[26]

The conflicting views of the mission churches and the government representatives in Ovamboland on the best ways to develop the Ovambo in his totality did not end there. There were two opposing concepts: on the one hand the missionary belief in creating a new western-oriented Christianized community, and on the other hand the government policy tending to perpetuate the *status quo* through indirect control without too much encroachment on traditional ideas and values. Although adjustments were made as time went on, a difference in principle continued to exist mainly between the Finnish Mission Church (later the Ovambokavango Church) and the South African Government representatives, in their outlook on modernizing Ovambo and especially on the ways of doing it. It must also be realized that the Ovambokavango Church was the largest single contributory factor in modernizing the country. In 1973 about 78 per cent of the Ovambos in the territory belonged to a Christian church, of whom 70 per cent were members of the Ovambokavango Church.

The comparative isolation of Ovamboland, with its closely-knit national society and the decades-old policy of the German and South African authorities not to interfere in the political, social and economic order and progress of the country, meant that the Finnish Mission Church could initiate extensive development and control, which in other African colonial territories were largely undertaken by the secular authorities. It was thus to be expected that the transfer to a secular authority of the task of development, which for decades had had strongly pious motives, would not proceed without tension. The Ovambo Christian had identified himself with the Finnish Mission Church's development programme, in which he could share and participate on an equal footing. At times there were bound to be strains between the Finnish Mission Church and the Ovambos, but these were outweighed by the trust that the latter reposed in the Finnish missionaries and mission co-workers. The Finns were idolized as models of Christianity, and the Ovambos became convinced that whites coming to work in their country must be good people. Every white was measured according to the Finnish yardstick.

The advent of direct administration for Ovamboland by the South African Government and its agencies plunged the Ovambos into a dilemma. As church activities became more restricted to purely religious tasks, and the work of the South African authorities was seen to differ in motivation, content and *modus operandi* from that of the Finnish Church, the involvement of the Ovambos with their Church and their affection for it intensified, and concurrently their antagonism to the South African regime as the "intruder" increased.

This antagonism was reciprocated. Perhaps the authorities never fully understood the latent undercurrent among the Ovambos, first of expectancy then of suspicion and criticism and ultimately of disapproval, and the function of the Finnish Church in their overall development. Misconceptions grew up on both sides, which the authorities interpreted as open hostility, incitement, subversion and perverseness. A certain jealousy was discernible too among the authorities of the firm hold the church still had on the daily life and thinking of the Ovambos, and of their complete loyalty towards their Church, which they had not passed on to the secular authority. Another hindrance was the Ovambo philosophy and way of life, which revealed differences from those of the Calvinist Afrikaners. The work of the Finnish Lutherans was fully appreciated, but as Dr. van Zyl, Chairman of the committee of investigation into non-White education in South West Africa (1958), said in 1970, "they are not our friends ecclesiastically."[27] An additional reason for the Government's antagonism to the Ovambokavango Church, was probably the attitude of Finland, the home of the majority of the missionaries, towards South Africa's policies, especially at the United Nations. As the result, the most important institution for opening up Ovamboland was under increasing suspicion and accused of ill-will.

Can a religious establishment such as the present Ovambokavango Church retard modernization? Generally, it does not appear to do so. The Finnish Mission Church in Ovamboland began its task without the direct protection of a colonial power that could assist it in the work of development. Not only did it replace traditional religious ideas with Christian values and a Western orientation, but it also acted as innovator and reformer in other spheres in the absence of—or perhaps because of the absence of—a colonizing nation. It strove for economic renewal and created new social codes of behaviour and new legal norms, thus inaugurating changes normally carried out by a secular authority.

It was only after the Second World War, when other ex-colonial territories in Africa were gaining independence, that the secular authorities began to take a direct interest in Ovamboland. The coming of a direct secular power structure ushered in a process of differentiation, in consequence of which more and more attempts were made to separate religion from the political structure. By this time, religious values already had a significant influence on the Ovambos' political philosphy, which the secular authority, the South African Government, evidently either did not perceive or underestimated. The clear connection between the Finnish Mission Church, as a religious and a developmental institution, and the social changes which had already occurred was not judged on its merits. Instead of stepping up the developmental contributions already made, the authorities competed with the Church in every field except religion. When the Finnish Mission Church found itself deprived of its developmental functions and increased secularisation resulting, a conflict ensued. There were now the possible alternatives of either the Church striving to dominate the secular authority, or the reverse situation, or a bipolar power struggle could ensue. This latter alternative is typical of Ovamboland and is reflected on various levels. While the traditional scheme of things was, and is, being fundamentally influenced by the Church and its value concepts, the secular authority was trying to revive and perpetuate the old traditional order. However, due to its degree of secularization, it was no longer possible to restore this order to its original state.

The South African Government does not attempt to restrict the ecclesiastical activities of the Ovambokavango Church, although it would clearly have been happier—and greater co-operation might have resulted—had the Church, which stems from the Lutheran faith, adhered to the Calvinism expounded by the three Afrikaans churches. It would be wrong to talk of religious strife in Ovamboland, but it would be equally incorrect to deny that differences do exist over the task of the church *vis-à-vis* the state.

Through the obvious disagreement between the Ovambokavango Church and the South African Government, it was to be expected that the latter would seek to limit or neutralize the influence of this church, mainly on the socio-political plane. The devotion with which the Ovambos support the Ovambokavango Church has caused them to regard any criticism of or attack on it as an attack on themselves. So strong an identification with their church has created and still creates problems in the socio-political development of Ovamboland. The Ovambokavango Church has been placed in the role of opposition, and in this it receives backing not only in Ovamboland itself and from non-white groups in the rest of Southern Africa, but also internationally. This support holds good for the Ovambokavango Church primarily as a religious institution, but it also applies in the socio-political field. Given that the church has a massive popular following and that it has at its disposal a recognized élite structure whose leadership is accepted, the result has been that in the absence of any other mass organization for canalizing political needs, it has inevitably acquired a political character;[28] it has certainly become involved in the political build up of Ovamboland. This appears to be a continuing phenomenon, fed by hostility to the South African government and its protégé, the traditional stratum of society, persists.

Group identity on the strength of membership of the Ovambokavango Church is a fact, and it affords the institution the opportunity of being a strong regulating force in most spheres of life. It appears that the Church's role and involvement in the political process is becoming more comprehensive and that the influence of religion on political culture in Ovamboland is increasing. This is true also of the social order. Thus religion in Ovamboland is a vital and decisive element, even if this was not the original aim.

(g) *The Modernizing Role of Religious Leaders.* The action of the various mission churches, as the oldest institutions for developing Ovamboland, has created an opportunity for an indigenous religious élite, as the first new or modernizing élite, to be formed. The entire progress of the country from traditionalism to modernity has indeed been marked predominantly by religious élite influence. As guardians of Christian values and moral authority this religious élite has begun to play a key role, chiefly in times of crisis and in the social transformation process. Its part in the transitional stage from traditional to modern values has been decisive, and furthermore it has not only limited its contributions to social matters, but it has also made contributions in the economic field and has taken a stand on political questions.

The religious élite has become prominent, especially since the South African Government participated directly in the development of Ovamboland and brought about tension between it and the local churches. Its chief spokesman is Bishop Auala, head of the Ovambokavango Church,[29] who expressed himself for the first time on the relations between church and state in 1969:

The Church undertakes to co-operate closely with our government and not to compete with it, if only the Government will permit the Church to do the will of God, to fulfil its task of preaching the Gospel and teaching His will to the people.[30]

This statement was the first sign of stress between the Ovambokavango Church and the Government. In his own attitude and instructions to his flock, Bishop Auala displayed tolerance towards the Government and favoured the preservation of peace. Bishop Auala's standpoint was again emphasized in September 1970, when he expressed disapproval of the decision by the World Council of Churches to make money available for freedom movements in Southern Africa. He reiterated that differences between peoples and their governments should be resolved peacefully and not by violence or terrorism.[31]

The judgement of the International Court of Justice in 1971 in favour of ending South Africa's mandate over South West Africa, led to the first political document in which the Ovambokavango Church officially expressed its views on the economic, social and political problems involved in Ovamboland's development. This document, in the form of an open letter to Prime Minister Vorster, contained numerous and varied complaints and was a motion of no-confidence in the Ovambo Legislative Council, which was deemed incapable of understanding and coping with the needs and problems of the people. In this letter spokesmen of the Ovambokavango and Evangelical Lutheran Churches of Namibia accused the Government of failing to develop Namibia generally, and of violating human rights. As an example they cited the South African racial policy which restricted the freedom of the population, and gave them a sense of insecurity. They expressed opposition to the Group Areas Act and called for the making of Namibia into a single unitary state; and alleged that the application of government policy made it impossible for political parties run by non-whites to co-operate responsibly and democratically in building a future for the whole of Namibia. The right to freedom of movement and freedom of speech was demanded.

There was finally a reference to economic questions with a complaint against job reservation, unemployment and low wages, and against the contract system with its adverse effect on family life. The open letter ended with the following comment:

The urgent wish of the Church Councils is that your Government, in conformity with the utterances of the World Court and in co-operation with UNO, of which South Africa is a member, will seek a peaceable solution to the problems of our country, and will ensure that human rights are made fully operative and that South West Africa will become an autonomous and independent state.[32]

The Anglican and the Roman Catholic Churches both identified themselves with the contents of this letter.[33] The significance of the support from Ovamboland's most important churches lay in their willingness to accept responsibility for interpreting the true attitude and feelings of the majority of the population. In this the religious élite looked upon themselves as spokesmen for the masses; had they not thus spoken out, they could well have forfeited the support of their followers.

Representatives of this élite repeated the charges in an interview with Prime Minister Vorster on 18 August 1973, following up the open letter. Fresh grievances mentioned were alleged maltreatment by the police and violation of human dignity though a policy of *baasskap* forcing them into submission.[34] Mr. Vorster replied that the concept of human rights was arbitrary, and that everyone placed a personal interpretation on it. He also ôpposed the idea of a single state for Namibia and asserted his belief both in the policy of separate development and in the retention of the identity of every population group:[35]

With all due respect I ask you as one Christian to another, because the greatest Christian virtue is gratitude, which means thankfulness and truth. The Ovambos had nothing: they were just an appendage. Separate development is not a denial of human dignity. Such dignity is implicit in the policy of separate development.[36]

In conclusion Mr. Vorster repeated his objections to church leaders interfering in political matters. He also gave Bishop Auala to understand that he regarded him as the Ovambos' leader on the spiritual plane, but that he should keep to his own métier. However, the Prime Minister added that it was the task of the churches to enlist their people's co-operation for homeland development.

This dialogue highlighted the basic differences in concept and interpretation between the religious élite and the Government. The more deep-seated differences were not ironed out at these talks, but in due course they became more acute. It seems too that there was a misunderstanding of the reason why the religious élite felt itself bound to make its views on political, social and economic questions known, and a lack of comprehension of the churches' role in the overall development process of Ovamboland. According to one of the church leaders, the open letter brought about a confrontation between Church and State unlike anything seen in the past: "The Church's clear standpoint did not only shock the government, but it also succeeded in making people more mindful of events in the country. A new political consciousness arose in the minds of our congregations, which can only be ascribed to the consistency of the Church in its public utterances. ... The Church would go ahead with revealing the political dimensions of the Gospel."[37]

Increasingly the religious élite voiced its opinions on social, economic and political matters in the development of the territory in its own church newspaper *Omukwetu*; as, for example, in comments on the International Court of Justice judgment in 1971, decisions taken at the United Nations, and reports on the labour strike and accompanying labour unrest. Despite the resentment of the South African authorities, the church leaders felt that in the absence of a daily press in Ovambo they were under an obligation to the members of their congregations to publish current as well as church news.[38] The authorities wanted to see *Omukwetu* purely as a church paper. The point of view of the religious élite was clearly enunciated in one issue thus:

There is no part of human life that is not affected by the Gospel. The church must be free to say something about political affairs, when they occasion difficulties for people, as is happening today, and it must be the mouthpiece of those who are forbidden to speak. It is clear that the churches have accepted this task in order to supply the true information.[39]

Their attitude on the different aspects of the modernization of Ovamboland was also much in evidence during the visit to the country of the two UN representatives, Dr. A. M. Escher and the Secretary-General, Kurt Waldheim. Old and well-known complaints were repeated in a memorandum handed to Dr. Waldheim by leaders of the Ovambokavango Church. Opposition was expressed first and foremost to apartheid and to the policy of Homelands for various population groups, and a request was made for independence for the whole of Namibia.[40] The memorandum emphasised the vigilant role of the church, whose task and duty it was to speak out on political problems.

During this visit, Bishop Auala made it plain to Dr. Escher that there was no hatred of whites, who had nothing to fear from an independent Namibia. South Africa should be allowed to proceed with its work of development in Namibia under UN supervision. However, he also referred to the growing impatience of the non-whites in the country with the existing political situation.[41] The objections of Ovambokavango Church members were quoted again in talks between Dr. Escher and Ovamboland's Anglican leaders. A fresh argument was advanced, blaming the unwanted Homeland development in Ovambo on the traditional leaders whose lack of education unfitted to them think independently and made them tools of the South African Government, which in reality ran the Homelands. In contrast to Bishop Auala, the Anglican leaders pointed out that South Africa was sowing hatred between Namibia's ethnic groups, and a demand was made for swift action by the United Nations.[42]

Since early 1973 the dispute between the religious élite and the South African Government, mainly on socio-political problems, has intensified. Bishop Auala contended in April 1973 that most members of the Legislative Council were, in fact, opposed to the principle of Ovamboland as a separate Homeland, basing his contention on information given to him by council members who had asked his advice.[43] The dispute appeared sharper during the second interview between the church leaders and the Prime Minister that same month. In a statement to the press it was affirmed that no agreement could be reached on several points and that the Prime Minister had again severely censured clergy who meddled in politics. In a memorandum delivered to Mr. Vorster on that occasion, complaints were made about the cancellation of visas and passports of church co-workers; the effects of separate development on family life; the alleged ill-treatment and torture of members of the Ovambokavango Church by the South African police and military; the obstruction and restraints on clergy wishing to visit congregations and parishioners on farms; and about restriction of movement as a result of pass-laws.[44] The church leaders thus emphasized anew that they saw plain speaking on social, economic and political matters as their duty and the delegation made it clear that this duty should be considered part of its function. Mr. Vorster strongly disagreed.

The greatest single factor in the deterioration of relations between the leaders of the Ovambokavango Church and the Government was the blowing up of the Church's printing-works at Oniipa on 10 May 1973. It was caused by a bomb explosion, identified as sabotage, for which Bishop Auala claimed that the South African Security Police were responsible. The blast, which destroyed all the machinery and the entire book stock, led to unparalleled solidarity between the people of Ovamboland and the religious élite, who were thereby enabled to increase their support.

Differences of opinion do exist within the religious élite on the role of church leaders in speaking out for or against the existing political authority and its policies, and those leaders evidently have the greater influence and backing who express hostility to the continuing political power structure and leadership in Ovamboland. Members of this élite who are prepared to be part of the existing regime are suspected of doing so either for personal advantage or because they feel that they can work for the benefit of their country by operating within the framework provided. They are the exception and are mistrusted, particularly by their younger and more progressive colleagues.

Wrangles that existed among this élite could still be smoothed out by the strong key-figure of Bishop Auala. His opposition to the election of the Legislative Council in August 1973 and in February 1975 was backed up not only by nearly all the ministers of his own church but also by the Anglican and Roman Catholic members of the religious élite.[45] The Bishop strongly criticized the principle of nominations to the Legislative Council, which, he maintained, were contrary to the will of the people.[46] The sole prominent ecclesiastical supporter of the election was the Ovambo Independent Church, represented by its leader the Rev. P. Kalangula, who in 1973 was nominated to the Legislative Council.

A recent manifestation among the younger members of the country's religious élite is a growing interest in Black Theology, which is meant to serve as a means to greater awareness of self-esteem and of liberation from a state of poverty, suffering, humiliation, exploitation and family disintegration. The concept sometimes accompanies identification with Black Power, with the Black Power salute as a symbol. In the thinking of, mainly, the younger members of the religious élite, a growing consciousness is taking root that only a black man can wage the real struggle for his compatriots. This exclusiveness indicates a strong awareness and resulting self-esteem among the religious élite, which serves to compensate for their lack of power *vis-à-vis* the whites.

Because thousands of Ovambos had been leaving Ovamboland from May 1974 onwards for Angola and Zambia, Bishop Auala issued a pastoral letter to the congregations in July 1974, which disclosed that many members of the church, chiefly of the modernizing groups, had left the country, and urged the remaining members to be patient, to be prepared to suffer and not to allow any of the necessary social and political changes to come about through violence. The letter also proscribed enmity among people, although the church realized that its members were being intimidated, which caused an increase in mutual hatred. This unfortunate state of affairs, said the Bishop, was being produced and accelerated by the government's apartheid policy, and yet he exhorted his followers to build bridges so as to serve the truth and preserve peace.[47]

This mass exodus, which incuded teachers, entire school classes, clergy, theological and other students, officials, clerks and nurses among others, led to joint discussions between the South African Commissioner-General in Ovamboland and church leaders at Oshakati in July 1974. In a detailed memorandum the Ovambo churches set out as follows the reasons why their adherents were emigrating:

"THE CHURCHES IN OVAMBOLAND EXPRESS THE PEOPLE'S OPINION
AS AN ANSWER TO THE COMMISSIONER-GENERAL'S QUESTION
WHY PEOPLE ARE LEAVING THE COUNTRY

The following churches are being represented in presenting this paper:
The Evangelical Lutheran Ovambokavango Church
The Roman Catholic Church
The Anglican Church
The Baptist Congregation

A. GRATITUDE

The leaders of the Churches are very grateful to the Commissioner-General for
having invited them, in these difficult times, to talks with the leaders of the
Government about why people are leaving the country.

B. REQUEST

The leaders of the Churches request the Commissioner-General to attend to it that
the discussions on June 27th, 1974 and August 6th, 1974 between the Churches and
the Government would not bring about distrust, hatred, persecution and misunderstanding, but good fruits of peace.

C. SURPRISE

The Churches are surprised at the Commissioner-General's idea of calling the
Churches to take up such matters for discussion that earlier were called politics into
which churches were not allowed to mingle with. The churches tried—long ago—to
communicate with the Government as to the general feelings of the people but
leaders of the churches who did do it were put to shame by the Government, some
were exiled, others were prohibited from p aching the Gospel where it is needed as
in Ovamboland. It is on account of the fact that the Church always wants peaceful
discussions that it has welcomed the invitation. The churches wonder whether
discussions of this sort are to be continual or just temporary?

D. THE VIEWS OF THE PEOPLE

During the meeting between the church leaders and the leaders of the Government
on June 27th, 1974, the churches were asked why people are leaving the country
without permission. The leaders of the churches consulted the parishioners in order
to supply a satisfactory answer. The following points of view reflect the nation's
opinion on why people are leaving the country and what is to be done:
1. As a mandated territory under the South African Government South West Africa
had to get all rights to develop towards self-determination and independence. The
consequent development is wrong and oppresses the South West African people. The
constitution and policy used in South Africa was not to followed in S.W.A., a
mandated territory.
2. This constitution has been enforced on the people. It does not conform to the will
of the people of the country. The policy of racial and ethnic segregation has been
strictly applied only in regard to the Blacks, depriving them of human rights whereas
the Whites as a unity have their separate means of progress and only they have all
the human rights.
3. The Odendaal plan has been carried out in the spirit of dividing the Blacks in
order to rule them.
4. The South West African people who have had a chance to education would have
liked to have a share of the politics of their own country. It is a great regret that
these people have been persecuted and that black political parties have not been

allowed and that political leaders are being tortured because of their thoughts of righteousness. This has caused hatred towards the Government.

5. The oppressive powers of the police have caused grievance among the Ovambos and all S.W.A. people. Those who oppose the inhuman constitution are being flogged, tortured with electric shocks, detained for long without trial, and the conditions of imprisonment are inhumane. This has caused fear and hatred towards the police instead of respect for it as helper of the people. The people expect the police to be defenders of peace but the terrorism-like actions of the police with their weapons have frightened the people.

6. The actions of the Ovamboland Government and its police have been found to have been instigated by the South African Government, not by the Ovamboland Government and police themselves. This has degraded the respect for the Black Government.

7. The so-called Proclamation R17/72 has badly oppressed the people by restricting the freedom of speech. Only one small political party has been accepted (the Ovambo Independent Party) but it does not act as a mouthpiece of the people. This proclamation does not conform to the agreement between the Honourable Mr. Vorster, Dr. Waldheim and Dr. Escher to grant each man freedom of speech, of movement, and of taking part in the political activities without persecution.

8. The Police are often wrongly informed because the informers are promised rich rewards. This practice has corrupted the nation.

9. The Police often intimidate parents when asking them for their children who left the country. The people want to know whether those who left their jobs at government institutions had resigned and whether their employers are being treated in the same way.

10. The practice of enforcing the identification cards is causing sufferings of shame as people are forced to give their finger prints like thieves and murderers.

11. The nation deplores the use of permits and travel documents which restricts heavily movement within the country. Passports are refused, or granted with difficulty. Whereas the Whites pay R3 for a passport the Black has to add a deposit of R200–400.

12. The Government often makes false promises. In 1968 the people were promised free elections in five years' time but nothing materialised. What happened was only to deceive the nation.

13. The difference in wages: The Black is paid according to apartheid, not work.

14. The difference in education: The people do not accept segregation in education (Bantu Education) which is enforced on them.

15. Expulsion of pupils and students who really want to study and who aim at helping their people is deplorable as well as is enforced transfers of teachers, especially those who oppose the Government.

16. The people have lost their faith in the Government which has refused to follow the will of the people and to change the wrong actions.

17. All these issues revealed by the nation have forced people to leave for exile. The nation expects the Government to change its methods and to follow the will of the majority of the nation and to give people freedom and human rights.

E. THE EFFORTS OF THE CHURCHES 1967–1974

Long ago the churches urged the government to take cognizance of what the people want. This was done as follows:

1. In 1967 the leaders of the Roman Catholic, the Evangelical Lutheran Ovambokavango and the Anglican Churches instructed the Commander of the S.A. Police in Ovamboland to stop torturing people with electric shocks. The two indigenous Lutheran Churches also addressed a memorandum to the Prime Minister in regard with the people's refusal to recognize the homeland policy.

2. In 1971 the Church Boards of the two Lutheran Churches addressed an open letter to the Prime Minister Mr. Vorster and this letter was publicly supported by the Catholic and Anglican leaders. Mr. Vorster was asked to take cognizance of the fact that the people of this country do not have human rights and that the laws used here have not been accepted by the people on whom they are just being enforced. In 1971 and 1973 these matters were orally repeated to him.

3. In 1973 two Bishops, the Anglican and the Lutheran, and one parishioner made an appeal to the Supreme Court in Windhoek to stop the inhuman and shameful floggings. The court, however, gave sanctions to public floggings of naked people. Still today people are being flogged.

4. In 1974 these same church leaders appealed to the Court of Appeal in Bloemfontein to stop the infamous floggings.

All these efforts of the Churches have been made for the sake of the truth of the Gospel and out of love of the nation and peace. We, as Church leaders and leaders of congregations speak on behalf of our parishioners who are members of the community and we appeal to the Government to inquire earnestly into the problems that trouble the nation."[48]

Some of the refugees found new homes in Europe, where several countries offered to help with their education. However, the largest number took refuge in Zambia, and the Ovambokavango Church called on two clergymen there to cater for their spiritual needs.

The Lutheran churches, including the Ovambokavango Church, regarded this exodus as a grave loss both to the black population and to the whole country. They regarded the expatriates as some of their best people and they declared that if their object had been to bring about a change in the present structure, their methods were open to doubt.

In May 1976 Bishop Auala appealed to both the South African Defence Force and SWAPO to lay down their arms; according to him, it was not too late for the two parties to hold talks to find a peaceful solution for Namibia. The appeal came at a time when South African security forces were intensifying their military operations to deter Angola-based insurgents from further attacks. The Bishop pointed out that the Ovambo population feared both the insurgents and the soldiers.

In a declaration published on 14 May 1977 the Ovambokavango Church, together with the Roman Catholic Church, the German Evangelical Lutheran Church, the Black Evangelical Lutheran Church, the Anglican Church and the Methodist Church, stated that new unrest and bloodshed in Namibia would result if the death sentence imposed on two SWAPO members by the Namibian Supreme Court should be carried out. Both were accused of having been accomplices in the assassination of Chief Elifas.

The Churches stated that the severe sentence has been unanimously deprecated for the following reasons:

In the past years we have been striving to proclaim the message of peace, reconciliation, love and justice. Even in the most difficult times the Church steadfastly persevered in this. If it was not for the calming influence of the Church, our country would already have been thrown into a bloodbath as has been the case in other African countries. We have tried to negotiate with political parties, both Black and White, as well as government institutions, to maintain peace in this country. However our work towards reconciliation has been made difficult by the harsh actions of the Defence and Police Force.

We are afraid that this unexpected judgement and death sentence in Swakopmund will lead to greater chaos and disorder and as Church leaders, we cannot guarantee that we will be in a position to control our congregations and to request them to keep the peace. We are afraid that new unrest and spilling of blood will result. Thus we ask those responsible in the country to help prevent it. Bitterness and hate are gaining the upperhand in many places in our congregations and the death sentence, described by Mr. Justice Strydom, as a "deterrent" can be the cause of new unrest in our Black Community.

We cannot see how such measures can contribute to the detente policy of the Prime Minister, Mr. Vorster. We can only see it as a hardening of fronts which could lead to the miscarriage of the detente politics which are supported by the Church.

Seen from a Christian view point, we condemn the death sentence as one of the most brutal measures to eliminate a God given life.

The Church further condemns any other method of violence, physical or institutional, of whatever type or from whatever source it may come. The church leaders want, as in the past, to contribute to the maintenance of peace in our country and ask that the best possible opportunity be given to the accused before the death penalty is carried out. Violence gives birth to violence and we fear the sentence will contribute to a further escalation of violence if it is not set aside.[49]

Another important document was the letter sent to the American Secretary of State, Dr. Kissinger, by the leaders of the Ovambokavango Church, the black Lutheran Church in Namibia and the Anglican Church in Namibia, in June 1976. It was stated in the letter that "the vast majority of the Black population of our country fervently desires that the South African Police, Army and Administration should rapidly leave this Territory". The church leaders noted that South Africa has "done some good and generous things here, such as in the fields of communications, water affairs and general economic growth". But these advances are overshadowed by "the discriminatory political policies which have been so callously implemented here". The churchmen referred to the "ever increasing rule of terror which has been inflicted on the people (especially arbitrary arrest, indefinite detention and brutal torture). These policies have destroyed human dignity and bedevilled relationships within the family and community and totally alienated the Black population. Thousands are fleeing the country because they feel unsafe in their fatherland". They added that "some of those who have fled the country feel that they have no option but to take up arms".

Dr. Kissinger was asked that the people of Namibia and the United Nations find a "way to co-operate in the working out of a plan or procedure for the peaceful and democratic transmission of power to the people of South West Africa". The churchman also asked for a general election in Namibia in which all parties should be allowed to participate peacefully. Referring to the Constitutional Conference in Windhoek, they said the vast majority of the Black population has no interest or confidence in these talks. For the most part, delegates to the convention [Constitutional Conference] were hand-picked by the South African Government. The churchmen alleged a "particular serious fraud" in the selection of the Ovambo delegates.

The Constitutional Conference was also regarded with suspicion by the church leaders because of the "dominating influence of White officials". They contended that the Constitutional Conference has only a negligible chance of success. The letter ended by stating, "We have repeatedly condemned the use of violence and brutality by anyone at all as a means of political persuasion. But we must now report with regret that our public statements and private arguments have failed to have the desired effect".[50]

Against the background of these statements, it can be seen that Ovamboland's religious leaders have played a pre-eminent role in forming values and giving direction in the process of modernization, but as we have seen, most of their actions are contrary to the aims and perceptions of the country's traditional power structure. A sustained disregard for their thinking and potential contributions in the modernizing process could have a disruptive and delaying effect on every side of the country's development. It is too strong and influential to be ignored for it already has the vigour and influence necessary to mobilize the population in favour of its proposals and values. Any oppression of the religious élite would doubtless lead to greater solidarity between it and the people.

If the Government does not abandon or at least amend its current policy of perpetuating the traditional authority and the idea of political independence for Ovamboland, a concept largely unacceptable to the religious élite, the gulf between the churches in Ovamboland and the South African and Ovambo Governments will widen rapidly, and may reach the stage where any understanding and form of co-operation will become still more difficult. Growing polarization is already clearly discernible. It is highly probable that in any conflict between church and state the Ovambos would side mainly with the Church. Thus if the development of Ovamboland is to proceed peacefully, more and more attention will have to be paid to the terms and suggestions of the church through its leaders.

2. Political and Administrative Modernization

(a) *German Administration.* Although Ovamboland was part of the *Schutzgebiet* (protectorate) which Germany had occupied since 1884, there was never any direct administrative control over the territory. The first relevant official German documents date from 1898, and the German Governor in South West Africa applied a system of indirect rule to the area. But in contrast to the treaty system, which was negotiated with all the indigenous tribes of South West Africa at the very beginning of the German colonization, this was only done with the Ovambo tribes much later, in 1908.

The fact that treaties were concluded with the Ovambo peoples only after twenty-five years of German colonization did not mean that the German Government was uninterested in Ovamboland. The chief reasons for the delayed interest in administering the territory were its geographical remoteness from the administrative centre of South West Africa and the numerous wars waged against other tribes in the country, which occupied all the German administrators. Just before these wars ended in 1907, greater interest was shown in exercising administrative control over Ovamboland. German officials had already paid visits there in order to acquire more intimate knowledge of the land and its inhabitants. In 1899 the regional head of Outjo, Captain Viktor Franke, was the first German official to go to Ovamboland, and endeavoured to induce the Kwanyama and Ndonga tribal chiefs, Uejulu and Kambonde, to accept German protection. At the prompting of Rautanen, the Finnish missionary, Kambonde did not enter into a written agreement with Franke. However, more German officials went on reconnaissance trips to Ovamboland and tried to prevail on the Ovambos to accept German protection amicably without military action.[51]

Meanwhile, military posts were established at Namutoni and Okaukueyo near the southern border of Ovamboland to ward off possible military attacks from that quarter; this appeared necessary because the Hereros had appealed to the Ovambo tribes for assistance in their struggle against the Germans, but actual conflict was forestalled through the intervention of the missionaries. The tribesmen adopted a neutral attitude, but one exception was Nehale, who attacked Namutoni on 28 January 1904 with a force of about 500 men.[52] This was the only military encounter encounter between Germans and Ovambos.

This attack led to increased interest in Ovamboland. A proclamation was issued in 1906 forbidding whites to enter the territory without official permission,[53] and the import of guns, ammunition, horses and alcohol into the area was also banned. Article 5 laid down that Africans could only be recruited as manpower with the consent of the Governor, but it was expressly stipulated that missionaries would still have free access to the territory.[54]

Thenceforth South West Africa consisted of a police zone and an area outside this zone comprising the northern native territories, including Ovamboland where the German Government was thus not represented by any soldiers and police. A second difference was that no direct administration was imposed outside the police zone, and the old tribal control system remained unaffected. The political organization of the Ovambo tribes was recognized as the basis for local rule, and association with the tribal chiefs was on a friendly basis.

What really interested the German regime in Ovamboland was its labour potential, which was urgently required for a variety of economic projects—the construction of a railway in the south, mining and farming. It was thus considered necessary by the German administration to place its relations with the Ovambos on a firmer foundation, especially since workers wanting to leave the territory had to obtain permission from their chiefs. Olivier thinks that one reason why the Germans did not impose direct jurisdiction over Ovamboland was its fear that, if it were applied, the supply of workers would be cut off.[55] The Germans were aware of the apprehension current among the tribal chiefs that their military forces might occupy the area.

To remove suspicion and improve relations, the German Government's representative, Captain Franke, concluded official treaties with the Ovambo tribal heads in 1908, which placed them under the authority and protection of the German Government in exchange for recruiting rights for contract labour in the south. Theoretically Ovamboland only became an integral part of the *Schutzgebiet* from 1908, when the German Government accepted responsibility for the control and administration of the territory, but as it did not interfere with the traditional local form of government, the old tribal authority remained unimpaired.

It was the wish of the German Government that the Ovambos should continue to live as a separate and homogeneous political community with its own legal system. The closing of the territory to any foreign elements such as white traders must be seen in this light, but infractions by Portuguese merchants from Angola were overlooked for the sake of peaceful co-existence. Yet the intentions of the Germans were less humanitarian than they appear. Avoidance of military conflicts was one reason, but another was the desire for cheap and abundant labour after many potential male African labourers from other tribes had lost their lives in warfare between the Germans and the indigenous people of South West Africa.

In fact, the Ovambo tribal heads were in due course to forfeit some of their power to impose sanctions. Acquaintance with a totally new European way of life exerted its influence on Ovambo contract workers even at that early stage. Through the impressions which they took home, their political, social and economic order was to be increasingly questioned. It was a slow process, which did not emerge during the German regime, but quietly gained momentum over the years. In this way the Germans indirectly influenced the gradual breakdown of traditional norms and authority, because they made no direct or tangible efforts to guide the traditional community along the road to modernization. They were satisfied with, and bent on, sanctioning and preserving the *status quo* and reaping material benefits from it. Their attitude towards missionary societies was often marked by suspicion, accompanied by the charge that education was unnecessary for natives. Coupled with this was the outlook that a "stupid" local inhabitant would make a humbler and more useful worker than an educated one—a viewpoint which originated in the *Herrentum* (autocratic) philosophy characteristic of the German colonial period.

(*b*) *South African Administration.* After the surrender of the German forces in 1915, South West Africa, and thus Ovamboland, came under the control of the South African Government. The country was under a military regime from 1915 to 1921 and thereafter under civil administration. South Africa did not annex South West Africa after capturing the territory, but administered it as an occupied area in accordance with international law, which forbids annexation before the cessation of hostilities. After the end of the First World War, the South African Government proposed that the country should be incorporated into South Africa as a fifth province; this proposal was unacceptable to the Peace Conference of Versailles, and instead South West Africa was declared a mandated territory ("C—category") with South Africa as the mandatory.

Three types of obligations *vis-à-vis* the League of Nations were enjoined on the mandatory for its administration of the area: the promotion of the interests of the inhabitants of the territory, and of the other members of the League, and the yearly submission to the League of Nations Council of a report on the country.[56] A mandate commission, set up by the League of Nations Council in 1921, supervised the fulfilment of the obligations.

Disputes soon arose between the mandate commission and South Africa on various matters directly connected with the welfare of the indigenous non-white population and the territory's status. The fault here lies partly in the vague wording of the original stipulations imposed on the mandatory, which were open to different interpretations. The ambiguity in Article 22 of the mandate caused questions to be raised as to who the "ultimate authority" was: this could have meant the mandatory, the Allies or the League of Nations. Further wrangles arose over what precisely was intended by the promotion of moral and material welfare. Besides, the League's inability to enforce the provisions of the mandate was soon apparent.

The claim of sovereignty likewise occasioned many problems. This question obtruded itself especially when South Africa began to exercise its mandatory responsibilities. It assumed that, as the mandatory, it had full administrative and legislative powers over the territory. Objections by the mandate commission became ever stronger when South Africa increasingly applied its laws, including "race laws", such as the "Colour Bar" Act of 1926, to South West Africa. More friction occurred between South Africa and the mandate commission over the creation of native areas, the educational development of the non-white population and the possible incorporation of South West Africa into the Union of South Africa.

From the outset, the South African Government allowed the northern areas outside the police zone to develop according to tribal traditions. Shortly after its occupation of South West Africa, a military expedition under the command of Major S. Pritchard was sent to Ovamboland in order to establish friendly relations with Ovambo chiefs. During his visit Major Pritchard, who was acting on behalf of the military administration as an "official in charge of Native Affairs", was asked by the Ndonga tribal head, Martin, to grant British protection to his tribal area. A similar request was made to Pritchard by the head of the Kwanyama tribe, Mandume, with the exclusive purpose of ensuring that the South African Government would defend him against any possible attacks by the Portuguese from Angola.

In a report after his visit, Major Pritchard suggested that the Union Government should institute administrative control over Ovamboland. One of his principal reasons for this suggestion was the general isolation of Ovamboland and the absence of any form of government administration and leadership. He concluded:

Circumstances are in our favour, and we should take advantage of the natives' frame of mind, and act. It will be difficult to imagine so unique an opportunity of establishing a political administration in a country in which, in other circumstances, resistance to authority might with reason have been anticipated.[57]

The result of these recommendations was that the military administration decided to extend its control over Ovamboland, and two white officials were stationed that same year at Ondangwa and Namakunde. Their duties were more political than administrative. They were instructed not to interfere in the traditional tribal administration, but to represent the Union Government's authority in Ovamboland. It was ensured that no whites except missionaries could settle in the area, and the autonomy of the tribes remained intact.

Tension quickly set in between Chief Mandume and the Union Government's representatives, which led to military action against him. He was defeated on 6 February 1917, and died in the battle. This also meant the end of the independent chieftainship in the Kwanyama tribe, as the deputy of the South African Government, Major Fairlie, was not prepared to accept the nomination or recommendation of a new chief. Fairlie favoured a co-operative headman system with a council of six senior headmen, of which he would be chairman at the trial of serious crimes. This arrangement was the first direct intervention in, and control over an Ovambo tribal organization by a white administrative and ruling power. According to Fairlie's definition of the new system of government among the Kwanyamas, "The Government of the people will be practically by the people. There are already in the west of Ovamboland small republics, so that this system of government cannot be entirely strange. Moreover, it is in part inaugurated in that there are headmen to represent the people".[58]

Although the system of indirect control remained for the time being limited to the Kwanyama tribe, it later spread over the whole region and thereafter was a feature of its administration. The principal headmen and sub-headmen were given advice and shown the methods of supervision advocated by representatives of the white regime. From the start, efforts were made to eliminate laws and tribal customs that ran counter to natural justice and public policy, and to reform them after consultation with the tribal authorities and with their consent. The system applied to the Kwanyamas was extended to the Mbalantu, Kolonkadhi and Eunda tribal areas. These tribes were all without a chieftainship system, but were under the rule of headmen, each of whom controlled a specific district in the tribal area. Through the aid of white officials, the various headmen were brought together within the tribal area—something previously forbidden under tribal laws—to form a tribal council. Under the leadership of the white officials, the headmen realized the advantages of such a tribal council system and began to accept joint responsibility for, and control over, their tribal areas as a whole. The remaining four tribes were still ruled by chiefs, but although they had their own councillors, they seldom made use of them and their rule was autocratic. The influence of the white officials, the example of the system of rule by headmen in the other tribes, and the growing fear among these chiefs that if they did not begin to heed the admonitions of the headmen they would lose their power over their subjects, gradually led them to appreciate the benefits of an advisory and co-operative political order.

Despotic practices by the Kwambi chief, Ipumbu, towards his subjects and his rebellious attitude towards the white resident-commissioner and the missionaries called for military action against him too, and in 1932, his kraal was bombarded by military aircraft of the South African Defence Force. Ipumbu surrendered, was dismissed from his office as chief and banished from his tribal area. No successor was appointed to him either, but a headmen's council, which was analogous to that in the Kwanyama tribal area, was established.

In consequence of these developments there are still today only three tribes in Ovamboland with a chieftainship system, while the other tribes have followed the system of headmen's councils,[59] the headmen being elected by their tribes instead of being nominated by white officials, and the choice requiring the approval of the white official responsible. This system continued with few changes till the early 1960s.

The period 1915–60 was characterized by stagnation and indirect white administration, which was anxious to subject the traditional order to the minimum of innovations and outside influences, and would brook no move by the traditional community to question the authority of indirect white control or to abolish it. In fact no initiative was shown by the white authorities in transforming traditional administrative institutions and adapting them to a modern framework, which would necessarily have made them more effective.

In general, the South African administrative regulations and governmental policy for Ovamboland remained rather vague, and no definite progress development policy was considered. The normal attitude was that there should be no interference with the traditional authority and tribal organization. In addition to the passivity of the authorities over any political and administrative advance in the region, a fairly biased view on the capacity of the Ovambos for progress was noticeable: it was said that they were law-abiding, peaceful people[60] who evinced no desire for change.

While there was failure to bring about adequate adjustments on a tribal level, neither were any efforts made to create a cohesive central administrative order. The result was that tribal particularism continued, and a collective unifying "national" identity was absent. The want of any effective administrative institutional development locally or centrally influenced every other sphere of human affairs in Ovamboland. No perceptible political and economic progress occurred during this period. Success was indeed achieved in the educational, medical and religious spheres, but the initiative came from private bodies (the churches), not from the white controlling authorities. The only economic asset employed was the region's labour potential, through which the white economy in southern Namibia benefited more than Ovamboland itself. The presence of indirect white control in the territory cannot be absolved from a utilitarian motive for exercising control over Ovamboland's labour force and exploiting it for the advancement of the white economic sector.

The exposure of workers to new influences had a drastic effect on the traditional establishment, which became acquainted with new values and systems. This change in outlook did not go unnoticed by government officials. In a government report of 1931, reference was made to the changed attitude among the population, especially the younger generation, which was inclining more and more to Western thought and customs.[61] These new values and influences could not be ignored; comparisons could now be made to the detriment of the traditional structure of Ovamboland.

It is worth noting that, whether consciously or unconsciously, the white authorities ignored the cumulative influences through which the traditional system and administration was called increasingly in question. It was probably accepted that a deliberate strengthening of a traditional system should be a sufficient guarantee to hold out against any disruptive influences, or at least to neutralize them. The traditional élite has likewise seen no reason for acceding to popular demand for change, which would imperil their own autocratic position. No reduction in status or power would thus be tolerated. Indirect white control was therefore welcome, as it helped to preserve and even extend the traditional *status quo* and power. Any innovations were treated with suspicion as irreconcilable with tradition. This élite little realized that even in that period a potential clash between traditional and modern values was germinating and this in spite of the indirect white administration, which desired to maintain the traditional power and influence at all costs. Conflict of interests was bound to arise.

This was to some extent sensed by the van Zyl Commission of 1935, which made the first thorough investigation of the situation in Ovamboland. The Commission found that the Ovambo tribal system left little scope for individual initiative and advancement, which "could easily cause the finely balanced social order to collapse". It was pointed out that the whites, when introducing new schools of thought to the Ovambos, should carefully observe their effect on the social structure. "It would be extremely simple to accomplish its ruin by speeding up the tempo of progress and thereby importing evils that could outweigh the advantages of the new progressive measures".[62] The Commission tested the view of Major Hahn, the former native commissioner in Ovamboland, who declared that the Ovambos were satisfied and happy because they were allowed to rule themselves. Interviews were conducted with the top representatives of the traditional élite, the chiefs and the headmen, who expressed their satisfaction with the form of administration then enforced.[63] It is noteworthy that the Commission indirectly conferred recognition on the existence and rise of new élites by taking evidence from clergy and teachers. In the final report, however, the evidence of the latter was not separately dealt with as was that of the chiefs and headmen.

The Commission's general conclusion was that the Ovambos were better off than they had been under the rule of their own chiefs unsupervised by Union state officials. Hence the Commission was convinced that the system of indirect administration was the best form of government for the Ovambos, and would remain so for many years. Ovamboland was seen as an excellent laboratory "for the study of both indirect control and the effects of a gradual introduction of more advanced methods to a primitive race";[64] this statement, which opened the way for the development of a more advanced administrative system, may be regarded as one of the report's most constructive observations. The existing form of indirect administration apparently did not fully satisfy the Commission, which seems also to have been displeased with the general level of development. This was abundantly evident in its recommendation "that the Mandatory [the Union of South Africa] should take more positive steps to develop the non-White races from their current backward position, in the direction prescribed in Article 22 of the Covenant of the League of Nations, and that financial means should be appropriated for this purpose".[65]

Little came of these recommendations over the next thirty years, as subsequent government reports clearly show, and no consideration was given to suitably adapted types of administration. The most important changes worth mentioning were purely of an administrative nature and did not affect the system of indirect control. One may cite particularly the establishment of a tribal trust fund, the imposition of an annual tax on all adult male natives of eighteen years and older and the appointment of Ovambo tribal secretaries, to be in charge of a central tribal office for each tribe. The tribal secretary, whose office is not a traditional institution, may be described as his tribe's chief administrative official.[66] He now forms part of the administrative echelon and his outlook is traditional, but his functions compete with those of the traditional leader.

A "political" event was the so-called plebiscite in 1947, when the non-white population was asked whether it favoured South West Africa's incorporation into South Africa or whether the trusteeship system should be continued under the United Nations. In its renewed attempt to incorporate South West Africa into the Union, the South African Government was supported by a decision of the white Legislative Assembly of South West Africa on 8 May 1946, which expressed itself in favour of incorporation.[67] The so-called plebiscite was held in order to produce further proof that the people of the country wished to be incorporated into the Union.

Meetings were held all over the country and in Ovamboland. The Government explained in a document to the United Nations that during the plebiscite the Africans were addressed and consulted by officials, who enjoyed their confidence and had the necessary experience of native affairs. The document went on: "Moreover, in view of native customs and native sensitiveness, arrangements have been made to consult the various tribes as units and not as individuals."[68] Consequently, the pre-printed petitions were signed by the chiefs, headmen or councillors on behalf of the whole tribe. It was stated in these petitions that South West Africa should become part of South Africa, that the tribe or people had made progress under the rule of the Union, that the desire existed for the South African government to continue governing the natives, and that no other government or nation except South Africa should rule the population of South West Africa.

The official result showed that 129,760 Ovambos were in favour of incorporation into the Union, and none against.[69] However, this was not the result of individual voting which was considered wholly foreign to the spirit of the tribal African. It was much more a consultation of the tribal units, "whereby the wishes of the individual could be determined by the tribal authority in the recognised traditional and customary manner".[70]

Both the figure of 129,760 and the way of conducting the plebiscite are open to question. As Ovamboland's population in 1947 was about 170,000, the stated number of those interrogated must have included women and children, who according to traditional tribal practice have no franchise. Neither can the block voting of tribes or tribal units be accepted without question as being representative, since the personal influence of white officials on the thinking and decisions of the traditional leaders has to be reckoned. It is doubtful whether the tribal leaders knew what was at stake and whether they were well enough informed. Probably there was insufficient current knowledge of the United Nations and its principles, and for the traditional leaders the choice was probably between the existing white authority and an unknown foreign alternative.[71]

No great value can therefore be attached to this poll, yet some recognition should be accorded to the attempt made to ascertain Ovambo opinion on the future of South West Africa, although it was only a block vote through the medium of the traditional leaders. In the end the so-called plebiscite made no changes to Ovamboland's existing form of administration. Among the population itself, especially the up-and-coming new élites, the plebiscite was not without results, for a consciousness of the existence of alternatives had taken root. Henceforth, these new élites-in-the-making would display a growing interest in the UN, and new expectations would be kindled. Africans fleeing from South West Africa and acting as intercessors at the UN on behalf of the black population of the territory contributed to this.

From 1959 onwards, still more witnesses from Namibia, most of whom had left the country illegally, appeared before the South West African Committee of the UN. Among the first of them were Ovambos such as Sam Nujoma, and Jacob Kuhangua, co-founders of the Ovamboland People's Organization.[72] Mburumba Kerina (Getzen), of Herero origin and a British clergyman, Michael Scott, who had travelled through Namibia on a fact-finding mission in the late 1940s, also gave evidence on Ovamboland's behalf. In addition, a petition was received from the Kwanyama tribal authority.[73] In general, the petitioners demanded the termination of South Africa's control and administration of Namibia and its take-over by UN trusteeship, which would lead to autonomy and independence.

The actions of Ovambo petitioners at the UN engendered an increasing political awareness, particularly among the budding new élites in Ovamboland. Apart from existing contacts between the petitioners and the Ovambos, chiefly adherents of the South West African People's Organization (SWAPO), the daily press and radio charted the growing importance of Namibia as a major political problem both inside South Africa and internationally. In particular, the members of the religious and educational élites realized from the beginning that the Namibian question was inextricably bound up with South African's domestic policy of separate development. The main interest centred round two interlinked aspects of this: the nascent independence of the whole of Namibia and the ending of segregation. The Namibian problem was no longer confined to mere political and legal issues, but had become invested with moral and emotional overtones. The result was that terms like human rights, human dignity, self-determination, independence, freedom of speech and movement, racial discrimination, oppression, exploitation and ill-treatment became an ever-larger part of the vocabulary of the various groups in Ovambo and also by contract labourers working in the south. With the mounting importance of the Namibian question, they all became conscious that they no longer stood alone in their views and demands concerning the political future of the territory. There was evidence of this in resolutions of the UN General Assembly and Security Council, and the Organization of African Unity, and the decision of Ethiopia and Liberia in 1960 to charge South Africa before the International Court of Justice with violating its obligations towards Namibia under the mandate. It was put to the Court that South Africa had neglected to further the moral and material welfare and progress of the territory's inhabitants to the best of its ability, and that it applied the principle of apartheid there. Objections were also raised to several alleged arbitrary, unjust and repressive measures implemented by South Africa which were deemed inconsistent with the precept of human dignity.[74]

South Africa denied and opposed these accusations, and the chairman and deputy chairman of the Special UN Committee for South West Africa were invited to conduct a personal investigation in the country. These two officials, Victorio Carpio and Dr. Martinez de Alva, visited Namibia in May 1962 and Ovamboland in particular. At the end of their visit they jointly declared that they had seen no signs of genocide or militarization, nor any trace of a threat to world peace in the territory in consequence of its administration by South Africa. Yet in their report to the Special Committee the two men objected to the application of apartheid in Namibia and to the nature of South Africa's administration of the area, which did not conform with the UN charter, the objects of the mandate and the Declaration of Human Rights.[75]

The pending indictment at the International Court of Justice and the growing international pressure against South Africa's administration of and control over Namibia, coupled with South Africa's desire to show that she set great store by the systematic social, economic and political development of the territory and its inhabitants, impelled the South African Government to appoint a commission of enquiry—the Odendaal Commission.

(c) *The Odendaal Commission.* One of the most significant events in the political evolution of Namibia's non-white population was the appointment of a "Commission of Enquiry into the Affairs of South West Africa", appointed by the State President on 11 September 1962, and its subsequent investigations. The Commission's terms of reference were as follows:

(1) Having regard to what has already been planned and put into practice, to enquire thoroughly into further promoting the material and moral welfare and the social progress of the inhabitants of South West Africa, and more particularly its non-white inhabitants, and to submit a report with recommendations on a comprehensive five-year plan for the accelerated development of the various non-White groups of South West Africa, inside as well as outside their own territories, and for the further development and building-up of such Native territories in South West Africa.

(2) With a view to this investigation, the attention of the Commission is particularly directed to the task of ascertaining—while fully taking into consideration the background, traditions and habits of the Native inhabitants—how further provision should be made for their social and economic advancement, effective health services, suitable education and training, sufficient opportunities for employment, proper agricultural, industrial and mining development in respect of their territories, and for the best form of participation by the Natives in the administration and

management of their own interests. The Commission is empowered to investigate any other matter which in its opinion may be of importance in this connection, including the financial implications and the manner in which any appropriation of funds should take place.[76]

The Commission's report appeared on 12 December 1963, the fruit of the most exhaustive socio-economic and socio-political enquiry ever conducted on Namibia.[77] In its conclusion and recommendations on the political development of the country's non-white races, the Commission foresaw slow evolutionary advancement as the best way to ultimate independence. The basis of this independence, through granting the right of self-determination to the non-whites of Namibia, would have to be the continuation and progressive expansion of the process already applied. Because of the heterogeneity of the population, the best method of eventually obtaining self-determination for the various peoples was to build on existing traditions and on the right to their own Homelands and own forms of administration. The Commission therefore advocated that each distinct ethnic group should have its own inalienable homeland "where it can govern itself according to its own expressed wishes and its own character and traditions, supplemented by what is best in Western democracy".[78] The Commission was convinced that the proposed new Homelands offered unlimited potential for the self-development and progress of the individual ethnic groups on their own native soil, but it warned that such a political change could not happen without equally important economic and social headway being made at the same time.

For Ovamboland, the Commission advised that the land area should be enlarged from 4,201,000 to 5,607,200 hectares, and that the territory should be designated a magisterial district for the exclusive use and occupation of the local indigenous communities and confirmed as the inalienable Homeland of the seven Ovambo tribes. Although these ethnic groups had "hitherto occupied separate area" and "had a separate authority for each area, each group in its evidence strongly urged that there should be one common Homeland with a Central Authority over and above the separate Community authorities. The Commission gladly accedes to this request and recommends accordingly that the said Ovamboland be enlarged as the Homeland for the said peoples".[79]

The Commission advocated the establishment of a Legislative Council for Ovamboland, made up of the following: (1) "*ex-officio*, the present functioning rulers, namely three chiefs or their authorised representatives and thirty-two headmen"; and (2) "as many elected members, elected in proportion to the number of voters of each population group, as may be determined by the members of the existing governing body: provided that such elected members shall initially not constitute more than 40 per cent of the Legislative Council".

The Commission also recommended:

That the Legislative Council gradually take over from the Department of Bantu Administration and Development the legislative authority and administrative functions, which are to be entrusted to the said Department for the time being, as recommended in Paragraph 222, or eventually all functions excluding Defence,

Foreign Affairs, Internal Security and Border Control, Posts, Water Affairs and Power Generation, Transport (with reasonable protection of the development of local transport undertakings), and that all legislation be subject to the approval and signature of the State President of the Republic of South Africa.

That the executive power of the Legislative Council be vested in an Executive Committee of seven members consisting of three chiefs, *ex officio*, or their authorized representatives, and four members elected by the Legislative Council, which will also designate the Chairman: provided that the four members elected by the Legislative Council need not necessarily be members of the Legislative Council.

That with a view to the administration of each community group, namely the Kuanyama, the Ndonga, the Kuambi, the Ngandjera, the Mbalantu, the Kualuthi and the Nkolonkati-Eunda, a community authority be established, constituted in accordance with their present functioning authorities, plus as many elected members, elected by the voters of the specific communities for each such community group mentioned above as the Legislative Council may determine, which Council shall also define the functions and powers of the said authorities.

That as soon as practicable, the Legislative Council institute for the Homeland by legislation a citizenship of its own, and that every Ovambo born in or outside Ovamboland, but within South West Africa, as well as any Ovambo born in or outside Ovamboland, but within South West Africa but now permanently resident in Ovamboland and not declared a prohibited immigrant in South West Africa, shall be entitled to such citizenship: provided that such a person shall forfeit his citizenship if he assumes the citizenship of another homeland.

That for the purpose of constituting a Legislative Council, the franchise be granted for the first election to all male and female Ovambo over the age of 18 years, provided they are resident in South West Africa and register as voters in Ovamboland, and that for subsequent elections, after the citizenship mentioned in Paragraph 306 above has been instituted, the franchise which may be exercised only within the Homeland, be granted to all citizens, both male and female, over the age of 18 years, provided they register as voters in the Homeland.

That for the purpose of the administration of justice, the Legislative Council institute by legislation inferior courts for the hearing of civil and criminal cases of minor import and a superior court for the hearing of civil and criminal cases of major import, the composition and jurisdiction of both courts to be determined by the Legislative Council: provided that all decisions of an inferior court shall be subject to appeal to the High Court and the latter's decisions shall in turn be subject to appeal to the Supreme Court of South Africa (South West Africa Division) and thereafter to the Appeal Court of the Republic of South Africa.

That when the Legislative Council has been instituted, the land within the boundaries of Ovamboland be transferred to the Legislative Council in trust for the population.[80]

It was evident from the report that the Government of the Republic still considered itself the guardian of Namibia, and that it would retain control over all developments occurring in the territory, the manner, direction, extent and speed of which it reserved the right to determine.

Ovamboland was the first area in Namibia selected for political independence. The reasons were clear: its isolation, its still operating tribal system, and the fact that it had over 46 per cent of Namibia's total population. Another reason advanced was that its independence as a self-governing territory would make it impossible for the Ovambos, as the largest single ethnic group, to dominate the other population groups in Namibia, with conflict as the result. According to the Commission, this would certainly have been possible within a unitary state. Reference was also made to the Ovambos' limited knowledge of the highly complicated economic and political system existing in the white areas. In consequence, ascendancy of the Ovambos in a single state would mean a lowering of the standard of administration and government, a situation which the whites, who were chiefly responsible for economic progress, would never tolerate. So the Commission deemed that a single central authority, representing all population groups, would not be suitable for Namibia. The alternative of Homelands with residential, political and language rights was accepted in its stead.[81]

The Commission spent eighteen days on its investigation in Ovamboland. During that time it held conversations with six whites of whom five were officials; seven white missionaries, seventy-five senior headmen, headmen, sub-headmen and tribal secretaries; nineteen traders, two nurses; nine Ovambo "officials"; twenty-six teachers and clergy and three members of SWAPO.[82] The Commission apparently sought to interview as representative a cross-section of the various interested groups in Ovamboland as possible. However, more than half the total number of people consulted were members of the traditional élite, which meant that proportionately too few members of the new élites were involved in the investigation. If, as this weighting indicates, the Commission started from the premise that the traditional value system was still the most promising framework for the Ovambo population, it laid itself open to the charge of having done so without the support of empirical proof. It could also have been objected that the existence of rival groups of political leaders was not fully recognized. While attempts were thus made to recognize the traditional leaders as political leaders, other élite groups opposed to restoring political rights to them were not properly acknowledged and consulted.

The fact that members of non-traditional groupings with influence and prestige in Ovambo society were consulted makes it clear that other groupings with functional roles in Ovamboland's development process were recognized. Evidently the Commission did not fully appreciate their influence, although the report indicated that differences of opinion on future political developments were to be found among the various groups and individuals questioned. Only a general impression of the conversations was given, and the opinions of the groupings in question were not quoted separately or analysed—which must be regarded as a shortcoming in the Commission's report.

Some of the recommendations showed that the existing administrative procedures were no longer considered appropriate for Ovamboland. The Commission was prepared, for the sake of progress, to advocate changes that would affect the power of the traditional leaders. Thus the recommendation that Ovamboland should become a single administrative area with one central administrative headquarters was incompatible with the traditional tribal laws, which forbade a tribal head to cross the boundaries of his tribal area. The recommendation that both men and women should vote, and the important provision that part of the Legislative Council-to-be should be elected was likewise contrary to tribal customs. Another provision—the setting up of lower courts and a high court—would limit the traditional legal system. The centralization of legislative, juridical and executive authority were equally vital recommendations because in this way the individual tribal authority would necessarily be curtailed, although it would continue to exist. The same was true of the suggestion that tribal land should be held in trust by the Legislative Council and no longer by individual tribes.

Viewed as a whole, all efforts were made to meet the traditional élite's wishes and to accept the traditional tribal system as a permanent basis for the political development of Ovamboland on its road to independence. Yet the Commission's political recommendations would satisfy neither the traditional nor the new modernizing élites—a fact which illustrates the dilemma of the country's political development. The traditional élite was still recognized as politically representative of the Ovambo nation, but while efforts were being made to retain its political status and authority, modernizing contacts with the whites were impairing the structure and substance of the traditional political order. About a hundred years of association with the whites, ranging from mere acquaintance to indirect and finally direct intervention in the political and administrative order, caused rivalry between Western and traditional value systems.

Against this development the traditional leaders were powerless. The rise and formation of the new élites cast doubts on the exclusive political authority of the traditional élites, who had no choice but to adapt themselves to the changes favoured by the White authorities. The old élite was too weak to offer a successful challenge to the White authority. It also realized that by competing with new élites for political influence, its declining political authority would be exposed. It therefore accepted the alternative of white protection for its traditional élite-status in a new adapted form.

The consequences were obvious. On the one hand, there was the incipient estrangement of the traditional élite from the new or modernizing élites, but on the other, the growing contacts with the white man and his controlling authority were degrading it from a body of rulers to subservient instruments. The despotic behaviour of the traditional leaders had to give way to controlled action under the aegis and supervision of the Whites. With that the period of indirect White authority ended and was superseded by direct White control.

III

THE IMPLICATIONS OF POLITICAL DEVELOPMENT

1. *Introduction*

The principle of a separate Homeland for the Ovambos was confirmed by the South African Government's acceptance of the Odendaal report. The Government made it clear that a new territory had not been created, but that an existing situation was being reaffirmed, and that any form of self-rule had to be based on the system known to the tribal group concerned. It was explained that new systems were not to be forced on people, but that current systems should rather be developed, extended and modernized and higher administrative bodies established with due regard to the prevailing circumstances and the wishes of the majority of the group.[1]

The intention was plain. Any constitutional development in Ovamboland had to be in accordance with the existing traditional system. As the spokesmen for the tribes, only traditional leaders were allowed, whose status and power were to be deliberately upheld, and who were recognized as the only valid political authority. These leaders were considered to represent the majority of the population. The use of tribal leaders in the planned constitutional development was in keeping with the South African Government's policy of making socio-economic and political advance in the tribal areas conform to the inhabitants' tradition, language and culture. Moreover, traditional and political practices and institutions in Ovamboland were to serve as the starting-point for administrative and national progress. The authoritative system peculiar to African societies was employed as a basis for the development of a centralized local political order.

The South African Government through its Minister of Bantu Administration and Development, M. C. Botha, stated that the development of local and central administrative and political bodies was not to be along Western lines, but that African traditionalism should be combined with such Western ideas as could readily be adapted to it;[2] traditionalism would still remain the point of departure and the Government would supplement it, albeit a little reluctantly, with elements from the Western democratic system.[3] The inevitability of part-adjustment to the Western system was to create a dilemma.

Because it was acknowledged that a traditional system would not at once be able to respond to all the new demands made on it, the role of the white

54

man as initiator and guardian came much into prominence, and in the process of constitutional development the power was—part directly and part indirectly—in the hands of the initiator and controller, viz. the South African Government. Lacking experience and knowledge, the traditional leaders, who were to take the intiative in the political and administrative development process, were not capable of acting as innovators. They were accustomed to ruling at the local level according to tribal tradition, and an all-embracing central authority was strange to them.

Although the constitutional recommendations of the Odendaal report were made known at many tribal meetings in 1964, their full scope was not at first realized by the traditional leaders. Explanations by white officials caused three Ovambo chiefs, thirty-three headmen and seven tribal secretaries to sign a petition, requesting the South African Government to carry out the recommendations of the Odendaal Report relating to the enlargement of Ovamboland and the establishment of a Legislative Council as soon as possible.[4] Once more the traditional élite acted exclusively on behalf of the whole population of Ovamboland without consulting it.

The offer of self-rule was made on 21 March 1967, with white officials to help in implementing it. Very soon the traditional leaders were to realize that the continuance of their power and status was coming to depend more and more on the support and goodwill of the South African Government, which had emerged as a higher authority within Ovamboland than the traditional political institutions. Another development was that the support and protection given by the white Government to the rulers led to the diminution of customary authority and support among their own people. Having had largely to waive his religious functions and powers owing to the influence of mission work, the traditional leader was now also to forfeit judicial, political and socio-economic authority, until he would become in practice, though not officially, a mere chief executive officer in the administration. Even the Government's promise that any political development would have to be based on the conventional system of government changed nothing. The powers that these leaders would gain at the centre would never, in the eyes of their people, compensate for the power he would lose in his immediate environment and local area of administration.

It seems that the leaders still viewed the new developments and proposals as a chance for recovering their waning authority and status. In this process they would tolerate no competition from other groupings in the Ovambo society, for the traditional power had to prevail. This attitude was apparent when the choice was left to them whether, as advocated by the Odendaal Report, elected representatives should be included in addition to themselves in the proposed Legislative Council. They rejected this possibility.

Under the direction of Chief Uushona Shiimi, these leaders accepted the offer of a central government on this basis "as a long-cherished ideal" and asked the South African Government in a letter to help Ovamboland in the process of obtaining self-rule. They stated in the same letter that they did not wish to be governed by any foreign powers.[5] The second request was directed at interference by the United Nations and the first implied that the Ovambos had no desire to rule over other population groups in Namibia.

The South African Government then proceeded to draft a bill on "the Development of Self-Government for Native Nations in South West Africa", which became Act No. 54 of 1968. In an explanatory memorandum the principle of using indigenous political institutions in the administration of Ovamboland was reaffirmed. It was explained that the bill aimed to enable the various groups to exist as separate and fully-fledged nations in every respect, each with its own territory and political system, and that development would depend on the inherent potential for growth of the different peoples and on the responsible guidance of the South African Government in its role as guardian.

Provision was accordingly made in the bill:

(*a*) for confirmation that certain areas are to be for the various peoples;
(*b*) for the fundamental principles of self-rule for every people by means of a system of central control, consisting of a legislative council and an executive council, and a system of local administration by subordinate authorities, of which the details in respect of each people shall be defined by Proclamation after consultation with the people concerned;
(*c*) for investing the central administration for each national group with legislative power and general powers over subordinate authorities;
(*d*) for integrating those members of a national group working outside their Homelands, with the central administration, by authorising an executive council in consultation with the Minister to appoint representatives in urban areas and other centres where there are large numbers from such Homelands;
(*e*) that the central administration should take the lead in connection with matters affecting the material, spiritual, moral and social welfare of the people in question.[6]

The broad objects of the bill were: to create homogeneous administrative areas; to train the peoples to acquire a sound understanding of the problems of soil conservation and agriculture; systematic development of a diversified economy in the Homelands; to extend education and build up their own legal system; to train the peoples in effective territorial administration; to promote the exercise of legislative powers by the peoples in respect of their own areas, initially on a limited scale but with the fixed intention of gradually extending these powers and systematically replacing white administrative and professional officials by qualified and competent indigenous members. These recommendations and objects are contained in the Act.

A feature of the Act was that it did not yet make any specific provision for ultimate independence. In the debates on the subject in the South African Parliament, repeated references were made to the fact that the decision on independence rested with Parliament. Opposition objections were mainly that, although the word "independence" was used in the introduction to the Act, it was not further defined in the Act itself, and no way was suggested as to how independence could be attained.

The Act immediately led to the issue of a proclamation, which gave recognition to each of the seven tribal and communal authorities of Ovamboland.[7] This recognition meant in effect that the South African Government had no power to appoint persons to these authorities, but that such power was still vested in the chiefs, headmen, sub-headmen and any other persons nominated by them.

Provision was made in Proclamation No. R.291 in the same Government Gazette for the establishment of a Legislative Council of Ovamboland. Its preamble stated that the native people of the territory were duly consulted over the establishment of a Legislative Council for Ovamboland, and the manner in which such a Council, and an Executive Council, should be organized. "Due consultation" was not further defined, but it probably meant consultation with the traditional leaders.

One can deduce from the Proclamation that considerable weight was given to representations from these leaders to compose the whole Council solely of nominees. According to Minister M. C. Botha, the Ovambo leaders wanted nothing to do with the franchise, and made it clear that they alone wished to rule.[8] In future, the Council would be constituted on a "federal" basis with a maximum of six members from each of the seven tribes, appointed by the various tribal authorities in accordance with their custom. Each tribal delegation was to operate as one voting unit in the Legislative Council. Any one of the nominated members could, with the consent and at the request of the tribal authorities, attend the meetings of the Legislative Council as a substitute for a nominated member. In order to become a member of the Legislative Council, the conditions were that the person had to be an Ovambo and over twenty-one years of age, with no criminal record, and neither guilty of high treason nor mentally retarded. A further stipulation was that the Council had to meet in session at least once a year.

The Executive Council was to consist of seven members, each tribe having the right to nominate one. Of the seven Council members one would be appointed by the Legislative Council as Chief Councillor and would hold office for the following five sessions of the Legislative Council. However, the State President had the right to dismiss the Chief Councillor from office at the request of the Council. The main duties of the Executive Council were the control and administration of the different departments in accordance with instructions given to the various Council members. The seven departments would be Education and Culture, Community Affairs, Justice, Economic Affairs, Agriculture, Public Works, Authority Affairs and Finance. A civil service was instituted, to consist eventually of Ovambo only; at first, however, white officials would be seconded to help with the spade-work. These men took up their duties in October 1968.

During meetings in all seven tribal communities, the six members for each tribe were appointed to the Legislative Council. On 30 September 1968 the forty-two nominated members assembled at Oshakati to acquaint themselves with the draft proclamation establishing and constituting the Legislative and Executive Councils. The procedural rules of the Legislative Council were explained to them.

The prevailing impression of the period up to the establishment of the Legislative Council was the over-emphasis placed on the traditional leader's reputed authority and status in the society. Nowhere was there any suggestion that the already existing modernizing groups had been recognized in the evolutionary constitutional process. They might well have had the chance to air their views at tribal meetings, but to obtain a hearing they were dependent on the permission of the leaders, who dominated the meetings. With the power of nomination at their disposal, leaders could ensure that none of their opponents would be admitted to the Legislative Council; they neither could nor would tolerate any rivalry. Their fear of losing absolute power was understandable, yet they could not halt the diminution of respect paid to them despite their bolstering by the white authority. The replacement of old institutions by new ones made the disintegration of traditional authority inevitable.

The creation of a central political and administrative structure caused several questions to emerge regarding tribal allegiance in Ovamboland, the attitude towards traditional authority—its exercise and its survival—and whether traditional tribal authority was preferable to a central political authority. These questions were tested with representatives of the different Ovambo élites. The question "*To what extent do you feel yourself bound to your tribe?*" explicitly referred to the particular Ovambo tribe to which the respondent belonged. The following replies were given (expressed in %):[9]

	T.	R./L.	O./C.	Comm.	N.	Trad.	Ov./Av.	Kat./Av.
Very Strongly	45.7	48.2	82.1	72.7	75.0	95.8	66.0	42.4
Strongly	13.0	3.7	14.3	9.1	20.0	4.2	10.9	22.6
Partly	30.4	18.5	3.6	18.2	—	—	14.1	16.7
Not at all	4.4	22.2	—	—	5.0	—	5.8	10.6
No reply	6.5	7.4	—	—	—	—	3.2	7.6

From these answers it is evident that loyalty to one of the seven tribes is on the whole still strong and almost the same as the average replies in a preliminary survey: "very strongly"—63%, "strongly"—10%, "partly"—12%, "not at all"—7%, no reply—8%. Only among the teachers as representatives of the educated and among the clergy representing the religious element is there a marked decline in tribal allegiance. The same tendency is revealed in the average answers given in Katutura. If all the information is taken into account, it seems clear that tribal particularism has not yet been overcome, but that it is slowly beginning to dwindle.

As a rider to this question, a test was carried out on whether the traditional Ovambo culture was still a requirement in the country's development process. By traditional culture was meant the aggregate of the spiritual quality and way of life, as passed on with adaptations from one generation to the next. The following replies were given during the in-depth interviews:

	T.	R./L.	O./C.	Comm.	N.	Trad.	Ov./Av.	Kat./Av.
Yes	43.5	40.8	71.4	81.8	90.0	83.3	62.8	9.1
No	15.2	18.5	17.9	—	—	4.2	11.5	62.1
Uncertain	21.8	18.5	7.1	9.1	10.0	12.5	14.8	24.2
To some extent	13.0	14.8	3.6	9.1	—	—	7.7	—
No reply	6.5	7.4	—	—	—	—	3.2	4.6

These replies correspond more or less to the tendency shown in the answers to the previous question. Once again, it is the ministers and teachers who object strongly to traditional culture as a requirement for any future development, and yet support for this culture is still predominant in Ovamboland taken as a whole. In Katutura the trend is altogether reversed, as the low percentage of affirmative replies indicates a wide cultural gulf between the Ovambos there and in the land of their origin.

In further questions, attention was paid to the attitude to tribal politics of the particular Ovambo tribes to which those interrogated belonged. The aim was to determine whether the tribe involved still displayed a definite allegiance or loyalty to and interest in political matters affecting it, so that subsequent comparisons could be made with questions on political affairs concerning the whole of Ovamboland and Namibia. Three further questions and answers follow:

Question: ARE YOU INTERESTED IN THE TRIBAL POLITICAL AFFAIRS OF YOUR TRIBE?

	T.	R./L.	O./C.	Comm.	N.	Trad.	Ov./Av.	Kat./Av.
Very	34.8	44.5	75.0	63.6	15.0	95.8	52.5	45.4
Little	36.9	14.8	25.0	27.3	30.0	4.2	24.4	15.2
Not at all	19.6	37.0	—	9.1	45.0	—	18.6	33.3
No reply	8.7	3.7	—	—	10.0	—	4.5	6.1

Question: DO YOU SUPPORT THE PRESENT METHOD OF ELECTING TRIBAL AUTHORITIES?

	T.	R./L.	O./C.	Comm.	N.	Trad.	Ov./Av.	Kat./Av.
Yes	6.5	11.1	42.9	63.6	5.0	95.8	31.4	21.2
No	91.3	88.9	53.6	36.4	80.0	4.2	65.4	75.8
No reply	2.2	—	3.5	—	15.0	—	3.2	3.0

Question: ARE YOU SATISFIED WITH THE PEOPLE SERVING IN THE TRIBAL AUTHORITIES (COMPOSITION)?

	T.	R./L.	O./C.	Comm.	N.	Trad.	Ov./Av.	Kat./Av.
Yes	8.7	7.4	35.7	54.5	30.0	95.8	28.9	21.2
No	84.8	81.5	60.7	45.5	70.0	4.2	62.8	71.2
To some extent	2.2	—	—	—	—	—	0.6	—
No reply	4.3	11.1	3.6	—	—	—	7.7	7.6

In the main there still appears to be reasonable interest in tribal political affairs and further proof of identification with those tribes to which the respondents belong. However, decreasing interest can be expected. This may be inferred from the answers of the strongest modernizing groups in Ovamboland—the teachers, clergymen and nurses. Over the current method of electing tribal authorities there exist wide differences of opinion between these teachers, clergymen and nurses on the one hand, and the traditional leaders on the other, with a middle group formed by the traders and officials/clerks. There is generally strong objection to the composition of the current tribal authorities and to their method of election. This is true of Ovamboland and to an even greater degree of Katutura.

The reasons for, and origin of, this opposition were ascertained in an open question. Opposition was expressed primarily to the principle of nominating members of tribal councils instead of holding free general elections. Another objection was that these tribal councils still mainly comprised the traditional leaders and their partisans, and they were accused of inefficiency, illiteracy and high-handedness. Members of the tribal authorities were also charged with living and acting in isolation from the thinking of the rest of the population. This antagonism, which was found predominantly among ministers, teachers, officials/clerks (except tribal secretaries) and nurses, was intensified by the allegation that the tribal authorities were adherents and exponents of South African Government policy, which was aimed at preserving and restoring tradition.

The favourable comments were made chiefly by the traditional leaders, who consider they know their people best and do most for them, and that they are the most highly respected section of society and the outstanding leaders, who act according to tradition. Their self-esteem is largely disavowed by the modernizing élite groups. The traditional tribal authority's continued responsibility for the maintenance of law and order, is strongly criticised and judged adversely. This tendency emerges from the following question:

Question: HOW IMPORTANT DO YOU CONSIDER THE CONTINUED EXISTENCE OF THE TRADITIONAL TRIBAL AUTHORITIES FOR THE MAINTENANCE OF AUTHORITY IN OVAMBOLAND?

	T.	R./L.	O./C.	Comm.	N.	Trad.	Ov./Av.	Kat./Av.
Very important	15.2	14.8	57.1	45.4	15.0	79.2	34.6	13.6
Less important	39.1	40.7	28.6	27.3	70.0	20.8	37.8	15.1
Unimportant	37.0	33.3	14.3	27.3	15.0	—	23.1	66.7
No reply	8.7	11.1	—	—	—	—	4.5	4.6

Question: DO YOU CONSIDER THE CONTINUED EXISTENCE OF THE TRADITIONAL TRIBAL AUTHORITY IMPORTANT FOR THE POLITICAL DEVELOPMENT OF OVAMBOLAND?

	T.	R./L.	O./C.	Comm.	N.	Trad.	Ov./Av.	Kat./Av.
Yes	13.0	22.2	50.0	63.6	10.0	87.5	35.9	4.5
No	73.9	77.8	32.1	27.3	15.0	12.5	46.8	86.4
To a certain extent	8.7	—	17.9	9.1	25.0	—	9.6	—
No reply	4.4	—	—	—	50.0	—	17.7	9.1

From these answers it is obvious that the modernizing groups, especially teachers, clergy and nurses, regard the continued existence of the traditional tribal authority as unimportant, and without any value for Ovamboland's political development. Again this attitude is reflected far more strongly in Katutura than in Ovamboland. The reasons given for this disapproval are the lack or low standard of education of the traditional leaders, their ignorance of and opposition to politics, their inability to be part of a dynamic modernizing process and their failure to recognize that no development can take place with the retention of all traditional values.

In support of the traditional tribal authority the traditional leaders, tribal secretaries and traders contend that traditional authority and political development cannot be separated, that tradition must be preserved and that the tribal authority is the foundation of all power.

That decline in influence must follow from the overwhelming antagonism to the traditional tribal authority is confirmed in the following replies:

Question: DO YOU THINK THAT THE INFLUENCE OF THE TRADITIONAL TRIBAL AUTHORITY IS DECREASING/INCREASING?

	T.	R./L.	O./C.	Comm.	N.	Trad.	Ov./Av.	Kat./Av.
Decreasing	76.1	48.1	57.1	36.4	45.0	12.5	51.3	57.6
Increasing	2.2	7.4	14.3	18.2	—	37.5	11.5	3.0
No change	19.6	33.3	25.0	36.4	5.0	50.0	26.9	30.3
No reply	2.1	11.1	3.6	9.1	50.0	—	10.3	9.1

The replies in both Ovamboland and Katutura indicate a decline in the influence of the traditional tribal authority, the implication of which is that its very existence is in jeopardy. The main reasons given are the growing literacy in Ovamboland, and the traditional leaders' weak and arbitrary exercise of authority. The importance attached to the traditional power by the South African Government in the development process is itself adduced as a contributory factor in the decline of the traditional tribal authority. The degree of influence of the current tribal authority, viz. the traditional leaders, on Ovamboland's political progress is significant. So too is the question whether the tribal authorities should have more power than the Legislative Council (see page 62).

Against the background of earlier answers, it was to be expected that in the majority view, the traditional tribal authority had relatively little influence on political development in Ovamboland (in Katutura it has none).

The replies to the question whether tribal administrations should have greater power than the Legislative Council, i.e. whether a local authority is more important for Ovamboland than a central authority, reveal a general rejection of such a proposition. Although a fairly high percentage gave no answers, which seems to indicate a repudiation of both kinds of authority, various progressive groupings expressed strong support for subordinating tribal interests to a central authority. The motivation for this attitude revealed a preference for a central authority for the whole of Namibia, rather than for a central authority for Ovamboland. If all these attitudes existed when the first Legislative Council was formed and became operative, it certainly began its work in a very unfavourable atmosphere.

Question: HOW STRONG IS THE INFLUENCE OF THE PRESENT TRIBAL
AUTHORITY ON THE POLITICAL DEVELOPMENT OF OVAMBOLAND?

	T.	R./L.	O./C.	Comm.	N.	Trad.	Ov./Av.	Kat./Av.
Very Strong	8.7	14.8	39.3	36.3	5.0	70.8	26.3	10.6
Strong	8.7	3.7	3.6	9.1	10.0	8.3	7.0	3.0
Moderate	30.4	25.9	17.9	27.3	45.0	20.8	27.6	9.1
Weak	50.0	29.6	32.1	27.3	15.0	—	29.5	74.3
No reply	2.2	25.9	7.1	—	25.0	—	9.6	3.0

Question: DO YOU THINK THAT THE TRIBAL AUTHORITIES SHOULD
HAVE MORE POWER THAN THE LEGISLATIVE COUNCIL?

	T.	R./L.	O./C.	Comm.	N.	Trad.	Ov./Av.	Kat./Av.
Yes	10.9	14.8	28.6	18.2	—	29.2	16.7	21.2
No	73.9	74.1	60.7	81.8	25.0	58.3	63.4	53.0
The same power	2.2	3.7	7.1	—	—	8.3	3.8	6.1
Don't know	—	—	—	—	40.0	4.2	5.8	—
No reply	13.0	7.4	3.6	—	35.0	—	10.3	19.7

2. *Composition and Functioning of the Legislative Council*

When the Legislative Council was established, Chief Uushona Shiimi of
the Ngandjera tribe was appointed as its Chief Councillor. It is remarkable
that the chief of a smaller tribe was chosen for this post and not the chief
of the mother-tribe, the Ndonga, or a senior headman from the
Kwanyama, the largest and most politically-minded tribe. In charge of the
seven departments was either the chief or the senior headman of each of
the seven tribes. The Executive Council, when constituted, had the
following members:

Department	Councillor in Charge
Authority Affairs and Finance, Chief Councillor	Chief U. Shiimi (Ngandjera tribe)
Community Affairs	Senior-Headman S. Iipumbu (Kwambi tribe)
Education and Culture	Senior-Headman W. Kanyele (Kolonkadhi-Eunda tribe)
Economic Affairs	Senior-Headman F. Kaluvi (Kwanyama tribe)
Works	Senior-Headman K. Mundjele (Mbalantu tribe)
Justice	Chief P. Elifas (Ndonga tribe)
Agriculture	Chief J. Taapopi (Kwaluudhi tribe)

The following changes of personnel were to occur between 1968 and
1973. In 1971 Senior-Headman W. Kanyele was given the post of Works
in place of Education and Culture, Senior-Headman Mundjele took
Economic Affairs in place of Works, and Senior-Headman Kaluvi
Education and Culture in place of Economic Affairs. These changes were

partly due to the inability of certain members to cope effectively with the portfolios awarded to them, the classic example being Senior-Headman W. Kanyele, in charge of Education and Culture, who had had no schooling himself. Drastic changes occurred on 14 January 1972 after the Chief Councillor, Chief U. Shiimi, had died in a motor accident at the end of the previous year. The death of Chief Paulus Elifas caused another change. Chief Filemon Elifas of the Ndonga tribe was elected in his place and became Chief Councillor, while Chief Jafet Malenga, the new Chief of the Ngandjera tribe, was elected to succeed Chief Shiimi. Senior-Headman Kaluvi, who as Councillor charged with Education and Culture did not prove a success because of his own inferior education, was dropped from the new administration and appointed as representative of the Executive Council in the white urban areas. He was succeeded by the first non-traditional leader in the person of the Revd. Kornelius Ndjoba of the Kwanyama tribe, and with this appointment the Department of Education and Culture could boast of having the best educated member of the Executive Council as its head. The failure of the two traditional leaders who had been put in charge of education necessitated the appointment of a better educated person, who was prepared to support the traditional authority.

The composition of the new Executive Council was then as follows:

Department	Councillor in Charge
Authority Affairs and Finance, Chief Councillor	Chief F. S. Elifas
Community Affairs	Senior-Headman S. Iipumbu
Education and Culture	The Revd. K. Ndjoba
Economic Affairs	Senior-Headman K. Mundjele
Works	Senior-Headman W. Kanyele
Justice	Chief J. M. Munkundi
Agriculture	Chief S. Taapopi

We now turn to the general background and educational level of the Executive Councillors.

The Chief Councillor, *Chief Uushona Shiimi,* born in 1919, grew up in the main kraals of different Ngandjera Chiefs, where in course of time he became a secretary of sorts to Chief Shaanika Ipinge, his maternal uncle. Now and again he temporarily attended school and obtained a maximum qualification equivalent to Standard I or II. He joined the army in 1942, was briefly stationed at Tsumeb, and then recruited soldiers for the Union troops because of unwillingness among the Ovambos to take part in the war. As the child of Chief Ipinge's sister, he became Chief of the Ngandjera tribe on Ipinge's death in 1948.

Senior-Headman W. Kanyele, born in 1911, began his career as a cattleherd, then worked in the south as a contract labourer, until in 1956 he was appointed private tribal messenger and guard to Senior-Headman Ashimbanga. That year he also became tribal messenger of his tribe, and from this position was nominated Member of the Legislative Council and

Councillor. He had no schooling, was married in traditional style and has two wives.

Chief Taapopi, born in 1936, also began his career as a cattleherd and contract labourer in the south, until in 1959 he was appointed acting Chief of his tribe, becoming full Chief in 1960. Baptised in 1961, he thereby became the tribe's first Christian Chief. At school he studied up to Sub B.

Senior-Headman S.F. Iipumbu, born in 1912, is the son of the late Chief I. Shilongo. In addition to his task of herding cattle, he went to school and attained Standard IV. After his father was banished in 1932, he was nominated by the tribe to succeed him as Senior-Headman. He is traditionally married to six wives and has about sixty children.

Chief Paulus Elifas was born in 1920. He had a traditional upbringing, but nothing is known of his educational qualifications. He has since died.

Senior-Headman Mundjele, who was born about 1910, also had a traditional upbringing, but no schooling. He is married traditionally and has two wives.

The last member of the First Executive Council in its original composition was *Senior-Headman Kaluvi*, but no information is available about his background. He is, however, known to have had very little education.

Chief F. S. Elifas, who replaced Chief P. Elifas as Executive Councillor after his death in 1970, was born in 1932. Except for a short period at Odimbo and Olukonda, he received most of his schooling at Oniipa and finished his education at the age of about twenty in Standard IV. He was assassinated in August 1975.

The first non-traditional member of the Cabinet was the *Revd. Kornelius Tuhafeni Ndjoba*, who managed the post of Education and subsequently succeeded Chief F. Elifas as Chief Minister. He was born on 10 November 1930 in the Kwanyama tribal area, and spent most of his childhood at Eenyika. He later received training in tribal matters from his maternal uncles, who were tribal chiefs. After his primary schooling, he went to a secondary school and in 1950 enrolled as student teacher at the Oniipa Training College. He obtained his teacher's certificate two years later. In 1953 he was appointed Principal of the newly established Eenhana Boys' School, where he taught till 1957. He then left teaching to study in seminaries at Oshigambo and Elim, and in 1968 he was ordained a Pastor in the Ovambokavango Church. During the same year he was appointed Member of the First Ovambo Legislative Council. On 30 May 1977 he was installed as a Senior–Headman of the Kwanyama tribe.

Six of the seven members in the Cabinet belonged to the traditional élite and their average level of education was equivalent to Standard I, but the addition of a non-traditional leader in the person of Ndjoba raised this average to about Standard II. Optimism, therefore, could not be felt regarding this Council's intelligence, effectiveness or ability to make and implement policy, even taking into account that political ability does not necessarily demand formal education.

After the reallocation of posts mentioned above, the educational level of the Executive Council, (a Cabinet from 1 May 1973) was as follows:

Senior-Headman Kanyele	No schooling
Chief Taapopi	Sub B
Senior-Headman Iipumbu	Std. IV
Senior-Headman Mundjele	No schooling
Chief F. S. Elifas (Chief Councillor)	Std. IV
Chief J. M. Munkundi	Std. II
The Revd. K. Ndjoba	Std. VI plus training as Teacher and Pastor

After the election of the Second Legislative Council on August 1 and 2, 1973, a new Cabinet was appointed as shown on page 66.

Although the new cabinet had a higher educational standard than its predecessor (equivalent to Std. IV) it still contained one illiterate. It had one traditional leader less as member, but the traditional leaders were still in the majority. If the educational qualifications only of traditional leaders in the Cabinet were taken into account, they would have been equal to Std. II. The rise to an average of Std. IV was due to the appreciably higher qualifications of the two clergyman serving in it.

The composition of the next Cabinet, after the election in January 1975, was as indicated in the table on page 67.

The educational level of the Cabinet of the Third Legislative Council was slightly lower than that of the former one, being equivalent to Std. III. The one illiterate, Chief Taapopi, was retained. In all, this Cabinet had one traditional leader less than the previous Cabinet, and F. Indongo, the richest trader in Ovamboland, was included in it. This was the first time that a merchant had held a Cabinet post.

After the assassination of Chief Elifas, the Chief Minister, on 16 August 1975, the Revd. K. Ndjoba was elected in his stead. With this step a non-traditional leader was appointed for the first time Chief Minister of Ovamboland. The new Cabinet was made up as as shown on page 68.

The average educational level of this cabinet was slightly above Std. IV, and was the highest to date. The successor of the murdered Chief Elifas as tribal head of the Ndonga tribe, Chief Immanuel Elijas, did not make himself available as a member of the Cabinet. T. Iimbili, who was elected to the Cabinet in place of Chief Elifas, had been an official in the service of the Department of Economic Affairs for Ovamboland in 1971–3, and afterwards for a year the private secretary of Chief Elifas. In 1973 he entered active politics and became Secretary-General of the Ovamboland Independent Party, having formerly been a member of the Legislative Council. There was an abortive attempt on his life early in December 1975.

The educational level of the Cabinet improved considerably when two new members were added to the Cabinet. The leader of the Ovambo Independent Church, the Revd. P. Kalangula, replaced Chief J. Munkundi

COMPOSITION OF CABINET: SECOND LEGISLATIVE COUNCIL

Profession	Name	Educational Qualification	Age	Religion	Tribe	Portfolio
Chief	F. Elifas	Std. IV	42	ELOC*	Ndonga	Chief Minister and Finance
Chief	J. S. Taapopi	Nil	36	ELOC	Kwaluudhi	Agriculture and Forestry
Chief	J. Munkundi	Std. IV	44	ELOC	Ngandjera	Justice
Senior-Headman	D. Shooya	Sub B	46	ELOC	Kolonkadhi	Works
Senior-Headman	J. Ashipala	Std. VI	48	Angl.	Kwambi	Interior
Clergyman	K. T. Ndjoba	Std. VI Teachers' Diploma and Theological Training	43	ELOC	Kwanyama	Education
Clergyman	T. Heita	Std. VI and Theological Training	52	ELOC	Mbalantu	Economic Affairs

* Evangelical Lutheran Ovambokavango Church.

COMPOSITION OF CABINET: THIRD LEGISLATIVE COUNCIL

Profession	Name	Educational Qualifications	Age	Religion	Tribe	Portfolio
Chief	F. Elifas	Std. IV	44	ELOC	Ndonga	Chief Minister and Finance
Clergyman	K. Ndjoba	Std. VI Teachers' Diploma and Theological Training	45	ELOC	Kwanyama	Education
Senior-Headman	D. Shooya	Sub B	48	ELOC	Kolonkadhi-Eunda	Interior
Clergyman	T. Heita	Std. VI and Theological Training	54	ELOC	Mbalantu	Justice
Chief	J. S. Taapopi	Nil	38	Prev., ELOC. Since 1975, D.R. Church	Kwaluudhi	Agriculture and Forestry
Trader	F. Indongo	Std. II	42	Roman Catholic	Kwambi	Economic Affairs
Chief	J. Munkundi	Std. IV	46	ELOC	Ngandjera	Roads and Works

COMPOSITION OF CABINET FOLLOWING DEATH OF CHIEF ELIFAS

Profession	Name	Educational Qualifications	Age	Religion	Tribe	Portfolio
Clergyman	K. Ndjoba	Std. VI and Teaching and Theological Training	46	ELOC	Kwanyama	Chief Minister and Finance
Chief	J. S. Taapopi	Nil	39	DR	Kwaluudhi	Agriculture and Forestry
Chief	J. Munkundi	Std. IV	47	ELOC	Ngandjera	Roads and Works
Senior-Headman	D. Shooya	Sub B	49	ELOC	Kolonkadhi-Eunda	Interior
Clergyman	T. Heita	Std. VI and Theological Training	55	ELOC	Mbalantu	Education
Trader	F. Indongo	Std. II	43	RC	Kwambi	Economic Affairs
Politician (formerly an official)	T. Iimbili	Std. VI	44	ELOC	Ndonga	Justice

as Minister for Roads and Works late in 1976. Chief Munkundi resigned in order to give more attention to tribal affairs. A new Department of Health was established on 1 August 1976. This portfolio is held by Toivo Shiyagaya, a well-educated and articulated person.

On 1 April 1977 the composition of the Ovambo Cabinet was as shown in the table on page 70.

Owing to a lack of information on the statistical particulars of the Third Legislative Council, only a summary and a comparison with its two predecessors in regard to the total number of members, average age, list of occupations, religious denominations and educational qualifications is shown on page 71. But it can be assumed that the Third Legislative Council, owing to larger number of elected members (42 altogether and 35 nominated) will on average be better educated. Ten members of the former Council were not re-elected.

At no stage did the educational level of the traditional leaders in the Legislative Council reflect the average educational standard of the Ovambo people, but remained below it.

It is noteworthy that only four occupations were represented in the First and Second Legislative Councils—traditional leaders, clergy, farmers and traders. The Second Council showed a large increase in traders who, beside the farmers, were the strongest supporters of the traditional leaders. The six ministers serving on this Council were largely prepared to back up the traditionalists. In both Councils the Ovambokavango Church had the largest number of adherents among the members, viz. 90 and 80 per cent respectively. It is thus clear that in the first two Councils, modernizing élites such as teachers, progressive pastors, officials/clerks and nurses were absent.

The range of occupations in the Third Legislative Council showed a change from its two forerunners. Of the members twenty-two traditional leaders, four traders, seven ministers and 2 farmers were nominated by the different tribes; and three traditional leaders out of fourteen candidates, three out of seven church office-bearers (three of whom withdrew before election days), one out of four housewives, three out of eight clerks/ officials, twenty out of thirty-six merchants, four out of eight ordinary labourers and eight out of thirty-two farmers were elected. The various churches put pressure on their clergy not to seek nomination or election, and one pastor resigned after the election. This caused a by-election in July 1975 which was won by J. Nangutuuala. Although he is the leader of DEMCOP, he did not stand officially as this party's candidate.

A notable trend in the election was the great popularity enjoyed by the merchants. At the same time the performance of the traditional leaders indicates a measure of resistance to them. It was the first time that women were elected to the Council. Although traders tend to be conservative in their political views, the large measure of support given to them can possibly be ascribed to the status and influence that accompany the possession of cash—to which more value is probably attached than to mere ownership of land and cattle.

It is striking that in the Third Legislative Council members of the modernizing élites were still poorly represented. Their opposition to the

COMPOSITION OF OVAMBO CABINET, 1 APRIL 1977

Profession	Name	Educational Qualifications	Age	Religion	Tribe	Portfolio
Clergyman	K. Ndjoba	Std. VI; Teaching and Theological Training	48	ELOC	Kwanyama	Chief Minister and Finance
Chief	J. S. Taapopi	Nil	41	DR	Kwaluudhi	Agriculture and Forestry
Clergyman	P. Kalangula	Matriculation and Theological Training	51	OIC	Kwanyama	Roads and Works
Senior-Headman	D. Shooya	Sub B	51	ELOC	Kolonkadhi-Eunda	Interior
Clergyman	T. Heita	Std. VI and Theological Training	57	ELOC	Mbalantu	Education
Trader	F. Indongo	Std. II	45	RC	Kwambi	Economic Affairs
Politician (formerly an official)	T. Iimbili	Std. VI	46	ELOC	Ndonga	Justice
Clerk/Official	T. Shiyagaya	Std. VIII and Teaching Training	48	ELOC	Ngandjera	Health

FIRST AND SECOND LEGISLATIVE COUNCILS: OCCUPATIONS AND RELIGION

	Total Members	Average Age	Occupation					Religious Denomination		
			Trad.	Cler.	Farming	Comm.	ELOC	Angl.	R.C.	Nil
First Legislative Council 1968–73	42	53	24	4	7	7	38	—	1	3
Second Legislative Council 1973–4	56	49	24	6	7	19	45	6	2	3

EDUCATIONAL QUALIFICATIONS

	Sub A or B	Std. I	Std. II	Std. III	Std. IV	Std. V	Std. VI	Form 5	Cler. Tr.†	Teach. Tr.‡	Nil
First Legislative Council	4	—	11	8	1	3	1	—	4	2	8
Second Legislative Council	1	—	2	5	6	3	3	2	4	5	25

† Training as a clergyman usually after Std. V or VI. ‡ Teacher training usually after Std. VI.

Legislative Council remained almost complete. This prevailing attitude provides confirmation of a tendency already shown by the answers given to questions during the in-depth interviews on the First Legislative Council:

Question: ARE YOU SATISFIED WITH THE COMPOSITION OF THE LEGISLATIVE COUNCIL (the first)?

	T.	R./L.	O./C.	Comm.	N.	Trad.	Ov./Av.	Kat./Av.
Yes	4.3	7.4	42.9	72.7	—	70.8	26.3	15.1
No	95.7	92.6	57.1	27.3	85.0	29.2	71.8	84.9
No reply	—	—	—	—	15.0	—	1.9	—

In the aggregate, the occupational composition of the Third Legislative Council (elected and appointed) was as follows.

Traditional leaders	25
Traders	24
Religious Occupations	9
Farmers	10
Labourers	4
Officials/Clerks	3
Housewives	1
Teachers	1

In anticipation of the answers to this question, the reasons for opposition to, or support for, the Legislative Council were more deeply enquired into as shown on page 73.

These answers reveal a deep antagonism to the Legislative Council, even on the part of some traditional leaders, who possibly feared that any strengthening of the central institution could harm the tribal one. Another reason may be the popular dissatisfaction over the composition of the Legislative Council—the first Council consisted solely of nominees, with no democratically elected members. The idea of democratic election has the overwhelming support of respondents, and the present system of partly nominating and partly electing the Council is supported by a minority only. Hence the strongest criticism appears to be directed not against the legislative body as such but against its composition.

It is clear that the first Legislative Council did not enjoy the full trust of the whole population, and in consequence the opinions of the majority were not represented, if the modernizing groups are taken as the yardstick. The strongest objections came from the teachers, clergy and nurses, but the Council had more support from the officials/clerks and traders, with their strongest backing from the traditional leaders, who in the first Council had the most powerful representation.

The fair amount of current interest in the activities of the Legislative Council is mostly confined to Ovamboland. In the answers to the other questions this tendency is apparent throughout, whereas in Katutura the Council is vehemently repudiated in all its aspects, and there is virtually no

Question: DO YOU THINK THAT THE LEGISLATIVE COUNCIL OF
OVAMBOLAND, MUST …

	T.	R./L.	O./C.	Comm.	N.	Trad.	Ov./Av.	Kat./Av.
… only consist of representatives appointed by the tribe?	—	—	14.3	9.1	—	25.0	7.1	16.6
… only consist of representatives elected by the whole population?	80.4	77.8	60.7	63.6	100.0	25.0	69.2	66.7
… consist of elected and nominated representatives?	10.9	7.4	25.0	27.3	—	50.0	1 8.6	7.6
No reply	8.7	14.8	—	—	—	—	5.1	9.1

Question: DO THE PEOPLE RETURNED BY YOUR TRIBE TO THE
LEGISLATIVE COUNCIL, REPRESENT YOUR OWN PERSONAL
ATTITUDE?

	T.	R./L.	O./C.	Comm.	N.	Trad.	Ov./Av.	Kat./Av.
Yes, completely	2.2	3.7	35.7	45.4	—	87.5	24.4	3.0
To some extent	23.9	29.6	35.7	36.4	5.0	12.5	23.7	12.1
Definitely not	69.6	63.0	25.0	18.2	80.0	—	47.4	77.3
No reply	4.3	3.7	3.6	—	15.0	—	4.5	7.6

Question: DO YOU SUPPORT THE INSTITUTION AND THE ACTIVITIES
OF THE LEGISLATIVE COUNCIL?

	T.	R./L.	O./C.	Comm.	N.	Trad.	Ov./Av.	Kat./Av.
Yes	8.7	11.1	57.1	72.7	—	95.8	34.6	24.2
No	84.8	85.2	42.9	27.3	90.0	4.2	61.5	75.8
To some extent	2.2	3.7	—	—	—	—	1.3	—
No reply	4.3	—	—	—	10.0	—	2.6	—

Question: ARE YOU INTERESTED IN THE ACTIVITIES OF OVAMBO'S
LEGISLATIVE COUNCIL?

	T.	R./L.	O./C.	Comm.	N.	Trad.	Ov./Av.	Kat./Av.
Very	19.6	25.9	57.1	72.7	10.0	91.7	41.0	12.1
Not much	32.6	22.2	32.2	27.3	20.0	8.3	25.0	24.3
Not at all	45.6	40.7	10.7	—	60.0	—	30.1	60.6
No reply	2.2	11.1	—	—	10.0	—	3.9	3.0

Question: DOES THE LEGISLATIVE COUNCIL SERVE A USEFUL
PURPOSE IN YOUR OPINION?

	T.	*R./L.*	*O./C.*	*Comm.*	*N.*	*Trad.*	*Ov./Av.*	*Kat./Av.*
Yes	10.9	14.8	57.1	63.6	10.0	91.7	35.9	7.6
No	76.1	81.5	21.4	18.2	65.0	8.3	51.3	87.9
To some extent	8.7	3.7	17.9	18.2	—	—	7.7	3.0
No reply	4.3	—	3.6	—	25.0	—	5.1	1.5

support for it or identification with it. From this it can be inferred that the
Ovambo inhabitants of Katutura now identify themselves politically not
with Ovamboland but with Namibia as a whole.

The hostility to the Legislative Council in both Ovamboland and
Katutura is based on the fact that its members are not in touch with the
thinking and wishes of the population. Another objection raised is that,
allegedly, most Council members are illiterate, stupid and incompetent.
Again this situation is imputed to the Council's being representative of
traditional thought only, and not reflecting the outlook of the better
educated and forward-looking section of the population although the latter
are thought to be in the majority throughout. However, due to the
nomination system they are not fully represented in the Council. Others
oppose the Council because it subscribes to the Homeland idea, whereas
they demand a Legislative Coucil for the whole of Namibia. Thus the
Council is regarded only as a mouthpiece of the South African Government
to promote the policy of apartheid.

The minority supporting the Council contend that the traditional leaders
are the natural leaders, who must be represented as such, and who act in
the interests of the people and bring development and progress to
Ovamboland. The Council, it is said, has united the country and conducts
tribal politics at a higher central level; it is also seen as a step from the
traditional to the modern, its composition being in harmony with the
thinking and wishes of most Ovambos.

Early on, the traditional leaders became sensitive to many of the
objections, which put them on the defensive. Even during the opening of
the first session of the First Legislative Council, the Chief Councillor, Chief
Shiimi, pointed out that the Council was not forced upon the Ovambo
people, but had come about through consultation with them. Yet he
intimated that the proposal to establish a Legislative Council had
originated with the South African Government. After this the Ovambo
leaders had decided to accept it enthusiastically.[10] With these observations
Chief Shiimi lent substance to the complaints of the modernizing section
that the Legislative Council merely reflected the wishes of the traditional
leaders, following its proposal by the South African Government. The
establishment of a Legislative Council was acceptable to the traditionalists
after it had been repeatedly stressed that their institutions would remain
unchanged, i.e. that at a local or tribal level the authority would be
preserved and strengthened, but that innovations would be introduced at
the centre. Although it soon became evident that these aims were
incompatible, the traditional leaders nevertheless relied on the South

African Government to abide by its promise of retaining the old order and continuing to support it.

The South African Government realized soon after its establishment that the Legislative Council did not have the undivided backing of the modernizing element. The realization had taken root that the new élites would ultimately have to be represented in the Council, but the South African-appointed White Commissioner-General for the indigenous peoples in Namibia, Dr. M. J. Olivier, openly stated that the inclusion of educated people in the Government of Ovamboland at the expense of the chiefs and headmen would never be allowed. He said that these chiefs and headmen would help to lead their subjects to self-realization, and that the guidance of a nation required devotion as well as erudition.[11]

The objections of the modernizing élites were thus noted, but nothing definite was undertaken to satisfy them, as appears from a further speech by Dr. Olivier, in which, *inter alia*, he said the following:

"There are no doubt people who think that the new government of Ovamboland must be a government elected by the people on the principle of one man one vote. Everybody has the right to cherish his own ideals, because this is a popular cause and the views of one's compatriots have to be taken into account. This is what the Government (the South African Government) has done. How the people feel on the matter has been determined by consultations, and efforts have been made to satisfy the majority, but consideration has also been given to the minority."

Dr. Olivier's remarks typified the approach of government spokesmen, who confirmed the view held among the modernists, above all the educated, that the South African Government regarded the traditional leaders as the most important spokesmen for the people, because it was assumed that they had majority support. Not only did the modernizing groups deny that the traditional leaders still enjoyed majority support, but they maintained that in the political development process no thought had really been given to the so-called minority. They also contended that they had not been involved in the political modernization process, which had been worked out to the advantage of a traditional interest group, which according to the modernists could actually claim only minority support. The opposition modernizing group also refuted the idea that the Legislative Council had been established democratically. They alleged the opposite, because if the principle of one man one vote had been applied, the majority of the people would have decided differently from the traditional leaders. This would have been a decision not necessarily against the establishment of a Legislative Council, but rather in favour of instituting it on an electoral basis.

Dr. Olivier spoke out against this and sided with the traditional leaders, who had decided against an election, making this significant comment:

"During the long period of consultation it became quite clear that although the principle of an election was accepted as a necessity, which would have to be introduced in the long run, it was still too early at that stage. The traditionalists and other responsible individuals, who took part in the deliberative discussions, indicated that an over-hasty introduction of the electoral principle could lead to disastrous results."[13]

Dr. Olivier considered the traditionalists as the best equipped for the social, economic and political development of Ovamboland, because they thought and acted positively and progressively.[14] It was just this which was rejected by the modernists who claimed to have more learning than the traditional leaders; these leaders, without adequate educational qualifications, were unsuitable to modernize a society. Dr. Olivier's accusation that "educated people" were endangering good order in Ovamboland and wanted to drive away the traditional leaders reflected a wrong assumption. The main complaint of the modernists was that they did not want to be ruled by those who had not acquired sufficient academic ability. Knowledge was their catchword and not tradition *per se*.

Obviously traditionalist opinion—and preference for the line of least resistance—was decisive in bringing about and composing the Legislative Council. No reason was given why it was then still too early for a partial election, nor did Dr. Olivier state who were the few responsible individuals who agreed that an election should not be called. His contention that new developments should be held over until the whole population was ready for them cannot be upheld because in a developing community a minority, usually comprising the educated, act as entrepreneurs and lead the population along the path to progress. A traditional élite, characterized chiefly by stagnation and adherence to the *status quo* or even to a *status quo ante*, seldom plays the role of a modernizing entrepreneur in a developing society after development contrary to their value concepts has already begun. Therefore Dr. Olivier's statement that progressive thinking and positive action distinguished the traditional leaders is highly disputable. The verbatim reports of the Legislative Council's proceedings are sufficient evidence of this.

3. *The First Legislative Council, 1968–73*

(a) *The Problems Discussed.* During the six sessions of the First Legislative Council, attention was focussed on quite a number of social, economic, political and judicial questions in Ovamboland, of which the most important were the legal system, land tenure, the labour problem and education. The Commissioner-General's proposal to concentrate on reforming the legal system so as to introduce a uniform system of laws for all Ovambo tribes did not receive the undivided backing of the tradition leaders. Its discussion led to a clash between them and the other members of the Council, because some of the traditionalists feared that reform would deprive them of their powers, and of some of their sources of income.[15] From the argument it appeared that the point at issue was not where and by whom justice was to be administered, but that compensation was to be paid to the headmen in whose district or ward a crime had been committed. Fines which the traditional leaders imposed had always been one of their chief sources of revenue. It was suggested that the South African Government or the Legislative Council should compensate them for any loss of income they might suffer. However, this could lead to partial loss of their authority due to their being deprived of the personal benefit of the fines, while at the same time they would become paid "officials" of the South African Government. The Select Committee on the Administration of Justice, which had to consider these matters, advocated that court records be kept for all lawsuits; that all fines be paid into the tribal fund instead of being collected by the tribal leaders, and that the penalties be the same for similar offences in all tribes.

Another problem closely affecting the tribal leaders was land tenure. A Select Committee on Land Tenure and Utilisation was appointed to sound out the feelings of every tribe on the old system of land ownership, and on the most suitable new system for the future development of Ovamboland. This investigation was made against the background of strong popular feelings, especially among the modernizing groups, that the old system of communal land ownership should be revised. These sentiments were also reflected in the answers given to the following question during the in-depth interviews:

Question: DO YOU THINK THE LAND IN OVAMBO SHOULD ...

	T.	*R./L.*	*O./C.*	*Comm.*	*N.*	*Trad.*	*Ov./Av.*	*Kat./Av.*
... be available for purchase by any Ovambo?	89.1	77.8	64.3	54.4	90.0	16.7	69.2	83.3
... remain under the control of the headmen?	4.3	3.7	25.0	18.2	5.0	79.2	20.5	6.1
... be under the control of the Legislative Council?	2.2	7.4	10.7	18.2	5.0	4.1	6.5	7.6
Uncertain/Don't know	—	—	—	9.1	—	—	0.6	—
No reply	4.4	11.1	—	—	—	—	3.2	3.0

This shows the fervent desire for permanent private land ownership, and they confirm a tendency already observed in the preliminary survey. There is a clear rejection of the system of communal land ownership and the dominant role played by the headmen and chiefs in allocating land, which the possessor only has in leasehold until his death. The wish for permanent private land ownership is strongest among the educated, with the traders again in an intermediate position. Almost 80 per cent of the traditional stratum, who derive most benefit from the old method of land ownership, repudiated the proposal that land should be removed from the control of the headmen, and showed equally little interest in placing that right in the hands of the Legislative Council. To the modernizing groups, the traditional leaders are identical to the Legislative Council and not a substitute.

As was expected, the eagerness for permanent possession of land is still greater in Katutura, where no private land ownership is possible, than in Ovamboland. While the Ovambos can invest their money in cattle and land cultivation, this possibility is totally lacking in Katutura. This was probably the main reason why so high a percentage of Katutura's inhabitants were in favour of the purchase and permanent ownership of land.

The Select Committee did not include Katutura in its investigation, but limited itself to meetings at tribal offices, to which it invited:

Reliable sub-headmen	30
Reliable nurses	2
Clergymen	5
Reliable traders	3
Clerks	3
Other reliable people	40

No definition is given of "reliable", which may mean that those invited were honourable and trustworthy people, or merely that they endorsed present government policy. If the "other reliable people" were mostly farmers, members of the modernizing groups would have been in the minority.

The most important recommendations resulting from the interviews were that the old system should be amended, so that the land would become the property of the Ovamboland Government. However, this change did not affect the essence of the problem of permanent private land ownership. There was still adherence to the principle that land should be held leasehold only until the decease of the owner. The only change was therefore that the monies owing no longer went to the traditional leader but via the tribal fund to the Ovamboland Government. In the view of the modernizing groups this changed nothing because, as already stated, the traditional leaders were identified with the Legislative Council.

An important recommendation of the Committee was that the remuneration paid to a chief, senior-headman or sub-headman should be augmented from the tribal fund in order to make good the income lost from sales of land. Thus they would become paid government officials. In 1974 the chiefs received a yearly stipend of R660 (formerly R492) and senior-headmen R480 (formerly R300). To go still further to meet the traditional leaders, it was also recommended that senior-headmen and sub-headmen should no longer pay for their respective districts and wards, while for their subjects a fixed though reasonable price for land was recommended, which was to be the same everywhere in Ovamboland. On the whole, recommendations of this committee were a mixture of old and new practices. In one sense the status of a chief, senior-headman or sub-headman was lowered to the level of a tax-collector, but in another sense the system of communal possession was retained, as opposed to individual permanent ownership. One innovation was that sub-headmen would have the same advantages as the chiefs and senior-headmen in receiving regular payments from the Government. These proposals did not satisfy the modernizing groups or meet their wishes, as the replies during the in-depth interviews made clear. The Select Committee, which conducted its discussions mainly with supporters of the traditional élite, obviously attempted to reach a compromise-which, however, appeased neither the traditional nor the modernizing élites.

In conjunction with this Committee, another Select Committee investigated the obligations, powers and conditions of service of headmen and sub-headmen. It was found that because of the lack of duly prescribed regulations, the tribal government was inefficient. It was also recorded that there were too many sub-headmen in Ovamboland—1,014 in all—which contributed to a cumbersome administration. The following proposals were therefore made by the Select Committee:

(a) When appointing a chief, the Council of Headmen must make recommendations and signify approval, with due allowance for the tradition of the tribe concerned.
(b) When appointing a senior-headman, the inhabitants of the district concerned must assemble and elect someone. The chief shall remain chairman and act together with the Council of Headmen, or, where there is no chief, the Council of Headmen shall so act.
(c) When appointing a sub-headman, the inhabitants of the ward concerned must assemble and elect somebody.

The obligations of chiefs, senior-headmen and sub-headmen were to be as follows:

(i) to ensure that tribal levies are regularly imposed in their areas;
(ii) to report any instance of insufficient food and water for man and beast;
(iii) to help with the recruitment of those seeking work;
(iv) to report contagious diseases among people and animals;
(v) to keep an eye on and report on strangers in their area;
(vi) to take action against the use of any drugs;
(vii) to see that law and justice prevail in their area;
(viii) to forbid unlawful gatherings;
(ix) to protect flora and fauna;
(x) to help combat veld-fires and to prosecute offenders;
(xi) to report births and deaths;
(xii) to help with the organization of campaigns for the inoculation of people and animals;
(xiii) to forbid any witchcraft;
(xiv) to report matters to a higher authority, which they themsevles cannot solve;
(xv) to maintain law and order in their own area.[16]

It was further recommended that these regulations should also be made applicable to chiefs and that, on the death of a sub-headman, his ward should be added to existing wards until the tribal council of the area in question decided that the wards had been sufficiently reduced in number. In the case of a sub-headman who, due to age or ill-health, was no longer capable of attending to his duties, the Headman-in-Council could decide to dismiss him from office.

These findings and recommendations of the Select Committee also indicated a reduction in the duties and privileges of the traditional leaders, levelling them to chief administrative and control officials within the districts and wards at the tribal area, representing the Central Government. Co-operation was expected but any autocratic or arbitrary action, and policy-making at tribal level, were forbidden.

The proposals of this Select Committee caused a paradoxical situation.

While the political powers of the traditional leaders were limited at the local level, they were increased at the centre. Why this was so is not very clear, more especially as this was not the South African Government's original intention, unless the central authority in the Legislative Council was to serve as compensation for the local limitations. Seeing that the prestige and status of the tribal leaders were still confined exclusively to the local level within their tribal area, a situation of conflict arose, which has already produced problems and will produce still more. Opposition forces within the tribal areas referred to the tribal leaders as puppets of the whites—an accusation which, while not reflecting the precise position, gave an indication of their state of dependence. This decline did not go unnoticed even among loyal followers in districts and wards, and could only lead to a depreciation in the status and prestige of the chiefs and senior-headmen. Compensation in the form of representation on the Legislative Council was ignored by the majority of their followers, who were too far away and lacked understanding of that institution. Many members of the Executive Council were to discover that a long absence from their tribal area carried the risk that they would lose their authority and status.

The modernizing groups approached the recommendations of the Select Committee with mixed feelings. In a way they were delighted over the traditional leaders' loss of power, but they were not happy about points (iii), (v) and (viii) concerning the obligations of these leaders, as they felt that such duties could lead to abuse.

Besides these important problems, attention was given to other innovations and improvements during the six sessions of the first Legislative council, and at each session the question of labour or the so-called contract system was raised. In the strikes and subsequent labour unrest, grievances over the existing system came to a head. Following from a strike, an agreement was concluded between the South African and Ovamboland Governments whereby the recruitment of contract workers was taken over by the latter government. This in turn was to create fresh difficulties for the Legislative Council, because since then the Ovamboland Government had been held fully responsible for the system, with its many flaws and attendant problems. Among the workers, the labour system was regarded as a scheme for exploitation, and the Legislative Council was alluded to as the exploiter of Ovambo manpower—a point of view also prevalent among the modernizing élites.

Educational questions aroused great interest in the Legislative Council. Complaints were made about the shortage of high schools, of trained teachers for secondary schools and of educational facilities generally,[17] and poor school attendance was also condemned. At once, there was insistence on compulsory education. Concern was also expressed over political activities in schools, and strong criticism was directed against troublemakers. The latter were referred to as terrorists and SWAPO supporters,[18] who were accused of undermining traditional authority, and of wanting to disturb law and order and kill the traditional leaders so that they themselves could rule. The United Nations was blamed for subverting Ovambos, who left the country only to return with weapons and new ideologies for the purpose of sowing unrest and committing murder.[19] Because of this and other considerations, a request was made during nearly every session for the establishment of an Ovambo police force.

The alleged moral decay of the youth also came under discussion. Increasing misuse of liquor, extra-marital sex, illegitimate births, child neglect, brothels and other evils were held responsible, and a Select Committee was instructed to examine the question. The report subsequently published can be regarded as the result of the most important investigation undertaken by the Legislative Council into definite aspects of Ovamboland's social order, which was exposed to new external influences because of economic developments and the construction of towns and workers' camps.

Other significant decisions of the Council included the safeguarding of roads, the erection of border fences, the recognition of Oshindonga and Oshikwanyama as official languages, budget procedure on central and tribal levels, the laying out of Ongwediva as the new capital of the territory, the appointment of urban representatives of the Ovamboland Government in the rest of Namibia, the institution of a pass system for Ovamboland and the appointment of a Public Service Commission for the country. At every session numerous motions of thanks and appreciation to South Africa were proposed for her help given in the development of Ovamboland.

(*b*) *Defects and Problems.* The Legislative Council was an entirely new institution for Ovamboland and it was axiomatic that functional problems should occur. Because of the low average literacy level of its members, the problems and defects were probably more conspicuous than they would otherwise have been. A better qualified Council would still have had its problems, but their range and intensity would probably have been less. But from the point of view of Ovamboland, a Council supported by the majority of the population would not have been observed so critically.

Besides their need to become conversant with procedure, the main problem, particularly for the traditionalists among the executive councillors, lay in the initiation and handling of motions and points at issue and replying to questions.

The speeches made by members of the Legislative Council during the sessions show that the higher the educational standard of an individual member, the more frequently and constructively did he intervene in Council discussions, the clergy most notably. The lower a member's educational level, the less he spoke in Council. During some sessions, illiterate members did not speak at all.

Contentious matters tended to be raised by modernists, and not by the traditionalists. Thus, for instance, the whole question of labour and increases in wages was raised as early as the second session by a member who was a churchman, but no response was forthcoming from the traditionalist executive councillors. Drawing up a budget was beyond the capacity of the executive councillors, who lacked experience and knowledge. Still more apparent was their inability to handle their portfolios. In consequence they were unable to play a leading and constructive role in debates. The upshot was that after the second session, preparatory meetings were held in every tribal area for the traditional members of the Legislative Council (the reason given for this was that the Council members should be encouraged to remember that theirs was the body that ruled Ovamboland).[20] At these meetings the white Chief Director gave notice of motions that were to come before the Council at the next session. It was thus made clear that motions were initiated by white officials, and that the Executive Council was incapable of initiating resolutions and proposing motions.

The incompetence of the executive councillors was shown up most clearly during the debates on their votes and whenever they had to reply to questions. At times irrelevant or unasked-for replies were given, which obliged the chairman to correct the executive councillor involved, or to call a brief adjournment. The councillors concerned more often requested adjournments themselves, and in time this became a regular pattern, with intervals being used for seeking advice from white officials. It was quite clear that the Council, as then organized, would not be able to manage for long without the help and advice of these officials.

As individual sessions progressed, a growing impatience took hold of the better-educated Council members over the lack of ability among the executive councillors. Criticism of the traditionalists became a characteristic of the sessions, at first discreet but later more open.[21] The unwillingness—sometimes the refusal—of the executive councillors to discuss the terms of measures and proclamations indicated that they were not familiar with their contents and objects, and did not grasp them. The sarcastic remarks that some councillors made on the incompetence of the executive councillors[22] caused the latter to become even more dependent on the white officials' advice. Indeed traditional leaders stressed increasingly that no development could take place in Ovamboland without the help and protection of the whites; this was repeatedly emphasized by the Chief Councillor.

The inefficiency of the traditionalist government leaders and members of the Legislative Council was highlighted also by the increasing proportion of the few non-traditional councillors that were being appointed to Council committees and commissions. Clergymen who were Council members were repesented on committees in a higher proportion than the traditional leaders. A clergyman was appointed chairman of the Civil Service Commission. This was partly in recognition of the churches' contribution to Ovamboland's development.

To summarize, it can be said that in the process of the territory's political advance the traditional élite was not capable of meeting the demands which the white authority made upon it. Mostly its illiteracy or semi-literacy restricted the political progress that had been envisaged and planned. The corollary to this was increasing resistance by the modernizing élite groups from one side, and greater support by the South African Government from the other. The white administrative personnel had to direct, initiate and determine policy, and even perform executive tasks, as well as fulfilling an administrative role. Hence its political role was much more significant than had originally been intended.

4. *The Second Legislative Council, 1973–75*

In May 1972, the Executive Council held joint talks with the South African Government. During these discussions, which were on constitutional matters relating to the development of self-rule, it was proposed that the next constitutional step for Ovamboland would be self-rule on the following basis:
(1) that the area known as Ovamboland be declared a self-governing territory;
(2) that provision be made for granting wider powers to the Legislative Council;
(3) that provision be made for a Cabinet with Ministers in lieu of an Executive Council with Councillors.
(4) that provision be made for the establishment of a High Court for Ovamboland;
(5) that the territory should have its own flag and national anthem.

After a visit to Cape Town, the Chief Councillor declared that the people of Ovamboland should play a larger part in the formation of a government when their country was proclaimed a fully self-governing territory, and he proposed an election, in which both men and women should elect a specific number of members for the Ovamboland Legis.ative Council. He also announced that the Legislative Council would be convoked for a special session to discuss its own reconstitution, a proper basis for an election, the establishment of a cabinet and the setting up of a Constitutional Committee, the task of which would be to work out the electoral system and make recommendations on the reconstitution of the Legislative Council and the institution of a cabinet. He suggested too that in order to involve Ovambos who were not members of the Legislative Council in this important matter, he as Chief Councillor would propose during the special session that membership of the Constitutional Committee should not be limited to members of the Legislative and Executive Councils. To enlighten the people further on these matters, the Executive Committee would hold meetings among the various tribes before the special session of the Legislative Council. Ovambos working in the south would also be informed. In order to establish who were in fact members of the Ovambo nation, the registration of voters would be considered urgently. In conclusion it would also be necessary to prepare the Ovamboland administration for greater self-governing powers. The Executive Council would consider this matter.[23]

The promised meetings were held in the different tribal areas from 3–7 July 1972. A feature was the informed and discerning type of question, particularly from the modernizing élites. Questioners wished to know who had requested self-rule for Ovamboland: the Executive Council or the whites. If the members of the Executive Council, it was essential to know whether they had asked the people, because the people were opposed to it. Why had the Executive Council not informed the people beforehand on what they had asked for in Cape Town, and were they sure that the Ovamboland Government had popular backing at home? It was also contended that there were citizens outside the Council capable of giving advice, who had not been asked. It was also asked in what way the new Legislative Council would change, and whether chiefs could take part in the election or would remain outside politics. Another question directed at the Executive Council was whether it had ever concerned itself with the welfare of the people.

Had the present Legislative Council ever promulgated a law in its five years' existence, and if so, would it make this law known before its resignation? The members of this Council were accused of doing no work either at their homes or during the sessions. The people had already been assured in 1968 that they themselves could decide on who would serve in the Legislative Council, but this had not happened, and they doubted whether it ever would. Yet another question was whether this new governing body would go fearlessly to the members of the tribes and whether political canvassing would be permitted in the tribal areas. Would political parties be allowed, or only a government party? Could they, the people, give vent to their opinions without fear of prosecution, and would they have the right to disagree publicly with the government?

Many questioners were uncertain what were the differences between an Executive Council and a cabinet, and between the present system and the new developments planned. Requests were made for educated persons to have seats in the Legislature. It was asked what was the meaning of registration and why there were limitations on freedom of movement. Would Ovambo get its own police force and army? One questioner expressed doubts regarding the truth of radio broadcasts. Others professed their confidence in the South African Government, and asked the regime to show the people what liberty was, how it was taught and how it manifested itself. Satisfaction was expressed with the new constitutional deal. There were those, again, who said that they would wait and see what happened before deciding whether it was good. Several questioners were interested in the new political changes planned, but only in so far as they would benefit from them economically in Ovamboland or in the south. Doubts were expressed about economic development, because the country had no mines.

Some enquirers wanted to know how there could be progress, if a people had nothing. What did an election mean and who would make the laws? Would the Ovambos, who were ruled traditionally, in future have to choose from among headmen and chiefs, or would anybody be eligible for election? Would the headmen with this new dispensation be permitted to stay at home more often? One enquirer was dubious whether the people were yet equal to handling the matters that were crowding in on them, especially as there was no money. Another asked whether the whole of Namibia was going to become independent, whether there would be human rights in the territory and whether apartheid would always remain.

This gives some indication of the presence or lack of confidence, trust and clarity among the population over the existing government and the proposed new political developments. Most dissatisfaction was found among teachers, clergy and some traders; the traditional leaders and many farmers gave the Executive Council their full support.

Councillor the Rev. K. Ndjoba took the lead at most tribal meetings although the Chief Councillor was always present. Apart from Councillor

Ndjoba's greater intellectual ability, a sound reason for this was that the Kwanyama-speaking tribes were not prepared to be addressed by the Chief Councillor in Oshidonga, his mother-tongue. The gatherings demonstrated positively that a section of the population was strongly opposed to the Legislative Council in general and to the Executive Council in particular. Antipathy was clearly manifested at several meetings to the traditional leaders over their participation in politics. The chief objections advanced were their frequent absence from home, their ignorance and illiteracy, and the fact that they were nominated and not elected.

After a series of meetings the Legislative Council assembled on 28 July for a special session. In his opening address the Commissioner-General mentioned the powers already granted to the Legislative Council and the measures that it could enact. Up to that time the Council had been able to pass measures in the following areas: education and culture, welfare, trading licenses, promotion of the economy, roads, dams, canals, agriculture, forestry, justice, labour, registration of the population, erection of buildings, taxes, budgets, conditions of service, salaries of the Legislative Council, procedure at sessions of the Legislative Council, conditions of service and salaries of government officials (viz. the Ovamboland Government Service), licensing of dogs, and fines for disregarding any of these laws. In due course other matters were added: e.g. nature conservation, the supply of liquor, estate duty and property tax in municipal areas, protection of the lives of persons and property, road traffic, registration of births, marriages and deaths, division or merging of tribes, the recognition, dismissal, discharge, conditions of service, duties and pensions of chiefs and headmen, establishment of towns, control of cattle diseases, and public festivals.[24] The Commissioner-General then stated that he had recommended to the South African Government—and this had been accepted by the Executive Council—that it confer more powers on the Legislative Council and declare Ovamboland a Self-Ruling Area. It was thus clear that the Commissioner-General, and not the Executive Council, had taken the initiative in this important matter.

Doubts were expressed in the Council over the exact meaning of the Afrikaans terms "*selfbestuur*" and "*selfregering*" the Commissioner-General explained that the former meant "management" but not "rule". The latter term signified the right to decision-making powers.[25] Though this explanation gave rise to problems of interpretation, the intention evidently was to grant the existing Legislative Council wider powers. The Council would no longer govern by proclamation, but by laws that would be published in its own official Government Gazette; these laws would still have to be signed by the South African State President. Due to this higher status the country would have a flag, a national anthem and a High Court. Moreover the Executive Council was to be replaced by a Cabinet, and the Chief Councillor by a Chief Minister with ministers assisting him.

The Commissioner-General also said that the people should have more say in the Legislative Council and that consequently the next Council should consist partly of elected members. At the same time he rejected a joint government for Namibia. In his opinion, every population group should confer separately and live within its national region.[26] So that prompt attention could be given to all these proposed constitutional changes, the Commissioner-General proposed the appointment of a Constitutional Committee. Lastly, he declared that when the time was ripe, still greater powers and authority could be requested.

When the motion for the appointment of a Constitutional Committee of fifteen members was introduced, the Chief Councillor explained that the Committee would consist of a representative from each of the seven tribal areas plus a chairman, all of whom would be appointed by the Executive Council. Seven additional members, each representing a group of professional people, would have to be appointed by the Legislative Council, but they could not be Legislative Council members.[27]

Thereupon the following members were appointed:

On behalf of the Executive Council:
  The Rev. K. Ndjoba (Chairman)
  Senior-Headman W. Kalomo (Kwanyama)
  Senior-Headman T. Mbago (Ngandjera)
  The Rev. G. Amupolo (Kwaluudhi)
  Senior-Headman W. Shitatala (Kwambi)
  The Rev. T. Heita (Mbalantu)
  J. Mbokoma (Ndonga)
  I. Nakamue (Onkolonkadhi)
On behalf of the Legislative Assembly:
  H.D. Namahuya (Education)
  P. Auala (Labourers)
  Mrs. J. Shiyagaya (Nurses)
  T. Shiyagaya (Officials)
  The Rev. K. Dumeni (Clergy)
  E. Namundjebo (Traders)
  F. Amukwa (Farmers)

For the first time recognition was given to the principle that all professional and tribal groups should be represented in one governmental committee. Most of the members were not personally hostile to the Legislative Council, though at least four of them had strong objections to it.

Meanwhile the registration of Ovambo votes began in Ovamboland on 23 October 1972, and in the south on 1 February 1973. It closed on 30 June 1973. The registration aroused political hostility, since to be registered would imply recognition of a homeland government for Ovamboland. A further complaint was that everybody, even the better-educated, had to place all ten finger and thumb prints on the registration card. This was considered humiliating for people who could read and write, and the question was asked whether the same principle applied when whites were registered. Objections were also made to the necessity to apply for registration as a member of the Ovambo people, and for the applicant to declare that he was a South African citizen. There was also opposition to supplying some of the required information, especially among the new élite groups, where there is antagonism anyway to the idea of independence for Ovamboland, rather than for Namibia as a whole. After many voters in the Kwanyama area had begun to register, it became evident that there was a possibility of domination by the Kwanyama; the hope arose too that political parties would be allowed, and therefore many who were at first unwilling to vote were finally persuaded to do so.

It appeared subsequently that most of the Ovambos who had registered were contract workers, actual and prospective, who had done so partly under pressure in order to be allowed to work in the south. The same registration cards which intending contract workers needed to obtain work in the south also served as the only legal proof of eligibility to vote. In the absence of a voters' roll, every voter had to bring his registration card, which was stamped on the back before he could cast his vote.[28] It was mainly the modernizing élite like clergymen, teachers and others, who refused to register. In July 1973 the number of registered voters was estimated at 80,000–90,000 Ovambos, which indicated that about half the electorate had registered.

Even before the Constitutional Committee brought out its report, the Amendment Act on the Development of Self-Government for Native Nations in South West Africa, Act No. 20 of 1973, was approved by the South African parliament on 30 March 1973. This Act was of special significance for the constitutional progress of the homelands in Namibia generally, and for Ovamboland in particular. This Act served as an amendment to the Act on the Development of Self-Government for Native Nations in South West Africa, 1968. Its scope was as follows: to redefine the areas for the various indigenous peoples of Namibia and to reserve and set apart those areas for exclusive use and occupation by Africans; to exclude certain matters from the powers of legislative councils; to exempt members of legislative councils from liability for certain actions; to arrange for the appointment and discharge of government employees of the said areas; to stipulate that the duties, powers, authority and activities of senior-chiefs, chiefs and headmen remain in force; to define the scope of certain laws on the registration of vehicles and licensing of drivers; to regulate the institution of claims against the homeland governments; to provide for specifying which would be the official languages of particular areas; to provide for the proclamation of any such area as self-ruling; to organize the area executive authorities and the powers of the legislative councils; and to extend those powers; to provide for the establishment of a High Court in each self-governing area; to regulate certain financial affairs of the self-governing areas, and provide for the transfer of certain assets of the area governments.

According to this Act, a Legislative Council is not competent to pass measures to set up or in any way control any military or quasi-military unit or organization, whether full- or part-time, within the self-governing areas, or to make any provision for the manufacture of weapons, ammunition or explosives.[29] Section 5A further specifies that a Legislative Council has no rights over the following matters:

the appointment, accrediting and recognition of diplomatic and consular officials and the conduct of deliberations in connection with the conclusion or ratification of international conventions, treaties and agreements; the control, organization, administration, powers, entry of and presence in the area concerned of a Police force from the Republic, charged with the maintenance of public law and order and the internal security in and the safety of the said area and the territory of South West Africa; postal, telegraphic, telephone, radio and television services; railways, harbours, national roads and civil aviation; the entry into the said area by persons other than members of the population group concerned; currency, banking and the control of stock exchanges and financial institutions, as defined in Section 1 of the Inspection of Financial Institutions Act 1962 (Act No. 68 of 1962); customs and excise duty and the control and management of customs and excise; and the amendment, repeal or substitution of this Act.[30]

Section 10D (1 and 2) lays down that ...

... a provincial or local division of the Supreme Court of South Africa, which has jurisdiction in an area or portion of an area for which a legislative council has been established, is competent to pass judgment on the validity of a measure of that legislative council, and that no magistrate's court or other lower court is competent to pass judgment on the validity of a measure of a legislative council.

Section 10 I (1) states that in each area the official languages will be English and Afrikaans, plus the language used in that area (in Ovamboland it is Oshindonga). Section 17 B provides for the establishment of a flag for a self-governing area, its design to be approved by the Legislative Council, and to be flown alongside the National Flag of the Republic. Section 17 C (1) provides that the Legislative Council of each self-governing area shall submit a recommendation for its own national anthem to the State President. Section 17 F (1–2) stipulates that every bill accepted by a Legislative Council must, immediately after acceptance, be sent through the Commissioner-General's office, together with an explanation of its scope and effects of and the reasons for its acceptance, to the Minister of Bantu Administration and Development, who then presents it for his assent to the State President, who in turn may agree to it and sign it, or, on the basis of advice, refer it back to the Legislative Council for further consideration.

These few excerpts from the Act illustrate close dependence of the Self-Governing Territory of Ovamboland on the Government of South Africa, and also on South Africa's overall control over security, i.e. safeguarding the area against external influence or attack such as might make it a security risk to the Republic itself.

The next step in Ovamboland's constitutional development came during the sixth session of the first Legislative Council, when the Chief Councillor introduced a motion stating that the Legislative Council agreed in principle to requesting the State President to declare Ovamboland a self-governing area on 1 May, 1973. In the same session the report of the Ovamboland Constitutional Committee, chaired by the Rev. K. Ndjoba, was tabled for the Council's approval. The report recommended that the Legislative Council be enlarged from forty-two to fifty-six members, among whom women could be included. As for the Legislative Council's composition, the Committee advocated that five members should be nominated by each of the seven tribal areas, but that one of the nominated members of the Kwaluudhi, Ndonga and Ngandjera tribes was to be the chief. Three members from each of the seven areas would be elected, and each area would be a constituency for this purpose. The Committee also proposed that the minimum age for membership of the legislative Council should be 26, except for a Chief or Senior-Headman, and for the franchise 21. It further recommended the institution of a cabinet, election of the Chief Minister by the Legislature Council, and the appointment by him of six ministers from the Legislative Council, one from each remaining tribal area.

Other recommendations of the Committee were that members should be able to vote individually in the Legisative Council instead of *en bloc* in a tribal delegation, and that the appointment of members by the tribal authorities should take place a considerable time before the nomination date of candidates for election. In conclusion, it was suggested that political parties be allowed with the approval of the Ovambo Government.

After discussion, the report was approved in principle, and the Constitutional Committee's proposals resulted in the Ovamboland Constitution Proclamation No. R104 and Election Proclamation No. R105 both of 27 April 1973. In the former proclamation it was also stipulated that Oshidonga was recognized as an official language of the Self-Governing Territory of Ovamboland, for certain purposes.

On 1 May 1973 Ovamboland was declared a Self-Governing Territory by Government Proclamation No. R104 of 27 April 1973, and the new cabinet was sworn in the same day. Chief Councillor F. S. Elifas became the Chief Minister with the former Councillors as Ministers. The following departments changed their names: the "Department of Authority Affairs and Finance" to the "Department of the Chief Minister and Finance"; "Education and Culture" to "Education" and "Community Affairs" to "the Interior". The other departments retained their previous names. The rank of the white directors of departments changed to 'secretary'.

Proclamation No. R117 of 4 May 1973 dissolved the first Legislative Council of Ovamboland with effect from 1 August 1973. It also provided that the appointment of members of the Ovamboland Legislative Council by the tribal authorities had to be made on or before 23 May 1972, and that a general election to choose them be held on 1 and 2 August 1973.

In the first edition of the Ovamboland Official Gazette (Vol. 1, No. 1 of 4 May 1973) which laid down the holding of elections for the Ovambo Legislative Council, it was stated that a nomination court would sit in every constituency (tribal district) at the various tribal offices (except in Kwanyama, where it would sit at only one tribal office, i.e. Ohangwena); it was also specified that if a ballot was to take place in accordance with Section 10 of the Ovamboland Election Proclamation of 1973, three members had to be elected in each constituency.

Accordingly, a nomination court sat on 30 May 1973 at each tribal office, and candidates were then proposed for election to the Legislative Council to fill the balance of twenty-one elective seats in the Council. The constituencies of Kwaluudhi, Ndonga, Ngandjera, Mbalantu and Kolonkadhi-Eunda each nominated only three members, who were therefore automatically elected to the new Legislative Council. Hence no elections were necessary in those tribal areas. In the Kwambi tribal area four candidates were proposed and in the Kwanyama area seven. Elections were held in these two constituencies only on 1 and 2 August 1973.

Confusion set in immediately, because some members of the Kwambi and Kwanyama tribes were living in other tribal areas and had to cast their votes there. As most Ovambos knew nothing of the meaning or method of voting, or why it had to be done secretly and in writing, or why some Ovambos were voting and others not, the value of these elections was queried right from the beginning apart from other political factors. Bewilderment was common to voters in Ovamboland itself and to contract workers in the south. This was true especially of urban areas, where members of the different Ovambo tribes lived side by side and only some of them were called upon to vote. In these places votes were cast at magistrates' offices. There were also polling booths in Kavango, Caprivi, Hereroland, Damaraland, Boesmanland and Kaokoland.

The election was received with hostility also because only the governing party, the Ovambo Independent Party, was allowed to nominate candidates. The application for recognition by the opposition Democratic Co-operative Party was refused while SWAPO was not allowed to take part in the election, one reason being that it repudiated the principle of separate homelands and strove for the independence of "Namibia" (not South West Africa).

Those nominated in the five tribal areas where there was no election were all proposed by the Ovamboland Independent Party, while in each of the other two tribal areas three of its candidates were nominated. Since the thirty-five members appointed by the traditional tribal administrations and the fifteen members, nominated by the Ovambo Independent Party and returned unopposed, supported the traditional authority and standpoint, the position even before the election was that fifty of the fifty-six members of the new Legislative Council upheld the traditional authoritative structure.

The twenty-six nominated candidates for the election represented the following occupations: two clergy, six farmers, eleven merchants and businessmen (of whom one was a business woman and the sole female candidate), two headmen, one labourer, one hospital orderly, one tribal messenger, one lorry driver and one retired person.[31] From this it is clear that the most important modernizing élite groups in Ovamboland like the teachers, clerks, officials, nurses, clergymen and traders, except for those nominated, were represented either by no one or only nominally. Thus the new Legislative Council, even before its election, was not representative of the whole population and already at that stage it had no backing from the modernizing élites.

The election was held on 1 and 2 August 1973 in a tense atmosphere. Just before it took place, several Ovambos were arrested after holding unlawful gatherings in Ovamboland to urge a boycott of the election.[32] Several of these meetings were organized by the SWAPO youth movement. On these occasions protests were made against the whole principle of Bantu homelands, and independence was demanded for Namibia as a whole. SWAPO and the Democratic Co-operative Party were to the fore in calling on the people not to vote, and the boycott also had the tacit approval of the churches.

In the Kwanyama and Kwambi tribal areas were respectively 31,500 and 11,300 voters, and in addition there were about 8,000 who were chiefly in the south on contract labour. As early as the first polling day, 1 August, it was apparent that the election would be a failure, when few voters turned out to vote at the fifty-nine ballot-boxes, a trend which continued on the second day. In Windhoek, out of thousands of voters, only four voted of whom three were Ovambo policemen.[33]

According to the official result of the election, there were 3,662 votes cast. Of these 2,474 were in the Kwanyama and 1,188 in the Kwambi tribal area, which was equivalent to 8.9 per cent of the voters in the tribal areas. In the Kwambi tribal area, where three of the candidates belonged to the Ovamboland Independent Party and one was an Independent, the last-mentioned and two from the Ovamboland Independent Party were elected. Two of those elected were headmen. In the Kwanyama tribal area, where three candidates of the Ovamboland Independent Party and four Independents stood, three Independents (all traders) were elected. The only woman candidate in the election was defeated. The election of the Independents indicated a decided rejection of the Ovamboland Independent Party in the Kwanyama tribal area, which was the most thickly populated tribal district. In the Kwambi region the only Independent was sponsored by the traditionallly orientated Independence Party. The same trend would probably have emerged in the other tribal areas had Independents stood there, but it is also a reasonable assumption that if one of the opposition parties, SWAPO or DEMCOP, had been allowed to participate in the election, the electoral chances of any single candidate from the Independent Party would have been slender.

Thus, of the fifty-six members of the new Legislative Council, altogether fifty-two were either part of the traditional structure or were appointed with the consent of the traditional leaders or by the Ovamboland Independent Party with its traditionalist orientation. The composition of the new Legislative Council, and the fact that opposition parties were excluded from the election, made it certain that the Council would not have the majority of the population and the modernizing élite groups behind it, or, above all, represent the modernizing groups such as the clergy, teachers, officials, nurses, scholars and students. In any case, a large portion of the Ovambo people viewed Ovamboland as an integral part of "Namibia" and not as a *separate* part of "South West Africa".

Reactions to the elections were various. To the Commissioner-General, Mr. De Wet, it proved that the silent majority in the country accepted the Ovamboland Government and the pattern of constitutional development. He denied emphatically that the low vote in anyway reflected a renunciation of the South African policy of separate development. In his view the low vote proved that the Ovambos were not acquainted with the new form of election, and that they did not think it necessary to vote because they were satisfied with the Ovamboland Government. As a further reason for the situation he mentioned the lack of electoral machinery and the fact that the Ovambos were accustomed to nominating their leaders. He felt that the "pan-Africanist SWAPO opposition" had only played a minor part in causing the low turn-out in Ovamboland, but that it had been a deciding factor in Walvis Bay and Windhoek.[34]

The fact that the whole election had passed off without incidents or demonstrations he saw as another sign that the silent majority accepted the Ovamboland Government.[35] He had already intimated that there was no necessity for a multi-party system in Ovamboland and that the Ovamboland Independent Party had grown out of a spontaneous need by the population. He described the adherents of the party as those who put Ovamboland first as their homeland and South West Africa second. The Ovamboland Independent Party was opposed to the idea of "Namibia" and to everyone who supported it. Mr. De Wet also said that the opposition parties had not nominated any candidates because they would thus have supported government policy. He stated as his firm conviction that political parties were something strange to the Ovambos, because they believed in a one-party system.[36]

The chairman of SWAPO in Namibia, D. H. Meroro, had predicted when the polling booths opened that the election would be unsuccessful, because the Ovambos would heed the call from SWAPO not to vote; and according to his interpretation, they rejected the government and its institutions.[37] The leader of DEMCOP, J. Nangutuuala, said that the outcome of the election demonstrated the Ovambos' rejection of the homelands policy, and that the Government of Ovamboland was not representative. He declared that the only reason why the South African Government could pursue its policy in Ovambo was that it had the weapons to keep the traditional leaders in power.[38] What the population of Ovamboland desired was a unitary state of Namibia with a central government.[39]

The South African authorities were disappointed. The traditional leaders were not supported by the masses, neither had the hastily founded Ovamboland Independent Party the necessary backing. At no stage was the party accepted outside the traditional strata or as the mouthpiece of the modernists, who would not identify themselves with its programme of championing an independent Ovamboland homeland. The opposition factions were in revolt against the dominance of the traditional leaders, which was out of all proportion to their actual strength and prestige in Ovamboland. These factions, whose main inspiration came from members of the modernizing élites, were officially forbidden to establish their own party, the Democratic Co-operative Party (DEMCOP). Although the party leadership found itself in a dilemma over whether its participation in the election would signify recognition of the policy of separate development, it was nonetheless ready to do so. Because the Ovamboland Government would not recognize DEMCOP officially, it was deprived of the opportunity to take part in the election. It is certainly fair to assume that had this opposition party fought the election, it would have received the most support. Most of the twenty-one elected candidates would have been members of DEMCOP, although it would still have been in a minority compared with the thirty-five nominated Council members.

In not allowing DEMCOP and SWAPO to participate in the elections, the authorities left them with no choice but to call on potential members in turn to boycott the election. Yet if they had been allowed, they would have motivated the electors and taught them how to vote, in which case inadequate knowledge would only have been a minor factor in a low percentage poll.

The election result unmistakably repudiated the official contention that the traditionally oriented Ovamboland Independent Party was the mouthpiece of the Ovambo population. The artificial power role assigned to the traditionalists, which evoked the ever-increasing resistance of the people, was disapproved of. The resistance was also directed at the South African Government's policy to develop Ovamboland as a separate homeland and not as an integral part of Namibia. The traditional leaders were seen as the agents of a policy that was widely opposed by the Ovambo people. These factors were evidently underestimated by the authorities, and it must have been clear that an election which did not include the parties that would express the popular antagonism to the policy of the South African and Ovamboland Governments was doomed to failure. The peacefulness of the election was no sign of acquiescence in the *status quo*. DEMCOP, SWAPO and the churches were against disturbances, but not against a demonstration of passive resistance. Before the election it was clear that open resistance to the election, involving SWAPO and DEMCOP, would break out afterwards. This was borne out by events.

In planning and carrying out the election the authorities ignored the elementary principles and conditions of a democratic modernizing process, such as the involvement of both supporting and opposing trends of thought, and so made its failure certain. Its outcome intensified the popular hostility to the Ovamboland Government. Thus the second Legislative Council began with the knowledge that only a minority of the population supported it.

One of the first laws approved at its first session was the Ovamboland Payment and Privileges of Members of the Legislative Council Act, 1973, which came into force retrospectively on 1 May 1973. It provided *inter alia* for the Chief Minister to receive an annual salary of R4,800, a minister R4,000, each Councillor R1,000, and the leader of the Opposition, if any, R1,800. Since 1 January 1977 the Chief Minister's salary has been R8,640 a year, a minister's R7,200, a councillor's R2,520, and that of the leader of the Opposition, if there is one, R2,800.

Another law, the Ovamboland Flag Act No. 7 of 1973, provided for the new Ovamboland flag—to be flown beside the South African flag on public buildings, as we have already seen. It was to consist of three horizontal stripes of equal width—from top to bottom blue, white and olive green, with seven vertical olive green staves in the centre of the white stripe.[41]

In the second session of the second Legislative Council, from 14 May to 6 June 1974, various votes on the estimates were approved and sundry motions were discussed and accepted. A motion was adopted proposing that the Legislative Council should consider a system of succession appropriate to current living standards. Against the objections of some traditional leaders, the motion provided for written wills within the traditional system of succession, which lent itself to many abuses and was especially prejudicial to women and children on the death of the husband and father.[42]

In the Council several problems produced a polarization between the traditional leaders and their supporters, and other members. Accusations by traditional leaders (e.g. Headman E. Mbango) that the churches in Ovamboland were aiding terrorist movements were refuted by members of the modernizing élites (e.g. the Rev. C. Ndjoba). Another member of the latter (L. Mukuilongo) assailed some of the traditional leaders holding ministerial posts for not replying to questions or performing their duties; he said this was due to the lack of opposition, which would have kept ministers on their toes. There continued to be frequent adjournments whenever ministers could not answer questions—a clear indication of incompetence.[43] For the first time misgivings were expressed in the Legislative Council over the effectiveness of certain white officials, the benefits enjoyed by white inhabitants of Ovamboland and their desire to live apart from the Ovambos. There were complaints against the high standard of white housing compared with the low standard of housing for Ovambos, and against whites benefiting from illegal financial and trade transactions and illicit hunting in Ovamboland; allegations of bribery were also made against Ovambo officials. There was criticism of the tribal police, who were assuming increasing, and sometimes unlawful, powers and acting in an arbitrary and high-handed fashion. Similar charges were made against tribal secretaries, who were accused of despotic conduct, embezzlement of tribal funds, inefficiency and excessive liquor consumption. These secretaries were also suspected of using the tribal police to bolster their own power. The chief accusation, however, was that the tribal secretaries were competing in terms of power with the traditional leaders and even ignoring and slighting them.[44]

During the closing stages of the session the members of the Legislative Council were surprised at the thousands of Ovambos, chiefly the young, who were emigrating from Ovamboland into neighbouring countries. This led to the adoption of a motion that the cabinet should investigate the "causes and effects of Ovambos leaving Ovamboland illegally via the northern frontier, and take steps to combat this, because it is in the interest of the country and of extreme importance and urgency".[45] During the discussion, the exodus was explained by antagonism to the Legislative Council and the Ovamboland Government, the influence on them of "terrorists" inside and outside Ovamboland, and the shortage of recreation facilities for young people in the country. In general the Council showed its lack of insight into the more deep-seated reasons for this exodus, for example in the remark of the Chief Minister, Chief F. Elifas, that he did not really know what the younger generation wanted.[46] The real causes of the emigration were expounded by the churches.

The Council was still able to govern only with the help and protection of the South African authorities, i.e. through the presence of whites in Ovamboland. This was bound to be counter-productive and endanger peaceful development. Any progress in the modernization of the country would depend more and more on how far all resources and points of view could be combined and accommodated in the development process.

5. *The Third Legislative Council, 1975–*

The low percentage poll in the first election in Ovamboland, and the popular dissatisfaction over the composition of the Legislative Council resulted in the second Legislative Council accepting, at a Special Session on 8 October 1974, the proposal that a new Legislative Council be elected which would consist of more elected than nominated members. To achieve this, the Legislative Council was enlarged. Probably as a sop to the traditional leaders, the number of five nominees per tribal area was retained, and the number of elected members raised from three to six per constituency. Thus the elected members would outnumber the nominated members for the first time, and the Council would consist altogether of seventy-seven members. At the same time there was agreement that the qualifying age for the franchise should be reduced from twenty-one to eighteen. In consequence the following motion was laid before the Council and adopted:

That this Legislative Council, in terms of section 7 of the Ovamboland Constitution Proclamation, 1973 (Proclamation R.104 of 1973), request the State President to—
(*a*) dissolve the Ovamboland Legislative Council with effect from 13 January 1975;
(*b*) provide for the conduct of a general election during the period 13 to 17 January 1975;
(*c*) that the designation of members of the Ovamboland Legislative Council by the respective tribal authorities mentioned in Section 3 (i) of the Ovamboland Constitution Proclamation 1973, shall take place on or before 25 October 1974.[47]

According to the official result, 66,000 of the 120,000 voters cast their votes, which meant a turn-out of 55%. Spoilt ballot-papers accounted for 1.52%. 64,500 Ovambos voted inside Ovamboland (equal to 70% of the territory's electorate) and 1,500 outside (equal to 4.2% of the voters there).

Theoretically, it should have been possible for all parties, including SWAPO and DEMCOP, to take part in the election, but both decided not to do so as long as proclamation R17 existed, which forbade the holding of political meetings without the authorities' consent. Yet the most important objection was that participation in the election would be the recognition of the ethnically based homelands policy, which both parties rejected in favour of a unitary state of Namibia. This was probably the primary reason too why expatriates did not accept the Legislative Council's invitation to return and play their part in the election. Both SWAPO and DEMCOP asked the voters to boycott it.

The Ovamboland Independent Party also did not take part officially in the election, although some of its members stood as independents (it is difficult to estimate the support obtained by these independent candidates). Nine members of the second Legislative Council who were not re-elected were members of the Ovamboland Independent Party, and only five of the 14 members of this party who stood as independents were returned. It can thus be concluded that had the Ovamboland Independent Party participated officially it would have received little support, and that there was widespread resistance to a party which strongly supported traditional authority.

Most of the electorate undoubtedly voted for individual candidates and not for one of the parties. The election results also clearly show that not all the voters made use of their opportunity to cast six votes for candidates in each constituency. Instead of a possible total of 396,000 choices (66,000×6 votes) only 274,166 choices were made, or an average of 4.1 per voter, to which must be added 1,827 spoilt ballot-papers.

After the boycott of the first election, the poll of more than 50% in the second election was surprising. SWAPO's appeal for a boycott of the election, apparently did not yield the desired results, at any rate in Ovamboland. Outside Ovamboland, where SWAPO was stronger and more effective, the boycott succeeded almost completely, the low percentage of 4.2% being very clear evidence of this. There was a variety of reasons for the high percentage poll in Ovamboland, one clearly being that for the first time the Legislative Council consisted of more elected than nominated members, which made the people feel better represented. Secondly, Ovamboland was better organized for this election than for the previous one, and the electorate was also better informed on electoral procedures. By contrast, SWAPO's organization in Ovamboland appears to have been less good than in the previous election. Some of its best leaders had by then fled from Ovamboland, leaving the party relatively leaderless.

It was maintained after the event by SWAPO and some church leaders in Ovamboland that the election had not been free and that many voters had been compelled to vote. They alleged intimidation and threats: voters, they said, were threatened with the loss of their work, pensions, medical care and the right to cultivate land if they did not vote. Various traditional leaders, assisted by the tribal police, alllegedly forced some members of their tribe to vote and put pressure on Ovambos seeking work at Oluno in the south. It was claimed that 2,000–3,000 were coerced into voting before they could apply for work, and every person who had voted received a mark on his identity card.[48]

From another source, the International Commission of Jurists, it was contended that in the presence of army and police units there was an element of compulsion, as people voted through fear of intimidation. Many voters were told for whom to vote, and the election was regarded as being neither free nor secret. A further contention was that visitors to the south were not granted leave until they had voted. Doubts were expressed about the percentage of 55%, because new voters had been added since the last registration who had not previously been included in the total of voters. Hence it was estimated that there were more than 120,000 registered voters.[49]

Efforts were made to investigate these accusations. One of the SWAPO officials in Ovamboland, Sam Shivute, tried to hold an enquiry in the country and collect evidence that would corroborate the allegations of intimidation and the use of force during the election. His attempts were hampered by the Kwambi tribal police, whose behaviour led to his wife applying to the Supreme Court in Windhoek for protection for herself and her husband. She aked for an interim order restraining the Kwambi tribal authority and all police or employees of the authority from assaulting, molesting or intimidating her husband or herself. To substantiate her application, she testified that her husband, as secretary of SWAPO in the north, was an important official in the party. However, the traditional leaders were vigorously opposed to him and his activities. She also said that he had endeavoured to obtain proof of the systematic terrorisation of voters during the last election, on the strength of which, he intended to challenge legally the validity of the election results. According to her, this led to his being persecuted by the tribal leaders and tribal police, and his life was threatened.[50]

This alleged misbehaviour by tribal leaders led the heads of the three most important black churches in Namibia, Bishop Auala, Preses L. de Vries and Bishop R. J. Wood, to accuse the authorities of blocking a legitimate enquiry into a charge of intimidation during the Ovamboland election. According to them,

a *prima facie* case that intimidation took place at all levels, from the highest official in the area to the lowliest tribal policeman, can already be deduced from the sworn affidavits. A powerful claim for the voiding of the election could undoubtedly be made. It is desired to test this claim in the courts of the land. ... If a reputable advocate and legal team of the highest repute are refused the necessary freedom to complete their investigations, the belief that the allegations of grave and extensive irregularities during the election are true, will be unavoidable.[51]

Even allowing for the coercion of some of the voters, it can be accepted that a fair percentage—at least 35%—voted voluntarily. That in itself is a large increase over the previous election. It is understandable, too, that SWAPO felt frustrated and angry over being unable to succeed in prevailing upon the entire population to boycott Ovamboland's latest election, as they had contrived to do during the preceding one. Yet from among the ranks of the modernizing élites they managed to find support.

The Third Legislative Council began its activities against this background. The Council, though not representative of members of the modernizing élites, ought to be able to maintain a higher standard than its predecessor by virtue of its composition. Yet the average quality of the cabinet in terms of educational qualifications remains low, and more problems are bound to crop up in the future than in the past. Thus greater efficiency and competence, particularly at cabinet level, will become ever more urgently necessary.

As a result of the presence of forty-two elected members in the Legislative Council, there is the possibility of opposition groups making themselves heard in the Council, but the chances of forming a new opposition party are slender. The third Legislative Council has to perform its tasks against a background of intensified international pressure for the creation of a single independent state of Namibia, and of a growing consciousness of political unity among the inhabitants of the area, the majority of whom support the idea of a single state and repudiate the principle of Homelands. Also in the background are the unrest and prevailing violence in the neighbouring state of Angola. These developments and viewpoints are bound to put heavy pressure on the third Legislative Council, and any attempt under the current political circumstances to request complete independence for Ovamboland as a separate state would hasten the process of political self-destruction, especially of the traditional authority. The Government of Ovamboland accepted the election result as a motion of confidence in the existing political dispensation for the country.

Mainly due to the improved composition of the third Legislative Council, the level of discussions in the Council during the first two sessions showed a marked improvement over that of its predecessors. Many subjects in the educational, economic and social fields which had been discussed previously were brought up again.

Serious accusations were levelled against the Minister of Education for inadequate education facilities at secondary school level. Council members alleged that many pupils who had successfully passed their final primary school examinations had no opportunity to continue their studies. Some council members also referred to the unsatisfactory formal qualifications and to the misconduct of many members of the Ovambo teaching staff.

Another matter causing serious concern during the first two sessions of the third Legislative Council was the checkpoint on Ovamboland's southern border at Oshivelo. The police were accused by council members of treating Ovambos in a disgraceful manner at the border post when they leave Ovamboland and when they return:

"Ovambos are shunted about and their belongings searched. Whether he is at fault or not, he is pushed about. It also happens that they are maltreated and cursed at before he is requested to produce his travel documents. ... Oshivelo has humiliated us. ... The wall at Oshivelo is a wall of hate. ... Oshivelo is an apartheid gate. ... we do not know why only Ovambos are stopped there, while Namas, Whites and so forth pass through there without having to be searched. ... I never have heard of any White person having had trouble at Oshivelo; the only people who have problems are the Ovambos."[52]

Many councillors strongly attacked the necessity of a border between Ovamboland and the "Police Zone":

"The border between us and the Police Zone is something which frightens us. ... This is the request of the whole of Ovamboland that Oshivelo should be removed. ... I was frightened when I saw those words on the wall at Oshivelo, namely South West Africa on the one side and Ovamboland on the other. I agree that the wall on which this is written must be removed to the border between South West Africa and Angola. ... Why is Ovamboland, according to the words of the wall, excluded from South West Africa, while Ovamboland is in fact part of the whole of South West Africa? There are eleven population groups in South West Africa and every one of those population groups has its own country or area where it lives—and even though that is so, those population groups are still part of South West Africa. I do not want to make out that I do not wish to be considered an Ovambo, nor that I am against the country Ovamboland. What affects me adversely is that a border has been established there—a border for my country made by another without even consulting me and after establishing a border for me and giving me a small country, he writes such names on the wall. I am not satisfied with it."[53]

Dissatisfaction was also expressed by some members about the relationship between the Whites in Ovamboland and the Ovambos. This was summed up by one of the members, Thomas Nakambonde, as follows:

"We Ovambos are satisfied and proud of this Government of ours, but there are a few things which worry us. It is said that we have only acquired self-government in name, but in reality that is not so, but if the government belongs to us then we expect and demand that there should be a few changes which will ensure that it is acceptable to the people.

"We anticipated that with the White officials who are in our midst, who are there to assist us, that between them and us there must be a better relationship and that we should understand one another better. When we speak of better relationships, or respect towards the other persons, then we wish to mention further that there are Whites whose names we do not know, but we always call them 'Sir', but they call us by our names. There are also White officials who call us 'boys'.

"We want that habit or that practice, where in the past White officials or Whites called us 'Kaffir', should cease. We must respect each other and there must be a good relationship between us. We will then greatly respect and appreciate our Government, especially if we see that our Ministers receive respect from the Whites, because they are the heads of the departments and the rulers of our people.

"We who are outsiders cannot properly understand what is going on when our Ministers receive speeches and then do not know where it came from or what is stated therein. Usually the Minister is then not prepared to answer questions emanating from the speech.

"We expect and wish that our Ministers should be empowered to reject matters not in the interests of the people. It is that alone which can create better relationships between us and White officials and in that way we will respect our own Government."[54]

The complaints of many members about the treatment of Ovambos by Whites, especially white officials, resulted in the unanimous adoption of a motion by the Council "that in the opinion of this Legislative Council the Cabinet should give consideration to the desirability that all services to every inhabitant, temporary or permanent, should be rendered in the same manner".[55] During the discussion of the motion it was stated clearly by several members that this motion intended to eliminate any form of apartheid.

Another motion dealt with the creation of a tax system for Ovamboland, which was agreed to.[56] Minister T. Iimbili introduced a motion "that according to the opinion of this Legislative Council, the Cabinet ought to give consideration to the desirability of depositing all tribal fines in the tribal fund".[57] This motion was directed against tribal leaders and tribal secretaries who had unlawfully misused tribal fund money for their own benefit. The motion was adopted.

In the absence of a department of foreign affairs, the lack of appropriate knowledge on foreign matters, especially on African countries, was felt by the Cabinet. It resulted in a motion being introduced by the Chief Minister, and adopted, "that according to the opinion of this Legislative Council, the Cabinet should consider the appointment of an individual for the purpose of collecting and reporting back to the Legislative Council on all matters pertaining to political and African affairs".[58]

Annoyed by the developments across the northern border in Angola, and especially by various terrorist outrages during the eight months from August 1975 to April 1976, viz. the killing of seventeen Ovambos, the abduction of twenty-one Ovambos and the destruction of ten shops and damage of other property in Ovamboland a motion was adopted by the Legislative Council "that efficient steps are taken to ensure that attacks from Angola will cease and that the border between Ovamboland and Angola be respected".[59] This followed a motion adopted at the first session of the third Legislative Council "to move all traders along the northern boundary of Ovamboland 1.6 kilometers southwards in order to exercise certain control measures over the border".[60] Another emerging problem for the Ovambo Government was the influx of more than 10,000 Angolan refugees into Ovamboland.

In 1975 an invitation was extended by the White Legislative Assembly in Windhoek to the Ovamboland Government to take part in a conference of all recognized ethnic leaders to discuss matters of common concern to all in Namibia. A motion was accordingly introduced in the Ovambo Legislative Council to consider the advisability of holding these discussions and of the Ovamboland Government being represented at a Conference.[61] When introducing the motion, the Chief Minister said that "no country can exist in isolation and it is of the utmost importance that we should at all times foster peaceful co-existence with our neighbours and even those who do not border on us".[62]

It was decided that Ovamboland should be represented at the talks, which became the Turnhalle Constitutional Conference, by the whole Cabinet accompanied by an appointed representative from each tribe. The following members of the Legislative council were appointed by the different Ovambo tribes: Headman Tara Iimbuli (Ndonga), Immanuel Hihulifua (Kwanyama), Ananias Kamanya (Kwaluudhi), Toivo Shiyagaya (Ngandjera), Thomas Nakombonde (Kwambi), Johannes Andjamba (Mbalantu), and Israel Nakamue (Kolonkadhi-Eunda).

At the end of the Second Session of the Third Legislative Council the Chief Minister of Ovamboland, the Rev. K. Ndjoba, reported briefly on the proceedings at the Constitutional Conference in Windhoek. He emphasized that although the Constitutional Conference was trying to work out a constitution for the whole of Namibia, the premise remained that every population group in Namibia should be recognized as a separate individual nation.[63] The constitutional status of Ovamboland and its Legislative Council would therefore never be doubted in any new dispensation for Namibia.

From the very beginning of the Turnhalle Conference, it became clear that the representatives of Ovamboland were participating for the sole purpose of defending and maintaining the traditional organization in Ovamboland and would not tolerate any interference in the country's political affairs. This intransigence is bound to lead to conflict, not only with the modernizing echelon inside and outside Ovamboland but also with other population groups in Namibia.

During joint talks between the Ovamboland cabinet and Prime Minister B. J. Vorster on 6 August 1975, Chief Elifas reiterated that he was still striving to lead his country to political independence and that he and his people relied on the South African Government to support them in this development. In reply Mr. Vorster assured the Ovamboland Government of his Government's co-operation with Ovamboland's independence aims, and he gave an assurance that no interference from outside would be permitted:

"I have stated as my point of view that every nation has its particular needs and interests in regard to which it must decide for itself. No interference from outside can be tolerated. South Africa does not demand one inch of their land from the peoples of South West Africa. As long as South Africa's presence is needed by the peoples of South West Africa, it is her duty to see that their rights are not taken away. I have assured the cabinet of Ovamboland that the existing system of government will remain untouched for as long as the Ovamboland people choose."

Mr. Vorster also made it clear that the South African defence force and police would stay in Ovamboland for as long as the Ovamboland Government considered their presence necessary for the maintenance of law and order and as a prerequisite for stable government and continued peaceful development.[64] The assassination of the Chief Minister, Chief Elifas, shortly after these joint talks must be seen as a political act by frustrated opponents, directed against the traditional authority and the South African Government.

6. Attitudes to Political Development

(a) *The White Administrative "Elite".* The attitudes, actions and influence of the Ovambo élites are largely determined by the dominant authority of the white administration in Ovambo. No Ovambo élite has the same enforceable ascendancy as these white administrators, who give energetic leadership in the overall modernizing process of Ovamboland and determine its content, its pace, and above all its direction.

By the terms of their instructions from the home Government, the temporary élite group of white South African officials in Ovamboland are bound to support the traditional élite, and seek to maintain, restore and extend their status and authority. The inadequacies of this élite when faced with the need to operate a modern administration were quickly recognized by the white officials, with the result that more supervisory and directive action was required from them.

Dissatisfaction with the state of political development was noticeable at a conference of the South African Department of Bantu Administration and Development held at Rundu in 1970. The South African minister, M. C. Botha, said at the conference that power must no longer be wielded individually by chiefs and headmen, but by a joint central authority. He felt, all the same, that because the authority in Ovamboland consisted predominantly, and by design, of traditional leaders, no real difference existed, except that resolutions passed in the Legislative Council no longer applied to individual tribes only but to the whole of Ovamboland. Minister Botha said that resolutions and motions were not to be announced by white departmental staff but that Executive Council members should make important announcements themselves whenever possible, and these could be relayed to the population via the government. The people would thus learn that it had a government, and the government would learn that it had a duty towards the people. He illustrated his premise as follows:

"We as guardians, acting through our officials, are at the same time giving the leaders of the people the chance to build themselves up to true leadership. Therefore, whenever there is something good which has to be announced, we must seize every opportunity of enabling the leaders to make such announcements to their people, by way of advice or drafting the necessary papers. Thus we build them up to be influential persons, we gain their goodwill, and we get their co-operation, often over very difficult matters that have to be undertaken in their areas."[65]

This statement made it plain that the traditional authority in Ovamboland needed to be strengthened. The initial development work would still have to be done by the white officials, but the Ovamboland Government would benefit all the same by announcing developments as coming from the Ovamboland Executive Council. The traditional leaders' authority and status would thus be enhanced, the implication being that they could not rely as a matter of course on popular support and that co-operation between the white officials and those leaders was also not automatic. This latter assertion is borne out by the fact that many decisions have been taken, which could have an adverse effect on the authoritarian status of the traditional leaders.

A further point made at the conference was that the white directors of government departments in the Homelands were not mere administrators as they had been under the old dispensation, but also politicians. Their task was to guide the people along the road to political maturity within the framework of policy, and especially to motivate them. It was expected of the directors that they would identify themselves entirely with the Homelands in which they were working: "Consequently the directors must strive to operate this system in a manner that will make it fit more and more into the cultural milieu and political pattern of the people."[66]

As far as Ovamboland was concerned, it was felt that government action was being retarded in that many possibilities offered to the Legislative and Executive Councils of Ovamboland by the Act for the Self-Government of the Native Nations of South West Africa were not being utilized. The following proposal was therefore made: "To obviate frustration, the functions entrusted to the local Government should be duly implemented and amplified, and resolute steps taken. Analyse the situations and get them to pass measures, so that there could be action and reaction. There must be no dilatoriness in any political situation. In order to manage and handle the situation purposefully, the guiding hand must always be one pace ahead."[67]

The most significant remarks at the conference came from the Commissioner-General, Mr. J. De Wet, who touched on key questions in the political development of Ovamboland.

"It becomes confusing if on the one hand there is a wish to retain tradition and to hold an election in a traditional manner, and on the other hand the people are asked to accept and have a modern, democratic outlook on certain aspects. Politically it can be a bit muddling if there are no clear guidelines regarding the future pattern—whether it is to be traditional or a mixture of both.

"There are those who no longer have a tribal allegiance, who have become erudite through education and have also acquired political aspirations. This cannot be stopped. The Commissioner-General, the Chief Director and the Directors will have to be given sound guidance and be clear about the path along which these people are to be led. This will then have to be explained to them so that they in turn can bring it home to their compatriots.

"Thought must also be given to the organizations or societies that will have to be brought into being in order to canalise the energies of others who also have aspirations (not necessarily political ones) and a desire to make their mark, in such a way that they are kept active and can assist in strengthening the government."[68]

This profound insight into some of Ovamboland's most knotty problems elicited no reaction during the conference, which in itself is illuminating. Mr. De Wet rightly showed that there were other instruments besides the Ovamboland Legislative Council, which could probably be used in the modernizing process. He recognized that the existing Council was traditional in its composition, but from his remarks it could be inferred that this was only temporary. This was the first time that official mention was made of the existence of detribalized Africans and educated people with political ambitions, whose opinions ought to be given some means of expression. The absence of any reaction to Mr. De Wet's remarks leads to the assumption that those quarters responsible for the development of the Homelands in Namibia hold a strongly biased view on that development. It seems that the Legislative and Executive Councils were considered the only valid political instruments for developing Ovamboland, with the chief role in this task being assigned to the traditional élite; the latter were incapable of coping with it, while those sufficiently well educated were either inadequately represented in the Council or totally excluded and left without any prospect of political participation. The result was more frustration, which was either ignored or underestimated.

Meanwhile there was continued support for the traditional leaders in the political progress of Ovamboland, at the expense of the modernizing élites, and the importance of the role played by white officials in this was accentuated. At the opening of the fourth session of the first Legislative Council, Mr. De Wet appealed for close co-operation between the Executive Council, the Legislative Council and the white directors. He went on to say that the co-responsibility of the Ovambo officials would in due course become full responsibility. In the meantime he considered it the task of these officials to win the confidence of the Ovambo people. To this remark he added the demand that the allegation that it was not the Legislative Council but still South Africa that ruled, should be stopped at source. He admitted that the existing régime in Ovamboland did not have popular support, and that concrete objections to it existed.

Mr. De Wet appealed to the people to honour and respect their leaders, to "take them by the hand, strengthen them and help them in their task of leadership". His appeal made it plain that the official attitude towards the traditional leaders remained that of regarding them as the political leaders of their people. Their incompetence and the lack of trust in them were acknowledged by him in his request to the people to guide the leaders in their task. This the modernizing élites were not prepared to do. His appeal intensified their antagonism not only towards the traditional élite, but also towards the South African Government officials. However, this élite could not command the economic and physical resources to enforce their views.

Whether or not the white administrators can succeed in their task will depend on the recognition and co-operation of all existing élites in Ovamboland. The ignoring or elimination of these groups will be counter-productive to the entire development process and will jeopardize the success of any development policy—partially or completely. The task not only of initiating and mobilizing development but also of allowing the population to identify themselves fully with it thus devolves on the white administration. An imbalance between the two will limit the influence and contribution of the white authority. Within the process of development, divergent opinions will have to be weighed up and accommodated. The support of only one élite (the tribal leaders) at the expense of the modernizing élites must expose the development process to unnecessary conflicts with disruptive consequences.

(*b*) *The Chief Councillor and Chief Ministers.* In a broadcast over Radio Ovamboland in September 1970, Chief Shiimi, the first Chief Councillor, delivered a policy speech in which he stated that Ovamboland was making good political progress. He agreed with the people's right to self-determination and went on:

"This right of survival of peoples is also laid down in the order of creation by the Almighty Creator, and who is man to want it otherwise? Is that not blasphemy? That is why as early as 1968 we informed the Government of the Republic of South Africa that we wished to manage our own affairs and to work out our own salvation; also that we did not thereby desire to govern or rule other peoples at any time. ... Thus we also expect that other peoples will not interfere in our affairs or dictate to us how we should regulate them. We have the right to decide how our country is to be administered: Ovamboland has the right to choose who will assist her. This is our reason for making it plain that we want the Government of the Republic of South Africa to help us along the road of development."[69]

It was the first time that an official Ovamboland Government spokesman had given a theological justification for the right of nations to self-determination. The repeated use of "we" implied the Legislative Council. In his radio message Chief Shiimi also attacked the Security Council, the International Court of Justice and President Kaunda of Zambia. According to him, the Republic of South Africa was and would remain Ovamboland's best friend; Ovamboland itself had decided on that. South Africa guaranteed law and order in the country. He also spoke out against the World Council of Churches, which he charged with giving moral and financial aid to so-called "freedom fighters"; he believed this body was supporting terrorism, which meant bloodshed and was the forerunner of Satan. He therefore dissociated himself from the resolutions of the World Council and expressed agreement with the South African Prime Minister's statements on the subject. The Ovamboland Government would take strong action against terrorism and eradicate it root and branch.

Lastly, Chief Shiimi complained that the United Nations was meddling in the country's domestic affairs. He rejected in advance any decisions the world body might make on Ovamboland, without consulting his government. His earnest wish was that the South African Government should assist, lead and advise Ovamboland at all times, because South Africa was the only neighbouring state in which his territory reposed full confidence and which would help it to become one of Africa's model countries.

From this speech it was obvious that the Chief Councillor ranged himself wholeheartedly on the side of separate development and of Ovamboland as a separate Homeland, yet he gave no indication as to the extent of his popular support. However, his ideas were identical to those of the local South African officials, and he enjoyed their support in full measure.

In a conversation in July 1971, the Chief Councillor was asked whom he envisaged as the future leaders of Ovamboland. He replied that the territory had always been administered in accordance with traditional law and this would continue, but future traditional leaders would also have to be educated. He was not worried about a few teachers whose ideas differed from his and who were dissatisfied with what the "Boers" and the South African Government were doing; their displeasure was mainly due to his having censured the advisory opinion of the International Court of Justice the previous month (June 1971) and expressing trust in South Africa, which had raised Ovamboland to its present stage of development. He had rejected the 1971 advisory opinion on behalf of the Ovamboland Government and people in the following terms.

"We believe and are convinced that the policy of separate development is Christian and morally correct, because it has brought us peace, prosperity and progress. Any change in the present order is unthinkable, and we reject it. We shall not allow people and organizations, who know nothing about us, to dictate to us. We are determined to continue building along the road of separate development, and we shall not let ourselves be influenced by the contradictory opinions of the outside world."[70]

Though Chief Shiimi professed to speak for Ovambo people, the reaction that followed his speech from modernizing groups clearly disproved his claim. The following answers were given during the in-depth interviews in 1972.

Question: DID YOU SUPPORT THE WORLD COURT JUDGMENT IN 1971?

	T.	R./L.	O./C.	Comm.	N.	Trad.	Ov./Av.	Kat./Av.
Yes	73.9	81.5	50.0	27.3	90.0	—	58.3	97.0
No	15.2	7.4	39.3	72.7	—	100.0	33.3	1.5
No reply	10.9	11.1	10.7	—	10.0	—	8.3	1.5

In this answer most of the educated groups—teachers, ministers, nurses, officials/clerks—disagreed with Chief Shiimi's interpretation of support among the population. The International Court's advisory opinion undoubtedly had the overwhelming backing of the modernizing elements and strengthened their antagonism to South Africa, whereas the traditional leaders agreed that the opinion should be repudiated. A meeting on 2 July

1971 of senior-headmen, chiefs and other members of the Legislative Council under the leadership of the Chief Councillor resolved that the best course was for South Africa to continue as guardian. Those present stated that they knew South Africa but knew nothing about the United Nations or its judges, who had never visited Ovamboland.[71] On this occasion the traditional leaders, and especiallly the Chief Councillor, expressed their concern over teachers who supported the United Nations and influenced the younger generation against the traditional leaders.[72]

Chief Shiimi confirmed during the conversation alluded to that some of the teachers regarded the South African Government as dishonest, paying meagre salaries and jailing people without trial. He was also aware that there were teachers who grumbled because the first Legislative Council consisted solely of nominees. However, it was the people who had appointed the Council, he said, and as soon as tradition was abandoned, there would be problems: this would soon be appreciated by the teachers who were dissatisfied with tradition because they were being stirred up by the Communists. To the question whether there were Communists in Ovamboland, he answered in the affirmative and cited both the influence of certain white South Africans in the territory and foreign radio broadcasts. "It is the whites", he said, "who come here and tell our people that there is help for them from beyond our borders. They are the types who incite our people to leave the country illegally." Shiimi was here referring to Ovambos who had left Ovamboland and taken refuge in African states.

For him Namibia was a neighbour of South Africa, not of the United Nations. On close questioning, however, he betrayed ignorance and uncertainty regarding the UN and its relations with South Africa concerning Namibia. He pointed out that he was a chief, well versed in traditional matters, but where the UN was concerned, he needed guidance because he was a simple man. The whites should rather supply the answers to questions about the United Nations. The chief's confusion was evident when he said that, according to the contention of certain people, the world body had handed over the mandate to South Africa, when in fact this was not so. He was also worried about the advisory opinion of the International Court, because he asked what would happen if the United Nations were to endeavour to enforce the judgement and Red China was encouraged to occupy Namibia.[73] He therefore wanted to know, in conclusion, how strong Red China was militarily, and what South Africa would do in the event of a Chinese attack on Namibia.

Uncertainty and even anxiety repeatedly emerged from the conversation, which was also characterized by a plea for the retention of the traditional organization in Ovamboland. To many—mostly simple—questions Shiimi was either unable to reply or was evasive. It was also apparent that he was not *au fait* with the thinking of the new élite groups, who to him were just ordinary Ovambos with specific professions. They were summarily condemned without any enquiry into the merits of their objections. Shiimi was well acquainted with certain subjects, such as unemployment and the shortage of high schools; but he felt that contract workers' complaints over their low wages in the south were only valid there and that on their return to Ovamboland, ceased to have any reality. The strike six months later proved this supposition to be false: he maintained that if the population had any grounds for dissatisfaction, they would surely inform him because of their faith in him as traditional leader. This was why the teachers had come to him with a list of grievances.

The last observation is most significant. Shiimi assumed as a matter of course that if anyone visited him with a grievance, it was primarily because he was a traditional leader, and not because he was Chief Councillor of Ovamboland. The two roles appeared to him synonymous; and he seemed not to appreciate the essential difference. The conversation also demonstrated the justice of the complaints, and confirmed the doubts of the modernizing element regarding the Chief Councillors' ability to deal with real problems. The gulf between the two was already too wide to be bridged, and frustration over, and hatred for, Chief Councillor Shiimi among the educated element increased. His death in a motor accident at the end of the year was regarded by his opponents as a fortunate stroke of fate.

The policy of new Chief Minister, Chief F. Elifas, did not deviate much from that of his predecessor. He inveighed on various occasions even more strongly against SWAPO, for whom he became an object of special hatred; he held the organization responsible for the fact that many Ovambos had left the country and sought asylum elsewhere, chiefly in Zambia. He doubted SWAPO's credibility because, as he said, Ovambos had left the country due to SWAPO's false promises.[74] He appealed to these Ovambos to return and help in the development of Ovamboland, and he rejected SWAPO's boycott of the Legislative Council elections.[75] He banned SWAPO meetings, which were aimed at dissuading the population from voting in elections.[76] He contended that SWAPO could not claim to represent the Ovambo people.[77]

When several Ovambos returned from across the border, Chief Elifas said in the Legislative Council:

"The Ovambo nation accepts them with open arms in their country where there is peace and stability. They will be accepted in the hearts of the nation provided they have returned with peace in their hearts. I trust that the people who have crossed our borders despite my warnings now realize that I was right in the first instance and that they will take heed of my warnings and not lend their ears to dissentients. I always knew that those who enticed my people over the border had ulterior motives and now my people have seen and experienced it for themselves. These organizations and churches must now stop confusing and misleading my people because now my people have experienced what is happening across the border where thousands of innocent people are being killed. Real freedom can only be found in Ovamboland and nowhere else."[80]

Chief Elifas consistently viewed SWAPO as a terrorist movement that promoted bloodshed, damage to property, intimidation, labour unrest and race hatred, and the undermining of government and tribal authority. In his opinion, it had contributed nothing to the development and welfare of Ovamboland, and he warned its "self-appointed" leaders to moderate their attitudes, otherwise resolute steps would be taken against them. He told members of the Ovamboland Government Service, who were using their position to further the interests of SWAPO, that their services were not indispensable.[78] He continued to promise active support for South Africa's political, economic and social development plans in Ovamboland. On several occasions he spoke out strongly against the dangers of Communism and terrorism. In 1974 he handed R30,000 to the South African defence and police forces for their peace-keeping role on the borders of Namibia in the name of the Ovambo tribes.[79]

At various times Chief Elifas affirmed that Ovamboland could only develop and progress if law and order were maintained. He stressed the Ovamboland Government's duty to ensure peaceful co-existence, and said that this also applied to every Ovambo. Chief Elifas further exhorted headmen to enforce their traditional authority, whenever it might be threatened. Ovamboland belonged to the Ovambo people, and there would be no other rule in the country. He urged SWAPO to take note of this, because he would not let Ovamboland be sold out to Communism, following the examples of Mozambique and Angola. No outside interference would be tolerated in matters affecting his people, and he was not prepared to govern his country under United Nations supervision. His compatriots could not share their rightful traditions, culture or way of life with others, and a greater national consciousness was needed.[81] Foreign courts should not interfere with tribal practices and customs; this warning was directed mainly at church leaders, who had applied in a white court at Windhoek for an interdict against the infliction of corporal punishment. On several occasions he requested clergymen not to meddle illegally in government and tribal affairs, and to refrain from subversive political activities.[82]

He accepted the result of the January 1975 General Election as a vote of confidence in himself and his government, and as a mandate for action against certain idividuals, including churchmen, on the grounds of incitement, intimidation and other kinds of subversion. Chief Elifas said that the reputation of some churches in Ovamboland had suffered through the actions of politically active clerics, and he appealed to the churches to confine themselves to their allotted task, which was outside the realm of politics, and work with the government.[83]

The Chief Minister said several times that Ovamboland was on the road to total independence. The Ovamboland Government was ready to send representatives to take part in an open conference on the constitutional future of Namibia, but he made it clear that he was not prepared to discuss the Ovambos' political development or right to self-determination. The internal government of Ovamboland, notably the power structure, was something which he regarded as his sole prerogative. Over the years, he said, the Ovambos had been able to maintain their own traditional administration, and this now had to be evolved into a modern government, suitable for the needs of a developing nation. He conceded that the advancement and adaptation of the Ovambo people would have to be encourged from outside, but the stimulus for it would have to come from within the Homeland.[84] He was resolved to lead Ovamboland to independence.[85] He clearly believed that he could retain and even extend the traditional administration even in the teeth of resistance from the UNO, SWAPO and the modernizing élite.

The Chief Minister stated that

"the privilege to govern Ovamboland is the God-given right of Ovambos only, with an inherent national sentiment for that which belongs to us and which must be retained at all costs. The time has arrived that the nation must take note of the fact that the anti-Christ with its evil forces is busy undermining the nation, in a subtle way and by false pretences leading our youth across the border. What is even more tragic is that those evil powers are assisted by clergymen from our own nation. Tragic indeed!"

The Chief Minister called on all the members of the Legislative Council to work harder on all fronts. He continued:

"For that reason my department has taken the necessary steps to activate tribal authorities in the country in order to ensure that service of a high standard is rendered to the nation. Senior-Headmen, Headmen, Chiefs and Legislative Councillors are not there only to enforce authority, but must also render service. If you perform only the former, be not surprised if the nation shuns you. During the course of this sitting many of you will no doubt ask why the Government has not done this or that. Do not be affronted when I ask you as Senior-Headman, Headman or Legislative Councillor what you have done to solve the problems. Modernization also means that the local tribal leaders will in future render service to our people."[86]

Chief Elifas repeated that he was not prepared to have Ovamboland governed under the supervision of the United Nations, but

"leaders from Africa who are interested in a visit to the territory in order to gain first-hand information about the country are very welcome to do so either personally or through their representatives. I will also be prepared to exchange ideas with the O.A.U. on the basis of the points of view which I have enunciated, but the role played by SWAPO cannot be accepted. If the Africa Chairman of the South West Committee and the Special Committee of the O.A.U. take a real interest in the progress of this territory and discuss these matters with me in South Africa, I will also ask the true leaders of the people of this territory to discuss matters with them. If they are desirous of meeting the leaders in their own countries in order to obtain first-hand information they are at liberty to do so and may be invited and we shall do everything in our power to make such a visit possible."

He concluded:

"We are a free country and the Government has been placed there by the Ovambo nation, which is a responsible nation, which knows exactly what it wants and how it wants to be governed. I will not do something which will cause tension in our country and I am prepared to do my duty in order to find solutions where necessary but it must be remembered that Ovamboland is for the Ovambos. ...[87] I am the leader of the greatest nation in South West Africa and I therefore say unequivocally that I, together with my Government, are nobody's puppet or parrot, neither of the UN nor the South African Government. SWAPO, on the other hand, is the marionette of people who have not yet done anything for the Ovambo nation, it is the mimics of other organizations and it is instigating anarchy. We will take care and ensure that law and order are maintained in our country in order to take us further along the road of development."[88]

Two months later, on 16 August, Chief Elifas was assassinated near

Ondangwa. His successor as Chief Minister, the Rev. K. Ndjoba, made it clear that he would carry on Chief Elifas's policy and strive for the political independence of Ovamboland. He also lashed out fiercely at SWAPO, whose declared enemy he had been for years. However, the modernizing élites regard him as a stooge of the South African Government, and even most clergymen in his church, the Ovambokavango Church, view him as a renegade who has forsaken his ministry for the sake of prestige and financial advantage.

In his first speech in the Legislative Council as Chief Minister, Mr. Ndjoba expressed his support for an independent Ovamboland but had, at the same time, shown his awareness of the increasing dangers to his country from among his own people, from Angola and from SWAPO. The following are some of his statements made during the speech:

"We are firmly on the road of development and because we now see for ourselves what can be achieved, we will brook no interference in our domestic affairs. As I have already said on many occasions, we are, however, always prepared to talk with interested persons on matters of common interest, as for example, economic interdependence, but let us respect one another's constitutional aspirations.

"Now the question arises—are we as a young nation and young government going to surrender that which we have worked for? Are we going to permit the Angolan sickness of division, anarchy, murder and bloodshed of innocent persons also to bleed our land to death? Are we going to allow SWAPO terrorists to force us on our knees? Are we, as a nation, going to sacrifice the future of our youth?

"Today from every angle of life onslaughts are made upon the life of the people. Intimidation is the order of the day; landmines are killing innocent Ovambos; properties built up over years are being burned down and, above all, your and my religion is being destroyed. A wedge is also being driven in between White and Black.

"I am the last person who is the yes-man of the White man, but I accept the White man if his intentions with me and my people are honest. I now challenge—will SWAPO, the communist or any other wedge-driver give my Government R14 million to balance our budget? That is what the Government of the Republic of South Africa is giving us gratis and without any conditions for development, and there is still hope for more later.

"We must be realistic and that is why I sketch the picture as it appears today: We will have setbacks, we will have to make sacrifices, but defeat—never! And why will we not suffer defeat? Only for one reason, and that is because our cause is right. We stand for peaceful development with a place in the sun for all our people.

"The identity of our people is one of our biggest assets, and we will most certainly not be subjected to foreign authority, and that which is our own we will not allow to go under. ..."[88]

On several other occasions the Chief Minister has made known his unyielding attitude towards SWAPO although he is prepared to receive back any member of SWAPO's external wing wishing to return in peace to Ovamboland. The Ovambo Government would provide all the aid they needed. When some former members of SWAPO's external wing returned to Ovamboland (e.g. J. Kuhngua, J. Kambode, M. Kerina, N. Neghumbo), he appealed to SWAPO's president, S. Nujoma, and his followers to lay down their arms and return to Namibia in peace.[89] According to the Chief Minister, SWAPO represents only a minority group which he will never allow to form a majority government: "SWAPO talks about a majority government, but the history of Angola has taught us that Unita and FNLA are the majority, and that the MPLA, supported by SWAPO, are the minority threatening the lives of the inhabitants of Angola rather than protecting them. Never will I allow a minority to decide over the future of Ovamboland."[90] The Rev. Ndjoba rejects the claim of SWAPO to be a Christian organization, even if clergymen serve on its head committee: "SWAPO is a Communist organization; it does not believe in God and His Commandments. SWAPO only wants to kill and to create disaster to the disadvantage of the Ovambo people. That is why my Government fights SWAPO with might and main."[91]

The Chief Minister has repeatedly made clear that he and his Government welcomes the presence of the South African Defence Force in Ovamboland. He has emphasized that his Government has actually asked the Defence Force to be present in Ovamboland and to act strongly against any SWAPO activities in Ovamboland and on the border. This includes, at his request, hot-pursuit operations "even if it means going right to Luanda,"[92] especially when people in Ovamboland are abducted or killed by SWAPO forces.

On the Constitutional Conference on the political future of Namibia, the Chief Minister said that he stood firmly by the principle of an equal say for all population groups in Namibia, and the principle that the rights of each population group should be guaranteed. He reserves to Ovamboland the right to remain autonomous, although he is in favour of it being represented in an all-embracing National Assembly. Thus he seems to see Ovamboland's political future as being within a confederation rather than as a unitary state, as proposed by SWAPO. So far the Ovambo Government has never renounced its right eventually to become an independent state.

(c) *The Ovambo Élites.* The validity of the assertion that the people supported the line of political development envisaged by the South African Government and the associated role of the traditional administration was tested among the different élite groups of Ovamboland. Unlike previous questions on tribal political affairs, this inquiry was centred on the political development of Ovamboland as a whole, i.e. the whole area within the Legislative Council's jurisdiction.

Question: ARE YOU INTERESTED IN THE POLITICAL AFFAIRS OF THE WHOLE OF OVAMBOLAND?

	T.	R./L.	O./C.	Comm.	N.	Trad.	Ov./Av.	Kat./Av.
Very much	80.4	44.4	82.1	100.0	35.0	87.5	71.2	48.5
A little	8.7	11.1	14.3	—	20.0	12.5	11.5	12.1
Not at all	8.7	29.7	3.6	—	25.0	—	11.5	33.3
No reply	2.2	14.8	—	—	20.0	—	5.8	6.1

In general, a high degree of political consciousness was found in both Ovamboland and Katutura, and most members of the élite groups felt themselves to be closely linked to political developments in Ovamboland and the rest of Namibia. This deep involvement is clear from the replies given in Ovamboland. The seemingly smaller interest on the part of Katutura (in reality intense, as will be apparent from other replies) must be ascribed to the resistance of most respondents there to the prospect of Ovamboland being isolated from Namibia as a whole. While interest in the politics of the entire territory is lively, there is scant enthusiasm for Ovamboland as a separate entity. Similarly the Ovambo residential area in Katutura is accepted as part of Namibia and not as part of Ovamboland, which lessens the sense of a separate Ovambo identity. The geographical distance from Ovamboland is an added reason for the slight interest taken in its politics.

The foregoing question, which tested general interest in political factors, was followed with one of the current political development of Ovamboland.

Question: WHAT IS YOUR FEELING ON OVAMBOLAND'S CURRENT POLITICAL DEVELOPMENT?

	T.	R./L.	O./C.	Comm.	N.	Trad.	Ov./Av.	Kat./Av.
Satisfied	4.4	14.8	39.3	63.6	15.0	95.8	32.0	10.6
Reasonably satisfied	21.7	14.8	14.3	18.2	5.0	4.2	14.1	7.6
Dissatisfied	71.7	70.4	46.4	18.2	40.0	—	48.1	78.8
No reply	2.2	—	—	—	40.0	—	5.8	3.0

With the exception of the traders in Ovamboland, who were comparatively satisfied, and the traditional leaders, whose satisfaction was virtually unanimous, all the élite groups in Ovamboland and Katutura displayed varying degrees of dissatisfaction with the present political development in Ovamboland. They explained their attitude by the following reasons: educated people were accorded no share in the territory's political development; there was hatred between the government and the people; Namibia should be developed in its entirety, and not Ovamboland separately; there should be human dignity and universal equality; apartheid should be abolished; the existing political development in Ovamboland was fostering division and not unity in Namibia; there was no equality before the law; the people had no share in the government; no political parties existed in Ovamboland; political development was proceeding too slowly; those taking part in politics and stating the truth were arrested, intimidated, interrogated, tortured, given electric shocks, imprisoned and restricted in their movements; the traditional leaders were told beforehand what to say, and did not express the real thoughts of the people; the members of the Legislative Council were nominated and not elected, and did not attend to matters that truly affected the nation; the Council was undemocratic and unsuitable; and political meetings were not tolerated.

Against this background of widespread discontent, the arguments advanced in favour of the current political development by the more satisfied groups like the traders and the traditional leaders are also important. These leaders emphasized the general progress that was taking place under the new deal and their right to leadership on traditional grounds. It was precisely this attitude and this self-assumed right that was being opposed by the modernizing élites.

The next question was designed to check on this.

Question: ARE YOU DISSATISFIED WITH ANYTHING IN THE PRESENT POLITICAL DEVELOPMENT OF OVAMBOLAND?

	T.	R./L.	O./C.	Comm.	N.	Trad.	Ov./Av.	Kat./Av.
Yes	91.3	85.2	57.2	45.4	85.0	33.3	71.2	80.3
No	2.2	14.8	32.1	45.4	—	66.7	22.4	13.6
No reply	6.5	—	10.7	9.1	15.0	—	6.4	6.1

The degree of dissatisfaction here is considerable. Most comments, especially by the modernizing élite groups, were identical to the replies given to the preceding question. These are elementary political objections to a governmental system which claims to accord with democratic standards. If it is in fact democratic, then it should be applied to the whole of Namibia and not to Ovamboland as a separate entity. Here again the most important demands made, serving as a yardstick by which the political development and institutions of Ovamboland would be measured, were for free elections in which everyone was allowed to elect the candidates of his own choice, (thus eliminating the system of nominees), and the right to freedom of speech and movement. Further, they demanded approved political parties, with the right to participate in the political process; protection against intimidation, and the recognition of human and equal rights, regardless of race, creed or colour.

New were the complaints directed by the traditional élite at the younger generation and some of the teachers; dissatisfaction was expressed over the thinking of the young and over the way in which the traditional spiritual life and traditional institutions, such as land ownership, were being affected. Differences between the generations were the subject of the following question:

Question: IS THE POLITICAL OUTLOOK OF THE YOUNG PEOPLE GENERALLY THE SAME AS THAT OF THE OLDER PEOPLE?

	T.	R./L.	O./C.	Comm.	N.	Trad.	Ov./Av.	Kat./Av.
Yes, the same	4.3	25.9	7.1	9.1	—	—	7.7	12.1
No, different	93.5	74.1	92.9	90.9	85.0	100.0	89.7	86.4
No reply	2.2	—	—	—	15.0	—	2.6	1.5

From these replies the conflict between the generations appears irreconcilable. Yet it seems equally clear that the divergence of views does not merely run parallel to age differences, but exists between a strong, dynamic young generation, interested in modern political development, and an older one which still clings to the traditional order. Both sides are well aware of this struggle. Besides their perceptible political differences, it is

Question: DO YOU VIEW THE GENERAL DEVELOPMENT OF OVAMBOLAND AS BEING ...

	T.	R./L.	O./C.	Comm.	N.	Trad.	Ow./Av.	Kat./Av.
... in co-operation with South Africa?	26.1	7.4	57.1	54.5	—	100.0	38.4	18.2
... in co-operation with the UN?	6.5	3.7	7.2	9.1	5.0	—	5.1	39.4
... in co-operation with the OAU?	2.2	11.1	3.6	—	—	—	3.2	4.5
... on its own?	13.0	—	10.7	—	50.0	—	12.2	19.7
... in co-operation with another country or organization that I may choose?	26.1	37.1	10.7	9.1	5.0	—	17.3	4.5
... in co-operation with South Africa and UN?[93]	10.9	14.8	3.6	18.2	—	—	7.7	3.0
... on its own and in co-operation with South Africa?	2.2	3.7	—	—	—	—	1.3	—
... in co-operation with the UN and the OAU?	10.9	7.4	7.1	—	—	—	5.8	6.1
... on its own and in co-operation with UN?	—	—	—	—	30.0	—	3.9	—
No reply	2.1	14.8	—	9.1	10.0	—	5.1	4.6

primarily the illiteracy of the older generation that divides it from the younger people. Knowledge, readiness to learn for the sake of rapid modern development, and acceptance of Western values are postulated by the latter as conditions for understanding their value concepts and ideas on political progress. The younger people think that the older generation are unequal to the task, and should therefore relinquish political control.

The question arises as to who should take the lead in developing Ovamboland—specifically, the political lead (see page 114).

South Africa is still acknowledged as the most important agent in Ovamboland's development. Co-operation with South Africa and the evolution of Ovamboland on its own—without any assistance from outside South Africa or Namibia—have the concerted backing of more than half the respondents. South Africa receives its support most solidly from the traditional leaders (100%) substantially from the merchants and officials/ clerks, especially the tribal secretaries, and almost a quarter from the teachers questioned. Least support comes from the clergy, with none at all from nurses.

The answers in Katutura indicate strong opposition to South Africa's

Question: WHO, IN YOUR OPINION, SHOULD TAKE THE MOST IMPORTANT DECISIONS ON THE POLITICAL DEVELOPMEMT OF OVAMBOLAND?

	T.	R./L.	O./C.	Comm.	N.	Trad.	Ov./Av.	Kat./Av.
White officials, i.e. the South African Government	—	—	10.7	—	—	20.8	5.1	3.0
The tribal leaders	—	—	—	—	—	—	—	1.5
The Legislative Assembly of Ovamboland	2.2	7.4	21.4	9.1	—	45.8	13.5	1.5
The UN	4.3	—	3.6	—	5.0	—	2.6	57.6
The whole population of Ovamboland	63.0	18.5	46.4	54.5	80.0	12.5	46.1	12.1
South Africa and the Legislative Assembly	4.3	3.7	10.7	18.2	—	20.8	8.3	—
The whole population of South West Africa	2.2	3.7	—	9.1	—	—	1.9	1.5
South Africa and UN jointly	4.3	7.4	—	9.1	—	—	3.2	1.5
The whole population of Ovamboland jointly with the UN	17.4	22.2	3.6	—	5.0	—	10.3	19.7
No reply	2.2	37.0	3.6	—	10.0	—	9.0	1.6

role in developing Ovamboland—and the high premium placed on assistance from the UN in its advancement. Even the development of Ovamboland on its own receives more support than co-operation with South Africa. The low level of South Africa's prestige in Katutura, reflected in less than 40 per cent élite group support for South Africa as a collaborator in Ovamboland's development, may be surprising if one considers the large amount of development aid South Africa has already given to the territory. The extent of mistrust expressed in these replies confirms a tendency observed in previous answers, from which the chief cause for such mistrust appears to be in the political sphere (see page 115).

Here again the initial choice between the five alternatives was extended when it emerged during the investigation that further alternatives would have to be put in order to accommodate the ideas of the respondents. From the answers a clear preference can be detected, which is different in Ovamboland from Katutura. The first three choices in the two areas are as follows:

OVAMBOLAND	KATUTURA
1. The whole population of Ovamboland (46.1%)	1. The UN (57.6%)
2. The Legislative Council of Ovamboland (13.5%)	2. The whole population of Ovamboland together with the UN (19.7%)
3. The whole population of Ovamboland together with the UN (10.3%)	3. The whole population of Ovamboland (12.1%)

The replies given in Ovamboland shows a trend towards wishing to decide on the country's own future and feeling itself equal to the task without interference from outside. Such external interference refers not only to the UN but also to the South African Government, neither of which are popular in the country. The outright rejection by the entire Ovamboland population of the Legislative Council, which has majority support among the traditional leaders only, illustrates the same mistrust of the Council as was expressed in replies to other questions. It is not regarded as representative of the Ovambo people.

By contrast the greatest confidence in the UN is expressed in Katutura, and after that in the population of Ovamboland. Every other alternative, such as the Legislative Assembly and the South African Government, receives a minimum of approval. The conclusion from this is that the Ovambos in Katutura are mistrustful of the ability of any organization other than the UN to solve Namibia's political problems. A further probability is that the Katutura Ovambos perhaps consider themselves as part of a greater Namibia and no longer of Ovamboland, an outlook already sanctioned by resolutions of the General Assembly, the Security Council and the International Court of Justice. All they now wait for is the assurance that their continued existence in Katutura and in Namibia as a single state will be assured.

Answers to earlier questions have revealed a critical attitude towards the policy of separate development. This anticipated standpoint led to the next fundamental question.

Question: DO YOU THINK THE POLICY OF SEPARATE DEVELOPMENT AS NOW APPLIED IN OVAMBOLAND IS A GOOD POLICY FOR THE TERRITORY?

	T.	R./L.	O./C.	Comm.	N.	Trad.	Ov./Av.	Kat./Av.
Yes	13.0	11.1	46.4	54.5	10.0	91.7	33.3	3.0
No	82.6	88.9	50.0	36.4	85.0	8.3	63.5	94.0
To some extent	—	—	3.6	9.1	—	—	1.3	—
No reply	4.4	—	—	—	5.0	—	1.9	3.0

Here is a predominant antipathy to the policy among all élite groups except the traders, the traditional élite and a proposition of the officials and clerks, especially tribal secretaries. Once again there is even stronger opposition to it in Katutura than in Ovamboland, for the reasons already given.

A strong cause of solidarity with other non-white groups throughout Namibia repeatedly emerges. Other complaints refer to the way in which the policy is applied, which is objected to on ethical and religious grounds—while, incidentally, the logic of separate development is doubted:

"Apartheid is a bearer of hate and not of love between white and black."

"Apartheid is inhuman and misanthropic. It is the blacks who suffer most from it."

"Separate development estranges people from one another."

"The policy lays no emphasis on human dignity; it is unchristian and contrary to divine law."

"The object is hate and humiliation, and the policy holds good only for so-called non-whites. It is Kaffirs there, whites here."

"Separate development causes discord, not concord. The whole of Namibia must develop together."

"Separate development causes dissension in Ovamboland and in the whole of Namibia. It was applied in order to save the day for the whites."

The answers in favour of the policy emphasize the development aspects and the benefits conferred by the policy, rather than segregation itself. These answers reveal a great determination to retain the old tradition at all costs, and to build further on it—an argument met with chiefly among the traditional élite. Some observations made by traditional leaders follow:

"Separate development is uplifting."

"It brings economic progress."

"It is good for the retention of traditions in Ovamboland."

"Nature made boundaries and languages. People cannot develop in higgledy-piggledy fashion, but all people on their own."

"Everyone stands by his own home and his own homeland."

"Ovambos are getting the opportunity to rule themselves."

"The policy is the only way of bringing about peace in South West Africa."

"Ovamboland must not be governed by a foreign people."

"God gave Ovamboland its own land, tongue and culture."

The prevalent attitude of strong disapproval of separate development, which emerged mainly among the modernizing élite groups, threw into relief the question whether the Ovambo élites wished the area to become independent.

Question: MUST OVAMBOLAND BECOME INDEPENDENT?

	T.	R./L.	O./C.	Comm.	N.	Trad.	Ov./Av.	Kat./Av.
Yes	26.1	33.3	53.6	81.8	10.0	95.8	44.9	13.6
No	71.7	66.7	42.9	18.2	55.0	4.2	49.4	81.8
No reply	2.2	—	3.6	—	35.0	—	5.7	4.6

These replies show a distinct difference in attitude between Ovamboland and Katutura. While the idea of independence is overwhelmingly rejected in Katutura, it has a fair backing in Ovamboland, except among the majority of teachers, clergy and nurses. A small majority of the officials and clerks give it their blessing, but a substantial majority of traders and traditional leaders strongly support the idea of ultimate independence for Ovamboland. On the basis of their reactions to earlier questions, it could be contended that if some of their most elementary objections were attended to, the modernizing groups would view the final independence planned for the territory more sympathetically.

The following points of view favouring independence are apparent from the answers: (*a*) the acceptance of self-government, partly because it is the aim of every developing country and partly because it is what South Africa wants; (*b*) the desire to escape from apartheid measures, and (*c*) the desire to achieve a thriving economy as soon as possible. The replies opposing independence reflect emotional reasons, such as the emphasis on brotherhood with other tribes, and also some rational considerations. It can be assumed that both economically and politically, Ovamboland is not yet in a position to be independent, and will not be in the near future. Moreover, it is unlikely that Ovamboland will ever be able to relinquish a relationship of interdependence with the rest of Namibia. The expressed wish for Namibia to be a unitary state is idealised, without any indication of its content and manner of operation, or of how unity is to be realized, or who will take the lead in the process.

(*d*) *The Problem of Political Leadership.* In the absence of political parties that could voice the people's needs, efforts were made to ascertain who, in the eyes of the élite groups, could be approached, to answer political questions and fulfil political needs, and from whom leadership could be expected in the political development of the country. Respondents were asked to consider the various professions and bodies involved in the general development of Ovamboland, and also to judge their own potential.

Another question gave a list of leading personages in Ovamboland and asked which of them exercised influence on the country's political development. The élite groups were likewise asked which ethnic group in Namibia they considered the most important politically; and finally an attempt was made to see if there was any attachment to a country outside Namibia or if any country was particularly admired because of its political example.

In the first question the respondents were given the whole spectrum of existing occupations in Ovamboland—ranging from students to employees of the Bantu Investment Corporation. The replies showed a preference for four occupations, first place being given to teachers, both in Ovamboland and Katutura. Ovambo clergymen were given second place and the chiefs and headmen and students respectively third and fourth places. The high grading of the last-named group may perhaps be due to its active involvement in the political affairs and development of Ovamboland and Namibia.

Merchants take fifth place in both Katutura and Ovamboland but with a very low percentage, while the other occupations and the Bantu Development Corporation are deemed of minor importance and considered as having little or no influence in the Territory's political development. White and Ovambo officialdom tie respectively for sixth place, at virtually the same level as the merchants. Support for white clergymen is negligible, though slightly higher in Katutura than in Ovamboland. Hence white clergymen do not have the political influence officially claimed, least of all in Ovamboland.

The traditional leaders are considered politically important mostly by themselves, and they are supported by their tribal secretaries and by a small percentage of traders and ministers. The Ovambo clergy and teachers are considered the most influential and important by everyone except the traditional leaders. The latter command least support from the teachers, nurses, officials and clerks (the tribal secretaries excepted), and students. While the traditional leaders credit themselves with roughly 90 per cent backing as the most significant political influence, their influence is rated by the other groups in the territory at only 15 per cent. These contrasting figures speak for themselves.

In a follow-up question the respondents were asked whether political influence should in fact be exerted by the various occupations, and by students and the Bantu Development Corporation, and on what grounds such influence could be claimed. It was clear from the replies that the preference accorded to specific occupations was based on the necessity for leaders to have had a good education. A further criterion was the extent of contact with the population and the ability to interpret their wishes. Ability to meet these requirements would determine the extent of the people's trust in different occupations. The answers showed that it was mostly clergy and teachers who fulfilled these conditions.

The respondents were asked, in conjunction with the previous question, to give their opinion on who best represented the political thinking and wishes of the Ovambo people. They were requested to state no order of preference, but merely the occupations and bodies involved.

The replies to the follow-up question, when compared with the previous one, showed no difference regarding the vocations considered best able to interpret the wishes of the Ovambo people. In both Katutura and Ovamboland teachers, ministers and students, in that order, are given top place in this respect. The traders and traditional leaders in Ovamboland receive a certain amount of support, other occupations being little favoured. In Katutura, the fourth and fifth places go to white ministers and Ovambo dealers, with about a quarter of the support to the first three.

After those questioned had identified the vocations from which they expected the best leadership, and who could best represent their political thoughts and wishes, they were asked "Do you think that you are personally able to exert strong influence on Ovambo's political development?"

Question: DO YOU THINK THAT YOU ARE PERSONALLY ABLE TO EXERT STRONG INFLUENCE ON OVAMBO'S POLITICAL DEVELOPMENT?

	T.	*R./L.*	*O./C.*	*Comm.*	*N.*	*Trad.*	*Ov./Av.*	*Kat./Av.*
Yes	80.4	44.4	82.1	81.8	60.0	95.8	74.4	73.9
No	10.9	40.8	10.7	18.2	35.0	4.2	18.6	15.4
Don't know	—	3.7	—	—	—	0.10	0.6	4.6
No reply	8.7	11.1	7.2	—	5.0	—	6.4	6.1

Although it was expected that most respondents would answer in the affirmative, two categories were guarded in their replies—the churchmen and (in Katutura) the students. Yet, viewed as a whole, every group felt confident of its ability to give political guidance.

An explanatory follow-up question sought to ascertain the motivation for claiming personal influence on political development. The answers revealed a strong awareness of leadership ability: by the modernizing élite groups on the basis of educational qualifications, and by the traditional leaders due to practical experience and conferred or acquired status. The modernizing élites referred to their knowledge of new developments and requirements in Ovamboland, and of conditions in the outside world, and claimed the ability to innovate. Both they and the traditional élites claimed to have the soundest knowledge of their people and their wishes. Thus each maintained that their leadership was accepted.

In a final question on political influence and thinking, the respondents were handed a list of personages in Ovamboland, who were considered of high repute in the social, economic and political spheres; because there was no recognized party in Ovamboland through which political needs could be channelled, and therefore such demands were probably being met by individual leaders, they were aksed to indicate three who commanded the highest admiration, by virtue of their political leadership in the development of the territory.

The following represented the respective occupations:

1. *Traditional leaders and (at the time of questioning) Executive Councillors (subsequently ministers)*
Chief F.S. Elifas (Chief Councillor)—Ndonga tribe (assassinated 1975)
Chief S. Taapopi—Kwaluudhi tribe
Chief J.M. Munkundi—Ngandjera tribe
Senior-Headman S. Impumbu—Kwambi tribe
Senior-Headman K. Mundjele—Mbalantu tribe
Senior-Headman W. Kanyele—Kolonkadhi-Eunda tribe

2. *Clergy*
Bishop Auala (ELOC)
Assistant-Bishop Dumeni (ELOC)
Rev. P. Kalangula (Leader of the New Independent Anglican Church)
Rev. K. Ndjoba (ELOC and Executive Councillor at the time on behalf of
   the Kwanyama tribe; Chief Minister since 1975)

3. *Teachers*
H.D. Namahuja (the only Ovambo inspector of education in 1972)
J. Otto (chairman of the Teachers' Association in 1973 and leader of
   SWAPO; fled abroad in 1974)

4. *Officials/clerks*
J. Nangutuuala (leader of DEMCOP)

5. *Traders*
F. Indongo (richest merchant in Ovambo; Minister of Economic Affairs
   since 1975)
L. Mukuilongo (member of the Legislative Council and chairman of the
   Traders' Association)

The respondents were allowed to give another name if they did not feel
that all the most important leaders had been mentioned. Three other names
were given—J. de Wet, the Commissioner-General, once; a certain Gabriel
Shihapo once; and (in Katutura) the restricted SWAPO vice-president
in Namibia, Nathaniel Maxuiriri, four times. The few alternative leaders
mentioned indicates that the most important ones appeared in the list.

Only four of these thirteen leaders received substantial backing, and
these can be divided into two groups. The first comprised Bishop Auala and
Johannes Nangutuuala, who were regarded as the two outstanding political
leaders. In both Ovamboland and Katutura, Bishop Auala took first place
and Nangutuuala the second. The other group, who obtained a fair amount
of support, comprised Chief Elifas and John Otto, the former being
considered the third most important leader in Ovamboland, and the fourth
in Katutura, whereas the latter occupied fourth place in Ovamboland and
third in Katutura.

Though the four men were respectively a minister, a clerk, a traditional
leader and a teacher, their selection can be assumed to have been due not
so much to their occupations as to their roles in Ovamboland's political
development—Bishop Auala as leader of the predominant Ovambokavango
Church, who in the past had repeatedly made political pronouncements;
Nangutuuala as leader of the (unrecognized) Democratic Co-operative
Development Party and of the striking workers (1971/2); Chief Elifas as
Chief Minister and leader of the Ovamboland Independent Party, and John
Otto as leader of SWAPO in Ovamboland. They all represented differing
political outlooks.

Of the four leaders named only Chief Elifas, representing the traditional
élite, supported the homelands policy and separate development. The other
three, who belonged to the new élites and were professionally trained to a

high level, were all opposed to the idea of Ovamboland becoming a separate homeland, and were interested solely in the political development of Namibia as a unit; their views differed only in degree. Bishop Auala was the most moderate of the three, with Nangutuuala rather less so but still a pragmatist, and John Otto the most consistently radical over Ovamboland's future as an integral part of Namibia.

Chief Elifas naturally received most of his support from the traditional leaders and some from the tribal secretaries and traders in Ovamboland. Only one of the traditional leaders was ready to include Nangutuuala and Otto in his preferences; four mentioned Bishop Auala as second and third choice. The palpable mistrust of the traditional leaders for the three leaders named can be regarded as a further sign of the deep and apparently irremediable suspicion and antagonism which exist between the modernizing and traditional leaders in Ovamboland. Of the other leaders on the list, the low grading of the Rev. K. Ndjoba, the cabinet member with the highest academic qualifications, is significant. He was the first member of a modernizing faction willing to become a member of the Executive Council and thus part of the traditional power structure. For this the modernizing élite groups branded him as a renegade. Significantly he only obtained substantial backing from the traditional leaders.

Viewing the Ovambo nation as the most numerous ethnic group in Namibia, and bearing in mind the recent role of the Ovambos (clearly reflected in the activities of SWAPO, DEMCOP, the Ovambokavango Church and Ovambo labour power), the people were asked whom they judged the most politically important ethnic group in Namibia. This question was also aimed at assessing the self-awareness and self-esteem of the Ovambo people, and the possibility of their co-operating with other ethnic groups in the country.

Question: WHICH IS THE MOST IMPORTANT ETHNIC GROUP IN NAMIBIA FROM A POLITICAL ANGLE?

	T.	R./L.	O./C.	Comm.	N.	Trad.	Ov./Av.	Kat./Av.
Ovambo	30.4	29.6	71.4	45.4	30.0	87.5	47.4	57.6
Herero	—	—	3.6	18.2	—	—	1.9	1.5
Damara	—	—	—	—	—	—	—	—
Bushman	—	—	—	—	—	—	—	—
Namas	—	—	—	—	—	—	—	—
Basters/Coloureds	—	—	—	—	—	—	—	—
Kavango/ Ovahimba	—	—	—	—	—	—	—	—
Ovambo/Herero	39.2	18.5	3.6	—	35.0	—	19.9	1.5
All together	15.2	37.0	3.6	18.2	—	4.2	13.5	7.6
No reply	15.2	14.8	17.8	18.2	35.0	8.3	17.3	31.8

Within the category "no reply", several combinations are included which were not furnished as alternatives and are therefore being separately recorded.

Alternatives mentioned in Ovamboland	No. of instances
Ovambo/Herero/Damara/Kavango	1
Ovambo/Herero/Damara/Basters	1
Ovambo/Herero/Coloureds	2
Ovambo/Herero/Damara	1
Ovambo/Herero/Ovahimba	1
Ovambo/Herero/Coloured/Kavango	1
Ovambo/Herero/Nama/Kavango	1
Ovambo/Kavango	1
Ovambo/Nama/Kavango	1
Ovambo/Damara/Kavango	1
Ovambo/Damara	2

In Katutura, 30.4% of the category "no reply" was provided by the following answers from teachers and students:

Alternatives mentioned in Katutura	No. of instances
Ovambo/Herero/Damara	5
Ovambo/Herero/Basters	2
Ovambo/Herero/Damara/Nama/Basters	3
Ovambo/Herero/Nama/Basters	1
Ovambo/Herero/Nama	1
Ovambo/Herero/Coloureds	3
Ovambo/Herero/Bushmen	1
Ovambo/Damara	2
Ovambo/Kavango/Coloureds	1
Ovambo/Coloureds	1

Some emphatic trends emerge from these replies. In Ovamboland it was only a majority of the officials and clerks and the traditional leaders who regarded the Ovambos as politically the most important ethnic group in Namibia. The rest were divided in opinion between the Ovambos or a combination of them with the Hereros, or all together. Ovambos were assigned a more important political role in Katutura than within its own borders, a tendency perceptible mostly among nurses, officials and clerks.

From the combinations given both in Ovamboland and Katutura, it is striking how the basic combination of Ovambo and Herero predominates; it was chosen by most students and by teachers—who in some cases preferred all the population groups together. One can infer from this that the two groups mentioned identify themselves least with the idea of an Ovambo nation, and most with Namibia as a whole. Generally, the bond with the Hereros seems to be the stronger, which must be because, except for the Kavangos, the Hereros are ethnically the most closely related to the Ovambos. Another reason may be that most Hereros consistently show solidarity with the political demands of the modernizing groups in Ovamboland and Katutura.

A follow-up question was aimed at ascertaining on what grounds the choices were made. The answer showed a high degree of self-esteem among the Ovambos, on account of their reputedly better education and greater experience and their economic contribution due to their numerical strength. The modernizing groups also stressed the Ovambo's role in airing political opinions that were officially unacceptable. While these groups emphasized the Ovambo's party political activities, the traditional leaders ascribed the pre-eminence of Ovamboland's political role to the experience gained in the traditional system. Similarly, the traditional leaders stressed the role of the Ovambos in Ovamboland only, while the modernizing élites were interested in the part played by their members in Namibia as a whole, in which they welcome the co-operation of the Hereros as political comrades.

Lastly, a test was conducted on the Ovambo's attitude to, and their connection with, the outside world:

Question: WITH WHAT STATE OR COUNTRY OUTSIDE NAMIBIA DO YOU FEEL THAT YOU HAVE THE STRONGEST TIES?

	T.	R./L.	O./C.	Comm.	N.	Trad.	Ov./Av.	Kat./Av.
Zambia	10.9	7.4	7.1	—	—		5.8	28.8
Transkei	—	3.7	7.1	—	—	12.5	3.9	—
Congo (Zaire)	2.2	—	—	—	—	—	0.6	—
Malawi	—	3.7	3.6	—	—	—	1.3	—
Egypt	4.3	—	—	—	—	—	1.3	—
South Africa	8.7	—	21.4	18.2	—	54.2	16.0	22.7
Tanzania	10.9	—	—	—	—	—	3.2	24.2
Other independent African States	2.2	—	7.1	—	—	—	1.9	3.0
The UN	—	—	—	9.1	—	—	0.6	1.5
No reply	60.8	85.2	53.6	72.7	100.0	33.3	65.4	19.7

Other countries quoted in Ovamboland were the USA (4), Ethiopia (3), Finland (2), the USSR (2), England (1), Germany (1), Western countries generally (1), Nigeria (1) and Angola (1). In Katutura, the USA (3), Finland (2), Sweden (2), Denmark (2), the Netherlands (1), Germany (1), the People's Republic of China (1) and Kenya (1) were also mentioned. The fact that the question elicited little interest in Ovamboland can be taken to mean that the country is largely beholden to itself and seeks no outside alliances. Katutura showed a stronger involvement with the outside world. The strong attachment to Zambia and Tanzania was probably due mostly to familiarity with radio broadcasts from these two countries. Additionally, both countries have been actively training guerrilla forces to fight against Southern Africa and affording asylum to political refugees and organizations like SWAPO.

As a rider, a further question was asked (see page 125). Additional answers in Ovamboland were Finland (5), Germany (3), France (2), Malawi (2) and Namibia (4), and in Katutura, Germany (2), Denmark (1), and Sweden (1).

The respondents were asked the reasons for their support, and it was clear that they admired countries for lack of apartheid measures, emphasis on human rights and democratic systems of government which eliminated

Question: WHICH COUNTRY DO YOU ADMIRE MOST IN THE WORLD?

	T.	R./L.	O./C.	Comm.	N.	Trad.	Ov./Av.	Kat./Av.
The USA	65.2	37.0	17.9	18.2	30.0	4.2	34.6	53.0
Finland	—	3.7	7.1	—	15.0	—	3.9	3.0
People's Republic of China	—	—	—	9.1	—	—	0.6	—
England	—	—	3.6	—	—	—	0.6	3.0
South Africa	—	3.7	7.1	9.1	—	45.8	9.7	10.6
Tanzania	—	—	3.6	—	—	—	0.6	4.6
Zambia	—	—	7.1	—	5.0	—	1.9	3.0
The Soviet Union	4.3	7.4	3.6	—	—	—	3.2	—
Egypt	2.2	—	—	—	—	—	0.6	—
No reply	28.3	48.2	50.0	63.6	50.0	50.0	44.2	22.7

colour discrimination. Technical achievement, economic progress, the granting of overseas aid—and adherence to Christianity—were additional criteria for admiration.

7. Administrative Reform.

Coupled with political development, there is a need in Ovamboland for an administration geared to change, adaptation, renovation and growth. In this process, it will have to carry out government policy, as formulated by decision-makers within the political order. However, in a developing country, where there is lack of experience and skill in many sectors of the political system, an administrative order can play an assisting, substituting and controlling role until other sectors are capable of performing these functions themselves.

Effective administration institutional development is thus essential for a stable and ultimately democratic regime in a developing country, but in Ovamboland there is a real danger that a bureaucracy may develop far more quickly and vigorously than the corresponding structures and capacities of the political organization; administrative talents may be encouraged at the expense of democratic political development. Both need the support of the community in equal measure, and they will be successful and effective to the extent that the people can identify with both political and administrative institutional advancement. The interdependence between the two elements is obvious.

Political development in growing communities, of which Ovamboland is a good example, thus comprises two important spheres of social organization. One one side there is a need to create government structures and administrative organizations to handle problems of public policy, on the other hand stable though sensitive and effective mechanisms have to be established to link the interests and needs of the society with political power.

(a) The Administrative Framework. From 1968 to 1975 the central administration of Ovamboland has consisted of seven departments: Economic Affairs, Justice, Interior, Agriculture and Forestry, Works, Education and the Department of the Chief Minister and Finance. Two new departments, that of Information on 1 April 1976 and the Treasury Department on 1 January 1977, have been established and added to the existing ones. A Tender Board for Ovamboland and a Motor Road Transportation Board with jurisdiction over matters concerning motor transportation within the borders of Ovamboland were formed during 1976. The administrative heads of the Government departments were called directors till 1 May 1973, since when they have been known as secretaries. All of them are at present white officials seconded to Ovamboland by the South African Government. The highest administrative posts are still occupied by whites, but the official policy is to fill all administrative posts by Ovambos in due time. In 1974 there were 773 posts in the Ovamboland Government Service, 679 held by Ovambos and 94 by whites. There is an urgent need in the Government Service for academically qualified Ovambos to take over professional jobs. In 1974, as a result of a decision by the United Nations "Council for Namibia", and because many members of the modernizing Ovambo élites have left the area, mainly for Zambia, this Council, with the concurrence of President Kaunda, decided to found in Zambia a training institute, the Namibia Institute, for public administration, one of its objects being to train expatriates, the majority of them Ovambos, who would then serve as administrative officials in Namibia after independence. In 1977 about 150 students were trained in the Namibia Institute.

Ovamboland's local government system is still underdeveloped. In each tribal area there is a tribal office under the supervision of a tribal secretary, but the Kwanyama tribal area, because of its size, has two additional sub-tribal offices. These offices represent the administrative headquarters of tribal government. Since 1974 efforts have been made to activate tribal authorities in order that fully-fledged magistrates' courts should eventually exist in each of their areas. In addition to the existing magistrate office at Ondangwa two additional magistrates' offices were established at Ombalantu and Ohangwena in 1976.

In theory, Ovamboland has ten "towns" (in addition to its squatters' settlements), of which only two justify that description, while the rest, although represented by tribal offices, consist only of a handful of houses. In 1972, with two exceptions, a school and between one and eight businesses were located near each tribal office; in two instances, there was also a church. The only actual towns were Oshakati (606 houses) and Oluno, near Ondangwa (153). In 1973 an Ovambo town with 450 house plots was laid out near Ruacana. The towns had no local government, but were administered from the tribal office by the appropriate tribal authority. Efforts were made during 1977 to promulgate local regulations and institute town councils consisting of Ovambos. An announcement to this effect was made by the Chief Minister when he opened the third session of the Third Legislative Council on 12 April 1977.

Other agents of administrative development are such institutions as Radio Ovamboland, the Post Office and the Bantu Investment Corporation and the "law and order" agencies like the South African police, the Bureau of State Security and the Security Service, side by side with the tribal police and the Ovambo Police Force. The training of officials and clerks largely takes place on an in-service basis inside or outside Ovamboland. The "law and order" agencies and the Post Office usually train their staff outside the territory, either in Namibia or in South Africa.

The changes in Angola resulting from the Portuguese coup in 1974, and the fear of increased military activity by SWAPO both from Angola and from Zambia, coupled with the murder of Chief Elifas, led to greater vigilance by South Africa. One consequence of this was the quartering of South African military forces in Ovamboland. Although these forces have in addition to their military duties engaged in various social and economic development services locally, the modernizing élites have seen this as a means of maintaining the *status quo* in Ovamboland and throughout Namibia. However, the traditional leaders welcomed the presence of the South African army—to which wider attention was drawn by incidents on the frontier with Angola since 1974. The relations between the military forces and the population are often subjected to great strain. They are referred to as an "occupying force" by members of the modernizing élites.

However, a spokesman of the South African Defence Force denied that any tension existed between the military and the Ovambo population, who were well-disposed to the Defence Force and had eventually realized that the armed men were their friends. In his opinion, the Defence Force's prestige was much higher with the Ovambo people than that of SWAPO. The South African military would provide aid until Ovamboland had become independent.[94] The number of South African soldiers present in Ovamboland varies, but there are several thousands at any given time.

Tight security control was imposed on Ovamboland in May 1976 when a virtual state of emergency was declared in the territory. Ovamboland was declared a security district in terms of new regulations which were a substitute for Proclamation R 17, which had governed Ovamboland in a state of quasi-emergency since February 1972. All adults, including chiefs and headmen, were obliged to report the presence of any person whom they suspected of being in Ovamboland unlawfully. Firearms and ammunition were to be handed over to the authorities.

This was but the latest move in a campaign to contain increasing insurgency in Ovamboland. Support for SWAPO was put by official sources as high as 70 per cent of the Ovambo population. According to the new regulations, any civilian failing to report the presence of an insurgent is guilty of a criminal offence, and is liable to be arrested with or without a warrant and held incommunicado until the authorities are satisfied he has answered all questions fully and truthfully. In effect, the authorities are entitled to hold suspected offenders indefinitely without trial. Consultation with legal advisers is specifically denied without official permission. Offenders tried and convicted are liable to a maximum fine of R600, maximum imprisonment of three years with or without the option of a fine, or to both a fine and prison. All non-residents are required to obtain a permit to enter Ovamboland. This category consists of people "absent for the purpose of employment or for the exercising of any trade, calling or profession, or who permanently reside outside the area." The definition clearly includes Ovambos who have left to join SWAPO outside Namibia.

The new measures supplement a decision to evacuate the population from a strip of land along the Ovamboland-Angolan border 1 km. wide. It is stipulated that people living in one area can be instructed to move to another for a specified period, without the right to return. Specified activities in any particular area (like trading and farming) can be prohibited and moved to another area. The regulations also empower the South African Minister of Justice to declare "prohibited" any areas bordering on a security district. No one may enter or pass through such an area, other than security forces or people exempted from the provision.

Depopulation of a 1 km.-wide strip along the Angolan border in order to block north–south guerrilla movements started in May 1976. By October the same year, more than 3,000 Ovambos had been resettled and compensated for moving out of the area, which is now known as no-man's land. At the same time a security fence was to be erected, stretching 450 km. along the border and along the 1,000-metre line. A security fence, eight foot six inches high, was to be built with barbed wire on the top. By January 1977, 60 km. of the security fence had been completed.[95]

Fear among the people was also aroused by the Ovambo tribal police who, till their disbandment in 1975, were in the service of the tribal authorities and thus at the disposal of the traditional leaders. It was alleged by several political and religious leaders that the tribal police often exceeded their powers. Examples given were alleged arbitrary mal-treatment of members of the public, intimidation, meting out of ignominious corporal punishment and suppression of political activity (e.g. that of SWAPO and DEMCOP members) directed against the traditional leaders and their political order.[96] During the Legislative Council elections in February 1975, church leaders accused the tribal police of forcing people to vote—on behalf of the traditional leaders.

Actually, the tribal police is manned by ordinary Ovambos, who since 1973 have undergone brief four-week training courses organized by the South African police. The tribal police, who are stationed at tribal offices, are not a fully trained police force, and do not have the same knowledge and expertise as Ovambos serving with the South African police.

Although they remained under the control and supervision of the Chiefs and Headmen they were paid by the Department of Justice, who arbitrated between the tribal police and the Headmen when differences occurred. An investigation in 1975–6 by the Department of Justice revealed that most of the headmen were unable to exercise proper control over the tribal police, who mostly disregarded them. The tribal police were thus seldom reporting to their supervisors except at the end of the month for their salaries. It was also revealed that only ten of the tribal policemen could read and write, and therefore suitable for further training.

In 1975 the tribal police was disbanded and was to be replaced by an Ovambo police force, which would man proper police stations at every tribal office. Intensive efforts were immediately made to obtain recruits with at least standard VI school qualification for training as Ovambo police. The following posts were created: one captain, three warrant officers, four senior sergeants, twelve sergeants and fifty-five constables. By 1976 the Department of Justice had recruited a platoon of thirty-three men for training; a second platoon was established in 1977. Tribal policemen unsuitable for further training were placed at tribal offices, to perform new defined duties under the control of the local magistrate.[97]

In 1976 the South African Defence Force started training Ovambo soldiers at a military camp near Ondangwa. Although no numbers of trainees have been disclosed, it is expected that they eventually form the nucleus of an Ovambo army. It is intended that these soldiers should help to defend the northern border of Ovamboland alongside the South African army against possible attack.

(b) Attitude of the Administrative Élite. As we have seen, an Ovambo bureaucracy is still in the state of development. There is still a scarcity of Ovambos suitably trained for administrative tasks, and the functions that Ovambo officials and clerks can and will be able to perform in the immediate future remain limited. Because of this, the whites have delegated relatively few responsibilities to Ovambo officials and clerks. Hence no form of administrative autonomy by Ovambos is possible at the moment.

If more and more administrative posts are filled by Ovambo officials and clerks, and if the Legislative Council does not improve its efficiency and standards, these clerks and officials in the government service can be expected increasingly to take on the policy-making and executive functions which should properly devolve on the Legislative and Executive Councils. If this happened, it would give this group of officials and clerks an opportunity to become a strong pressure group in Ovamboland's development.

In a young country, a bureaucratic or administrative élite is generally accepted as an important modernizing element, and there is general recognition of its value in formulating and applying policy. In Ovamboland, however, officials and clerks, as part of the administrative élite, look down on the ruling traditional élite and, as the in-depth interviews have shown, largely reject the current political framework. In its political outlook, the administrative élite is the same as the religious and educational élites. The ideas of the teachers and clerks are reflected more closely in "urban" areas, like Ondangwa and Oshakati, than in the rural areas.

As has already been stated, the full and assistant tribal secretaries also belong to the administrative élite. But these officials, who serve as intermediaries between the traditional élite and the population, and depend for their livelihood on the approval of the traditional leaders, display generally a more or less accommodating attitude to the latter. During the investigation some of the tribal secretaries aligned themselves with the thinking of most of the administrative élite, but dared not do so openly. Since then the tribal secretaries have assumed power at the expense of traditional leaders.

The relatively small numbers of the administrative élite and the continuing presence of white officials and clerks in Ovamboland cause an ambivalent state of affairs for many members of this Ovambo élite. On the one hand there is subordination to the white officials, and on the other there is a strong dislike of white authority. This is clearly seen in the lack of enthusiasm for the planned development of Ovamboland. The ban on active participation in politics by government officials and clerks intensifies the existing tension and frustration, and because of the opposition to the existing political framework and planned expansion, there is unwillingness among these people to be nominated or elected to the Legislative Council. The composition of the first and second Legislative Councils bears testimony to this.

With more white officials being replaced by Ovambos, the latter should exhibit more of their own initiative than they do now. But this will only happen in the fullest sense when an authority exists with which the officials can feel *rapport*, and from which they can expect constructive and expert leadership in the modernizing process. Meanwhile, the majority of them are becoming more politicized, and already engaging in action against the current power structure, consisting as it does chiefly of whites and the traditional élite and their supporters.

To sum up, administration in Ovamboland is still in its early stages, especially at the local level. Because of the superior qualifications of the officials and clerks compared with the majority of the Legislative Council, the bureaucracy is in a position to develop into an instrument of power, which can compete with the government in the political development of Ovamboland. This situation will probably come about when the country has a more effective and differentiated administrative and political organization, entirely in Ovambo hands. Only then will there be a possibility for independent and autonomous action.

8. *The United Nations*

The judgment of the International Court of Justice at The Hague in 1971, in the form of an advisory opinion, significantly influenced the political thinking of the modernizing élite groups in Ovamboland. The Court expressed the belief that the revocation of the mandate by the General Assembly of the United Nations had been legal. The basis for this finding was that a contractual obligation existed between South Africa and the League of Nations (which had been succeeded by the United Nations), but that South Africa, in applying apartheid in Namibia, had definitely broken its mandatory obligations, so permitting the UN to terminate the treaty.[98] The implication of the judgment was that South Africa was legally obliged to withdraw from the administration of Namibia, and that member-states of the UN were legally obliged to oppose South Africa's unlawful presence in Namibia and to do nothing that would accord recognition to this illegality.[99]

It has been contended that 1971 was the turning-point in the Namibia dispute: first, the Hague Court gave its legal imprimatur to the political resolutions of the General Assembly and the Security Council, viz. the revocation of the mandate and the order to isolate Namibia diplomatically; and secondly the whole dispute over the territory was transformed in that year from an international matter into an international-cum-domestic one.[100] The judgment of the Hague Court and its implications strengthened the political consciousness and thinking of the Ovambos; since then they have displayed radicalism and a greater self-assurance in their political outlook, utterances and actions. This process was given a fillip by the visit of the UN missions to Namibia in 1972.

This visit too ushered in a new phase; the Secretary-General and the South African Government were now in direct negotiation over the future of Namibia.[101] Their different positions are reflected in the respective names used for the area. South Africa retains the name "South West Africa" and thereby reserves its inalienable right to decide the country's future in co-operation with the population. At the UN, on the other hand, the official name is "Namibia", which signifies that the world body, on the strength of earlier resolutions, claims the right of control over it henceforward. Both maintain that they are striving for an identical objective—independence—but they differ in the manner of attainment. While South Africa prefers its separate development policy for Namibia, the UN's policy is to develop it as a unitary state with an equal franchise and other equal rights for all its inhabitants, irrespective of race, creed or colour.

In March 1972, Dr. Waldheim and his entourage paid a brief visit to Namibia, with the main accent on Ovamboland. There he had talks with the Ovamboland Executive Council, the leader of the Ovamboland Independent Church, the Rev. P. Kalangula, and government officials. Both the Executive Council and Mr. Kalangula expressed their satisfaction with the South African Government. Dr. Waldheim also had a discussion with the exiled Bishop Colin Winter of the Anglican Church in Namibia, during which Bishop Winter accused the South African Government of oppression and discrimination and made a plea for the right to self-determination of the entire population of Namibia. Bishop Winter also handed Dr. Waldheim various petitions from Africans in Namibia and informed him that he intended to appear before the UN as a petitioner on behalf of the country's African inhabitants.[102]

On his arrival in Ovamboland Dr. Waldheim was greeted by fifty placard-carriers demonstrating their opposition to South African Government policy. He declared himself willing to meet five of them as well as representatives of the various church denominations—meetings which he subsequently said had been informative. According to a press report, he said it was not possible for him, nor was it his duty, to investigate allegations of intimidation and torture after the labour strike in December 1971, or the dispatch of police and army reinforcements to Ovamboland.[103] During this tour Dr. Waldheim saw several development projects, visited the Oshakati hospital, attended a banquet with the Executive Council, and called on the Headman and Chairman of the Legislative Council, G. Kautuima, at his kraal, where he was shown the way of life of a traditional Ovamboland kraal under the guidance of the Councillor in charge of Education and Culture. It seemed that the government was trying to bring Dr. Waldheim into contact mainly with the traditional leaders and to show him development schemes.

In his report to the Security Council on his visit to Namibia and the joint discussions with the South African Government, Dr. Waldheim supported the protest against the development of Ovamboland as a Homeland, and expressed the hope that the Government would not proceed with any measures which would be disadvantageous to the contacts esatablished. He reiterated that the national unity and territorial integrity of the whole of Namibia should be the basis of any further contact. He said that the South African standpoint of self-determination and independence for the different peoples of Namibia was not acceptable, and in conflict with the Security Council's resolution 309 of 1972. As such it could not serve as the foundation for further negotiations. Yet Dr. Waldheim did say in his report that he favoured further contacts, and that the proposal he had made that a personal envoy should continue the negotiations on his behalf was acceptable to South Africa. Problems arose at once when SWAPO made it plain that it would have to be recognized in the nomination of the Secretary-General's representative. South Africa objected very strongly to this.[104]

On 25 September 1972 a Swiss diplomat, Dr. A.M. Escher, was appointed as the UN representative, and he paid a visit to Namibia on 12–28 October 1972. During his visit to Ovamboland he was able to hold talks with several SWAPO leaders, and received a deputation consisting of eighteen of its leaders and members. Thirteen of the delegates belonged to the Ovambokavango Church, three were Anglicans and two Roman Catholics, a proportion representative of the population. At least four of the delegation were teachers and four were in the service of the Ovambokavango Church; there were three traders, two officials and one labourer. The leader was John Otto, then leader of SWAPO in Ovambo and former secretary-general of the movement in Namibia. Another important political leader in the delegation was Johannes Nangutuuala, leader of the unrecognized DEMCOP. The only female member of the delegation represented "the women of Namibia".[105]

The deputation criticized the creation of separate Homelands, which, its members maintained, would lead to the fragmentation of Namibia and the destruction of non-white unity. They considered the so-called Homelands "concentration camps", which had to supply cheap labour and where the old, the sick and feeble were sent—to be exposed to hunger, indignity and injustice. The delegation demanded the unconditional withdrawal of the South African administration from Namibia, and rebuked the USA, France and Britain for continuing their trade relations with the territory, contending that those countries were setting a higher value on its mineral wealth than on the fate of its people. The delegation likewise objected to the application of apartheid and to the restrictions on freedom of movement and speech for non-whites.[106]

Other non-Ovambo SWAPO leaders who met Dr. Escher were D. Meroro, chairman in Namibia, Jason D. Mutumbulua, secretary, Ben Namalabo, member of the executive committee, and Gottlieb Nathaniel Maxuiriri, the organisation's restricted vice-president. Their complaints were almost the same as those of the SWAPO delegation in Ovamboland. They stated emphatically that they visualized Namibia's political future as a unitary state, and they were prepared to accept as a caretaker measure an interim UN administration to lead the people to self-rule. They insisted that when the territory became independent, the whites would be entitled to full citizenship and that there was no enmity towards them.[107]

After visiting Namibia, Dr. Escher had talks with the South African Prime Minister, Mr. Vorster, and told him that according to his impressions the majority of the Namibian population would support the establishment of a united and free Namibia. His point of view was that the people of the territory should be at liberty to express themselves on self-determination and independence in accordance with the principle of equality and on the assumption that the area would exist as a unit and not as separate parts.[108] Dr. Escher also mentioned the hope which had been expressed that the UN would bring a free Namibia into being.

In a concluding *communiqué* Mr. Vorster again emphasized that it was not the appropriate time to discuss self-determination and independence in detail; this could best be done when the necessary conditions had been created and the inhabitants of Namibia had more administrative and political experience. To a question from Dr. Escher whether practical steps could be considered that would lead to the exercise of self-determination, the Prime Minister replied that experience in self-government was an essential element for possible self-determination; owing to the circumstances, this could best be attained on a regional basis. Dr. Escher's answer was: "This seemed to me acceptable in principle, provided that the necessary conditions for the exercise of self-determination were fulfilled, and at the same time an authority for the whole territory would be established."[109]

The Prime Minister also declared that he was willing to institute an Advisory Council consisting of representatives of the various regions and ethnic groups in Namibia, and said that he would personally assume full responsibility for the whole territory. When Dr. Escher asked whether the Government was contemplating the repeal of laws restricting freedom, including existing limitations on freedom of movement and speech and the right to hold meetings, Mr. Vorster replied that restrictions on freedom of movement had become essential largely in order to exercise influx control, which was in the interest of all the inhabitants in the country, but he was willing to consider the possibility of abolishing restrictions without impairing influx control. He agreed with the idea that there should be lawful political activity which would include freedom of speech and the holding of meetings.[110]

In his recommendations to the Security Council, Dr. Escher concluded that Mr. Vorster, through his readiness to appoint an Advisory Council for the whole of Namibia, had thereby given his consent to certain measures involving the "territory as a whole"; this could be interpreted as conforming with the aim of retaining the unity of Namibia. As for the Prime Minister's promise to make certain other concessions over freedom of movement, political activities, and the holding of meetings, Dr. Escher considered that this would help to create suitable conditions for the practice of self-determination; hence it would be a good thing to maintain contacts with South Africa.[111]

Even before the report was discussed in the Security Council, the Prime Minister clearly stated during a speech in Windhoek on 20 November 1972 that the people of Namibia would ultimately have to decide whether they preferred a federal or unitary state for their country. He postulated adequate experience in self-government as a pre-condition for realizing the full consequences of any such decision. Neither the UN nor the South African Government—in other words, no power from abroad—could dictate their choice to the inhabitants of Namibia.[112] From this it may be assumed that the Prime Minister had, more or less finally, abandoned the thought of political union between Namibia and South Africa.

One of South Africa's most vital declarations on the future development of Namibia was handed to the Secretary-General on 1 May 1973. South Africa had agreed to the following:

(1) Freedom of speech and political activities including the holding of public meetings in the process of leading Namibia to self-determination provided public security was not disturbed. According to Dr. Waldheim, this principle would be valid for every political party in the territory.

(2) The possibility of enlarging Namibia's administrative districts in order to relax restrictions on people and to bring about greater freedom of movement.

(3) South Africa made no claim to any part of Namibia.

(4) South Africa had no wish to retard self-determination for Namibia and would, in collaboration with the Secretary-General and in consultation with the inhabitants, take steps to ensure the attainment of self-determination and independence.

(5) Judging from current developments, South Africa anticipated that it would not take more than ten years for the population of Namibia to reach the stage where it would be ready to exercise the right of self-determination.

(6) South Africa did not foresee the eventuality of individual population groups suddenly hiving off as separate independent entitites.

(7) South Africa stressed that Namibia had a separate international status and that Walvis Bay would remain South African territory.

South Africa's full supplementary declaration read as follows:

Desiring to enable and assist the population of South West Africa to exercise their right to self-determination and independence, the Government of South Africa will fully respect the wishes of the whole population of the Territory with regard to the future constitutional organization of the Territory. It has no intention of imposing any constitutional system. Any exercise to ascertain the wishes of the population in this regard will not be comprised by any existing political and administrative arrangements, South Africa will not impose upon the population of South West Africa any given system contrary to the wishes of the latter or contrary to the Charter of the United Nations, which in article 1 (2) calls on member States to develop friendly relations among Nations based on respect for the principle of equal rights and self-determination of peoples.

All political parties of South West Africa will have full and free participation in the process leading to self-determination and independence.[113]

Although the statement of the Secretary-General to the Security Council reveals several new lines of thought, such as the enlargement of administrative areas and the possibility for the population to exercise the right to self-determination within ten years, there is a note of ambivalence in South Africa's promises. Freedom of speech and political activities will be permitted, provided they do not disturb public order. Because either South Africa or the Homeland government has to decide who is disturbing public order, the statement opens the way to arbitrary rule. As an example one can cite the recognition accorded to the traditionally-minded Ovambo Independent Party and the non-recognition of the opposing Democratic Co-operative (DEMCOP) Party, which was forbidden to hold meetings.

The South African Government's intention to allow no constitutional development in Namibia against the principles of the inhabitants and those of the UN is open to several interpretations. Against the background of earlier assertions by the Prime Minister that the principle of several ethnic groups in one country is recognized by the UN Charter, and because in Ovamboland the Legislative Council is supported mainly only by the traditional groups which agree with the South African Government's intention to create a separate Ovambo Homeland, there is apparent confirmation of the view that South Africa still regards Namibia as a territory of different ethnic groups, each with the right to self-determination and independence.

In December 1973, the UN Security Council decided (by Resolution 342 of that year) to abandon the negotiations between the Secretary-General and the South African Government. The dominant idea was now to bring more direct pressure to bear through UN member-countries on South Africa and forcing it to withdraw from Namibia. This was confirmed in a further resolution of the Security Council in December 1974, in which a request was made *inter alia* "that South Africa take the necessary steps to effect the withdrawal, in accordance with resolutions 264 (1969) and 269 (1969) of its illegal administration maintained in Namibia, and to transfer power to the people of Namibia with the assistance of the United Nations". It was resolved "to remain seized of the matter and to meet on or before 30 May 1975 for the purpose of reviewing South Africa's compliance with the terms of this resolution and, in the event of non-compliance by South Africa, for the purpose of considering the appropriate measures to be taken under the Charter".

The acceptance by the Security Council of a proposal that South Africa should be forced to evacuate Namibia was vetoed by the three major Western powers in June 1975, because they did not see the issue as a threat to world peace. However, during the OAU conference of July 1975, the Secretary-General supported the demand by OAU member-states that the independence of Namibia should be considered a matter of pressing urgency. Compliance with this demand was regarded by these states as the acid test of the credibility of South Africa's détente policy (Dar-es-Salaam Declaration 1975); the solution of the problem was regarded as a similar test of the UN's effectiveness.

South Africa restated its point of view in two important declarations on Namibia. On 27 May 1975, the Minister of Foreign Affairs, Dr. H. Muller, said in a letter to the Secretary-General that South Africa's considered opinion was still that the peoples of Namibia themselves should decide of their own free will and without interference either from South Africa, from the UN, or from any other country. This standpoint was confirmed in a speech by Prime Minister Vorster at Windhoek in May 1975. Both he and Dr. Muller referred to the first round table constitutional conference, which was due to begin in that city on 1 September 1975, and at which all population groups would be represented.[114] Both men made it clear that all options were open to the people.

On 13 November 1975 the General Assembly's Trusteeship Committee approved an omnibus resolution calling for South Africa's immediate withdrawl from Namibia and measures to bring this about. The Committee strongly condemned South Africa for its persistent refusal to withdraw from Namibia and its "manoeuvres to consolidate its illegal occupation by organising a so-called constitutional conference, with a view to creating divisions among ethnic groups and furthering its policies of Bantustans". It also strongly condemned the "military build-up by South Africa in Namibia and forceful removal of Namibians from the northern borders for military purposes". The Committee demanded the immediate withdrawal by South Africa of all its military and police forces and administration so as to enable the Namibian people to achieve freedom and independence. It decided that free national elections should be held in the Territory urgently under the direct supervision and control of the UN. On 27 November 1975 the General Assembly voted 110 to nil for a resolution demanding South Africa's withdrawal from Namibia and Namibian independence.

In reply to the UN demands, the South African Prime Minister re-emphasized that South Africa's clearly-stated policy over the years had been that the peoples of Namibia themselves would decide the future of the territory. He added: "If South Africa is not going to interfere there, she has the moral right to say to others and the United Nations: 'You will not prescribe to these people.' To those who have misgivings at the moment I would point out it is notable that the Whites have taken the initiative for the constitutional discussions. The National Party Government left it to the peoples of South West Africa to determine their future but until this has happened, it has the right and the duty to maintain law and order there."[115] According to Mr. Vorster, South Africa was governing the territory in terms of the mandate granted by the League of Nations. On this occasion the Prime Minister also referred to the first constitutional (Turnhalle) conference, which had begun on 1 September 1975. All the ethnic groups in Namibia had been invited to take part through their representatives in discussions and to make proposals for the country's political future. The Ovamboland Government was represented by fifteen delegates.

Right from its beginning, the Constitutional Conference was denounced as unrepresentative not only by many political parties in Namibia, including DEMCOP and SWAPO, but also by the outside world. The Commissioner of the UN Council for Namibia described it as an attempt by the South African Government to divide the people of Namibia and ignore UN resolutions affecting the territory.[116] A first official statement, the so-called Declaration of Intent, was issued at the end of the first session of the Constitutional Conference in Windhoek on 12 September 1975:

We, the true and authentic representatives of the inhabitants of South West Africa, hereby solemnly declare:

That in the exercise of our right to self-determination and independence we are voluntarily gathered in this Conference in order to discuss the constitutional future of South West Africa;

That we most strongly condemn and reject the use of force or any improper interference in order to overthrow the existing order to enforce a new dispensation;

That we are firmly resolved to determine our future ourselves by peaceful negotiations and co-operation;

That mindful of particular circumstances of each of the population groups it is our firm resolve, in the execution of our task, to serve and respect their wishes and interests;

That mindful of the interdependence of the various population groups and the interests of South West Africa in its entirety to create a form of government which will guarantee to every population group the greatest possible say in its own and national affairs which will fully protect the rights of minorities and which will do right and justice to all.

And further we declare:

That we are resolved to devote continuous attention to social and economic conditions which will best promote the welfare, interests and peaceful co-existence of all the inhabitants of South West Africa and their prosperity;

That we are resolved to exert ourselves towards the promotion of and deference towards human rights and fundamental freedoms of all without discrimination merely on the basis of race, colour, or creed.

We therefore resolve:

(*a*) to draft a Constitution for South West Africa as soon as appropriate and if possible within a period of three years.

(*b*) to devote continuous attention to measures implementing all the aims specified in this declaration.[117]

Interference from outside and from the UN was strongly condemned by the Conference. At the same time it asked that action should be taken against agitation and intimidation from inside the country. A Constitutional Committee, appointed by the Conference to work out a constitution for Namibia, issued a joint declaration on the intended constitutional development process for the territory on 19 August 1976. Five points had been agreed upon by the Committee:

1. *Self-determination and independence.* The Committee has agreed that 31 December 1978 can, with reasonable safety, be set as the date for the independence of South West Africa. Meanwhile, it is obvious that many matters will have to be negotiated with South Africa, such as Walvis Bay, the South African Railways, water and electricity supply, monetary and financial affairs, security, etc.

As soon as there is consensus on a basic constitutional formula and the above mentioned negotiations have been completed, we intend to establish an interim government based on the constitutional formula agreed to which will handle the transfer of functions and establish a permanent government according to a constitution which will be finalised during the interim period.

2. *Territorial integrity.* The Committee reaffirms the interdependence of the different population groups and its strong desire to keep South West Africa as a single unit.

3. *Constitutional system.* Since we do not wish to anticipate a final dispensation at this stage, it would be premature to divulge details about a constitutional system now, but the Committee can already announce that it envisages a system of

government, particularly in the central body, which will provide complete protection for minority groups.

4. *Peaceful solution.* We wish, once again, to deplore any attempts at solving the problems of our country by violence, and urgently appeal to all civilized nations to combat any attempt at a violent solution of our problems with all the power at their disposal.

5. *Social and economic affairs.* Herewith we wish to repeat our appeal to the South African Government and all bodies concerned (private or public) to expedite the implementation of the resolutions of the Conference in regard to these matters.

The Constitutional Committee's request for an interim government and independence for Namibia before the end of 1978 was denounced by the UN Council for Namibia, which stated its strong condemnation of "the latest ill-advised stratagem of the South African Administration in Windhoek as totally lacking in legitimacy, ambiguous and equivocal". The Council said the proposals did not even approach any requirements for genuine self-determination and independence laid down by the UN and did not mention the elimination of apartheid legislation. The suggested independence date constituted an "unjustifiable prolongation of the illegal South African occupation".[117]

By late 1976 the Constitutional Committee decided on a three-tier government for an independent Namibia. According to its chairman, Mr. D. Mudge, the first tier of government would be representative of all ethnicities in the territory and would be responsible for matters of national importance. All sixty members of the first tier, the National Assembly, would be appointed by the second tier which had been devised explicitly to give the various ethnic groups the maximum say in their own affairs and cultural matters. The second tier would consist of ethnic bodies elected by the members of the various ethnic groups. The third tier, local government, would consist of local bodies such as municipal councils. In the case of Windhoek, the capital, there would be three municipal councils, one each for the Whites (greater Windhoek), the Blacks (Katutura) and the Coloureds (Khomasdal).

It had been agreed that the Ovambos, representing nearly half the total population of Namibia, would have twelve representatives in the National Assembly, the Whites six, the Damara, Herero, Kavango, Coloured, Nama and Caprivian groups five each, and the Bushmen, Basters and Tswana groups four each. All the population groups would be represented in the council of ministers, appointed by the National Assembly.

The constitutional proposals of the Committee, approved by the Constitutional Conference, have been forwarded to the South African Government for legislation. It is also necessary for South Africa to revoke certain legislation and to transfer its responsibilities to Namibia, although the Constitutional Committee proposed that for the interim period (till full independence on 31 December 1978) defence, foreign affairs, internal security (defence, police), transport and telecommunication should remain in South Africa's hands.

The three-tier plan, which stresses the importance of ethnicities and ethnic areas, gives a permanent place to homeland governments, such as Ovamboland, as a second tier of government. Spokesmen of the Ovamboland Government have said that this does not exclude the possibility of complete independence for Ovamboland, or partial independence within a confederal framework. In the meantime the Chief Minister, the Rev. K. Ndjoba, has given an assurance that the Ovamboland government would operate as an autonomous body in an independent Namibia.[119]

The interim government, especially with the three-tier plan, has been attacked and condemned by opposition forces inside and outside Namibia as another "grand apartheid plan" which avoids a unitary state system and free national elections under UN supervision. This condemnation was expressed in Security Council resolution 385 of 30 January 1976 which also condemned South Africa's military build-up in Namibia. On 20 December 1976 the UN General Assembly by a vote of 107 to 6, with twelve members abstaining, formally declared support for armed struggle for the indigenous people of Namibia to achieve self-determination, freedom and independence in a united country.

The General Assembly also adopted eight resolutions on Namibia by large majorities. They included the adoption of a nationhood programme for the territory, which would involve comprehensive aid "covering both the present period of struggle for independence and the initial years of independence". Simultaneously the Assembly decided to grant observer status at the UN to SWAPO as the authentic representative of the people of Namibia.[120]

The five Western Security Council members (the United States, Great Britain, Canada, West Germany and France), in an effort to counter the demand by African states in the UN's Special Committee on Decolonization to apply a mandatory arms embargo, without any qualifications whatsoever, and a ban on new investment and loans in South Africa to force her to comply with UN resolutions on Namibia, compiled a declaration of principles. In this declaration the South African government was asked to terminate all systems and plans, under whatever name, which forcibly separate elements of the population on the basis of race, whether within a unitary state or in the form of separate political units; to end its illegal occupation of Namibia, and to comply with the Security Council resolutions on the territory. This declaration of March 1977 led to intensive diplomatic consultations between the five Western members of the Security Council and South Africa in which the former sought to convince South Africa of the urgent need to apply the Security Council's resolutions.

The debate between South Africa and the UN brought into the open two contrary points of view on the political destiny of Namibia: those held respectively by the Turnhalle Constitutional Conference, a champion of development on ethnic lines, and the protagonists of a unitary state as proposed by the UN and SWAPO. A compromise remains difficult and therefore polarization with the eventuality of an open conflict more likely.

9. Conclusions

Developments in Ovamboland prove the theory that social changes strengthen political consciousness, multiply political demands and demand wider political involvement.[121] These changes necessarily undermine the traditional sources of political authority and traditional political institutions, but they also complicate the problem of creating new bases of political associations and new political institutions, which can combine legitimately and effectively together.

In the administrative and political development of Ovamboland there is a striking imbalance between the local and central levels. Central power has developed at the expense of an efficient local administrative system. Attention has been paid primarily to changes in the broad framework of centrally controlled institutions. An identical administrative and political system has been drawn up for all the tribes, as well as a uniform system of taxes, land tenure and administration of justice. From this basic contradiction arise: on the one hand, central modern administrative, political, legal and economic systems have been created, while on the other, these changes have been based on more or less unaltered sub-groupings—namely tribes—and on traditional attitudes and loyalties. The people as a whole were denied full participation and integration in a common central political system. The substitutes devised at a local level are so inadequate that they cannot satisfy cherished hopes.

The limited ability of the leading traditional government strata, and the strong influence of the white officials on the Legislative Council's decisions, which in turn are implemented by the Executive Council, have caused a rapid increase in the resistance of opposition groups. Ill-will towards the traditional leaders, who are regarded as tools of the South African Government, was enhanced by the failure to accommodate these groups in the first Legislative and Executive Councils of Ovambo. The modernising élite groups were strengthened in their resistance by the judgment of the Hague Court in 1971, by the UN and by other international bodies. The mounting tension between the South African Government and religious denominations in Ovambo, especially the Anglican and Ovambokavango churches, has accentuated the antagonism felt by the modernizing echelon towards the traditional élite and the South African government, whose presence in Ovamboland is more and more unwelcome.

With no official channels (e.g. recognized political parties) for settling conflicts, grievances could only be voiced during tribal meetings or by means of petitions, but this was seldom resorted to, possibly owing to fear of intimidation and persecution. The non-party modernization process in Ovamboland caused political instability, no matter how strongly this was at first denied by the traditional élite. The valid objections of the modernizing élite to the Legislative Council, which was non-party and not fully elected, aggravated the political instability. It was natural that the traditional élite should fear that by allowing political parties and only elected representatives in the Legislative Council, they would suffer a further decline in their power.

The opposition to the traditional élite did not remain confined to the modernizing élite groups, but took root also among the ordinary people who expected from the new system a greater measure of participation, and consultation by the traditional leaders, than subsequently appeared to be the case. The leaders did not accept the challenge of introducing democracy and modernization into tribal affairs—perhaps through inability to do so—and looked on the new deal as a reaffirmation of their authority.

It is worth noting that the basic complaint of the modernizing élite was not against the traditional leaders *per se,* but against their high-handed assumption of political decison-making on behalf of, and not with or by, the people. For this they were considered unsuitable, mainly because of their low educational standard. This gave rise to demands, usually by the modernizing élite, that the traditional echelon should refrain from taking political decisions and confine itself to ceremonial duties. Since the traditional leaders support the current political framework and are mainly responsible for formulating and applying the policy which the modernizing élite group opposes, a mounting conflict between the two groups seems inevitable, and compromise between them even more remote. It also seems that the modernizing groups are in a better position than the traditional élite to mobilize a majority of the population for their objectives.

Efforts were made to remove or at least to neutralize some of the tensions from the second and third Legislative Councils, by introducing a partly elected Legislative Council. However, this change came too late to satisfy the modernizing élites, who were also dissatisfied that only a party under a traditional leader like Chief Elifas was allowed. This ensured that no problems were ever solved, and that no further political development on that basis—especially full political independence for Ovamboland—could succeed. The apparent intention to give the population at large more say in the making and implementing of decisions is still in the embryonic stage, but nothing adequate is contemplated. This is due to a lack of dynamism, and inclination to favouritism on the part of the traditional forces, and suppression or disregard of the modernizing ones.

The result is that the complaints of the modernizing élite groups—the most serious of which is that a static group under the traditional leaders is being artificially kept in power—go unheeded. The modernizing élite do not concede that the old leaders have any capacity for dynamic innovation, and feel that they themselves are being compelled to play the passive role, having been denied both their rightful share in the political development process and the chance to display their own inherent dynamism and progressiveness.

IV

SOCIO-ECONOMIC DEVELOPMENT

1. Introduction

The advocates of modernization accept that no country can claim to be modern without being economically advanced and pursuing a progressive economic policy. The dynamics of a developing country are largely measured by the will and the capacity to be economically progressive.

It is essential for any developing country to make a survey of the economic situation, resources and activities which can help to provide the requisite framework for economic and socio-political advance. A feature of developing countries is socio-economic stagnation in which daily needs and little else are catered for. Such a state of affairs goes with low literacy. The higher the literacy level and the corresponding level of knowledge and skill, the greater will be the input into the development of economic industries, and the further will it be removed from a subsistence economy marked by low productivity, low *per capita* income and low social and economic mobility. Another characteristic of a poverty culture is unemployment because of a surplus of unskilled and illiterate labour. The resultant low average level of productivity and income contributes to a meagre circulation of money, small savings and little capital formation. Low taxation income makes a developing country dependent on investment, subsidies and loans from abroad, with strong economic dependence on outside sources—a position which applies especially to Ovamboland where there is close economic interdependence with South Africa and Namibia, while it strives at the same time for political independence. Ovamboland's heavy economic dependence on others raises the question of the degree of political independence that is actually attainable.

The absence of a broadly-based, relatively well-qualified and moneyed middle class capable of acting as entrepreneurs, of modernizing the agrarian subsistence economy and of stimulating new economic enterprises, as well as bringing about greater economic and social equality between rich and poor in the community, is keenly felt in developing countries like Ovamboland. It is in the interests of people at this socio-economic level, on whom a heavy responsibility rests, to further dynamic economic development. However, they are faced with the immense task of meeting increasing expectations within a brief period of time. If they do not succeed and cannot mobilize the necessary help from outside, there is a grave danger that mounting hopes will change into mounting frustration, which in turn will imperil not only the economic but also the social and political order.

142

2. *Economic Development*

Ovamboland's economic development is still in its infancy. Its tempo and scope are inadequate and do not keep pace with the political development planned and already implemented. *Per capita* income and the GNP are low while unemployment is high. Agricultural development in the territory has its limitations and is heading for more family units than can be accommodated in the farming sector; only a portion of them can be absorbed into the industrial sector, and there is little prospect of the absorption capacity of the economy being able to keep up with the increase in population. Dependence on contract labour with its political, economic and social problems is not a satisfactory alternative.

(a) Agriculture. Agriculture has always been Ovamboland's biggest industry, and it is precisely here where little actual progress has been made. Owing to its particular topography and situation, Ovamboland makes heavy demands on its farmers. The uncertainty of the annual rainfall, the sandy soil with its poor drainage, and the lack of both implements and knowledge to make the best use of the soil are among some of the major retarding factors. As much of the country is under water during the rainy season, arable land is limited.

A feature of Ovamboland is that the native tiller of the soil still has a great deal of leeway to make up before there can be development in agriculture, mainly because he still sticks firmly to traditional customs and agricultural practices. Furthermore, agriculture is still traditionally considered women's work, and a male cultivator has a very low status in his community. This, and the fear of being ridiculed by girls, is one reason why most young men are not interested in tilling the soil. The agricultural college founded at Ogongo in 1972 is still has a relatively low attendance by Ovambos.[1] In the search of contract labour in the south farm labour remains the lowest type of work. Another important cause is that youngsters with a reasonable education consider farming beneath them.

Some of the foregoing views were tested during the preliminary survey and the in-depth interviews with members of the different élites. In the preliminary survey, in which 462 people took part, 85 per cent maintained that too many people were farming in Ovamboland. The in-depth interviews produced the following replies:

Question: DO YOU THINK THAT THE OVAMBO FARMER CAN EARN ENOUGH FROM HIS HARVEST AND HIS CATTLE?

	T.	R./L.	D./C.	Comm.	N.	Trad.	Ov./Av.	Kat./Av.
Yes, enough	4.3	25.9	17.9	18.2	—	20.8	13.4	13.6
No, not enough	93.5	74.1	82.1	81.8	95.0	79.2	85.3	84.9
No reply	2.2	—	—	—	5.0	—	1.3	1.5

To a further question, whether the yield from farming could be increased by improved farming methods, 70 per cent answered in the affirmative, 6 per cent that it could not be improved much and 21 per cent answered no (3 per cent giving no reply).

Although the great majority thought that farming methods could definitely be improved, the forty-two farmers who answered this question were more divided than any other of the occupational groups. There are a number of reasons for this, and the hardest problem encountered by the Ovamboland farmers was tested in a supplementary question. Although, as we have seen, too little land is available in the territory to guarantee a livelihood for all families, it was not lack of land that was mentioned as the biggest problem in the 462 replies but too little water (44%), tractors (13%) and fertilizer (9%); and only 8% mentioned shortage of land. The rest named a combination of these four elements as the chief difficulty.

Periodic droughts and irregular rainfall are evidently of more immediate urgency to the Ovambo than the land problem, as the South African Government has realized ever since it began to develop Ovamboland. This has led to a water development scheme which provides, among other things, for the construction of dams and canals, the building of a hydro-electric power station at the Ruacana Falls, and a constant flow of water from the Kunene River to the remainder of the territory. Thought was given to the possibility of irrigation, but owing to the very poor soil and drainage, this will be confined mainly to the north-west of Ovamboland, where 2,500 hectares of irrigable land is available. However, it was announced in 1977 that no irrigation would be laid on because the costs were too high.

Other problems which hamper the extension of agriculture in Ovamboland are over-grazing and inferior livestock. Cattle have always been considered the best means of saving, and they confer prestige on their owners. A factor of exceptional importance here is that cattle are privately owned, whereas land is the communal property of the tribe and is only held by the Ovambo farmer on a leasehold basis. Because of the long distance to the nearest market and the poor quality of the animals due, *inter alia*, to cattle sickness, Ovambo's livestock has not become the economic asset expected.[2] Efforts are being made by the South African Government to improve the livestock and to create better grazing conditions. Furthermore, a meat processing factory has been established. The development of a fishing industry and the promotion of forestry in Ovamboland have also developed into important issues.

From this it may be inferred that in agriculture Ovamboland has entrepreneurship at two levels. On the one hand there is still the underdeveloped Ovambo cultivator with a few entrepreneurs, while on the other there is the dominant role played by the South African Government through its agents as chief entrepreneurs. No co-operative system has developed, nor is there any need for one, because there are no surplus products. The transition from a subsistence to a market economy will not occur quickly, even with all the advice, aid and ready credit facilities that are available. The problem in the central part of the country is serious due to its overpopulation, and it is only the south-western and eastern areas that offer possibilities for expansion. Nearly 40 per cent of Ovamboland is uninhabitable because of insufficient water resources.

It was estimated in 1970 that 25,599 Ovambo farmers could be settled on a basis of economic units, but that a total of 59,520 families in the territory were largely dependent for their income on the yield from their farmlands. In other words, there were altogether 33,921 "surplus families" who, in theory, could not be absorbed into agriculture.[3] If the high annual population increase of about 3 per cent and an anticipated yearly economic growth rate of at most 5 per cent are taken into consideration, a mounting development crisis can be expected. This crisis can only be averted by establishing economic alternatives, which, with the possible exception of contract labour, are limited for the time being.

The replanning of Ovamboland is full of promise. The First Regional Planning Committee met at Ondangwa on 7 June 1971, and as an initial experiment the general physical planning of the tribal area of Kwanyama East was entrusted to it. Besides the white Secretary of Agriculture as chairman and a senior white agricultural official, there were four senior-headmen and two other traditional representatives on the committee. The preponderance of traditional leaders as committee members was probably because senior-headmen are still responsible for allotting land in their particular tribal areas, and the system of hereditary land tenure was still impeding agricultural development. However, the committee has the right to co-opt individuals from other occupational groups if necessary.

The land in question comprises 190,000 hectares, subdivided into thirty-seven farms or wards, one of which is a quarantine camp. The main purpose of the committee is to replan the area for better agricultural use. Each ward of 5,000–6,000 hectares will be redivided into five tracts consisting of a dwelling with gardens and four grazing camps, each camp to be grazed in turn. Boring for water will be carried out in the residential or central section of the five tracts, in order to supply the needs of man and beast, and this residential area may become the nucleus of urban growth. In the meantime, a Second Regional Planning Committee has been constituted for the tribal area of Kwaluudhi West. This attempt at improvement of the soil can be regarded as a matter of social justice as well as a means of gaining political support. It will give rise to a redistribution of income, especially when land is jointly cultivated in such units, but it is still uncertain whether the aggregate income will show the expected rise.

The success or otherwise of the undertaking will depend largely on two other factors. In addition to the necessary change from a system of communal land ownership to one of individual and permanent private ownership, the current matriarchal right of inheritance will have to be altered. The modernizing élite groups in Ovambo feel very strongly about this, as is apparent from the answers during the in-depth interviews set out at the top of page 146.

With the exception of the traditional leaders, the present system of matriarchal right of inheritance is rejected with equal vehemence by all the other groups. They are not only opposed to the way in which traditional leaders are succeeded on their decease, but also to the principle whereby, when the head of a family dies, the matrilinear relatives are the heirs and not the dead person's own family. Opinion on how the present system of inheritance might be changed was tested in another supplementary question:

Question: DO YOU THINK THE PRESENT SYSTEM OF INHERITANCE ...

	T.	R./L.	D./C.	Comm.	N.	Trad.	Ov./Av.	Kat./Av.
... still serves its purpose?	—	—	10.7	—	—	62.5	11.5	13.6
... should be changed?	97.8	100.0	89.3	100.0	100.0	37.5	87.8	84.9
No reply	2.2	—	—	—	—	—	0.7	1.5

Answers: IN-DEPTH INTERVIEWS ON INHERITANCE

	Ovamboland	Katutura
	%	%
Wife or husband and children should inherit	60.9	57.6
Wife/children and family of husband should inherit	21.2	1.5
Only the blood relatives should inherit	1.3	—
The individual should have the right to decide who may inherit, e.g. by testamentary disposition	3.2	12.1
It is an old tradition, which should remain	3.9	—
The system is obscure and primitive	1.9	—
The future will tell	0.6	—
No reply	7.0	28.8

The rejection of the matriarchal system in favour of the patriarchal principle was clearly expressed in these replies. A further alternative suggested was that the decision as to who should inherit should rest with the individual himself. The only significant resistance came from the traditional leaders in the following answers:

	%
Wife or husband and children should inherit	8.3
Wife/children and family of husband should inherit	37.5
Only the blood relatives should inherit	4.2
It is an old tradition, which should remain	20.8
The future will tell	12.5
No reply	16.7

Although the traditional systems of land inheritance and ownership were overwhelmingly repudiated, the population was thoroughly conscious of the traditional leader's power and authority in the economic sphere, especially in the allocation of land. During the preliminary survey in 1971, a choice of four highly respected occupations in Ovamboland society was given which it was thought would be able to help in finding a solution to economic problems. Of the 462 replies 61 per cent gave pride of place to the traditional leader, 17 per cent to the clergymen, 11 per cent to the merchant, 6 per cent to the teacher and 2 per cent to a combination of all four, (3 per cent gave no reply).

It is obvious from these answers that the traditional leader is trusted when economic problems arise. This must be ascribed mainly to his still being responsible for the allocation of land. It is the clergy, the officials and clerks, the traders and the teachers—i.e. the competing status groups—who have least confidence in him. The percentage who consult the clergy over economic problems is high.

Material welfare in Ovamboland is still gauged largely by the (temporary) ownership of land and cattle, although more "modern" criteria like money and a profession are increasingly helping to determine prestige. This supposition was examined in the following question:

Question: WHO/WHICH AMONG THE FOLLOWING HAVE THE HIGHEST REPUTATION IN YOUR OPINION?

	T.	R./L.	O./C.	Comm.	N.	Trad.	Ov./Av.	Kat./Av.
Someone who owns much land	—	7.4	—	—	—	29.2	5.8	12.1
Someone who owns many cattle	—	3.7	7.1	9.1	5.0	29.2	7.7	21.2
Someone who has much money	19.6	14.8	21.4	18.2	45.0	29.2	23.7	13.6
Someone who has a specific occupation	28.1	33.3	14.3	36.3	—	—	19.2	48.5
All together	2.2	18.5	3.6	—	—	—	4.5	4.6
Cattle and land	4.3	7.4	14.3	9.1	—	4.1	6.4	—
Land, cattle and occupation	10.9	3.7	3.6	—	5.0	—	5.1	—
Money and cattle	19.6	11.1	35.7	18.2	25.0	8.3	19.9	—
Money and occupation	10.9	—	—	9.1	5.0	—	4.5	—
No reply	4.3	—	—	—	15.0	—	3.2	—

In both Katutura and Ovamboland the traditional material values, land and cattle, are less highly thought of in determining prestige than the more recent status symbols of money and an occupation. While the traditional élite still sets the greatest store by land and cattle, the modernizing groups, except for the nurses in Katutura, generally accept money and occupation as the most important status symbols.

The following differences between Ovamboland and Katutura should be noted:

	Ovamboland %	Katutura %
Combination of money and occupation	47.4	62.1
Land and cattle	19.9	33.3
Combination of money, occupation, land and cattle	29.5	4.6
No reply	3.2	—

Money and an occupation are thus more highly considered as standards of prestige in Katutura than land and cattle—even more so than in

Ovamboland. It may indicate that, compared to Katutura, Ovamboland is still in a state of transition as far as the determination of material values as a sign of prestige is concerned. In Katutura the Ovambos have already become part of a more advanced development within the framework of an urban culture, where money and an occupation clearly predominate. The fairly high rating of land and cattle in Katutura compared with Ovamboland can again be attributed to the Ovambo townsman's lack of opportunity to possess tangible status symbols such as land and cattle—his longing for them thus being all the greater.

A test was then carried out to ascertain the most highly esteemed occupation in Ovambo society. One or more occupations could be selected from the eleven listed. The respondent had to state the occupations which he considered the most important in his community.

Ovamboland	*Katutura*
1. Teacher	1. Teacher
2. Clergyman	2. Clergyman
3. Doctor	3. Doctor
4. Headman/Chief	4. Nurse (Male or Female)
5. Trader	5. Headman/Chief
6. Nurse (Male or Female)	6. Trader
7. Farmer	7. Official/Clerk
8. Police	8. Police
9. Official/Clerk	9. Farmer
10. Tribal secretary	10. Witch-doctor
11. Witch-doctor	11. Tribal secretary

While the respondents in Ovamboland still ascribe considerable prestige to the chief or headman (though considerably less than to the first three professions), their status is lower in Katutura, signifying further dissociation from the traditional authoritative structure. The reason for the prestige of the trader being slightly higher in Ovamboland than in Katutura is probably that in Katutura a merchant and his wealth have less symbolic value because trade outside Ovamboland is chiefly in the hands of whites. The involvement of Ovambos in Katutura in commercial occupations is very limited.

The occupation of clerk or official is of fairly recent origin in Ovamboland and still gaining status. From the somewhat low status accorded to this group, it seems possible that there is a connection with the status of the white official, against whom there is so much antagonism and political prejudice, which may have rubbed off on the Ovambo official or clerk. The reputation of the witch-doctor is considered worth mentioning only by the clergy, with whom his practices come into some competition. The medical profession has reduced his influence and activities to a minimum.

A significant general tendency that can be seen is the low status accorded to farming, which is still the main occupation in Ovamboland. The chief objections are not so much to farming *per se* as to the limited progress it offers because of various factors. Some of these may be overcome by changes in the systems of land ownership and inheritance, but there are some factors that can only be altered with difficulty. A growing money economy, which by degrees is replacing possession of cattle as a sign of status, has strengthened the attraction of other occupations that have arisen with the modernizing process. The higher incomes connected with these new occupations, the greater prestige associated with them and, above all, the greater independence they give from the traditional authoritative structure, have caused the calling of farmer to decline in status and have made of it a reputedly unprofitable career. The chances of retrieving this loss of status in the foreseeable future are slender.

(b) Commerce and Industry. One of the most vital problems in Ovamboland's economic advancement is the provision of work, to guarantee a viable existence for the country. The region's difficulties in this respect increase every year. Two principal reasons—a chiefly agrarian economy and overpopulation—have already been cited. To these can be added lack of capital, a defective physical and social infrastructure, absence of exploitable minerals and limited knowledge of industrial development. The exploitation of such resources as the Otjivalunda salt-pans, the iron-ore deposits on the border near Obombo, and the lime deposits beside the Kamanyag road is being investigated, while prospecting work for precious metals is being carried out west of Oshikango. Drilling for oil is taking place in the Oponono lake area, but so far to no avail.

Another problem is Ovamboland's isolation. There is no direct access to the sea, and markets are far away. A further obstacle to development is that Ovambo contract labourers, during their term of service in the south, are mostly employed as auxiliary workers and labourers; they receive no vocational training, which in turn militates against Ovamboland's development. These questions are assuming large proportions: in 1975, approximately 50,000 breadwinners were dependent on the industries of Ovamboland and the rest of Namibia because they could not be absorbed into the agricultural sector of Ovamboland.

For decades past, and especially since economic, social and political development was first undertaken there by the South African Government, the population of the territory has become acquainted through its contract workers with a higher standard of living, which has fostered the desire to enjoy its benefits much more quickly than it can be satisfied. The overpopulation of rural areas has also helped to arouse increased expectations. This entails a shift of the population to other areas, especially cities and towns (mainly outside Ovamboland). This phenomenon is of course present in any society in the process of modernization.

People were asked, in a preliminary survey, where they would most like to work. Altogether 53 per cent of the 462 replies named a town in Ovamboland, 36 per cent a town or city in Namibia, 5 per cent a farm and 6 per cent gave no answer. This showed a clear desire to work in a town or city. The disinclination for farm employment is revealed in the acceptance of contract labour in the south.

The high average percentage of 36 per cent preferring work in a town or city of Namibia may indicate that there is doubt whether sufficient work is available in the towns of Ovamboland, and in another sense it points to the attractions and employment possibilities that are to be expected in Namibia's urban centres. Possibly, as more and better opportunities are provided in Ovamboland's towns, the attraction of working there will increase. The present inconvenience and hardships experienced in contract labour may be an additional incentive to working in Ovamboland rather than in the south. The older the contract labourer, the stronger this consideration appears to be.

As a follow-up to the previous question, an endeavour was made during the in-depth interviews to ascertain the residential preferences of the élite groups. The original alternatives presented were either city/town in Ovamboland or traditional kraal in Ovamboland or city/town in "South West Africa". The modernizing élites objected to the use of the word "kraal" for an abode, and to the concept of South West Africa instead of Namibia and to the questioner's mentioning Ovamboland as separate from Namibia. Consequently the idea of the traditional kraal was replaced by "rural areas" in the questioning, and where it was insisted upon, the respondent had to choose between South West Africa and Namibia. No choice of alternative names was given in Katutura.

Question: WHERE WOULD YOU LIVE, IF YOU HAD THE OPTION?

	T.	R./L.	D./C.	Comm.	N.	Trad.	Ov./Av.	Kat./Av.
City/town in Ovamboland	13.0	—	17.9	18.2	5.0	4.2	9.6	10.6
Rural areas in Ovamboland	21.8	48.2	46.4	63.6	10.0	95.8	43.6	10.6
City or town in Namibia	8.7	14.8	14.3	—	5.0	—	8.4	68.2
Any place in Namibia	—	—	—	9.1	—	—	0.6	1.5
Any place in Ovamboland	2.2	—	3.6	—	—	—	1.3	—
Any place in Ovamboland or Namibia	4.3	18.5	—	9.1	—	—	5.1	3.0
City or town in Namibia	32.6	18.5	14.3	—	55.0	—	22.4	3.0
City/town in Ovamboland as part of Namibia	2.2	—	—	—	20.0	—	3.2	—
Rural areas of Ovamboland as part of Namibia	4.3	—	3.6	—	5.0	—	2.6	—
No reply	10.9	—	—	—	—	—	3.2	3.1

More than 70 per cent in Katutura prefer living in a city or town in South West Africa/Namibia as against a little more than 60 per cent in Ovamboland who prefer to live in their own territory. In Katutura 82 per cent of those questioned opt for living in a city or town, while in Ovamboland the figure is 44 per cent. The latter figure is significant in that less than 5 per cent of Ovamboland's total population inhabit towns there. The choice of a city or town in Namibia is most often found among teachers, clergy, nurses and officials or clerks in Ovamboland, whereas the traders and traditional leaders show a preference for residing in Ovamboland. Whereas there is really no town in Ovamboland with its own characteristic urban culture, those who choose domicile in Ovamboland do not in general care to live in its rural areas, the sole exceptions being nurses, whose choice is probably attributable to the fact that hospitals are not to be found in the country districts, but in or near the towns.

A long time will have to elapse before the wish to live and work in a town, especially outside Ovamboland, can be fulfilled. The influx of Ovambos into the city areas of Namibia is considered undesirable by South Africa and not in line with its Homelands policy. The South African Government has therefore tried to stimulate industrial development in Ovamboland, which it is incapable of managing on its own. The necessary capital, knowledge and entrepreneurship are lacking. Seeing that Ovamboland as a Homeland is too far removed from the Namibian markets, and the cost of inducing white industrialists to move in there from outside is too high, South Africa has been obliged to act as entrepreneur through its own agency, the Bantu Investment Corporation (B.I.C.), which as become the largest single employer in Ovamboland, with 199 white and 1,530 Ovambo employees in June 1972. Its intention to provide work for 5,000 Ovambos by 1975 did not materialize. This is equal to one-tenth of the estimated number to be dependent on industries in Ovamboland by the same year. But it is still too little to make the province self-supporting in employment opportunities. Its dependence on work opportunities in the south will thus become all the greater.

The B.I.C. has come to realize increasingly that Ovambo entrepreneurship cannot develop merely through the supply of capital. Experience has shown that the Ovambos do not take easily to the world of industry, and the B.I.C. has consequently obtained the right to start industries and other undertakings in Ovamboland itself. In addition to establishing a limited number of factories, developing quite a number of businesses, establishing a savings bank and opening up tourist resorts, it has given much attention to commerce. To achieve these aims and greater economic independence, the B.I.C. has been divided into an industrial and a development section. The Bureau for Training falls under the latter, and offers several commercial, accounting, managerial and personnel management courses.

One of Ovamboland's most striking characteristics is the large number of licensed and unlicensed traders. According to official information, the territory had altogether 1,438 licensed and 5,575 unlicensed traders in June 1975 ('trader' meaning any person who had premises selling consumer goods). Most dealers in Ovamboland offer only a restricted range of commodities in their shops. The 7,013 merchants in Ovambo served a population of about 380,000 people (one to every 50.3 inhabitants) but most of these traders are still carrying on supplementary occupations such as those of farmer, teacher or even clergyman. The reason for so many becoming traders is rooted in the idea that it is the way to wealth. (In 1973 a Trades Licensing Board came into being, and except for the chairman all its members are Ovambos. It has the task of permitting and licensing businesses. Section 1 of the Ovambo Trading and Licensing Measure of 1972 specifies that no person may carry on a trade without a licence.)

The Director for Economic Affairs estimated the buying power of the Ovambos in 1972 at 1 Rand per person per month,[4] but it has risen since then. It has also been calculated that a business in Ovamboland will pay its way only if it can attract about 600 customers. This is not happening, but the shortage of patrons is compensated for by higher prices, which are causing increasing dissatisfaction. The situation is aggravated by the allegations by dealers that the South African Government should be held responsible for the low purchasing power on account of low wages. The B.I.C. is again accused of exploitation and of being established in order "to make the Ovambos suffer".[5]

The prevailing discontent is increasingly influencing the political attitudes of the economic élite and the inhabitants generally, yet there is certainly no uniform political outlook discernible among Ovamboland's traders. Many of them have profited through the economic development of the region and are not prepared to criticize the government too sharply. They are also dependent on the consent of the traditional leaders for establishing their shops and carrying on business. So they avoid any unnecessary confrontation with the South African and Ovamboland Governments. These utilitarian political attitudes are reflected in the strong representation of merchants in the Legislative Council.

As the most mobile group, the dealers are reasonably conversant with local political thinking. Because of the emergency measures (Proclamation R17), which have been in force for Ovamboland since the beginning of 1972, and which forbid all gatherings except those of a *bona fide* nature, the shops have increasingly become the meeting place for political malcontents. As many of the dealers, too, are dissatisfied, some of them have become willing stirrers of ill-will, and because of their mobility they are also important as bearers of political news in the country. A tough anti-government school of thought is to be found among a number of dealers, especially the "urban" ones, and among teachers who run shops besides following their profession, but these dealers are not yet a pressure group in the political world. This is also true of the traders' association, which was founded in 1969 and replaced by the Chambers of Commerce in 1973. The aim was to set up a Chamber of Commerce within each tribe with a central Association of Chambers of Commerce in Ovamboland, but these Chambers have not enjoyed unqualified support from members of the commercial élite, some of whom are not disposed to accept an institution inaugurated by the Ovamboland Government, to supersede the old Christian Traders' Association, which had been initiated by the Ovambokavango Church.

The contribution to the modernizing process of the economic élite, still mainly represented by the traders, should not be underrated. The initiative it shows in the economic mobilization and advancement of Ovamboland will help determine the stability with which the country develops, and it will only show that initiative when the economic expectations of the population can be satisfied. High hopes were raised when the Planning Advisory Committee for Ovamboland was founded in 1973. Its objectives are short- and long-term planning and co-ordination of every aspect of economic development in Ovamboland, and advising the Cabinet. Several important recommendations have already been accepted by the Cabinet, e.g. a National Development Plan for Ovamboland to be drawn up as soon as possible, an enquiry into the creation of employment opportunities, and a pattern of capital outlay.

Besides the factors already outlined, Ovamboland's economic development is being handicapped by inadequate input by the Bantu Investment Corporation. Despite good intentions and some constructive achievements, the B.I.C.'s operations are still deficient in scope and too much geared to profit-seeking; and they are being thwarted by the antagonism of sections of the population, principally the new élites, the chief cause of which is the association of the B.I.C.'s policy with the official policy of the South African Government. Other specific problems arise from time to time in management, such as overlapping and friction between development authorities, difficulties of communication and understanding between the authorities in Ovamboland and Pretoria, and a lack of co-operation between the various development bodies in Ovamboland itself. Criticism might diminish if the B.I.C. were replaced by an Ovamboland Development Corporation. A request to that effect was made in 1975 by the Ovamboland Minister of Economic Affairs, F. Indongo, to the Department of Bantu Administration and Development. On 1 May 1976 it was agreed that Ovamboland would have its own Development Corporation (the O.D.C.) with its own board of directors consisting of four Ovambos and four South African Whites. Eventually the O.D.C. will take over the undertakings of the B.I.C.

The B.I.C. in the meanwhile would benefit if more Ovambos were directly involved as leaders in decision-making in the developing process, for in 1976 most of its managerial posts, both executive and planning, were still in the hands of whites. Hence the participation of Ovambos remains minimal. If they could be involved more numerously on the managerial, executive and planning level, they would probably identify themselves more with the South African development projects for their country, which they often label as "white" plans and attempts at colonization. The lack of identification with these schemes by Ovambos retards economic progress, and the slogan "it is done *for* Ovamboland" will have to give way to "*with* the Ovambos for Ovamboland as an integral part of Namibia".

If the present limited raising of living standards persists, the sharp distinction between "white" Namibia with its high-production economy and developed money sector and Ovamboland's low-production economy and even less developed money sector, will be perpetuated. The parallel existence of a strongly capitalist system in the "White" sector of Namibia and a still underdeveloped Ovamboland will also beget many difficulties and threaten the country's present socio-economic and political order.

(c) Labour. The biggest source of income for Ovamboland is still the

contract work beyond its borders, mainly in the rest of Namibia. One of the major reasons for migratory labour is the lack of economic undertakings at home that can accommodate the existing labour force. This migratory or contract labour means that Ovambo workers are out of the region for at least twelve months. The accompanying economic, social and political problems, both in Ovamboland and in the area of employment, are great.

Although contract labourers do not form part of the modernizing élites that we have considered in this enquiry, they are instrumental in Ovamboland's modernizing process. They represent the region's most numerous and most effective bargaining power. This has been recognized by members of the modernizing élites, who have helped to articulate the needs and complaints of the labourers. The modernizing group and a section of the traditional élite have identified themselves with the demands and grievances of these labourers and shown almost total solidarity. The strikes and labour unrest were therefore bound to receive the full support of the modernizing élites. This open resistance was intended to demonstrate, on the one hand, the state of dependence of the Ovambo labour force and its bargaining power, and on the other, dissatisfaction with the labour system and its social, economic and political implications.

In this situation the modernizing élites used the workers as a means of pressure in order to expose the defects in Ovamboland's development process and to insist on changes. As this problem did not only affect the élites and the workers, they could rely on the active support and solidarity of the greater part of the Ovambo community, as became apparent during the strikes and labour troubles. In a non-party modernization process, members of the modernizing element saw the whole labour question as a chance for them to articulate and publicise social, economic and political requirements. Hence the labour disorders and strikes had a high political content. Under the leadership of members of the modernizing élites, the Ovambo labour force has grown into one of the foremost pressure groups in the modernization of Ovamboland, and we must therefore thoroughly explore the entire labour problem and the role of the labour force in the development process.

As early as 1891, during the German regime, Ovambos in the Police Zone had been indentured.[6] This was because of the scarcity of labour, and because at this time diamonds and ore had been discovered, railways built, and agriculture developed in South West Africa.

For most Ovambos it was a totally new experience to work away from their homeland, as they came into contact with new and strange types of work, surroundings and climatic conditions. They were not accustomed to working long, regular hours, and the harsh climate on the coast caused many deaths. Care of these labourers by their employers was often defective, and the authorities often looked askance at the employers for taking the law into their own hands and administering corporal punishment.

The Ovambos in their turn came to know a new world in material and spiritual sense, and the idea of manliness was more and more connected with a term of employment in the south. Moreover, certain commodities only obtainable in the south had an irresistible attraction. A missionary in Ovamboland summed up the situation thus:

The young men, who in the old days were left free of duties in the home so that they could be the warriors of the chief, the protectors of the tribe, and the hunters of wild animals, are now seeking a new way of proving their manhood. Every year thousands of them leave the familiar places, the homes of their forefathers, to seek work in the white man's lands, in the mines and on the farms; to see towns and trains, mountains and the sea, and to bring back the white man's money, smart clothes, gay materials for their wives; sugar, coffee and buckets; bringing with them too, new ideas, a realization of other ways of life and sometimes disillusionment with the old tribal ways and customs. Through the coming and going of these young men Ovamboland is on the march, the march from the traditions and loyalties of the past thousand years, to the bewilderment and complexities of the twentieth century, a shattering metamorphosis unless sustained by new values and faith in the living God.[7]

The returning Ovambo was out of time with the values of his society, and exerted a strong acculturative influence on the traditional pattern of life.

The contract system in the German era amounted to the use of a cheap labour force without any obligations being incurred in Ovamboland that could have led to an improvement in the economic and social conditions in the country. Limited attention was given to improving working conditions, but the German employers cannot be absolved from the charge of having exploited Ovambo workers. Working hours were excessive, wages extremely low, and there was corporal punishment.

Since the South African Government assumed power in South West Africa, the recruitment of workers in Ovamboland has been intensified, because the region has been regarded as a labour reservoir for the economic development of Namibia as a whole.[8] In 1925 two recruiting organizations were founded: the Northern Labour Recruiting Organization (N.L.O., mostly representing the mining interests in the north), and the Southern Labour Recruiting Organization (S.L.O., mainly representing the diamond mines). Other employers were able to join these organizations for recruiting in the northern areas.[9] In 1943, the two organizations amalgamated to become the South West African Native Labour Association (Pty.) Ltd., with its head office in Grootfontein, and from that year SWANLA has had the sole right to recruit workers in the northern areas, on condition that labour is made available for all types of work.

Ovambos seeking work at the head recruiting office in Ondangwa were tested medically and then graded into three classes—A, B and C. Class A workers were considered fit for heavy work such as mining, Class B for surface work and industry and Class C for general and farm labour. Although various ordinances have been promulgated for protecting the Ovambo workers against ill-treatment and to regulate his working hours and conditions, there are no legal provisions on wage rates, although the Administrator has the right to lay down minimum wage scales.

The distribution of contract workers from 1942 to 1974 was as set out in the table on page 156.

Except for 1973/4 and 1974/5, the total number of contract workers includes Ovambos from Angola, and the Kavangos, and out of an

Year	Industry %	Agriculture %	Mining %	Domestic Service %	Total Number of Workers
1942	1.7	80.0	13.6	4.7	7.678
1952	20.0	42.8	30.8	6.4	18.586
1962	27.3	37.3	29.6	5.8	34.822[10]
1971	39.2	25.1	29.5	6.2	43.400[11]
1974	42.3	21.4	32.5	3.8	30,094[12] (only Ovambos)
1975	—	—	—	—	40,031 (only Ovambos)

aggregate of 43,400 in 1971, about 40 per cent were from Angola and roughly 7 per cent from the Okavango. According to this calculation approximately 23,000 Ovambos from Ovamboland were working in the rest of Namibia in 1971, a figure which had already climbed to more than 40,000 by 1975.

The majority of the Ovambos working the south are unskilled, and although no job reservation legally exists in Namibia,[13] there is an industrial colour-bar. Repeated periods of contract labour in the south have meant that some workers have reached the stage of being semi-skilled, while a small percentage have become skilled. As a consequence of swift economic progress in Namibia, Ovambos are performing more and more work previously done by whites, but without formal vocational training. An opportunity to provide development aid through in-service training outside Ovamboland which could then be useful and productive inside the region is not being exploited. The reason for this is partly the unwillingness of the white employer and partly the relatively short time (12–18 months) that the Ovambos stay in the south.

The tribal authorities have always guarded against the practice of workers remaining away Ovambo for too long, the maximum period of absence being fixed at eighteen months. Those returning must remain in Ovamboland for at least three months before they can enter into a new contract. The official reason is that too long a sojourn outside the country is apt to break the ties with the Homeland and disrupt the traditional values. With married men, there is the fear that they will not support their dependants.

Any Ovambo who stays in the south without the necessary permission, or has the necessary leave to remain there but neglects to support his dependants at home, can be repatriated. Another reason for repatriation is the cancellation of a contract, which can only be done by the appropriate authority, usually the magistrate. Thus there are few possibilities open to the employee for lawfully breaking his work contract. The upshot is that Ovambos often desert from their jobs. This is considered an offence, making them liable to prosecution, the punishment generally being repatriation.

Organized labour, in the form of trade unions, does not exist, but there is no official ban in Namibia on forming them. The comparatively brief sojourn and resulting lack of permanence among this labour corps and the wide distribution of workers all over Namibia, with few places offering any concentration of Ovambo labourers, are probably the main reasons why no organization has ever been founded to protect the collective interests of the labour force. But although they are not collectively organised, deep dissatisfaction has taken root among the Ovambo workers over the years, with overt signs as early as the 1950s. Strikes at various mines—the copper-mine near Lüderitz in 1954, the Brandberg West and Otjisondu mines in 1956 and the Tsumeb mine in 1962—were the start of increasing labour disturbances.

(d) The Strike of Ovambo Workers and the New Labour Agreement.
Large-scale labour unrest broke out in Windhoek and Walvis Bay on 13 December 1971, which subsequently spread to the whole country. Traditional leaders (members of the Executive Council) were brought to Windhoek to persuade the strikers to resume work, but had to abandon their efforts, since the latter made it plain that their advice was not acceptable to them. Some 13,500 striking Ovambos, more than half of all the Ovambo contract workers in Namibia at that time, were immediately repatriated, but the authorities later doubted the wisdom of this step. The sudden return to Ovamboland of thousands of discontented workers caused labour unrest everywhere in the territory and aroused a popular feeling of solidarity.

The Ovambos who returned began to organize themselves, against the wishes of the traditional leaders, and a joint meeting under the leadership of Johannes Nangutuuala, leader of the unrecognized Democratic Co-operative Development Party, attended by 3,500 strikers, was held at Oluno near Ondangwa on 10 January 1972. The strikers' grievances at that stage were reflected in a statement issued by their strike committee, with Nangutuuala as chairman, containing the decisions taken at the meeting. The full unamended text of the meeting is given here, including errors of grammar and spelling:

"1. Firstly the meeting discussed the report of the elected Contract Committee which met on 3rd January, 1972.
2. The resolutions of the Contract Committee follow:
3. What is the Contract System? Contract means an agreement between at least two parties. When the word "contract" is used that an Ovambo is on contract, it should mean he is on an agreement with his employer. But this contract used by SWANLA in Ovamboland has no agreement between the employer and the employee. That agreement is just between SWANLA and the employer. SWANLA sells Ovambos to the employers and so the Ovambos have come to be slaves of SWANLA and employer, and because of this wrong and bad system this agreement has been changed into wire instead of the contract.

Evils of the Contract System:
(*a*) This system makes use of forced labour such that a person has no right to do a job of his choice.
(*b*) it has meagre wages, and because of these our people are forced to leave a job with the intention of getting better payed jobs,
(*c*) it breaks up the family life and spoils the upbringing of the children,
(*d*) because of this system the employee and his family have no right to visit each other,
(*e*) the system caused the Ovambos to be looked down upon by the other Africans in (SWA) Namibia, and is causing hatred among the Blacks of Namibians,
(*f*) what is the anal examinations for Blacks when they are going on contract? Do the Whites also undergo this anal examination when they come to Ovambo on contract? For which type of disease is this examination done which is never found and is continuous?
(*g*) because of this evil system the employer values the work done by an Ovambo instead of a person who does the work,
(*h*) because of this system an Ovambo is not under the protection of the law.

The Contract system is a form of slavery:
I. All the people irrespective of race or colour are created by God with the same human dignity and are equal before Him—this system undermines the God-given human dignity of an Ovambo worker.
II. The so-called homeland became the trading markets where the Blacks are brought, and in this trade SWANLA became richer and richer and the Blacks poorer and poorer.
III. This slavery brought about the erection of the compounds equaling jails with surrounding walls on top of which sharp pieces of glass are built. In compounds workers sleep on hard beds made of cement bricks which cause lame and death.
IV. In consequence of this slavery system Ovamboland has only one exit to the police zone, quite exactly as the compounds and stays are built, and such an exit in our country is only out off Owambo and Kavango.
V. The system brings ill-treatment throughout the employment period.

The favourable system for looking for labour:
(*a*) We Ovambos, do not want any improvement of or new name for wire. But we want to do away with the wire, and to have a true contract in meaning of the word.
(*b*) We totally reject any form of buying and selling people, because of their colour.
(*c*) We want an agreement in the work with the following rights:
    (i) freedom of doing a job of his choice with the corresponding salary according to his skill,
    (ii) freedom of leaving unwanted and low paying jobs, and looking for another job of his choice, without police interference.
    (iii) freedom of having his family with, and visiting or to be visited by his family,
    (iv) his salary must be according to the work done regardless of his colour irrespective where he is working in Namibia (SWA),
(*d*) there must be labour offices all over in the so-called homelands and in every town, where people can look for jobs of their choice. The employers must send applications notifying the type of work and scales of wages to those offices.
(*e*) Vacants must be advertised and announced over the radios,
(*f*) Neither the employer nor the employee must pay anything to the labour offices,
(*g*) any-one getting a job along other channels has a right to get admition in anyone of those labour offices,
(*h*) the Government is reminded to create new job, and to give the first preference to Africans especially in the so-called homelands,

(*i*) the Government must allow many types of business enterprises other than the infamous BIC which is exploiting our people,

(*j*) there must be a mutual respect in the work without regard race or colour,

(*k*) the meeting is aware of the lies which have been told that the wire system and the low salaries have been laid down by Ovambo Captains and chiefs,

(*l*) The employee must receive his full salary such that he is able to buy his food and pay for his transport,

(*m*) Instead of the notorious travelling passes or the proposed Reference Books we want the Identification Cards with the following items:

    (i) the Name,

    (ii) the Citizenship (SWA Citizenship),

    (iii) the Sex,

    (iv) the Number,

    (v) the Passport Photo

N.B. It must be well understood that to ask for the freedom of the choice of labour is not to cause disorderliness and chaos in the economy of our country, but our objective is for human rights to work in peace and order like other people all over the world. An example: The African where excluded from using liquor because of the suspected chaos, but now it is clear to a fool that the Africans do not more misbehave than other people in this country.

A delegation has been elected from the Contract Committee to represent the contract workers at the discussion that will take place at Grootfontein on 19th–20th January 1972.

The resolutions of the Committee were unanimously passed by the mass meeting of 10th January 1972, at Oluno-Ondangwa. The mass meeting has given a serious warning to those people who have used a secret channel similar to the now-rejected contract system to recruit the Ovambos. The recruit Offices at Oluno-Ondangwa is particularly warned not to go ahead with the recruitment of Ovambos before the discussion of 19th–20th January 1972 at Grootfontein."[14]

The significance of this resolution was manifold. For the first time in the history of Ovamboland a rudimentary, secular mass organization was founded, which represented the interests of a specific interest group and clearly did not view itself as of a traditional nature. The resolution was supported by several thousand workers, and Johannes Nangutuuala was empowered to act as spokesman for an articulate *ad hoc* pressure group, with more power and active backing from the broad masses than the Legislative Council of Ovambo could command. Both the Council and the South African Government at once saw a potentially dangerous threat in Nangutuuala and his organization. No meeting of the Legislative or Executive Council and no traditional leader had given such articulate and pertinent expression to demands of a socio-economic and socio-political nature, as appeared in this resolution. Any successful solution to the labour problem would have to take account of what was set out in the statement.

Besides the well-known complaints against the contract system (translated into Ovambo as the "wire system")—e.g. forced labour, denial of freedom to choose employment and place of work, the breaking-up of family life, and poor salaries—further complaints were made. There was the attitude of other black groups in Namibia, who looked down upon the contract workers. The Ovambo workers also objected to the lack of legal protection and the humiliation of anal medical examination. It was stated plainly that the strikes were not in favour of an improved contract system, but demanding an entirely new system for the regulation of labour.

The strikers obtained a surprising amount of support for some of their demands from the Legislative Council, at a special sitting, when free discussion on the contract system was allowed. There was considerable sympathy with the strikers among some of the members, but most members were at a loss to decide whether to promise their support to the strikers or to the South African Government.

Because of the strike, a large section of the population became radicalized, but without at first showing militancy. The singing of hymns at meetings and on the departure of the striking Ovambos for their homeland was an outward sign of this (as well as being an indication of the Ovambos' religious outlook and self-discipline).

It was obvious from the start that, for both practical and ideological reasons, the South African Government could not accede to some of the requests of the strikers' committee—such as freedom of movement in obtaining work and permission to take families to the place of work. Any concession over the second point would not only necessitate the provision of more living accommodation at places of work, but would nullify the principle of keeping "European" urban and other centres white, and call in question the whole concept of Homelands development. The Ovambo worker was still regarded as a temporary migrant with permanent domicile only in his homeland with its traditional structure, irrespective of where his loyalties might be.

Even before joint talks were begun in Grootfontein, the holding of meetings by strikers and other prospective workers was forbidden by order of the Legislative Council. This resulted in tension and increased antagonism towards the Legislative Council. While the joint discussions were beginning, the United Nations Council for Namibia, after hearing evidence from a SWAPO representative, issued a statement which expressed full solidarity with the strikers in their struggle against oppression and exploitation, and support for their rightful demands. The Council moreover called for an immediate end to the contract labour system, which in its opinion, violated the Declaration of Human Rights. An appeal was likewise made to all foreign companies with interests in Namibia to cease making use of contract labour and not to be a party to any agreement for terminating the strike which ignored the workers' legitimate claims.[15]

The new labour agreement between the South African and Ovamboland Governments was signed on 20 January 1972. A South African Government spokesman pointed out that this had been brought about primarily through negotiations with an independent Ovamboland Government;[16] this strong emphasis on the territory Government must primarily be seen as a retort to the accusation that the agreement was concluded only under pressure from the contract workers.

The main negotiations were between the Government of South Africa on one side and the employers on the other, and the final wording of the agreement, which must be regarded as coming from both parties, was then submitted to the Ovamboland Executive Council and accepted by it. Hence no negotiations were conducted with the strikers' committee.

The Grootfontein agreement made provision for the setting up of machinery for the investigation of labour disputes with a view to settlement,[17] for arrangements to be made for workers to send money to dependents, and for future revision of the agreement. It did away with the division of workers into categories according to medical fitness, with a compulsory period of service and with the obligation to stay with one employer until the conclusion of the original term of service. The Grootfontein agreement did not provide for new wage scales, although higher pay was promised. Several other essential demands of the strikers' committee were not met, partly on account of ideological principles, as we have already seen, and partly because of pressure from White employers on the South African Government. Among the most important of the rejected demands was complete freedom of movement in Namibia, the right of a worker's family to accompany him to his place of work, and the right to seek suitable work for himself in Namibia. Work had to be accepted at the Labour Bureau of Ondangwa on the basis of take-it-or-leave-it, and bargaining, especially over wages, was impossible.

The provision in the new system whereby recruitment and distribution of workers was to be undertaken by the Ovamboland authorities (first the Department of the Interior and afterwards the Department of Justice) and not by private organizations, was to have far-reaching implications, the most important being that the Ovamboland Government would be held responsible for any problems that might arise subsequently. As the Ovamboland Government was, in any case, not supported by the masses, any strife would further harm the reputation of the Legislative and Executive Councils. This has, in fact, happened: the contract labourers hold the territory Government accountable for the prevailing low wages, but the Government has disclaimed any responsibility for this.[18]

Difficulties concerning employment also emerged. The Kwanyamas complained that they were discriminated against in favour of other tribes (e.g. the Ndongas), because the largest number of strikers came from their tribal area. It was also alleged that bribery occurred at the recruiting office of Oluno, and that employers only wanted "stupid" Ovambos and not those with a school education higher than Standard IV. The deduction was that "stupid" Ovambos did not strike, whereas those with advanced schooling were the dissatisfied ones and the fomenters of strikes.

Johannes Nangutuuala, chairman of the Workers' Committee, in a letter to the Legislative Council, in 1972, gave the following reasons for the discontent in Ovamboland: meagre salaries causing suffering to workers; dissatisfaction over food, sleeping accommodation and the lack of recreational amenities; the inability of workers' families to visit them freely; the lack of choice of work; insufficient work for non-whites and an absence of educational opportunities; the shortage of employment bureaux, which had been envisaged in the labour agreement; the lack of protection for workers from employers; and the daily occurrence of assault and arrest among the workers in Namibia. Nangutuuala requested the establishment of a workers' society (trade union) and the holding of a joint meeting of members of the Legislative Council and of the Workers' Committee, so

that arrangements could be made for members of the latter body to visit
the various employment areas in Namibia.[19]

The Legislative Council did not comply with this request. Nangutuuala's
opposition to the Council was well-known, and a reply to him would have
been an acknowledgement that he was the spokesman for the Workers'
Committee, which had no official recognition. The complaints he had
enumerated were accordingly not discussed in the Legislative Council, and
he and his Workers' Committee were denied any right of bargaining. In
this way the Ovamboland Government allowed an opportunity to involve
him and his Labour Committee constructively in the socio-economic
process of development to slip by. The result was a growing tension, which
spread to the workers from whom Nangutuuala had substantial support.

In 1973, a Labour Co-ordinating Advisory Committee was founded
under the chairmanship of the Commissioner-General for the purpose of
putting labour matters in Namibia on a healthy footing, but little is known
about this Committee's activities and effectiveness. Little is known, either,
of the adjustments in wages following the strike. In the fishing industry,
the basic remuneration, after the Grootfontein agreement, was raised to 12
cents an hour for normal working time, 18 cents for overtime and 24 cents
for Sunday work. In addition, the employer paid R10.75 per month on
behalf of every Ovambo employee for board and lodging in the Walvis Bay
compound. The building industry decided on a minimum pay of 7 cents per
hour, and the average weekly wage for an unskilled labourer in 1972
amounted to R9.50. In 1972 the diamond mine at Oranjemund paid a
monthly starting salary of R27.30 to R31.20 with a total average monthly
salary of R43.42 to R50.00, with free accommodation. The Tsumeb
Corporation laid down a minimum salary of 70 cents a shift for underground workers,[20] while the average monthly wages for domestic servants
in Windhoek were calculated in 1972 at about R22.17. Railway workers
received a minimum salary of R6.50 per week plus additional benefits. Bus
drivers in Windhoek were given monthly salaries of R58.00 and Ovambo
municipal police R59.00 with free accommodation.[21] The South West
African Agricultural Union (all White) recommended its members in 1976
to increase the monthly net remuneration for farm labourers (in 1975
between R12.50 and R24 per month) considerably. The first Committee of
the Constitutional Conference at Windhoek recommended in 1976 a gross
minimum salary of R106 per month for unskilled workers. After deduc-
tions, the net amount must not be less than R54 per month. These "high"
salaries were found unacceptable by many white employers. However,
considerable adjustments have been made to take account of the increased
cost of living.

(e) Labour Unrest. A characteristic of the 1972 strike in Namibia outside
Ovamboland was the orderliness with which it proceeded. Collective
discipline was applied, and incidents necessitating the use of compulsion or
force were few. Although there was tension on both sides which sometimes
reached breaking-point, the South African police tried to avoid an open
conflict which would have obliged them to resort to violence and mass
arrests. It appears, however, that the authorities were caught unawares by

the strike and surprised at its extent. Clearly there was lack of communication between the workers and the authorities over grievances, and the magnitude of workers' grievances had been underestimated.

In this situation of high emotion and escalating aggression, scapegoats were sought. The inability to deliver a direct attack on the white man was accepted and substitutes were found in the traditional leaders, who were seen as tools of the whites and jointly responsible with them for the current state of affairs. The first indications of this were seen when the striking Ovambos returned to their homeland. The direct occasion for this was a remark allegedly made by a SWANLA spokesman at Grootfontein to the strikers that the headmen and chiefs were really answerable for the poor wages, since the existing salary structure had been agreed on with them.

The ill-feeling against the traditional leaders which was already prevalent received new impetus, and they were subjected to violence. In January 1972, two senior-headmen, V. Uejulu of the Kwanyama tribe and I. Shiwedha of the Ngandjera tribe, were assaulted by striking contract workers.[22] The special significance of this act by unemployed Ovambos was that both headmen were members of the Legislative Council.

At once the South African Government reacted by sending police reinforcements to Ovamboland—which it described merely as a precautionary measure.[23] On January 17 the Executive Council prohibited all public meetings in the country, except for tribal meetings and those under the supervision of the Legislative Council, and the South African police were instructed to disperse any forbidden gatherings and prosecute the participants.[24] Thus the strikers were deprived of the right to record protests through meetings. The close co-operation between the Legislative Council and the South African police in controlling the strikers was to be another blow to the prestige of the Council. After the ban on open protests, hundreds of kilometres of wire on the Ovamboland borders, especially along the northern boundary with Angola, were cut. This action was not only sign of political resistance, but a gesture of unity with the Ovambo tribes in Portuguese territory.

The first open clashes occurred in the Kwanyama tribal area, where illegal meetings were broken up by the South African police. At these meetings, a demand was made for the removal of all whites from Ovamboland, and traditional leaders were attacked again. Several sub-headmen were injured in the attacks and the wife of a sub-headman was murdered. Kraals, mainly belonging to traditional leaders, were burnt down and schools forced to close or warned not to carry on with "Boer" teaching.[25] One of the burnt-out kraals belonged to Senior-Headman F. Kaluvi, a former member of the Executive Council, and the Ovamboland Government's representative for labour matters in Namibia. A general complaint by the strikers was that the Headman had allowed the "Boers" to enter the area. The strikers also intended to burn down the house of the Rev. K. Ndjoba, then Executive Councillor in charge of Education[26] and subsequently Chief Minister.

The South African police repeatedly stepped in, and during the ensuing skirmishes a number of Ovambos were shot dead.[27] The Commissioner-General, J. de Wet, stated that the police had acted only to protect workers wishing to return to their places of employment and to preserve the traditional political system.[28] If the latter was one of the main considerations, then it was instrumental in further discrediting and breaking down the traditional political structure. A traditional structure that had to depend for its survival on weapons in the hands of whites was in danger of imminent demise.

The South African Government also admitted through its Minister of Police, S.L. Muller, that headmen and chiefs were being threatened with violence and murder.[29] Not only Ovambos and SWAPO,[30] but also whites, were being blamed for the strike and the ensuing labour troubles. There was reference to whites who were not South African citizens, possibly with Finnish mission workers and the Anglican Bishop Colin Winter in mind.[31] The assumption here was that the unrest was mostly connected with certain individuals and a particular political organization, thus ignoring the underlying socio-political and socio-economic causes.

It would be wrong to contend that the strike and the labour resentment were initiated or organized by the churches, although it is a fact that they continually spoke out on the disadvantages of the contract system and particularly on its adverse effects on the social life of the Ovambo people. These churches were in daily contact with the distress caused by the contract labour system, and were the only institutions that had the full confidence of the Ovambos and were accepted by them as leaders; thus they clearly stated the correct reasons for the existing collective discontent. They were prepared not only to show up the undesirable side of the system, but also to seek remedies with the limited opportunities and means at their disposal. Church leaders felt that mere preaching was not enough, but that the churches had a social responsibility to fulfil. Thus they were openly taking a stand against malpractices, human suffering and other social implications of the contract system. An open letter was written to the Prime Minister, and the strike had the wholehearted support of, *inter alia*, the Ovambokavango Church. One of its missionaries, Miss R. Voipio, who had thoroughly studied the contract labour system, wrote the following:

Although the churches had nothing to do with organizing the strike, it can rightly be said that their influence was manifest in the episode. Heathens do not strike. People in their primitive state have neither the courage nor the means to organize a large-scale strike. The Mission taught the Ovambo nation to read and write. Without the Mission the higher education nowadays enjoyed by many Ovambos in Government schools would also have been impossible. Such advanced education has brought young Ovambo men and women into touch with developments in other countries by enabling them to read books and newspapers, and to listen to the radio. The slogan "freedom" has its attraction also for those who have no desire for violent revolutions. We must also remember that the Christian Gospel itself, which stresses the value of every individual before God, has contributed to the development. People have been made conscious of their human dignity and have begun to demand that they be treated like human beings. What was in many hearts for years has now been revealed.[32]

Miss Voipio stated plainly that the Christians of Ovamboland were ready to fight for their rights by striking, but that they were not willing to commit violence or bloodshed.[33] She did not comment on the sporadic violence that occurred in Ovamboland, but it can be inferred from her views that she did not approve of it.

The situation in Ovamboland led to the enactment of Proclamation R17 of 4 February 1972, which forbade entering or leaving the country without authorization. It banned and made punishable subversive and intimidatory declarations, and prohibited boycotts and meetings of more than five persons. All weapons not in the possession of the state or the South West Africa Administration had to be surrendered within forty-eight hours.

To undermine or interfere with the authority of the state, the Government of Ovamboland, the Bantu Commissioner, state officials and a chief or headman, was regarded as a crime. It was also an offence to subject a chief or headman to disrespect, contempt or mockery. Legal competence was given to chiefs and headmen to hear and punish most of the offences named in the proclamation. These measures, which still exist, have had far-reaching implications in Ovamboland. Strikers' meetings and political gatherings are still forbidden except in *bona fide* cases, which the Legislative or Executive Council may define. The upshot of this has been that existing non-political institutions like churches and religious organizations, youth societies and teachers' associations have been used more than before by the modernizing élites to channel current political requirements.

The provisions conferring on headmen and chiefs the right to prosecute and punish, and making it compulsory to respect them and not meddle with their authority, have aggravated the antagonism against them. The fact that such explicit regulations have been introduced is an indication that the South African Government has noted the loss of authority by the traditional power élite, and thereby attempted to restore its diminished authority and prestige. But the very opposite has happened: an ever-larger section of the population has been turned against the traditional leaders. (Another factor contributing to this has been the alleged conduct of the police and their collaboration with the traditional authoritarian structure.)[34]

The effective implementation of Proclamation R17 has so far prevented any widespread disorders from breaking out in Ovamboland hitherto. Proclamation R17 was indeed infringed in the territory during 1973, when leaders of the modernizing élites, Johannes Nangutuuala and the then SWAPO leader in Ovamboland, J. Otto, were accused of trying to subvert state security by issuing statements of a political character and holding an illegal political meeting. Between 1,500 and 3,000 people gathered outside the courtroom in support of these leaders and demonstrated their sympathy with them, the demonstration finding political expression in the singing of songs like *Namibia* and *We shall overcome.*[35] Proclamation R17, which is hated by most Ovambos, could also not avert the assassination of the Chief Minister, Chief Elifas, in August 1975.

(f) Social and Economic Aspects of the Contract System. Various social problems arise through the absence of Ovambo workers from their homeland for periods of at least twelve months. About 80 per cent of the contract labourers working in Namibia are married, and about 60 per cent

of the most productive manpower is employed outside Ovamboland, hence the negative effect on home and family life in the territory can be seen to be widespread. Miss Voipio believes that the contract system of labour has changed Ovambo marital and family life. She expresses surprise that the morals of the Ovambo people as a whole should still be high, a phenomenon which she ascribes mostly to church influence, but she reports that in another direction there is an increase in harmful social phenomena. There can be no adequate fulfilment of the obligations of family life owing to the defects of the contract system, because a man between the ages of sixteen and forty-five spends between two-thirds and three-quarters of his time away from his home on contract work in Namibia.[36] Married spouses become strangers to each other, and a contract worker is seldom present when his child is born and baptised. Problems are also created in bringing up the child, as the mother already plays a dominant role in this respect in the matriarchal society of Ovamboland. A measure of mutual estrangement, suspicion and mistrust thus exists between father and child when they see each other after long periods and only for a short time; as a rule, the father enters into his next labour contract after six months at home at the latest. Broken homes are often the result.

Other attendant evils are divorce and adultery. The husband's long absence leads to extra-marital intercourse, more among the men than among the women, and frequently to a broken marriage. In some cases it means keeping a mistress at the place of work, and the liability of then maintaining a double ménage is very heavy. More and more children are born out of wedlock and they cannot be taken back to Ovamboland to grow up there. Moreover, a lawful marriage cannot be entered into with a woman from another tribe, because the Ovambo contract worker has no right to permanent residence in the rest of Namibia. Problems are also experienced in taking a woman from another tribe back to Ovamboland. Although the wife of a contract worker in Ovamboland is exposed to the same unnatural sexual life, she does not err to the same extent as her husband, because the church still has a very strong influence on her way of living. It is in fact the only entity which stands by her in this social plight. At the same time, Ovambo ministers try to help men at their places of work in Namibia. These efforts, however, are made difficult, especially in the compounds, where humanity *en masse* makes individual care almost impossible.

Prostitution and excessive consumption of alcohol are ever-increasing evils. Less money is being sent to Ovamboland, where it is needed for the maintenance of families and other relatives, because of this; and there is an increase in venereal disease as well. Homosexuality, which was formerly almost unknown in Ovamboland, is also on the increase, especially in the mine compounds and in the Katutura compound near Windhoek.[37]

On a wider social terrain, the repeated absence of Ovambos for long periods has contributed to the breaking-down of traditional obligations and bonds. Notwithstanding all efforts, mainly on the part of the traditional leaders, the gradual drift away from tribal traditions and traditional values cannot be halted. This natural course of events, which has meant that tribal particularism is being more and more overcome through the experience of

Ovambos in the south, has brought in its wake changes in the social structure and organization. Contacts with Western cultural standards inside and outside Ovamboland have induced acculturation with Western norms and the consequent creation of a syncretistic culture.

Women in Ovamboland tend not to marry before their fiancés have worked in the south and so proved that they can support them. Contract labour, however, often provides the man with the opportunity of evading the sanctions of traditional norms, though this motive is becoming less important because traditional values are being replaced. The church (especially the Ovambokavango Church), rather than the traditional leaders, is expected to give a lead in solving social problems and attending to spiritual care. Thus it is also expected to assume the initiative and call the attention of the secular authorities to the detrimental effects of the contract system.

Churches, chiefly the Lutheran and Anglican, were accused by the authorities and by whites generally of playing a large part in the strike, or even of instigating it. An open letter sent to the Prime Minister on 30 June 1971 by the non-white Lutheran Churches in Namibia was quoted in support of this contention. Point 5 of the letter contained the following objection:

Through the application of job reservation, the right to free choice of occupation is restricted, and this makes for unemployment and lower pay. There is no doubt that the contract system disrupts healthy family life, because the ban on a person settling where he works prevents family associations. It is contrary to articles 23 and 25 of the Declaration of Human Rights.[38]

The church's identification with the defects and drawbacks of the migratory labour system reaffirmed it in the eyes of the Ovambos as the most credible institution in the development of Ovamboland. The Ovambo workers expressed relief and gratitude that the church, especially the Ovambokavango Church, had been the leader in the resistance. This did not come about through political considerations and violence, but for religious and social reasons. When youths committed acts of violence in Ovamboland, Bishop Auala rebuked them and forbade the use of force. The actions of the Ovambokavango Church during the strike and the labour unrest bound the Ovambos still more closely to it. Outward signs of this bond were that every strikers' meeting both in Namibia and in Ovamboland was opened with prayer and a Scripture reading, and the striking Ovambos returned to the homeland singing hymns. Even the letters exchanged between leaders in Windhoek and Walvis Bay were begun and ended with quotations from the Bible. It has been observed that the contents of these letters read like St. Paul's Epistles to the Ephesians.[39]

The strike and labour troubles brought on a worsening of relations between Ovambo and white, which was commented on by white political and church leaders in Namibia. It was said that the incidents unleashed a fierce antipathy among the whites generally against everything Ovambo. These sentiments were also directed against the black churches, especially the Ovambokavango Church, but above all against foreign missionaries. Another sequel to the strike was the further deterioration of relations between the Ovambokavango and Dutch Reformed Churches.[40] However, the strike did bring home to the whites that the Ovambos were not satisfied with the contract system. The whites also realized that the Ovambos—through their numbers, and because they (the whites) were dependent on their manpower—had become an economic and political force to be reckoned with.

The social relations between the Ovambo and the white employer had changed. The latter felt aggrieved because of the strike, but could not manage without Ovambo manpower, and therefore had to accustom himself suddenly to Ovambo bargaining power. The success of the strike had made the Ovambos more conscious of themselves, though rather in socio-political respects than in terms of economic gain. Yet their unsatisfied demands still contain the germs of further tensions. Releasing or neutralizing these even to a limited extent would require adjustments, principally in conceding the right of women to visit their husbands at their places of work in the south (or even to stay on farms), and supplying better residential and recreational facilities in localities where thousands of Ovambos are quartered in compounds.

Miss Voipio points out that mistrust and even hate of the whites has become a social manifestation among the Ovambos. This is no longer confined to the younger generation, but is being encountered to an increasing extent also among the middle-aged. According to her observations, the demands, mainly among the younger fraternity, are growing parallel with bitterness and lack of confidence.[41] The future of the labour situation, like the satisfaction of justifiable political and economic demands such as freedom of movement and equal pay for equal work, largely depends on whether mutual trust and social justice can be created, and whether relations between employer and employee can be improved.

We have seen that because of recurring droughts, poverty and the absence of a money economy in Ovamboland, the Ovambo man is obliged to work outside his tribal area. The assertion that he voluntarily negotiates for contract work is correct, because no one forces him to work in the south, but on the other hand he is compelled to do so by economic circumstances. The main reason is still poverty, combined with the fact that the Ovambo has to provide for dependants, buy cattle, clothing, land and food, pay yearly taxes and satisfy other material needs. Ovamboland is undoubtedly dependent for its economic survival largely on income from migratory labour.

During the preliminary survey the question was asked whether it was good for Ovamboland that some of its people work beyond its borders. Although "good" was not qualified, 77 per cent of the 462 replies were affirmative, while 19 per cent were negative and 4 per cent gave no answer. Ovamboland has no option but to send the bulk of its male workers elsewhere for employment, but this was evidently considered good in so far as these workers spent most of their earnings in Ovamboland. The possibility that contract labourers were not remitting sufficient money to Ovamboland for the maintenance of their families was tested. Out of 462 respondents, 58 per cent replied that the amount was insufficient, 36 per cent that it was sufficient, and 4 per cent did not reply. Although sufficiency is very relative, it can be assumed on the basis of the wages earned by contract labourers in the south that their remittances were not adequate to cater for daily needs. Besides the low wages, the attractions of urban life in the southern areas, obligations towards "kept" women there, expenditure on liquor, and the number of dependants in Ovambo, were also responsible for the insufficient amounts ultimately reaching Ovamboland.

To the question "What is your opinion of the contract labour system?" 44 per cent of the 462 respondents replied that it should be abolished, 26 per cent said it was good and should remain, while 23 per cent thought it had many disadvantages, but was necessary. (7 per cent gave no answer.) Some of the strongest objections came from the contract workers themselves. Strong disapproval was also registered by the clergy, no doubt because of the growing moral deterioration due to the system.

Many Ovambo men view the contract system as one of exploitation, but are not opposed in principle to working in the south. Their chief objections are still low wages, restricted freedom to choose employment, working hours, problems experienced at labour bureaux, the type of accommodation sometimes supplied, communal living that deprives them of privacy, treatment at places of work, the system in general and a lack of bargaining opportunities. They also complain that qualifications are not considered when wages are fixed. Payment is made mostly for the type of work and not according to the qualifications of the worker, who is thus subjected to wage fluctuations from one labour agreement to another. A worker who has earned a reasonable income from a previous contract because of his skill is apt to find, when entering into a subsequent contract, under another employer, that his earnings are far less. It is generally impossible for the Ovambo worker to qualify for a specific occupation except in the mines, and in this way a chance to make a larger qualitative economic contribution to the country's welfare is nullified. Planned training for employment to make the Ovambo more proficient in a particular job and place him in the same type of work when he concludes a fresh agreement would go far to obviate wastage of labour. Although no job reservation exists in Namibia, the Ovambo is not admitted to a number of vocations. On certain occasions white employers have threatened to take action if Ovambos were allowed to do work "traditionally" performed by whites only.

The Ovambo's claims, such as freedom to choose employment, freedom of movement and equal pay for equal work, represent the most elementary democratic principles. These demands are so deep-seated in the minds of the Ovambo nation that even the Legislative Council has fully identified itself with them.[42] The South African Government finds itself in a dilemma, mostly over the request for freedom of movement. To grant this would hamper control in the towns, where employment opportunities for everybody do not exist. The economic, social and political consequences bound up with such a move would be to the disadvantage of the Ovambo, as a shortage of work opportunities and an over-supply of labour would keep wages low and give him no radical economic improvement. The employer will therefore have to concentrate rather on higher wages, the betterment of working conditions, more effective use of Ovambo labour and the maxim of equal pay for equal work.

Understanding of the Ovambo labourer is also essential in view of the readjustments repeatedly required of him. He is constantly moving between a heavily traditional economy in Ovambo and a modern economy in the south, under white control.

A difficulty encountered particularly when labourers are serving their first contract is that they are not used to regular working hours. Similarly, when an Ovambo has to perform tasks which are carried out at home exclusively by women, a drastic adjustment is required.

Another aspect which is a matter of principle to the Ovambo is the regulation of Sunday work, for most Ovambo have deep religious scruples over working on Sundays. The *mutual* elimination of ignorance among both whites and Ovambos would obviate many misconceptions and tensions.

The supposition of the Odendaal Commission that the white economy in Namibia would eventually be able to manage without non-white labour[43] by increasing mechanization is not realizable in the foreseeable future. Indeed the strike proved how dependent the white economy is on Ovambo labour and how dependent Ovamboland is on the economy in the south. The full acknowledgment of this interdependence must be the foundation for any further negotiations and adaptations leading to the advantage of both parties.

(g) *Political Characteristics and Implications of the Contract System.* The idea is current that the strike and the ensuing labour unrest must be attributed to agitators and intimidators, who are seen as belonging in the ranks either of the churches or of SWAPO. Most of the strikers were church members and probably the majority of the strike leaders were both churchmen and members of SWAPO, yet it would be wrong to hold either of the two responsible. The strike was the spontaneous act of people frustrated and dissatisfied with the labour system, with the white authorities and employers and with the Ovambo homeland government. It should not be viewed as the result of action by individuals or institutions.

From the early stages of the contract system, there was close co-operation between headmen and chiefs on the one hand, and the recruiting organization SWANLA on the other. The former derived financial benefits not only through SWANLA, but also through returning contract workers, who were expected to give presents to their headmen. When the Legislative Council was established, the contract labourers believed that the traditional leaders would side with them over their grievances and bring these to the notice of the South African Government. When the support they needed was not forthcoming, the traditional leaders were held jointly responsible for the evils of the labour system.

A further objection was that senior-headmen and chiefs, who received regular remuneration from the South African Government, did not have to do contract work themselves. Thus this traditional élite stratum was seen as the confederate of the South African Government, taking no interest in the lot of the contract labourer. To the strikers the traditional leaders were symbolic of those people who were blocking the Ovambos' road to progress. They were the collaborators of the white police. The strikers took it amiss that the Executive Council and members of the Legislative Council did not demonstrate their sympathy with the strikers but, according to an announcement by the Commissioner-General, they actually asked for more white forces to be sent to Ovamboland to suppress the labour unrest. It also gave rise to the view that the traditional leaders were only able to maintain their waning status and authority with the aid of the whites and the white South African police. This opinion became permanently rooted among the strikers as well as the various modernizing élite groups, whose confidence the traditional leaders cannot ever be expected to regain.

The strike and the succeeding labour troubles, together with the changed labour system, stimulated political consciousness among the bulk of the Ovambo population. With no trade union through which to work, and because of their unwillingness to use the Legislative Council as mediator, the workers, on the strength of their successful strike, became aware that they had developed into a pressure group, which could act as a bargaining force.

The strikers and other modernizing groups were assisted in their outlook and actions by the support they received from most of the population, from the churches as demonstrated in the Open Letter to the Prime Minister and the accompanying reaction, and from abroad. Overseas assistance included that of the Anglican and Lutheran Churches in other countries, the Lutheran World Confederation in Geneva, SWAPO and South African political organizations in exile, the Security Council and the UN Council for Namibia, the Organization of African Unity and other international bodies. All of these displayed their solidarity with the strikers. This further strengthened their self-awareness and conviction of the justice of their cause. At the same time the influence and capacity for real action of the institutions and organizations mentioned above were overrated; the strikers and their sympathizers among the modernizing groups expected that the UN, at least, would intervene directly and give forcible effect to the resolutions it had passed.

Although there was some disappointment when these hopes were not realized, the visits to Namibia of the UN Secretary-General and, subsequently, of his personal representative gave fresh momentum to the expectations of direct action by the world body. Salvation was seen in a UN occupation of Namibia, and the simultaneous withdrawal of the South African Government from the territory. One of the most important demands of the strikers and the groups in sympathy with them would thereby be met; namely, that the intention of developing Ovamboland as a separate independent Homeland, with no permanent residential and employment rights for Ovambos in the rest of Namibia, would thus be abandoned. The strikers did in fact say that they accepted Ovamboland as their homeland, but that they considered the whole of Namibia as their fatherland, where the principles embodied in the Declaration of Human Rights had to be fully applied. In the claim of the Ovambos to the whole of Namibia as their fatherland, the argument was advanced that they were still the most important labour force in Namibia and that the economic prosperity and progress experienced by the country over the years was in no small measure due to their labour. On the strength of this, they demanded that they should be allowed to participate on a just basis in the economic well being of all Namibia, especially in those areas which they had helped to build up.

The strike and the labour turmoil have led to unprecedented solidarity among the Ovambos across tribal frontiers, and with the growing self-awareness, their political refractoriness can be expected to increase. For the time being it will be peaceful resistance because of church influence and lack of weapons, but the goal for the future is full and equal partnership in Namibia.

Any programme drawn up to find a solution to the socio-political and socio-economic problems of Ovamboland and of the rest of Namibia will have to aim at countering profound differences that now exist between White and Black, employer and employee, church and state, traditional leaders and their tribesmen, and between the Legislative Council and the people of Ovamboland.

3. *Education*

The development of education is decisive for continuous growth in a transitional society on the road to modernity. When a static society like that of Ovamboland, which still has widespread illiteracy, education is the chief criterion for upward mobility. In Ovamboland the first agents of education were the missionaries. At the outset their primary task was teaching people to read and write and to understand the Bible. Moral standards were imparted as well as the tuition, and pupils were encouraged to acquire more knowledge so that they themselves could act as teachers. This education, however elementary at first, had an immediate impact on the social order, for the new differentiated knowledge created new values and ideas. It enabled the people to compete with the dominant tribal leadership. The esteem accorded to missionaries was later transferred to those members of the population who, in their turn, acted as disseminators of knowledge. As a result of all this, the old values were challenged and the traditional authority was affected. The traditional leaders reacted with strong antagonism, yet in spite of this, education became the most important instrument for change within the old order, altering outlooks and helping to create new social economic and political structures.

(a) *Problems of Educational Development.* The history of formal education in Ovamboland can be traced back to 1870, when the Finnish missionaries arrived. Previously there had been traditional tribal schools, where boys and girls were initiated separately into tribal practices in order to become mature members of their respective tribes. From about 1900 onwards, attention was given to formal education and the training of local teachers. The Finnish Church was far from perfect in developing a system of education in Ovamboland, but it laid a solid foundation on which the South African Government could continue to build.

From the time when South Africa became more involved in developing

Ovamboland, all education and the training of teaching staff was gradually taken over by the South African Department of Bantu Education. Since 1973 education in Ovamboland had been regulated according to the Ovamboland Education Act No. 11 of 1973, in which provision is made for the control, administration and supervision of education and matters in connection with it. At the moment there are three types of school in Ovambo, i.e. regional, private and community schools. Apart from some private schools still run by the three leading religious denominations in the country, the majority are community schools. The function of administration was carried out by Ovambo management committees and councils up to 1 November 1974. Every community school had a committee with advisory powers, and came under the jurisdiction of a school board with limited executive authority. The school board and school committee members were nominated by the local parents' associations, by traditional leaders, and by the churches and the Ovamboland Government. The duties of these school boards were mostly advisory and administrative. It seems that they functioned reasonably well, but that the working of the school committees left much to be desired.

The new Ovamboland Educational Act of 1973 made provision for the abolition of the school board system and for the direct appointment of teachers by the Ovamboland Government. School committees, however, would remain. Through school committees, the population continue to be essentially involved in educational matters. These committees remain subject to the instructions and policy of the Department of Education in Ovamboland, and their duties are administrative and advisory. The first Executive Councillor in charge of Education was illiterate and the second had only a moderate knowledge of reading and writing, but their successor, the Rev. K. Ndjoba, subsequently became Minister of Education, and the best-educated member of the cabinet. He was succeeded by another well-educated clergyman, T. Heita. The Minister is assisted by an Education Advisory Council established in 1972, headed by an Ovambo, Hans Namuhuja.

The well-intentioned tactical appointment of a more competent man at the head of the Department of Education and Culture had come too late to rectify earlier damage. A large body of the teachers had regarded the appointment of Executive Councillors with little or no schooling as an insult to their professional status, and suspicion was thereby engendered concerning all the department's actions.

In 1976, 84,000 pupils were taught by 1,938 teachers in 327 schools, yet there is a shortage, chiefly of secondary school teachers, and compulsory education is still out of the question. It is mainly women who train as teachers. A large percentage of the teaching corps is either poorly qualified or without any teaching qualifications, 21 per cent of the teachers being unqualified at the end of 1975. In most other cases the highest qualification is Standard VI plus teacher training. In the post-primary schools, most of the Ovambo teachers possess a junior certificate or in some instances matriculation plus a teaching certificate. The first Ovambo teachers with academic degrees—two men and one woman—were appointed at the Ongwediva Training College in 1970. One of these held a

B.A. degree, then the highest academic qualification of any Ovambo in Ovamboland. In 1972 there were only nine teachers with a teaching diploma, who had matriculated. The result of this is that at the Ongwediva Training College and the high schools, mostly white personnel still have to be employed. In 1975 the College had a staff of thirty-six, of whom twenty-seven were whites, chiefly married women, and nine were Ovambos. Only five of the whites were qualified teachers. The Ovamboland Government requested the South African Government in 1975 to continue making white teachers available so that they could help with instructing Ovambo pupils and training Ovambo teachers.

In 1972 there were seventy-two Ovambo teachers with a junior certificate plus teacher training, 987 had a Standard VI education with teacher training, and 350 teachers were unqualified. From this one can deduce that less than 1 per cent of the Ovambo teaching staff had a qualification of matriculation standard or higher, 5 per cent had a junior certificate, and the qualifications of 94 per cent were below this level. All four Ovambos who had academic degrees in 1972 were engaged in teaching. By the end of 1976 the qualifications necessary for teachers had not significantly improved.

The low percentage of academically trained teachers in Ovamboland can be attributed to other factors, such as lack of opportunity and initiative, and an environment which gives the Ovambo little encouragement to realise his full intellectual potential.

At the end of 1972 the following 252 schools existed in Ovamboland: 124 lower primary schools, twenty-one higher primary schools, 100 combined lower and higher primary schools, three secondary schools, two high schools, one teachers' training college and one school for the deaf and blind. In 1976 there were eight secondary schools and two high schools. At the end of 1972, primary schools had 63,770 pupils there were 693 pupils in secondary and high schools, while 216 were training as teachers.[44]

The development of education in Ovamboland since 1960 has proceeded as shown at the top of page 175.[45]

The average number of pupils per teacher in 1976 was 43.34. It is noteworthy that the ratio of female to male pupils was about 3 to 2.

Typical of a country in the early stages of its growth is the pyramidal distribution in percentages of pupils among the various sub-standards and standards. The statistics for 31 March 1970, serve as an example (see page 175).[46]

According to this summary, the pupils in Form I to Form V represent no more than 1 per cent of the total, which is quite inadequate to satisfy the demand. It is remarkable how many pupils leave school after Sub. A, and that only 10 per cent of Sub. A pupils proceed to Standard VI, and even fewer move up from Standard VI to Form I.

Out of 1,691 pupils, 1,022 passed Standard VI (final year of primary school) in 1972,[47] and in 1974, 2,500 pupils sat for the Standard VI examination. In 1975, 5,622 candidates wrote the final examinations of the primary school (since 1975 Standard V). Of these only 31 per cent passed the examination. In 1972, 103 candidates out of 114 passed the Junior Certificate examination (Form III) and in 1973 there were 141 passes. All

Year	Government Schools	Pupils	Teachers	Mission Schools	Pupils	Teachers
1961	85	21,010	445	43	5,109	134
1962	121	25,442	557	28	2,758	98
1963	146	27,161	604	11	1,382	59
1964	155	31,484	646	12	1,463	49
1965	166	32,870	695	6	269	21
1966	176	39,223	776	5	406	22
1967	181	42,068	892	5	360	20
1968	194	46,601	966	5	414	18
1969	213	54,382	1,129	5	401	25
1970	214	57,140	1,201	5	420	30
1971	217	60,445	1,241	5	742	26
1972	252	64,679	1,459*	5	(included in totals)	
1973	259	±70,000	±1,500	5	"	"
1974	261	75,861	1,555†	5	"	"
1975	296	±80,000	±1,685	5	"	"
1976	327	±84,000	1,938	5	"	"

* Includes 38 Whites.
† Includes 40 whites.

DISTRIBUTION OF PUPILS, MARCH 1970

Class	No.	%
Sub. A	18,437	32.35
Sub. B	11,263	19.75
Standard I	8,977	15.75
Standard II	6,154	10.80
Standard III	4,395	7.70
Standard IV	3,318	5.85
Standard V	1,956	3.45
Standard VI	1,784	3.12
Form I	346	0.60
Form II	130	0.20
Form III	48	0.08
Form IV	25	0.04
Form V	19	0.03
Teacher training I	72	0.12
Teacher training II	96	0.16

eight pupils from the Oshigambo High School passed the matriculation examination (Form V) in 1972, whereas the whole class of about twenty matriculants from the Ongwediva High School, the only other high school going to matriculation standard, was suspended because of political unrest. In 1973 there were nine successful matriculants. Only twenty pupils attended the matriculation classes in 1975. Of these only two qualified for study at a University.

It was estimated in 1971 that 25 per cent of the population was of *school age*,[48] but this was possibly an under-estimation. In 1972 the total of pupils *attending school* accounted for 18.91 per cent of all Ovamboland's inhabitants, calculated on the census figure for 1970. If it is thus accepted that an estimated 75–80 per cent of children[49] of school-going age attend school, the total population of school-going age in 1976 must be reckoned at about 105,000 which, because of the prevalence of large families averaging six children each, is perhaps somewhat low. Compared with the formula of the Odendaal Report, based on 23 per cent of the entire population as school-going, with an annual literacy growth of 2 per cent, there has since been an increase in respect of both percentages. At the time of writing, rather more than 25 per cent of Ovamboland's total population is estimated to be literate.

Compared with primary education secondary education has yet to come into its own. One persistent problem remains the lack of duly qualified teachers. Out of seventy-three teachers at secondary schools in Ovamboland in 1976, only four were matriculated. That meant that ninety-four, 5% of the teachers at secondary schools, were inadequately qualified. Meanwhile the existing demand for secondary education cannot be met, and this leads to political discontent, especially among those who have completed their primary school years. Attention will have to be given to making the right use of these pupils, many of whom cannot continue their school careers and who tend to over-estimate their own worth. This mass frustration may assume serious proportions.

The decision of the authorities that, apart from the planned secondary schools in every tribal area, there will be a high school at Ongwediva only seems to be unsatisfactory, although there is a private church high school at Oshigambo. On the one hand, the authorities possibly fear that sufficient employment opportunities do not exist for pupils with a junior or senior certificate, while on the other hand there is a need for these qualified pupils to fill mostly professional posts. The educational development possibilities in Ovamboland are not by any means being fully exploited. The high daily school attendance figure (81 per cent of pupils in 1969, 84 per cent in 1971[50]) gives an indication that still larger numbers wishing to advance from Standard V to matriculation will have to be reckoned with. The Ovambos are exceptionally eager to learn, although compulsory education does not yet exist. As economic conditions improve, fewer pupils will leave school at an early age.

The need for educational development in Ovamboland was made clear during the in-depth interviews when the following question was put to the various élites:

Question: DO YOU CONSIDER THE EDUCATIONAL DEVELOPMENT OF OVAMBOLAND AS ...

	T.	R./L.	O./C.	Comm.	N.	Trad.	Ov./Av.	Kat/Av.
... Necessary?	93.5	66.7	92.9	100.00	95.0	100.00	90.4	66.7
... Not so necessary?	—	11.1	—	—	—	—	1.9	12.1
... Unnecessary?	—	11.1	7.1	—	—	—	3.2	18.2
No reply	6.5	11.1	—	—	5.0	—	4.5	3.0

The craving for knowledge, though noticeably less in Katutura than in Ovamboland, is thus confirmed. The hesitation among some clergy, who possibly rate spiritual development most highly of all, is inexplicable. The definite suspicion among pupils and officials/clerks in Katutura is also noticeable. A reason for this may be that Ovamboland is seen by outsiders as a "backward area". Another reason could be the protest factor, because there were objections to the question referring only to Ovamboland and not to the whole of Namibia. Hence educational development is regarded as necessary not for Ovamboland as a separate territory, but for all Namibia. A further reason could be dissatisfaction with the Bantu education system.

Yet the majority made it clear that there was a need for educational development, and the constantly improving, though still inadequate, educational system has contributed to this attitude. It was bound also to evoke rising hopes. Any progress in Ovambo's educational methods must be expected to be partly detrimental, in that an advanced educational standard breeds a dislike of manual work. However, the qualifications being obtained at present are still far too low to warrant effectively absorbing their holders into white-collar work. Thus Ovamboland has an inadequately educated stratum, whose aspirations and expectations are not being fulfilled, and whose resentment is often fuelled by leaders opposed to the present political set-up and promising a better situation for the stratum in question as soon as the current political order and the traditional power structure have been abolished.

A notable characteristic of Ovamboland's educational system is an imbalance between what may be loosely be called academically and practically oriented instruction. Technical vocational training, in particular, is inadequate. The trade school at Ongwediva has accommodation for only sixty pupils. Furthermore, the in-service training provided by the Bantu Investment Corporation does not meet Ovamboland's requirements for its current and planned economic development. In August 1971 the trade school came to a virtual standstill because of political unrest there; only nine pupils continued with their training, or were allowed to proceed with it.[51] The full complement was back in 1973.

Primary school teachers are trained at the Ongwediva Training College, while secondary teachers are trained outside Ovamboland. However, the number of students qualifying for the teaching profession is too small to meet the growing demand. The many reasons for this scarcity include dissatisfaction with salaries, the insufficient amenities at schools, shortage of books and visual aids, and the fact that not enough pupils are allowed to continue after Standard V. There are also political grievances and an unwillingness to attend schools far away from home. Further decentralization of secondary education remains a necessity. It seems too that the school syllabus does not measure up satisfactorily to Ovamboland's particular needs and needs revision.

The official policy of increasingly using one of the two Ovambo languages, Oshikwanyama and Oshindonga, as the medium for teaching is not wholeheartedly supported by the teachers. Although Afrikaans has been the most important language of instruction in the territory since 1925, efforts are being made to encourage mother-tongue instruction in primary schools and to make it compulsory. Afrikaans has begun to decline in acceptability among the modernizing élites because of opposition to the South African Government. The tendency is to replace it with English, no matter how imperfectly used. The use of Ovambo languages for instruction is seen by teachers as a handicap to a community that wishes to modernize according to Western norms and move away from traditionalism. It is also seen as a deliberate attempt by the authorities to prevent the Ovambos from becoming part of the international world and Western-minded policies. The emphasis on the local languages is seen by the teachers as a forced retrogression to an accentuated tribal identity.

There is adult education on a very limited scale and pre-school nursery schools are still at the planning stage, but with growing urban development the provision of both is becoming urgent. More attention will also have to be given in time to the care of orphans and neglected children, who until now have been looked after by the mother's family and seldom receive schooling. In February 1977 a school complex for 120 deaf and blind pupils was officially opened at Eluwa. Ovamboland's former educational system is supplemented by various youth societies, chiefly under the direction of the Ovambokavango Church, the Scouts and Guides, the Teachers' Association and a branch of the International Federation of Business and Professional Women.

The Teachers' Association, to which almost all teachers in Ovamboland belong, was founded in 1971. Most of this association's ordinary and executive members are strongly opposed to the South African Government's policy in Ovamboland and the development of the territory as a separate Homeland, and are striving for the independence of the whole of Namibia.

(b) *Political Attitudes of Teachers.* As propagators of new and predominantly Western values in Ovamboland, teachers have to compete with traditional values and thus with the traditional leaders. At present they form part of a fairly isolated and frustrated educational élite, to which no opportunity is offered for channelling and realizing its own needs and political concepts, which are at odds with the existing political set-up. The traditional leaders are aware of this. During the sessions of the second Legislative Council the teachers were accused of influencing the children to despise the government. It was also alleged that they were teaching children to disregard the tribal authorities, and that some of them, the younger ones especially, were instructing pupils in matters which had nothing to do with the school curriculum.[52] One member of the Legislative Council said that the teaching was good, but that some pupils gave off an "odour" of a different character. Letters had been sent out, which "damned old people" (i.e. the older, traditionally-minded generation) and no one knew who had written them.[53] Another member maintained that terrorism was the first thing to find favour among the teachers, and that they were busy teaching worthless politics to the children.[54]

Teachers are in the grip of a growing perplexity that is being transmitted to the pupils, who pass it on. One cannot expect a teacher to educate youth in Western ideas without giving attention to the implications of Western democratic and political values and wishing to put them into practice. In this process he is unable to stop his pupils from becoming his own disciples.

The teacher will have a constructive role to play when the imbalance between the existing educational level and the accompanying level of socio-economic and socio-political culture has been removed, and opportunities have been provided for making effective use of knowledge gained in all spheres, including the political. There is a lack of motivation among the educational élite in the development process, which is mainly due to its attitude towards South African Government policies for Ovamboland, but the upward mobility natural among teachers is being denied adequate scope, especially on the political plane. The absence of political parties able to represent the ideas and values of the teaching élite is keenly felt. Strikes, demonstrations, and unrest among teachers and pupils, and the exodus of hundreds of the latter since 1974, mainly to Zambia, have become the substitute for non-existent institutions of political bargaining.

The Teachers' Association plays a definite part in articulating and canalizing political grievances and needs, and the leaders of the first executive committee of this organization were mostly followers of SWAPO or DEMCOP. At the same time, most of the teachers individually and their Association as a body had strong ties with Ovamboland's various churches, with whom they co-operated closely.

During the in-depth interviews it was evident that the teachers were politically the most homogeneous group. In fact there was no variation in the degree of intensity with which the traditional power structure was rejected by them in all of Ovamboland's tribal areas. Their political ideas have a great influence on the thinking of the population as a whole, and the students transmit these ideas. The high regard in which teachers are held by the people because of their actual or supposed erudition emerged from the investigation. Erudition is a chief goal to strive for in Ovamboland.

The political views of the teaching élite are even more explicit than those of the religious élite, with whom there is a continuous interaction. The traditional leaders view the teachers as the principal agitators against the traditional authority and its values, but are powerless against them. In this respect, the educational élite's attitude is paralleled in other African states. There is a further parallel in that most teachers have been trained in religious institutions. The churches have thus done most to determine the values of the educational élite, although in the last few years there have been increasing influences from outside the country. Developments in international affairs are carefully watched, mainly through the newspapers and radio. The teachers listen closely to foreign stations, particularly those in independent Africa, and are the foremost interpreters of the information gleaned. Thus their leadership is far from being confined only to the field of education.

Although civil service regulations forbid Ovambo teachers to dabble in politics, the authorities have not been able to stop it at any stage of the country's development. The thinking of the teachers since Ovamboland came to be developed as a separate Homeland became explicit in a letter addressed to the former Chief Councillor, Chief V. Shiimi, following the judgment of the International Court of Justice in 1971. This letter, signed by thirteen teachers and seven officials, endorsed the finding of the court on behalf of the Ovambo nation. The signatories stated clearly that they disagreed with the Chief Councillor's point of view and alleged that the finding was accepted by the Ovambo people.

In addition to the accusation that no human rights existed under the South African Government, the following points were made:

(a) According to the South African System of Separate Development, we as 'Blacks' are not recognized persons before the law.
(b) We are denied the right to vote.
(c) We have no press freedom.
(d) We have no freedom of movement.
(e) Education based on Separate Development retards healthy progress in South West Africa.
(f) Unemployment—everyone has the right to employment without any discrimination.
(g) We suffer through unfair salaries.
(h) The contract system is a form of slave trade and ruins marital happiness.
(i) Why are the peoples of South West Africa ruled through police authority, although we are said to live in peace? Electric shocks and beatings are physically and mentally inhuman. Arrest and detention without trial are illegal.
(j) Trials in South West Africa are devoid of all justice.
(k) South Africa's doctrines of disregarding us and UNO, although it is itself a member of that body, are misleading. According to UN doctrine, 'THE WILL OF THE PEOPLE MUST BE THE BASIS OF THE AUTHORITY OF A GOVERNMENT—ALL PEOPLE ARE BORN FREE AND EQUAL WHERE DIGNITY AND RIGHTS ARE CONCERNED'.[55]

The people's close bond with the Church and acknowledgement of its authority in the development of Ovamboland were apparent during a meeting of parents and teachers in August 1971, at which it was decided not to support the "Boer Government", but rather Bishop Auala in his stand against the South African Government. At another gathering, convened by teachers and pupils in September 1971, the 500 members present proposed the establishment of a new government.[56] These two examples illustrate the political dissatisfaction among the educational élite, and the role of the teachers in the articulation of popular demands. This was also evident during the strike and other labour disturbances in 1971/2. Another illustration is afforded by the sharp criticism expressed by teachers at the meetings in preparation for new constitutional developments, and during the 1973 election, against the South African and Ovamboland authorities. The teachers also took part subsequently in protest marches and gatherings. On these occasions they repeatedly voiced their strong dislike of current political developments in Ovamboland and emphasized the principle of one united independent Namibia. During his visit to Ovamboland, a teacher handed a protest letter to Dr. Escher, the representative of the UN Secretary-General. Teachers were also partly responsible for the increasing attendance by pupils at public protest meetings.

It can be assumed that teachers will demand a still more prominent role in the future political development of Ovamboland. Significantly, no member of the teaching élite was prepared to be nominated or elected to the first, second and third Legislative Councils.

(c) *Political Attitudes of Students.* Pupils and students as an élite-in-the-making have a definite function in the territory's modernization process. As the future leaders of their society, they are reliable indicators of the nature of their society in the course of modernization. A definite prestige already attaches to them in Ovamboland society on account of their actual or supposed knowledge. Their education in Western values will form the basis of Ovamboland's future development. A process of modernization invariably relies strongly on youth, because young people are usually the most eager to assume modern roles.

Like the professional élites, the pupils and students in Ovamboland are a discontented and strongly politicized group. During the in-depth interviews and preliminary surveys, it was clear that the continued existence of the traditional authority and institutions was more fiercely repudiated by the pupils and students than by any other groups. They were far more outspoken in their rejection than the teachers or clergy, who had conditioned their own thinking and values. The pupils and students pay more attention to political questions than to social and economic matters. Because of their youth and their strong emotional concern with political problems, their actions are often less responsible than those of the other élite groups, but this does not impair the solidarity existing between them and the modernizing élites.

The involvement of these young people in politics, dates from the establishment of the First Legislative Council. A students' strike early in 1970 at the Ongwediva Training College was ascribed largely to political causes. The next occasion for public protest was the judgment of the International Court in 1971. Immediately after this, and because the judgment was rejected by Chief Councillor Shiimi, the pupils and students of Ongwediva drew up a written protest repudiating Shiimi's view that Ovamboland wished to remain under the control of the South African Government. To bear out the complaints against South Africa, recourse was had to the Declaration of Human Rights. The following allegations were made, and are reproduced exactly as written:

1. The segregation police estranges the inhabitants of SWA and resulting enimies among them.
2. Everyone should have a right of freedom of movement without restriction within boders of the whole of SWA and her aborad. Pass Laws and other discriminatory laws restriction this freedom should have been abolished. (Article 13; 1 and 2)
3. The doors of education should have been opened to everyone in Namibia (SWA). (Article 26; 1 and 3).
4. Students are forbidden to work in holidays, it is against Article 23; 1 and 1.
5. People are dismissed from work because their opinion in speaking and writing. It is against, (Article 19)
6. Salaries according to colour cause people to be slaves and also great poverty. It is against, (Article 23; 2)

7. Houses in the locations are very small are not looked after and carelessly constructed.
8. The arbitrary removal of people from their places is wrong and is against human rights.
9. The changing of newspapers articles and addresses in Radio Ovambo like the wrong interpretations given about UNO is totally faulty.
10. The imprisonment of defenceless people before being to law in a public trial is unfair.[57]

In this protest document, the students and pupils acted as spokesmen on social, economic and political matters. They resorted to frequent marches and boycotting of school lessons in order to draw attention to their protests.[58] During Dr. Escher's visit, they handed him a memorandum stating that the South African Government was using the Ovamboland Legislative Council to oppress the population. They inveighed against the arrest of students and the expulsion of pupils from schools for political activities. The creation of African Homelands was also condemned in favour of a unitary state, Namibia. Lastly, an appeal was made to the Security Council to ensure that the South African administration withdrew from the area.[59]

The Ongwediva Training Centre was the main hub of protest marches and meetings. The students and pupils of that institution formulated their own charges and demonstrated their support for the political leaders among the modernizing élites.[60] Moreover they took an active part in protest meetings organized by the SWAPO youth association inside and outside Ovamboland. Rejection of the results of the 1973 election was a predominant motive in these protests. There were clashes with the police, for which corporal punishment was meted out by the school authorities.[61] In most cases of resistance, pupils were supported by their parents but censured by the traditional leaders in such statements as "Our children are no longer our children" and "The conduct of our youth has changed from good to bad".[62]

As the Ongwediva Training Centre is the leading education institution in the territory, the thinking and actions of many of those studying there may be taken as representative of much student thinking in Ovamboland—a surmise which our investigation has confirmed. It seems probable that Ovambo pupils and students will continue in future openly to adopt definite attitudes on the political development of their country as part of Namibia, and that their demands will become increasingly forceful and articulate. Political consciousness has come strongly to the fore since May 1974, when whole classes of teachers, pupils (mostly secondary level) and students left the country and took refuge in Zambia.

4. Attitudes to Press and Radio

In the absence of any local daily or weekly newspaper in Ovamboland, the most important instruments of communication and news are the fortnightly church newspaper *Omukwetu* of the Ovambokavango Church, the Department of Information's monthly local information paper *Eume*, and Radio Ovamboland.

During the in-depth interviews, the members of the various élites questioned were asked if they read much, and their answers are as follows:

	T.	R./L.	O./C.	Comm.	N.	Trad.	Ov./Av.	Kat./Av.
Yes	97.9	96.3	100.0	81.8	95.0	83.3	94.2	84.9
No	—	3.7	—	9.1	—	16.7	3.9	12.1
A little	2.1	—	—	9.1	—	—	1.3	—
No reply	—	—	—	—	5.0	—	0.6	3.0

The replies revealed an exceptionally keen desire to read, and an enquiry was made into the most popular types of reading-matter:

Question: IF YOU READ A LOT, WHAT DO YOU READ?

	T.	R./L.	O./C.	Comm.	N.	Trad.	Ov./Av.	Kat./Av.
Only books	—	—	14.3	9.1	5.0	4.2	4.5	16.7
Only Magazines	—	—	—	—	25.0	4.2	3.9	4.5
Only Newspapers	6.5	—	10.7	18.2	—	29.2	9.6	16.7
Books/Magazines/ Newspapers	67.4	74.1	50.0	27.3	50.0	25.0	53.9	42.4
Books and Magazines	6.5	14.8	10.7	18.2	15.0	—	9.6	3.0
Books and Newspapers	8.7	7.4	10.7	9.1	—	12.5	8.3	6.1
Magazines and Newspapers	10.9	3.7	3.6	9.1	5.0	8.3	7.0	—
No reply	—	—	—	9.0	—	16.6	3.2	10.6

The percentage of newspapers read in Katutura was higher than in Ovamboland, because they were more readily obtainable there.

Reading habits were of course closely related to the educational standard found in the various élite groups. The traditional élite, where its members were able to read, showed one-sided reading habits, which were largely centred on the three Ovambo publications, *Eume, Omukwetu* and *Medu Letu*, the last of which has since ceased to exist.

Religious literature has the widest circle of readers, the most important reading matter among all élite groups being the Bible and the church magazine *Omukwetu*, followed by *Eume*. Next to these two, a considerable variety of magazines published in the Republic of South Africa are read, Afrikaans literature predominating over English. The three newspapers with the largest circulation are *Die Suidwester* (National Party), *Die Suidwes-Afrikaner* (United Party) and the *Windhoek Advertiser*, an independent English daily paper, all published in Windhoek. The radio is the next most important medium of communication in Ovamboland, and it is estimated that roughly 15,000 Ovambo had their own sets in 1972. Radio Ovamboland[63] maintain that 100,000 Ovambos listen to its broadcasts every day at varying times, a calculation that more or less corresponds with an opinion poll undertaken by the writer early in 1972. Of the 144 people who replied, 47 per cent stated that they regularly tuned in to Radio Ovamboland, 6 per cent sometimes and 42 per cent never (5 per cent no answer).

The common tendency obtained from all population groups in the opinion polls was tested on the élite groups. A very general question was put, which did not refer specifically to Radio Ovamboland:

Question: DO YOU LISTEN TO THE RADIO?

	T.	R./L.	O./C.	Comm.	N.	Trad.	Ov./Av.	Kat./Av.
Yes, regularly	71.7	70.4	82.1	54.6	65.0	75.0	71.8	71.2
Now and again/not regularly	23.9	18.5	14.3	36.3	20.0	20.8	21.2	21.2
Seldom	4.4	7.4	—	—	10.0	4.2	4.5	3.0
Never	—	3.7	3.6	9.1	—	—	1.9	—
No reply	—	—	—	—	5.0	—	0.6	4.6

A follow-up question asked which radio stations were the most popular, and which type of programme had first choice. The popularity of specific radio stations indicated as follows:

In Ovamboland
1. Radio Ovamboland
2. Radio South Africa
3. Voice of America
4. Radio Tanzania
5. British Broadcasting Corporation
6. Springbok Radio
7. Radio Lourenço Marques (now Radio 5)
8. Voice of the Gospel

In Katutura
1. Radio Ovamboland
2. Voice of America
3. Radio Tanzania
4. Radio South Africa
5. Springbok Radio
6. Radio Lourenço Marques (now Radio 5)
7. British Broadcasting Corporation
8. Voice of the Gospel

In addition to these, Radio Zambia (5 times), Radio Botswana, Radio Ghana, Radio Herero and Radio Moscow were also mentioned in Katutura.

According to the replies the traditional élite listen more or less exclusively to Radio Ovamboland, which is also the chief preference among the traders. Both the traders and the traditional leaders can usually speak only one of the two Ovambo languages, and their knowledge of Afrikaans and English, if any, is scanty. It was thus to be expected that Radio Ovamboland would be most popular with them. However, their preference is also due to the content of the programmes. Definite antagonism to Radio Ovamboland is confined largely to the modernizing élites. They, in turn, are keen listeners to radio stations abroad. Radio Tanzania and Radio Zambia, as the "Voice of Namibia", give daily broadcasts in one of the Ovambo languages and are very popular. The same popularity may well be extended to further "Voice of Namibia" stations planned by the UN Council for Namibia to be established at Kinshasa, Brazzaville, Algiers and Cairo.[64] By early 1977 they had not yet started to broadcast. It is surmised that Radio Tanzania and Radio Zambia have correspondents among the modernizing élites in Ovamboland and Katutura. The two South African commercial transmitters have more support in an urban area such as Katutura than in Ovamboland, no doubt largely due to the quality of reception.

As regards the popularity of programmes, the order of preference was as follows:

Ovamboland	Katutura
1. Religious programmes	1. Religious programmes
2. News*	2. Political programmes
3. Political programmes	3. Educational programmes
4. Educational programmes	4. Sports programmes
5. Musical programmes	5. Musical programmes
6. Economics programmes	6. Economics programmes
7. Sports programmes	

* Not included in questionnaire for Katutura.

The most conspicuous feature is that in both Ovamboland and Katutura religious programmes take first place, which confirms the impression that religious values and the role of the church are paramount in Ovambo society. The daily religious programmes are produced mainly by the Ovambokavango Church. Hymns are much more in vogue than traditional songs, for which there is almost no demand.[65] The low rating of economic programmes, despite Ovamboland's many economic problems, may mean that the Ovambo farmer still clings to his economic convictions and methods, and remains suspicious of economic innovations. Another reason may be that the agricultural programmes, as broadcast currently over Radio Ovamboland, are still too abstract for the average Ovamboland farmer.

5. Medical Development

With the coming of the first Finnish missionaries to Ovamboland in 1870, immediate attention was paid to curing disease. This was no simple matter, owing to the tropical climate and the belief in witchcraft and ancestor spirits. The rules, fears and taboos bound up with this belief were used and misused by the witch-doctors, who thus had a formidable hold over the people. Sickness and death were never ascribed to natural causes, but to the action of ancestor spirits or sorcerers. The medical work of the missionaries contributed to their success on the spiritual plane. They eventually erected hospitals and clinics in all tribal areas, and the South African Government continue to build upon their pioneering efforts.

Both the South African regime and the missionary societies devoted more and more attention to training indigenous nursing staff, although there were many stumbling-blocks which had to be removed at the outset. Since illness was regarded as supernatural, it was not easy at first to cultivate the right attitude among the people in general, and among the medical personnel in particular, towards the treatment of disease. Nurses, for example, met with much opposition, and local nurses were accustomed only to nursing their clan members or nearest relations, not the sick in general.

There is still a great shortage of qualified Ovambo nurses, but it is the prime career for women in Ovamboland. Since 1975, the minimum qualification for entry to the nursing profession has been a matriculation certificate; previously it had been Standard VIII. In 1972, about 700 women were practising nursing.

The traditional belief that the woman is inferior by nature had force for as long as no possibility existed for her to follow a vocation suitable to her sex. With the advent of the Finnish Mission, the position of Ovambo woman began to change. Her role in the development of Ovambo society and the increasing mobility of that society have helped to emancipate her from her subordinate status. The periodic absence of her husband in the south has contributed to her attitude of self-independence and self-esteem. But women still have a limited choice of vocation. Nursing was the chief profession open to her besides those of teacher, church worker or clerk.

As participators in Western education and as apostles for Western standards, female nurses have become part of the modernizing élites. In their attitudes towards social and economic progress, they associate themselves very closely not only with other modernizing groups, but also with political development. Instances of this were a strike at Oshakati Hospital, and the arrest of nurses during disturbances after the 1973 election. Both incidents were the result of motivated political action against the existing political framework in Ovamboland. During our in-depth interviews, it appeared that a large body of nurses were adherents of SWAPO or DEMCOP. Their identification with the various churches, especially the Ovambokavango Church, is also very strong.

The nurses, as a rule, are thoroughly aware of the contribution they can make to development in Ovamboland. Their political attitude, however motivated, cannot be ignored.

V

POLITICAL PARTIES

The first political party to represent the views of the Ovambos was the Ovamboland People's Organization, which later became the South West Africa People's Organization (SWAPO) of Namibia; this and the Democratic Co-operative Development Party (DEMCOP) and the Ovamboland Independent Party (OIP), both founded later, clearly reflected the state of affairs till the mid seventies. All three parties grew out of a situation where the White authorities still had the largest say in the administrative and political development of Ovamboland. Although the direct authority of the South African administration gave way to an indirect authority and the establishment of a Legislative Council, the Council's subordination to the South African government was still an absolute fact. The three parties were therefore the product of a situation in which the social, political and economic modernizing process is still dependent on the goodwill of the white administration. SWAPO and DEMCOP attempted to alter the position of subservience to the white authority, whereas the Ovambo Independent Party, a primarily traditional organization, opted for conformism.

1. *The Status of Political Parties in Ovamboland*

The traditional élite in Ovamboland over the years has been antagonistic to the institution of political parties, which have been seen as a menace to its political power which traditionally is derived from descent, social status and ownership of land. Traditional leaders, even with the changing circumstances in Ovamboland's modernization process, have thus not taken the lead in founding a party.

Neither SWAPO nor DEMCOP received the required recognition from the South African and Ovamboland authorities. A situation in which modernization was taking place without parties consequently arose, which made for political instability. With the declining authority and influence of traditional political institutions, there was no recognized party that could act as a substitute for them. In a modernizing society political parties are capable of supplying a measure of stability, when a weakening of traditional political institutions occurs, but in Ovamboland the attitude of the white authority and the traditional power structure has ignored this possibility. These authorities have over years repeatedly maintained that there is no need in Ovamboland to found political parties. During the in-depth interviews with members of the various élites, the following question was asked:

Question: DO YOU THINK IT WOULD BE GOOD FOR OVAMBO'S
POLITICAL DEVELOPMENT TO HAVE POLITICAL PARTIES?

	T.	R./L.	O./C.	Comm.	N.	Trad.	Ov./Av.	Kat./Av.
Yes	95.6	85.2	71.4	45.4	100.0	33.3	76.9	74.2
No	2.2	11.1	25.0	45.4	—	66.7	20.5	25.8
Don't know	2.2	—	3.6	9.1	—	—	1.9	—
No reply	—	3.7	—	—	—	—	—	—

The replies reveal overwhelming support for the idea of political parties. The traders in the territory and the nurses in Katutura were equally divided on the usefulness or otherwise of political parties in their country, and a majority against the utility of these parties in the political development of Ovamboland was shown by no section other than the leaders. The traditional leaders' fear that their authority might be impaired by political parties was noticeable; they clearly felt that their lower educational standard would reduce their ability to contend with political parties led by better educated members of the modernizing élites. This backwardness, which seems impossible to remedy, is strengthening the traditional élite's resistance to the emergence of political parties headed by members of the modernizing group; at best they will accept a party that respects and represents their own values and guarantees their authority. Under further questioning concerning support for or opposition to political parties, the modernizing élites emphasized the need for parties, representing both government and opposition, to be allowed in any process of political development, as this was a democratic right and the parties were lawful channels for expression of criticism. These opinions were strongly represented and were directed mainly at the Legislative Council because, according to the answers, it tolerated neither criticism nor opposition. Many answers also indicated that the Council had no right to exist because it was not a democratic institution. It was only a nominated body, which allowed no political parties, and furthermore it denied the people a voice in, and control over, its activities. According to the replies, such a situation would be unthinkable if political parties were permitted. Parties were credited with a dynamic force, which would constitute a counterweight to a stagnating Legislative Council that was blocking development or, at the very least, retarding it.

The replies of the modernizing élites showed strong sentiments concerning the role of a political party in the task of modernization. By contrast, the traditional leaders contended that party political development brought strife and division, and might cause a worsening of the general situation in Ovamboland, and a rejection of the traditional authority. Fears were also voiced that political parties would disturb Ovamboland's unity.

This fear is allied to an underlying objection to SWAPO and DEMCOP because, on the one hand, the traditional leaders and the South African Government, wish to confine nationalism to Ovamboland, i.e. one ethnicity as a frame of reference, whereas on the other hand, the two parties viewed nationalism on a much broader basis, i.e. with the inclusion of all the ethnicities of Namibia. The active suppresion of the latter concept was to rouse forces that are still gaining ground. Because of the hostility of the South African and Ovambo authorities towards SWAPO and DEMCOP, and their efforts to hamper and suppress the parties, the sympathy and support of the population for these parties has correspondingly increased, especially for SWAPO.

Ovamboland's three parties all have effective organizations but in both DEMCOP and the Ovambo Independent Party there are opportunist forces, which see these parties merely as means to an end. In the OIP, especially, there are elements that want to make use of the party for ulterior reasons. That party depends for its survival on the protection of the white authorities, and therefore it favours the continued presence of the whites. In the case of DEMCOP there are other reasons. Because SWAPO cannot conduct its activities in Ovamboland openly, some of its leaders and members have been working through DEMCOP, which, although it has no official recognition, is allowed to be politically and organizationally active. Thus SWAPO has been making use of DEMCOP for reasons of its own. If SWAPO is ultimately able to operate in the open, it will probably become the most important party and replace DEMCOP, OIP and any other existing party.

Only when a number of the Legislative Council members came to be elected in Ovamboland in August 1973, the protecting white authorities and the ruling Ovambo administration acknowledged that for an election a political party was necessary. The refusal to recognize neither SWAPO nor DEMCOP, because their objectives, and DEMCOP's leader personally, were unacceptable, encouraged the traditional élite to found the traditionally-oriented Ovambo Independent Party, which had to serve as alternative for the other two parties. The OIP was outrightly rejected by the modernizing élite groups and by the other two parties, as was proved by the election results. The OIP never demonstrated any vitality, and has to rely for support on the traditional élite coterie and on individual followers and supporters. Although its programme subscribes to modernization, this is within a framework that is only conditionally acceptable to Ovamboland's modernizing forces.

Besides the fact that the OIP's principles are unacceptable, the party is regarded as an artificial means whereby the traditional forces retain and affirm their power and status. Arrayed against it are the leaders of SWAPO and DEMCOP who come from groups in society—teachers, officials, clergy, nurses, etc.—that fulfil a vital role in the modernization process. Many of these leaders have not progressed much beyond Standard VI, but the traditional leaders are predominantly illiterate. SWAPO and DEMCOP have been able to recruit their most prominent members from organizations that preceded the establishment of parties, and were mainly non-political; and many of DEMCOP's features can be traced back to these sources, e.g. the traders' association, the teachers' association, students' and youth organizations, the strikers' committee, religious societies and the churches. Churches and other religious organizations undoubtedly encouraged the growth of DEMCOP and, to some extent, that of SWAPO too. Since the authorities would not allow opposing political parties in the territory, the frustrated Ovambos had to find alternative means of channelling their current political needs. These recognized pre-existing institutions, which had already aided Ovambo's modernization process, could be trusted to represent the interests of the modernizing forces in the population and aim at a single Namibian state. They were prepared to strive for a unifying national ideal which would guarantee freedom of speech and movement.

The phenomenon of modernizing parties being established or assisted through the churches is not new in Africa, but in Ovamboland the extent of such support has been exceptional. Because of the confidence which the population, and especially the modernizing élite groups, placed in it, the Ovambokavango Church became politicized against its will because of the absence of a suitable party. It has consistently refused to become a political institution, but it could not evade the compulsion placed upon it to pronounce on political matters as well. It has spoken out on social and political questions in the hope of changes coming about which would prevent an open conflict and violent confrontation. The Ovambokavango Church has always condemned a resort to violence and has championed peaceful resistance, while Bishop Auala is revered as a father-figure and as the true leader of the Ovambos. If he had declined to sign the Open Letter to the Prime Minister, which set out the chief complaints of the modernizing elements against the South African Government, he would have lost his credibility in the eyes of the Ovambo people, and impaired his Church's reputation. Essentially an apolitical figure the Bishop now had to express his views on matters which should primarily have been the task of a political party. Such a party (viz. SWAPO) did indeed exist, but without official recognition. So the populace asked the recognized churches to make their voices heard. This was done not only through the Open Letter but also through its church newspaper *Omukwetu* which, for want of a daily press, served as a substitute for a newspaper and gave current political news in addition to church news. Some of the modernizing elements conceded that this was done intentionally to counter the white-controlled monthly government-owned information paper *Eume*, and the broadcasts from Radio Ovamboland, which were described as biased. The destruction of the church press at Oniipa by a bomb explosion in May 1973, was seen by the church as a deliberate effort to silence it and to restrain it from making political utterances. The very opposite happened. The violently emotional reaction to this deed in Ovamboland consolidated the more or less invincible position of the Ovambokavango Church as a leader in the process of modernization. Church leaders denied that the explosion was the work of Ovambos.

For a while DEMCOP drew a good deal of support from members of the Ovambokavango Church, the influence of which was apparent in DEMCOP's programme. The party had originated as a political institution from the irreconcilability of divergent social forces in Ovamboland, and represented the concensus of a large section of the people. It seems likely that, although not officially recognized by the authorities, DEMCOP also temporarily had the support of adherents of SWAPO, which is not allowed to organize or canvass for members in Ovamboland.

The programmes of DEMCOP and SWAPO both devote much attention to long-term socio-political and socio-economic questions, but they hardly suggest how to help solve Ovamboland's day-to-day problems. The main complaint by the South African and Ovambo authorities against SWAPO and DEMCOP is that they are merely destructive and disregard positive measures for self-help.

It will damage future party political development in Ovamboland if the authorities persist in encouraging support only for a traditional oriented party thereby withholding a rightful share in the modernizing process from other political parties in the country. As long as opposition parties are deprived of their just and democratic participation in Ovamboland's affairs, the less likely is any development to succeed, however well-intentioned it may be. Resistance to the traditional leaders will only increase and give rise to instability and ultimately unrest. The Ovambo Independent Party, will never attract the forces necessary for the modernization of Ovamboland, as these forces are nowadays a part of the unrecognized "extra-parliamentary" opposition or outside the country. Such a situation may for a time delay or even nullify the modernization process, which will be to the advantage of neither Ovamboland, Namibia nor South Africa.

In a nutshell, SWAPO and especially DEMCOP, although forbidden to take part in the process of government, are regarded by the majority of the population as instruments and symbols of modernity. The popular backing they receive is such that they issue statements on questions such as national integration, power-sharing, legitimacy and the control of conflicts which they themselves help to foment. Both parties view themselves as the foremost entrepreneurs in the process of politicization.

In their claim to be the most popular parties, they are supported by the effective communication that exists between themselves and the population, and the response they receive. They are in a position to mobilize the masses and to change the patterns of behaviour. In their advocacy of a joint Namibian fatherland, bridging language differences, they are sustained by international recognition and support. This holds good especially for SWAPO. The Ovamboland Independent Party will remain a sectional party with a minimal following. Its link with the traditional power structure, the presence of traditionalist elements in its executive, and its collaboration with the white authority make its failure in Ovamboland a certainty which even a good party programme could not avert. As its existence depends on white protection, it is likely to perish once that protection is withdrawn. Its support might have been greater if opposition parties had been tolerated, but it could never have evolved into a party with mass appeal. The OIP does not attract the genuine modernizing forces, because, apart from the factors mentioned above, it does not stand for the political ideals of most of the modernizing élites. It does contribute to political awareness in Ovamboland, but only counter-productively; the more politically conscious the population becomes, the more will it turn against the OIP. The party is definitely not the microcosm of the future Ovambo society and is not seen as a symbol of modernity. Its ideal that

Ovamboland should become an independent homeland is rejected by most of the modernizing section and indeed by most of the population.

This situation prevailed till 1976, when Nangutuuala, the leader of DEMCOP, was abducted by SWAPO forces while on a visit to Angola, and the OIP, although apparently officially not dissolved, has been succeeded by the new National Democratic Party. Since the abduction of its leader, the importance of DEMCOP has declined rapidly, leaving SWAPO the strongest party in the territory.

The new National Democratic Party under the leadership of the Chief Minister of Ovamboland, the Rev. K. Ndjoba, maintains that it is an open, multi-racial party. Little is known of its activities or of its support in or outside Ovamboland. The opening of membership to all races seems to indicate an acknowledgement of the failure of OIP, which was purely Ovambo-oriented. As the credibility of the traditional leaders remains low, the National Democratic Party can be expected to enjoy minimal support. It is regarded in Ovamboland as a party of the territory's government.

2. *SWAPO*

The first party to represent Ovambo interests exclusively—the Ovambo People's Congress—was established by Herman Toivo ja Toivo and Andreas Shipanga in 1958 among Ovambo workers in Cape Town. One of its most important demands was the ending of the contract labour system, which was called a system of oppression and exploitation.[1] After making contact with an expatriate, Mburumba Kerina (alias Getzen), who appeared as a spokesman for black Namibians at the United Nations, Toivo was sent back to Namibia, where in due course he was placed under house arrest. On the advice of Kerina, he then set about establishing a country-wide political organization to replace the OPC, and the outcome was the founding of the Ovambo People's Organization in April 1959.

As Toivo was politically disabled by his banning to Ovamboland, Sam Nujoma (president), Louis Nelegani (vice president), and Jacob Kuhangua (secretary general) became instrumental in the re-organizing of the Ovambo People's Organization. One of its main aims was to fight the contract labour system and act as spokesman for the politically voiceless workers. The immediate concern became the working conditions and wages of the Ovambo contract workers.

Fearing possible resistance from the traditional élite, Kerina recommended that all tribal heads should become vice-presidents of the party, with himself as president and Toivo as secretary-general. The purpose was to create the impression that the party sided with the traditional leaders, while it simultaneously canvassed promising young members.[2] It was proposed that the party should make the following demands: (i) direct representation of all Namibia's inhabitants in the government of the country; (ii) the franchise for everyone irrespective of colour, race, creed or national descent; (iii) the immediate abolition of Namibia's white representation in the South African Parliament; (iv) the immediate placing of Namibia under UN trusteeship; and (v) that the USSR and the USA be requested to enforce UN resolutions on South Africa militarily.[3]

Kerina stated plainly that if the traditional leaders were not prepared to co-operate, their kraals should be burnt down.[4] He subsequently brought more pressure to bear on the party not to continue to exist on an ethnic foundation, but to make the OPO into a party uniting all non-whites in Namibia. The outcome of this was the founding of the South West Africa People's Organization (SWAPO). Kerina was anxious to act as representative abroad for the whole of Namibia but although the party had altered its name, it remained primarily an Ovambo organization. With the change of OPO to SWAPO, Kerina became chairman while Nujoma remained president.

SWAPO's success in the early days after its formation was rather circumscribed, mainly because the traditional leaders in Ovamboland have regarded the party from its foundation to the present, as a threat to their authority and have therefore always opposed it. For a time their resistance was so effective that some leaders of the party became frustrated and left the country, the most prominent of them being Sam Nujoma, president of SWAPO in Namibia, who fled in 1959. Since then he has been president of the movement abroad, with his headquarters in Dar-es-Salaam, Tanzania. Some hundred Ovambos followed him into exile in 1961–2.[5] Most of them wanted to study abroad, but only twenty had the necessary qualifications for further studies. The majority of them were trained as guerrillas.[6]

While support for SWAPO in Ovamboland continued to be limited, it received more and more support in the south. Its strongest backing was among contract workers in Windhoek and Walvis Bay, and for this reason SWAPO was also referred to as a workers' party. The activities of the organization in the early 1960s were mostly characterized by politics of protests. Numerous petitions were sent to the United Nations, expressing the hope that it would intervene in Namibia to secure the country's independence. Self-rule with a democratic black government was demanded.

When these demands remained unfulfilled, SWAPO decided to take the initiative politically and militarily on a basis parallel with United Nations intervention. It began a military training programme abroad, whereby Ovambos underwent instruction as guerrilla fighters in Africa, Asia and East Europe, the purpose being to develop a trained military cadre as the nucleus of the People's Liberation Army of Namibia (PLAN). A military élite is thus forming outside Ovamboland, and the population of the territory is thoroughly conscious of Ovambos receiving military training in this way, especially in Angola and Zambia. In 1973, SWAPO had four bases near the Zambian border on the Caprivi Strip, at Sinjembele, Imusho, Sesheke and Mwandi, a development condemned by the traditional élite. The modernizing élites are less ready to reject the use of violence to "liberate" Ovamboland. However, the religious élite has repeatedly opposed recourse to violence for solving the country's problems.

Ovamboland is thus noteworthy for the absence of an Ovambo military élite, on its home territory, while one does exist abroad. The strength of this élite, mostly consisting of officers, is not known, and its influence on Namibia is still chiefly propagandist. As the well-forested areas of the territory lend themselves well to guerrilla warfare, and a political climate has arisen that possibly favours guerrilla warfare, an increasing penetration of Ovambo guerrilla forces can be expected. About 4,000 SWAPO adherents received military training abroad. But only when these troops have achieved permanent military success in Ovamboland will a military élite be present in the country and directly influence development.

It was not possible to conduct an opinion poll among the Ovambo military élite in this investigation, but the external wing of SWAPO made the views and intentions of this élite sufficiently well-known to warrant valid conclusions concerning its attitude on current political developments in Ovambo. Once it had set guerrilla forces in motion, SWAPO abroad relinquished the principle of peaceful resistance. The trained cadre had to serve as the nucleus for organizing the underground mobilization of the black people to take part in the liberation struggle. As early as September 1962, this statement appeared in a SWAPO bulletin: "We are now irrevocably committed to a course of armed revolution."[7] That policy is being maintained.

Yet inside Namibia SWAPO has consistently supported peaceful resistance, and its local leaders have fastened their hopes on the success and possible actions of their leaders abroad. It is mainly since the judgment of the International Court of Justice in 1966 in South Africa's favour that a start has been made to translate frustration into violence. Even before the judgment, trained Ovambos were infiltrating the dense bush of the Kwanyama tribal area, and the instruction of local SWAPO followers in terrorism and guerrilla warfare had begun. The training camp at Ongulumbashe was discovered by the South African authorities and destroyed on 26 August 1966. Some of the trained infiltrators escaped. Two headmen were attacked in November 1966, and a senior headman a month later. From this is was clear that the SWAPO infiltrators were directing their aggression primarily against the traditional élite. This was also apparent during the so-called terrorist trial, *The State vs. Tuhadeleni and Others*, at which twenty-seven Ovambo guerrillas and ten SWAPO leaders in Namibia were formally charged with terrorism. The chief indictment was participation in terrorist activities, and there were two alternative charges under the Suppression of Communism Act. The accused were charged with having attempted to overthrow the existing government in Namibia and replace it with a government of SWAPO members. Four of the most important SWAPO leaders in Namibia were among the accused: Nathaniel Maxuiriri, acting president; John Otto, acting secretary-general; Jason Mutumbulua, acting secretary for foreign affairs; and Herman Toivo ja Toivo, the party's founding member.

During the trial one accused was found not guilty and one died of natural causes in detention. Another, G. Mbindi, complained of ill-treatment by the police during the trial, and was discharged before judgment was given. When sentence was passed, there were thirty-four accused left out of the original thirty-seven. Of these, twenty-one were ordinary labourers, three were farm labourers, three were farmers, two were teachers, one was a mechanic, one a clerk, one a trader and the occupations of two were unknown.[8] Thus at least four of the accused belonged to the ranks of the modernizing élites in Ovamboland although SWAPO has remained predominantly a workers' party.

Just before judgment was given, Toivo made a long statement in court,[9] which was the most significant political declaration by a member of a modernizing Ovambo élite at that period. Toivo was born around 1924 in Ovamboland, where he was educated at the Finnish technical school of Ongwediva. He joined the Native Military Corps in the Second World War, after which he returned to school for a time, and then worked in a gold mine on the Witwatersrand, as a clerk at a manganese mine, and as a railway policeman in South Africa, before finally taking a job in Cape Town where, as already mentioned, he entered politics. His political activities led to his deportation from Cape Town to Namibia in 1958. From then till 1961 he was under house arrest in the home of Chief Shihepo, whose successor refused to keep him detained any longer. Until his arrest he had been working for SWAPO full-time, having become the first professional Ovambo politician. It is against this background that his statement in court became an important document for its epoch and of great political significance. His statement became the political credo of many of SWAPO's followers. It can probably be assumed that it reflected to a great extent the political attitude of part of the rising new generation of Ovambo élites of that era.

At the beginning of his statement Toivo said that the accused were not South Africans but Namibians, who were being judged by foreigners. South Africa was always considered an "intruder" in Namibia, and Toivo could not see himself and his fellow-accused as terrorists—only, at the worst, rebels. He asserted that in this case South Africa was not only passing judgment on a matter it did not understand, but that it also saw the situation as an opportunity for justifying its policy. He wished to assure the court that South Africa did not rule Namibia with popular consent.

In his opinion SWAPO was the most important political organization and party in Namibia. Its members realized that the whites regarded the black not as politicians but only as agitators. Yet he wanted to impress on the court that although many blacks had no schooling, they knew very well the meaning of restrictions on freedom, pass laws, a just wage and choice of employment. They also knew that people wanted to be ruled by those whose authority they recognized, and not by others who governed them simply by virtue of possessing superior weapons.

Toivo objected to use being made of paid officials and headman during the court proceedings as witnesses to prove that SWAPO did not speak on behalf of the whole population. He then said: "If the Government of South Africa were sure that SWAPO did not represent the innermost feelings of the people in South West Africa, it would not have taken the trouble to make it impossible for SWAPO to propagate its peaceful policy."[10] Toivo maintained that South African officials wished to believe that SWAPO was an irresponsible organization.

He also declared in his statement that South Africa had had the sacred task of leading Namibia to independence and preparing the population for that end. Yet South Africa, believing in the superiority of the white race and that God had chosen it to rule in the world, had abused its trust under the Mandate and over a period of fifty years had failed to promote the development of the non-whites in Namibia. He accepted that it was not easy for people of different races to live peaceably together but he believed that it was possible and that endeavours should be made to that end. According to him, the South African Government was sowing enmity when it separated people and stressed differences, whereas he and his people were agreed that through living cheek by jowl mutual fear would vanish. "We also believe," he said, "that this fear which some of the Whites have of Africans is based on their desire to be superior and privileged, and that when Whites see themselves as part of South West Africa, sharing with us all its hopes and troubles, then that fear will disappear. Separation is said to be a natural process. But why then is it imposed by force, and why then is it that Whites have the superiority?"[11]

Toivo emphasized his strong opposition to the roles of the headmen. He stated that they had become accustomed to oppressing the population and that the whites' indirect administration contributed, because only someone who had white approval could become a headman. Other headmen, who had a feeling for their people, were compelled to accept white policy. He was convinced that neither South Africa nor the United Nations could bring progress, which could only be achieved through the work and struggles—and even the experience and mistakes—of the people themselves.

Toivo vehemently denied that any of the accused were Communists. They were not interested in ideologies, and using weapons from Communist countries had nothing to do with adopting Communist doctrines.[12] He said that documents compiled by SWAPO leaders called on the Almighty to lead the crusade for freedom. His people were united, Toivo said, in their desire for the right to liberty and justice.

They simply wanted the same freedom as other African states, and here Toivo vented his disappointment at the judgment of the International Court of Justice in 1966, because of which his compatriots had begun to fight for Namibia's independence. He explained that they did not expect independence to bring an end to their distress, but the people as a whole were entitled to self-rule. The question at issue was not whether South Africa was treating the non-whites well or badly, but that Namibia was their land, in which they wanted to be their own masters.

Toivo dealt with the scruples of people who, while sympathizing with SWAPO's aims, condemned violence. He himself was not by nature a man who counselled violent methods, which were a sin against God and one's fellow-human beings. SWAPO was still a non-violent organization, but the South African Government did not really care whether it operated with or without violence, but were opposed to any sort of resistance to apartheid. Since 1963 SWAPO had been forbidden to hold meetings, and Toivo admitted that this interdict had been imposed by the tribal authorities in Ovamboland—but, he said, these authorities were working with the South African authorities, who had never been in favour of political freedom. Another of his objections was that non-whites could not vote and had no right to express political opinions in their own country. Was it so surprising, he asked, that for reasons such as these, people resorted to weapons? Who would not readily defend himself and his belongings against robbers? His people believed that South Africa had robbed them of their country.

Toivo also mentioned that he considered himself an out-and-out Namibian, who could not remain an onlooker in the campaign his compatriots were waging. He had cast in his lot with the militants, because peaceful resistance had led to nothing. Just as he had been prepared, as a soldier in the Second World War, to lay down his life for South Africa, so was he now ready to risk his life for his people. He knew that the struggle for independence would be won some day, and that only when human dignity had been restored to him and his people, and they had been granted equal status with the whites, would there be peace between white and non-white.

He and his fellows believed that South Africa had the option of living in amity. However, if it should choose to crush them by force it would not only be betraying its charge, but would live securely only for as long as its power exceeded that of his people. Toivo gave a warning that no South African could live safely in Namibia because he would know that his safety was based on the use of force. If he did not use force, he would be unable to maintain himself.

He ended by saying that he and his people felt that their troubles and sacrifices had not been in vain. They were confident that events would convince the white South Africans that he and the inhabitants of Namibia were in the right and they in the wrong. Only when these whites understood this and acted accordingly would he and his compatriots be able to call off their struggle for freedom and justice in the land of their birth.[13]

Definite conclusions may be drawn from Toivo's statement. SWAPO claimed to interpret the political feelings of the Ovambo population, but felt frustrated in giving effect to them. The objective was plain: independence for the whole of Namibia as a single unified state, and there were to be no political divisions between the various ethnic groups in the country. This included the whites, with whom there would be co-operation, if equality existed between them and the blacks. A political solution had to be found, without the use of violence. For Toivo it was not primarily a matter of realizing specific ideological aims, but the principle of human dignity. Here he put his trust in God and in the standpoint of his church, the Ovambokavango Church.

In his opposition to the South African Government's policy in Namibia, Toivo singled out the traditional leaders as objects of his hostility. To him they were an obstacle in the process of political development, and he denounced their collaboration with the South African Government.

His views coincided more or less with those of the majority of the modernizing élites as disclosed during the in-depth interviews. One could thus infer that there was no essential difference between the opinions of the modernizing élites in Ovamboland and the political standpoint of SWAPO in Namibia.

The action taken by the South African authorities against SWAPO led to the movement inside the country remaining quiescent for a number of years, but helped to consolidate it abroad, where it sought new methods of opposing South Africa. The prosecution and sentencing of SWAPO's leading figures hampered, at least temporarily, the rise of an independent political élite in Ovambo, but this was taking place abroad in the meantime. Thus the direct influence of SWAPO leaders on the political development process of Ovamboland was limited. Yet beyond Ovamboland's borders this political élite-in-exile acted efficiently and influenced world opinion.

The Advisory Council of SWAPO met in Tanga, Tanzania, from 26 December 1969 to 2 January 1970, and reviewed its activities. It decided on the following:

— Greater sacrifices for the liberation of Namibia;
— Armed struggle was the only effectual way to liberate Namibia;
— Censure of the Western powers and Japan because of their economic, political and military aid to South Africa in oppressing the population of Namibia;
— Pressure on the UN to carry out its resolutions, especially resolution 2145 (XXI) of 1966;
— SWAPO should be recognized by the UN as the sole true representative political movement in Namibia and should be given material and moral support to prosecute the armed revolution in that country;
— Thanks to, and solidarity with, all organizations and countries that were assisting SWAPO in its struggle for the liberation of Namibia.

The following SWAPO office-bearers were appointed as part of an expatriate Ovambo political élite:

President	Sam D. Nujoma (Ovambo)
Vice-President	Bredan Simbwaye (Ovambo)
Acting Vice-President	Mishek Muyongo (East Caprivian)
Administrative Secretary	Moses M. Garoeb (Damara)
Assistant Administrative Secretary	Lucas Pohamba (Ovambo)
Acting Secretary for Foreign Affairs	Peter Mueshihange (Ovambo)
Acting Secretary for Information and Publicity	Andreas Z. Shipanga (Ovambo)
Secretary for Defence and Transport	Peter Nanyemba (Ovambo)
Assistant Secretary for Defence and Transport	Richard Kapelwa (Herero)
Secretary for Labour	Solomon Mifima (Ovambo)
Assistant Secretary for Labour	Luther Zeire (unknown)
Acting Treasurer	Joseph Ithana (Ovambo)
Secretary for Education and Culture	Nickey Iyambo (Ovambo)
Assistant Secretary for Education and Culture	Ben Amathila (Ovambo)
Secretary for Health and Social Welfare	Dr. Philip Indongo (Ovambo)
Assistant Secretary for Health and Social Welfare	Dr. Libertine Appolus (Nama)
Secretary for Economic and Judicial Affairs	Peter Katjavivi (Herero)
Assistant Secretary for Economic and Judicial Affairs	Ernest Tjirianga (Herero)

Organizing Secretary	Gottfried Geingob (Damara)
Assistant Organizing Secretary	Maxton Joseph (Ovambo)
Youth Inspector	Homateni Kaluenja (Ovambo)
Assistant Youth Director	Alpo Mauno Mbamba (Ovambo)
Director of SWAPO Women's Council	Dr. Libertine Appolus (Nama)
Chairman (Council of SWAPO Elders)	S. S. Kaukungua (Ovambo)
Deputy Chairman (Council of SWAPO Elders)	Jackson Mazazi (unknown)[14]

Where acting appointments were made, this was done in the place of SWAPO members who were either serving prison sentences in South Africa or were still living in Namibia. A noteworthy characteristic of the distribution of posts in SWAPO abroad is that at least two-thirds went to Ovambos, which once more bears out that even outside Ovamboland, SWAPO is a predominantly Ovambo political organization, although it acts on behalf of Namibia as a whole.

The portfolio structure illustrates that SWAPO regards itself as an alternative government for Namibia, and is accordingly keen to gain experience in administrative matters. It is not possible to appraise the effectiveness of the administration, as too little is known about its activities. Because of the lack of opportunity for putting into practice the tasks assigned to these posts, they must be assumed to be largely nominal.

For finance SWAPO-in-exile depends mostly on well-disposed international organizations such as the United Nations, the Organization for African Unity and the World Council of Churches, but it also depends on various African, Arab, Asian, European, Communist and other Western countries.[15] SWAPO is the only Namibian political organization that is officially recognized and supported by the UN and the OAU as the political spokesman for its country.[16]

From SWAPO's actions abroad, it has become clear in recent years that violent action is considered the only means of toppling the white regime in Namibia, and the possibility of bloodshed has been pertinently brought up by SWAPO at the United Nations. In contrast to Toivo's attitude, co-operation with the South African Government is ruled out. Guerrilla warfare must be seen as a military means to the attainment of political ends. According to one SWAPO spokesman, however, the organization must remain primarily a political one, responsible for training cadres in Namibia to work underground and induce the population to take an active part in the struggle.[17] This spokesman, in common with other SWAPO leaders, inveighs against the traditional leaders as puppets of the whites with little or nor influence left over their own people. Nujoma says that tribal loyalties and the traditional leaders no longer constitute a problem for SWAPO.[18].

SWAPO's increasingly militant attitude abroad caused the Executive Council in Ovamboland in June 1972 to address an urgent request to the South African Government to declare SWAPO a forbidden movement in the country. In its request the Council mentioned that this decision had been taken in the light of SWAPO's objectives and the role it had played during the unrest and strike in Ovamboland. This request was repeated early in 1976. In 1972 the following questions were put during the in-depth interviews with members of the various élites in Ovamboland:

Question: WOULD YOU SAY THAT SWAPO SERVES A USEFUL AND IMPORTANT PURPOSE IN THE POLITICAL DEVELOPMENT OF OVAMBOLAND

	T.	*R./L.*	*O./C.*	*Comm.*	*N.*	*Trad.*	*Ov./Av.*
Yes	87.0	70.4	35.7	18.2	85.0	.—	56.4
No	4.3	14.8	57.1	63.6	—	100.0	34.0
Don't know	2.2	3.7	3.6	18.2	—	—	3.2
No reply	6.5	11.1	3.6	—	15.0	—	6.4

Question: SHOULD SWAPO BE PROHIBITED IN OVAMBOLAND?

	T.	*R./L.*	*O./C.*	*Comm.*	*N.*	*Trad.*	*Ov./Av.*
Yes	4.3	11.1	53.6	63.6	—	91.7	31.4
No	87.0	77.8	39.3	18.2	80.0	8.3	59.0
Don't know	2.2	—	3.6	18.2	—	—	2.6
No reply	6.5	11.1	3.6	—	20.0	—	7.0

These replies make it clear that, for a majority, SWAPO is playing a useful and important part in Ovamboland although it is not allowed an active role in the country. In line with this reply, about the same percentage of people oppose a possible ban on SWAPO in Ovamboland. The organization receives its strongest support from the teachers, clergy and nurses, and its opposition from the officials and clerks, merchants and, most of all, traditional leaders.

The answers show that SWAPO is working diligently and is being supported in Ovamboland, but its chances of forming a recognized élite there remain limited. These questions could not be posed in Katutura, but it can probably be taken that support for SWAPO there is stronger and more radical than in Ovamboland. The total opposition to SWAPO among the traditional leaders is attributable to its rejection of the traditional authority and the Legislative Council, and to its attacks on and threats against, the traditional leaders. The latter have attributed the assassination of Chief Elifas to SWAPO. Although SWAPO in Namibia has denied this accusation, the movement outside the country has neither admitted nor repudiated it. Many SWAPO leaders were arrested after the murder and detained for questioning.

Up to the present, the South African Government has made no pronouncement on the possibility of banning SWAPO, no doubt because the SWAPO leaders in Namibia have openly spoken out against the use of violence, and it is better to tolerate a hostile organization than to drive it underground. A third reason may be South Africa's obligation to Dr. Waldheim and the United Nations to give political organizations in

Namibia the opportunity to state their case. The Waldheim report to the Security Council apparently did not come up to the expectations of the SWAPO leaders in Namibia, who had anticipated intervention by the UN against the Ovamboland elections in August 1973 and February 1975, which acted as a spur to further opposition activities inside and outside the territory.

In Ovamboland, SWAPO ignored the ban under Proclamation R17 of 1972, on the holding of public meetings, especially after the refusal of a request it had made to the Ovamboland Government to let it stage protest meetings against the decision to make Ovamboland self-governing. The outcome of this was that 3,000 SWAPO supporters demonstrated at the offices of the Chief Councillor, Chief Elifas. This led in turn to the detention of three SWAPO leaders, among them the head of the organization in Ovamboland, J. Otto,[19] who at that time was a teacher at Oluno. Otto fled from Ovamboland in 1974 and became one of SWAPO's most articulate spokesmen in the outside world. Three new SWAPO leaders in Ovamboland came to the fore in his place: Reuben Hauwanga, Sam Shivute and Skinny Hilundwa, all members of the modernizing élites. Hauwanga has begun medical studies, Shivute is in the service of the Ovambokavango Church, and Hilundwa is a clerk, formerly employed by the Anglican Church.

In 1975, Hilundwa defined SWAPO's policy as being opposed to racism, tribalism and the tribal chieftainship, because all three were barriers in the way of a unitary state of Namibia. But he did not consider SWAPO to be an anti-white organization; it was only in favour of one man one vote. However, SWAPO was opposed to participation in Ovamboland elections, as this would imply recognition of the Homelands policy. The Ovamboland Government would not agree to public meetings being held in protest against the 1975 election in the territory, and a meeting held at Oluno on 5 January 1975 was broken up by the tribal police.[20]

During SWAPO's mounting protests against Ovamboland as a self-governing area and against the homelands concept, its youth movement came to prominence, being actively concerned with protest demonstrations that took place in 1973 in Ovamboland and in the south. This youth movement begged the Ovamboland people to boycott the coming election, and criticised the traditional leaders and their anti-SWAPO activities. The traditional leaders were also warned that some day, when Namibia had a free government, they would "need God's help as things would go hard with them";[21] they were dubbed "Black Boers" because of their collaboration with the South African regime. The "Boer" government was termed a second Satan and anti-Christian.[22] All blacks were asked to unite, to speak with one voice, to break the laws of the "Boers" and to become more politically conscious.[23] Opposition was expressed to the traditionalist Ovamboland Independent Party, which was not acknowledged as a valid mouthpiece of the Ovambo people.[24] But the chief complaints and demands appeared in the form of a pamphlet which is reproduced here unedited:

Alas for us! Oppression! Perplexity and distress have devoured us. Horror and murder of our people in Namibia by the South African Government and its police troops have come to an intolerable point.

1. We, the oppressed people of Namibia make worship to our God in our trouble; and an urgent appeal to the whole world by means of a national labour strike from Monday, August 20th, 73. Namibia must be liberated!

2. The political prisoners of Namibia who are locked up in our prisons must be set free immediately.

3. We must have freedom of speech in our country.

4. Freedom of movement is not conceded to the black people. The pass system is indescribably oppressive. In our country people are not paid according to the nature of work, qualification or experiences. On the contrary they are paid according to their colour and race.

5. The migratory labour system through which people are brought degrades humanity and is necessarily an evil!

6. The homelands policy in Namibia must be ended at once. Namibia is one country.

7. We are sick and tired of *FM transmissions* which disseminate deceitful propaganda which is aimed at making homelands matters look attractive.

8. The discriminating educational system is preventing the natural academic and cultural development of our people.

9. The sorts of small houses met with in locations are humiliating for anybody.

10. BIC is the organization that works for nothing else but to disrupt the economy of a black man.

11. The treatment of the black patients in state hospitals in unsatisfactory.

12. The propagation of the Gospel among our people has been considerably hampered by the government:
   (*a*) missionaries are expelled from the country,
   (*b*) free sermon is obstructed.

13. Generally speaking the South African Government is nothing less than a big liar: the so-called concessions that it has made to UNO have never materialised. In north Namibia the emergency regulations are still in force and mass of arrests is the order of the day. People are still always being manhandled by the illegal police.

Wake up, oh the people of Namibia! Let us stand and work together. Unity will bring us to victory. We all know UNION IS STRENGTH! Show your freedom-fighting existence with this strike.[25]

The SWAPO youth movement showed by its actions that the party's younger members were becoming dissatisfied with the more moderate activities of the older members. It demanded more radical and militant exploits—in which it was supported by SWAPO abroad.

Since more young people joined the central committee of SWAPO, the senior party members identified themselves, from 1974 onwards, more and more with the activities of the party's youth organization. Junior SWAPO members were encouraged to educate the blacks politically and, to make them feel proud of being black and move away from tribal thinking and a sense of inferiority. It seems that increasingly hopes for change were being pinned on the younger generation. It was reckoned that the young were in the majority, that they were more adaptable to altered circumstances, that they would make decisions which would point the way for the rest of the population, and that they were the backbone of the country's economy. At the same time they were warned not to indulge in violence, but to seek a peaceful solution. In 1975 participation, on a purely ethnic basis, in a joint constitutional conference on Namibia's political future, was rejected.

Moreover various conditions were laid down for participation in any constitutional talks: (*a*) all political prisoners in the area and on Robben Island, including Herman ja Toivo, were to be freed; (*b*) all Namibians living in exile in foreign countries were to be allowed to return without any fear of prosecution and victimization; (*c*) South Africa must withdraw its armed forces and police from Namibia and Proclamation R17 must be repealed; (*d*) SWAPO was to have the opportunity of showing the strength of its following in Namibia; (*e*) any election and joint talks were to be held under the supervision and control of the United Nations; (*f*) a constitutional conference must be held outside Namibia in Lusaka or New York—however, SWAPO would not take part in any discussions arranged on ethnic lines; (*g*) South Africa must publicly accept the right of Namibia's inhabitants to independence; (*h*) South Africa must announce that Namibia's territorial integrity was absolute and not negotiable; (*i*) the restriction order on SWAPO's acting president, Maxuiriri, was to be rescinded;[26] (*j*) South Africa must accept the historical fact that SWAPO is the sole authentic representative of the Namibian people.

The activities of the SWAPO youth movement led to action being taken against the organization and the arrest of many of its supporters and leaders, including pupils, students, other members of the modernizing élites and nurses.[27] Various young leading lights in SWAPO, such as the chairman of the SWAPO Youth League Jeremia Ekandjo, its secretary and temporary acting chairman E. Taapopi, and J. Kashea, were sentenced to terms of imprisonment in 1974 for instigating violence. The political operations of SWAPO inside and outside Namibia disproved an official point of view that the Ovambos were one of the least politically aware groups in Africa.[28]

Just before the first sitting of the Windhoek Constitutional Conference in September 1975, SWAPO issued a discussion paper containing constitutional proposals for Namibia's future.[29] It was clearly stated that the document's contents were proposals only, as the people of Namibia would have to decide for themselves. In the preamble to the proposals it was stressed that Namibia had special problems of history, geography and economic development and that these must be taken into account. Interim measures should include elections for a constituent assembly under international supervision. At this constituent assembly the freely elected representatives of the people would agree on a constitution. When that constitution was accepted, free elections for a Namibian government would be held under it.

The executive authority would be a president, directly elected by the people for five years and assisted by a cabinet of ministers from the Legislature. For the latter a single chamber would be entirely adequate. However, the people might wish to have a House of Chiefs, without legislative power, as a second chamber. SWAPO suggested a directly-elected legislature of 100 members, elected for five years by a simple majority vote in 100 constituencies all with approximately equal numbers of voters. SWAPO rejected as inappropriate to Namibian conditions any system of proportional representation; it believed that protection for minorities should be achieved by other constitutional means. All those born in Namibia, or resident there for five years prior to independence, should be entitled to citizenship, and all Namibians over the age of eighteen should have the vote.

The National Assembly would have sole law-making power and control of public expenditure. There would be an independent state auditor.

The principle of an independent judiciary could be guaranteed by the appointment of a Judicial Commission and by security of judicial tenure. There would be both central and customary courts. To avoid the undesirable consequences of perpetuating South African Roman-Dutch based law, a high-powered legal commission with international representation would be appointed to advise on the adoption of a completely new legal system.

Acquired legal rights, including pension rights, would be maintained both in the event of the adoption of a new legal system and on the handover of sovereignty at independence. The attorney-general should be a political appointee, but the public prosecutor would be wholly non-political. A Constitutional Court would be established as the final arbiter and guardian of the Constitution. To it would be referred all human rights and other constitutional issues. The judges of this court would be subject to a special appointment procedure and would have a minimum tenure of ten years.

A Public Service Commission would be appointed to superintend appointments, conditions of service, etc., in the various areas of the public service, to ensure, as nearly as possible, impartiality and efficiency.

SWAPO expressed itself in favour of a rational system of local government while being totally opposed to any national "regionalism" based exclusively upon tribal affiliations.

A comprehensive bill of rights was proposed closely following the two United Nations Covenants of 1966 on Human Rights. This would be fully enforceable against the executive and the rest of the state administration at the instance of the citizen, and would take priority over the terms of the constituion. There would be comprehensive and effective anti-discrimination legislation. The evil of racialism in all its forms would be eradicated. SWAPO would advance for consideration the appointment of a minister whose portfolio would include responsibility for the furtherance of human rights in the country. It also advanced various possibilities of judicial appeal in matters of human rights to external or international organs. It also proposed the appointment of a Complaints Commissioner, (Ombudsman) whose sole function would be the investigation and resolution of complaints of unfair administration in any area of the public service.

SWAPO would favour—and would put forward for public consideration—the idea of an independent Namibia rejoining the Commonwealth. Sovereignty in Namibia would remain with the people. They would be the final protectors of their liberty and receive education in the schools in the nature and meaning of their constitution.

Education would be free and compulsory. English would be recognized as the official language. Health services would be free.

The paper left it to the future government to decide if its economic policy would be socialist or capitalist. In the original draft, SWAPO proposed socialist policies within the context of their applicability to Namibia. No mention was made of land nationalization, but SWAPO believed that agricultural areas could be most fruitfully utilized through state contributions, including the building of dams and subsidizing farmers in equipment and fertilizers. Farming co-operatives were favoured. The original draft mentioned state participation in major areas of production (presumably mining), without saying whether or not the state interest would be a controlling one.

The revised draft envisaged that the South African enclave of Walvis Bay would be included in the inviolate territory of Namibia. Relations with South Africa would be diplomatically correct.

On the anti-White attitude which exists today and will probably continue to do so after independence, SWAPO had the following to say:

An aspect of apartheid-colonialism is that we have been ruled, often with great viciousness, by a white minority group. There is a danger that memories may be too long. Just as some whites will be unable to accept black majority rule, so also some blacks will be unable to accept the good faith of those whites who sincerely want to work for the democratic non-racial state of Namibia. Our Constitution must achieve the reconciliation of all Namibians of goodwill, providing effectively for their reasonable fears, as well as for their fulfilment, within the needs of the whole society. Those who did not wish to assume Namibian nationality would, as in any other state, be aliens. They would not enjoy the full privileges of citizenship. But this, of course, would not mean that all aliens would be required to leave. They would have rights of residence in compliance with the aliens' law. Nationality is a complex matter and detailed laws would be enacted on the subject. These laws would operate within the constitutional framework and without discrimination on grounds of colour, creed, race or sex.

The discussion paper on the constitution of an independent Namibia concluded as follows: "Whatever the guarantee, in the end freedom depends upon those who wish to enjoy it. Namibia will be as free as Namibians want it to be."

SWAPO's constitutional proposals are clearly opposed to any division of Namibia into, for instance, independent homelands for the various population groups, although the existence of minority groups is recognized. But cultural diversity must be accompanied by political and administrative unity. The principle of one man one vote stresses this view.

The influence of the constitutions of Britian, the United States, West Germany, Sweden and certain African states—Tanzania, Zambia and Botswana—is discernible. The insistence on a constitutional court elevates the judicial power as a guarantor of the individual's rights against prejudice and discrimination. The eventual creation of a second chamber for traditional leaders is a conciliatory gesture to those leaders in an endeavour to obain their support, although their role is to be advisory only. The idea of a welfare state receives considerable support in the constitutional proposals.

The strong trend towards non-alignment is common to most developing countries. On the one hand, the special emphasis on the role of the United Nations can be interpreted as a recognition of the world body's contribution to the independence process in Namibia and, on the other hand, as a way of ordering South Africa to withdraw from the country, and abandon its supervision of the country's social, economic and political development. This antagonism is also shown in the rejection of Roman-Dutch law as the country's future legal system. The acceptance of English as the official language can be seen in the same light—in fact, the majority of Namibians use Afrikaans as the *lingua franca*. Relations with South Africa would be reserved and diplomatically correct.

In the economic sphere, as already mentioned, a socialist form of development programme is clearly indicated. The aim appears to be a mixed economy with the state possibly as a controlling and regulating supervisor. The South African enclave of Walvis Bay, the most important trading port in Namibia, is regarded as an integral part of Namibia. The possibility of membership of the Commonwealth is an indication of a close relationship with Britian in particular, and with the West in general. At the same time solidarity is professed with all African states by way of active participation in the OAU.

These substantive proposals by SWAPO must be seen in the light of SWAPO's claim to be the representative and lawful political spokesman of the whole population of Namibia. SWAPO's proposals are clearly aimed at dialogue, and at removing the impression that it is a predominantly radical and militant organization. In its proposals there is room even for the Whites in Namibia. However, these proposals make it clear that SWAPO sees Namibia's future solely in terms of rule by its own leaders. As it has consistently refused to take part in an election within a homelands framework and would only do so on a national basis, it is still incumbent upon SWAPO to prove its strength and support. Nevertheless it can be accepted as having more followers than any other political party in Namibia.

While increasing its military activities on the northern border and inside Ovamboland, SWAPO has rejected any possibility of participating in the Turnhalle Constitutional Conference. However, Sam Nujoma, its president, was prepared to attend a conference with the South African Government under UN auspices on neutral ground. He insisted, however, that such talks should be preceded by the release of all political prisoners and a South African commitment to withdraw her armed forces from Namibia.[30] SWAPO was willing to accept members of the Turnhalle Constitutional Conference as members of the South African delegation to the proposed conference.

When the plans for the three-tier government, which the Constitutional Conference accepted, became known, SWAPO rejected them outright. It accused the Constitutional Conference as being a 'puppet meeting', and said that nothing emanating from it could be supported as long as the people of Namibia were not included when changes were determined. SWAPO repeated its claim to be the sole legitimate and authentic representative of the people of Namibia, and emphasised that world and especially African opinion was waiting for South Africa to comply with UN Security Council resolutions proposing free elections under UN supervision and control.

According to SWAPO, the "so-called independence" decided on by the

Constitutional Conference is "illegal, undemocratic, racist and colonialist". It further claims that "the Namibia envisaged by Turnhalle will in no sense be sovereign or independent".[31] At a conference held in March 1977 at Windhoek, SWAPO resolved "that the world should take note of the following, which constitutes a collective threat to world peace and a gross violation of human rights: the Turnhalle Constitutional Conference and the proposed interim government; the application of Proclamation R17 in northern Namibia; the Terrorism Act; perpetuation of atrocities in Namibia, and aggression against neighbouring African countries."[32] SWAPO announced that it would "redouble its efforts to recover Namibia for the Namibian people, to bring about a speedy withdrawal of the South African occupation regime from our country, in view of the new and greater danger posed by the 'interim government' proposals that have been produced by the Turnhalle conspiracy."[33] This announcement must be seen against the background of several recent visits by SWAPO's president to the Soviet Union and Cuba, and prolonged discussions with the heads of government of Tanzania, Zambia, Angola, Mozambique, and Botswana, and of other African states that have assured SWAPO of their support in their struggle to liberate Namibia. According to SWAPO, these countries are now satisfied that the alternative, peaceful solution is out, and that these governments have now become committed to aid SWAPO in an intensifying warfare.

Although aware of not insignificant losses suffered at the hands of South African Security Forces, SWAPO is convinced that its military force can never be beaten. It feels the strategic balance to be in its favour because of the attitude and assistance of the "front line states" particularly Angola, where SWAPO and the MPLA have joined forces. SWAPO, however, denied that it would impose a revolutionary military dictatorship if it were ever to come to power in Namibia. One of its spokesmen emphasized that SWAPO was still essentially a political movement and that the People's Liberation Army of Namibia would simply fall away and leave the stage to civilian leaders at the conclusion of the armed struggle.

Concurrently SWAPO had to overcome another problem: disunity and divisions within its external wing, especially in Zambia. It appeared that a leadership struggle had developed between Andreas Shipanga, one of SWAPO's co-founders, and a former member of the Executive Committee, and Sam Nujoma. Shipanga and his followers who belonged mainly to the youth wing, accused SWAPO's political and military leadership of corruption and tribalism, and of withholding arms and medicines from its guerilla fighters. They also called for new leadership elections, which in 1976 were more than two years overdue.

The accusations were repudiated by Nujoma and the call for elections was refused. Nujoma, in turn, accused Shipanga and his followers of collaborating with the South African Government through some Western European governments. The Zambian Government then arrested Shipanga and his followers at Nujoma's request without their being given the opportunity to defend themselves, although Nujoma promised that they would stand trial in a court-martial set up by SWAPO. After being detained for some months at Nampofu in Zambia, Shipanga and his ten closest followers were transferred to the Ukongo Prison in Tanzania where they continued to be held in custody.[35]

Early in 1977 Sam Nujoma extended an invitation to "those Namibians inside Namibia who have either been misled or bribed, to resign from the Constitutional Conference, renounce their treacherous activities and genuinely join in the struggle for the liberation of Namibia. They can then work as individual citizens, either joining SWAPO or working within the framework of the SWAPO policy. Then they will be acceptable at a conference between South Africa and SWAPO on the Namibian side. But time is running out. Later they will be treated as traitors and punished. ... The struggle is demanding sacrifices. We are not interested in those groups who play along with Mr. Vorster and also pay lip-service to our ideals and struggle."[36]

When asked about Communist and Soviet influence, Nujoma was adamant that SWAPO did not belong to any bloc. "We do receive large donations from Soviet Russia and the Nordic states. But that does not mean that we automatically follow their foreign and international policies. We are an African party, which believes in neutrality and non-alignment."[37]

It is doubtful whether Namibia's ultimate constitutional and political order could be determined, let alone be applied, without SWAPO's support. To ignore SWAPO would be to bring confrontation closer.

3. DEMCOP

In 1970 Johannes Jefta Nangutuuala founded a party—at first called the Democratic Co-operation of Developments, and later the Democratic Co-operative Development Party (DEMCOP). Nangutuuala was born about 1930 and is an active member of the Ovambokavango Church. He qualified and then practised as a teacher, later becoming a clerk of the court at Ondangwa. In 1971 he had to give up his clerkship, as well as teaching, because of his political activities. After this he was employed for a time as a clerk by the Ovambokavango Church before devoting himself to full-time party work from 1973 onwards. Nangutuuala, is a man with a strong personality, eloquent and a demagogue, who recognizes SWAPO as the father of his party.

DEMCOP has a detailed party programme. Its preamble states that a government's task is to develop a people, especially in the political sphere; if the people are politically backward, they will have a hard time when they ultimately have to rule themselves. There must be political parties for this purpose to help the government carry out its functions in accordance with the will of the people. Nangutuuala regards a political party as a check on a government: "Under a democracy every member of the people has a say in the affairs of its government, which is only possible if there is a political party."[38] It is DEMCOP's task in the development process to ensure co-operation and contact between government and people.

In the programme is contained a promise that DEMCOP will co-operate with the South African Government in whatever way will promote the prosperity and development of the people. It will work with the South

African police in the task of maintaining law and order, on condition that the police do not overstep their limits but act according to the people's wishes. Co-operation is also offered to headmen and chiefs, provided they believe in development and do not hinder progress. Nangutuuala declares in the programme that chiefs should not become ministers by virtue of their hereditary office; the office of chief is an honorary one, not a "hard-working governing office". Hence the chiefs must not be allowed to take part in the process of government, although he proposes that one of them should became president of the country. In another article of the programme, thanks are expressed for the help given by the Churches in the development of the country; he promises that their great work will never be forgotten by the people. However, this work will also be needed in the future.

We still need their advice and help today, so that we can attain the right progress. This party expresses its good hope to these Missions for good co-operation between them and the government of the people to build up the people in its development task. Every one among the people tries to obstruct the work of the Mission is going to call down upon himself the curse of God and the people. The Mission is the hounds of God who bark in the darkness to the heathendom, and they frighten the beasts and enemies of progress in these non-white lands.[39]

The programme also thanks the business fraternity, who are regarded as the source of the people's wealth and as examples of how to combat poverty. They assured them of the Party's help in their task of development.

Thirdly, the teachers are praised for their efforts, which, despite their wretched salaries, are "the foundation of the people's progress"[40]; ignorance, in the programme's words, is the mother of all the weakness of development. It is therefore the Party's duty to encourage learning.

Fourthly, thanks are accorded to the workers—mostly the contract labourers, who have been "the mothers of all the people's riches and welfare from the time of the Germans up to the present day". They are assured that the many difficulties they experienced during their period of contract labour will be watched over by the Party. "If the people forget them, then the people forget themselves." Indirectly, the programme sounds a note of caution on the exploitation of contract labourers: "They must not only be the makers of wealth for the bosses but also for the people."[41]

In welcoming other parties in Ovamboland, DEMCOP affirms that the purpose of political parties in a country is not to fight one another, but to develop every facet of the land for the sake of progress. Co-operation with Africa, with other countries of the world and with the UN will be gladly accepted if it contributes to peace and progress. South Africa and the United Nations are asked to make known their honest and ultimate intentions to the people, because "we no longer want to be a topic of discussion for the world without there being any end to it".[42]

DEMCOP makes a request, against this background, for the franchise to be granted to the people in order to remove any obstructions in the way of development. The programme mentions that people in a democracy have the right to free expression of opinion including criticism of the government. The police are admonished not to dispute this right; if they do so, then they dispute the progress of the people, and will arouse animosity towards themselves.There must be general harmony, because this is viewed as the key to the nation's advancement.

In another article, the Party dissociates itself from the policy of separate development and refuses to assume any attitude in favour of or against it. The South African Government is reminded not to compel the inhabitants of Namibia to adopt the policy, which is blamed for generating hatred and contempt for the non-white, and such evils as salary differences between people of different races with the same qualifications. Reference is also made to the daily humiliation sufferred by non-whites; this breeds hatred, which does not help development.

The Party is opposed to Communism, but the government is warned not to brand anyone who criticises it as a Communist. The people only wish their voices to be heard—to advise the government. In the field of economics, communal ownership must be replaced by private ownership, but there is a warning that if the wealth of the whites is increased at the expense of the non-whites, Communistic tendencies will appear among the poor. "It means there must be wealth for everyone, which is true communism."[43] Wealth must be divided equally between white and non-white, and properly balanced every national group.

The party programme urges caution over suspecting anyone of being a terrorist, but it expresses disgust at terrorists who come to shed blood. These the people will deal with on their own—therefore the South African Government must arm the populace and not fight the terrorists itself. The police are not to become terrorists: "If they bully such people as women, children and innocent old folk, who have nothing to do with terrorism, then they are transformed by their deeds into terrorists. The maltreatment resorted to by terrorists is the same as that applied by others to the people."[44] The Ovambos are tired of a state of affairs where a person who justifiably rebukes those in power is accused of terrorism and finds proceedings taken against him.

An appeal is made to the South African Government to allow non-whites "to grow politically", so that they do not lag behind the other non-whites of Africa: "If the non-whites of South Africa continue to be childlike and unsound in their politics, then South Africa will stand disgraced among her fellow-leaders of the world."[45] Progress can only come if there is co-operation between the South African regime and the people. Things must not be given to the inhabitants that they do not understand and then reject: "If the people do not realize the value of a certain thing, which they recieve from the South African Government, the latter must wait until the people do realize its benefit. But if the government just says, 'take it, take it' the people will no longer be able to rely on that benefit, and such a present from the government is then merely thrown down the drain."[46]

Lastly, the programme asserts that the Party will deplore any steps taken by the South African Government to stir up bad feeling, such as taking action against DEMCOP without sufficient reasons. If the Party should make a mistake, the people will correct it. But those who defame the Party will be brought before the court and fined. The programme concludes: "Friendship, peace and honest co-operation in developing the nation is all that is necessary. This is what our Party expects from working together democratically."[47]

The structure of the Party's organization is set out in the last section of the programme. It proposes the appointment of advisers on finance, "people's affairs", labour, education, "wealth", justice, agriculture, water, transport, defence and police, foreign affairs and church affairs.[48] These will be expected to supervise progress in their respective tribal areas and notify the party of what is required for development. The party will then make requests from the government. The Party programme closes with this observation:

This party will begin its work in the footsteps of the said principles trusting the God of Israel who will lead every people as He Himself wishes. May this God himself open the doors and all the roads for the advantage of the party to work for His people. May His Will be done by this party and may He give us our daily bread. Amen.[49]

While care was clearly taken in the programme's formulation, it equally reveals the deeply felt needs and distress of Ovamboland's popul..tion. Behind many of the ideas the real thinking of the mass of the people lies hidden, which is not reflected by the Legislative Council in its debates. Nangutuuala is thoroughly acquainted with the basic principles of democracy, which, he says, are not being implemented in Ovamboland. That the nation still has a long way to go is continually admitted by the emphasis he places on development. He rightly sees a party as one of the most important instruments in accomplishing this development. His criticism of the traditional power structure, though carefully worded, is obvious; in his view, chiefs and headmen are the custodians of tradition, not political representatives or persons of authority.

The party programme also illustrates the strong ambivalence of Nangutuuala's attitude. On the one hand he supports the maxim of a unitary state in Namibia, but on the other hand he applies his arguments to the example of Ovamboland and how this part of Namibia should develop. Often, when he refers to Namibia, he actually means Ovamboland.

The stress laid on the role of the churches in developing Ovamboland, in the concluding paragraph of his party programme, reflects their influence on Nangutuuala himself. This can also be interpreted as tactics, because he realizes that his party can make no headway in Ovamboland without the support of the churches, particularly the Ovambokavango Church.

The various modernizing forces that have a role in Ovamboland's development receive clear recognition in the party programme. He mentions the traders, teachers and clergy, but does not directly allude to officials and the medical profession. The function of the contract workers in developing Ovamboland economically is emphasized, confirming the country's dependence on their incomes.

The South African Government is frequently criticized, e.g. over its plans for separate political development of Ovamboland and over the need for it to work in concert with the people and not solely the traditional leaders. Implicit here is the objection that the South African Government either is not conversant with the thinking of the people, or intentionally disregards it. The success of separate development must therefore depend on the harmonious working together of the South African Government and the entire population of Ovamboland. The nation's wants are frankly postulated: freedom of movement, higher salaries, and the right to criticize. The programme regards police behaviour and the casting of suspicion as the greatest impediments to such progress. If the people are understood and trusted, the South African Government need never fear terrorists, because the people will deal with them. Terrorism is a danger only when it can rely on hatred within the nation, and obviate hatred there must be mutual respect which will depend on the actions of the whites and the degree of respect they accord the people. This can be achieved through DEMCOP.

Development priorities emerge in the type of advisers who would be appointed to the several tribal areas. As matters stand at present, Ovamboland does not yet have all these departments in its central government, but Nangutuuala realizes they are necessary for the full evolution of a democracy. He believes that these must be present in every tribal area, central interest not being sufficiently represented at the local level. Although the programme is unequivocally opposed to separate development, there is the implication that it will be acceptable if the stipulated conditions are met.

Since 1970 Nangutuuala has been trying to have his party recognized, but without success. This could be because DEMCOP does not represent traditional interests and because its programme attacks separate development. Another factor could be the alleged personal antagonism between the Commissioner-General, J. de Wet, and Nangutuuala, who put his signature to several letters of protest. One of these, signed by himself and a number of teachers and officials, was sent to the former Chief Councillor, U. Shiimi, after the latter's unfavourable comment on the judgment of the International Court of Justice in 1971. Nangutuuala was also jointly responsible for drawing up and signing a memorandum to Dr. Escher when he visited Ovamboland in 1972. In this protest, Nangutuuala and members of SWAPO objected to the principle of homelands in Namibia. However, Nangutuuala made more of a name for himself as leader of the strikers' committee. He declared his absolute willingness to take part in the 1973 election, though stating bluntly that he would use the Legislative Council to express his distaste for separate development. He also declared that he was ready to work with SWAPO for the attainment of wider common objectives.[50] One of his objectives with which SWAPO did not agree was a united Ovamboland as part of either Namibia or Angola.[51] Nangutuuala contended that in either case the districts of Tsumeb and Grootfontein should be added to present-day Ovamboland.[52]

He claimed that his party was particularly well supported by the more educated people, such as clergymen and teachers. He believed that the government dare not let these people come to power because South Africa would then be unable to carry on with its Homelands policy in Ovamboland. Nangutuuala looks on Ovamboland's present rulers as innocents, who are being led astray in politics.[53] He also thinks the population would repudiate the policy of the present government were a democratic election to be held.[54] He called the August 1973 election a farce, and warned the South African Government that the time had come when weapons could no longer be used to keep a minority in power.[55] This warning was mostly directed at the traditional regime. There was no constitutional government in Ovamboland, he alleged; a minority was ruling while a majority suffered. But Nangutuuala rejected the use of violence and terrorism and declared himself in favour of dialogue and co-operation with the whites. He ascribed the dissatisfaction of the Ovambos not only to the apartheid policy, but also to the behaviour of the ordinary whites in their daily contacts and dealings with blacks.

Nangutuuala expressed the following thoughts when he was interviewed by the present writer in June 1972 and July 1975. In his current political philosophy he supported the concept of an independent unitary state of Namibia. While he saw the Legislative Council of Ovamboland as a modernizing agent for the system of traditional government, he was dissatisfied with it: in his belief, it was not working in the interests of the Ovambos, but for personal gain. It was too passive in its actions, and up till then it had carried out no reforms. It had been constituted against the will of the people, and many of its members had been nominated to suit the wishes of white officials. Nangutuuala was convinced that the South African Government was using the Legislative Council to force acceptance of the Homelands policy on the people, and he regretted that the members of the Legislative Council had not been elected on a party political basis. Separate development was the cause of dissension in Ovamboland and Namibia, its purpose being to save the day for the whites.

Nangutuuala viewed the current political development as being on the whole advantageous to the whites only and tending to uphold apartheid. In the process the Ovambos are denied their human rights and the freedom to express their own opinions. For him the traditional tribal authority was despotic and undemocratic, as the traditionalists and the Legislative Council did not heed the will of the people, who had not been consulted when it was constituted. Lastly, he again asserts that the will of the people must be the basis of the country's government.

In spite of occasional emotional political outbursts, Nangutuuala at the time of our investigations was the most important political leader in Ovamboland, wielding the most influence because of the restrictions on SWAPO. At that time he had a big following throughout Ovamboland, which was prepared to endorse his leadership. Had it been allowed to do so, DEMCOP could have contributed to the political development and modernization of the country. To have recognized the party would have been better than rejecting it, because DEMCOP did not show the same extremism as SWAPO. In their actions against the Ovamboland and South African Governments, Nangutuuala and his party, unlike SWAPO, preferred peaceful resistance to the use of violence, and legitimate political participation above everything. This is still not allowed, formal opposition being expressed in the refusal of the Ovamboland Government to recognize DEMCOP. Nangutuuala was thus deprived of the right to nominate candidates on behalf of his party to the Legislative Council, and thus he and his party have been prevented from assisting effectively in the forming of a functionally viable political élite.

Nangutuuala and his party took no part in the election for the third Legislative Council in January 1975. At a mass meeting in November 1974, for which he made use of the Chief Minister, Chief Elifas, as chairman, apparently on a wrong pretext, he attacked the Ovamboland Government and rejected the January 1975 election. The influence of Nangutuuala and his party declined after reaching its height during the strikes of 1971 and 1972. He again came temporarily into prominence in 1973 when, after he had allegedly insulted the traditional tribal authority, the Ndonga tribal court administered corporal punishment (20 strokes) upon him which led to an interdict against the tribal court by the Supreme Court in Windhoek.

When Nangutuuala said in 1975 that SWAPO should not regard itself as the only voice of the people, he lost much of his support. Yet he and his party declared themselves ready in February 1975 to join with SWAPO and other parties in becoming part of the newly founded Namibia National Convention (NNC), and together with these organizations he was doing his utmost to strive for a single Namibian state. When a vacancy arose in the Kwanyama constituency, Nangutuuala made himself available as a candidate for the Legislative Council at a by-election in July 1975. This aroused strong opposition—especially from SWAPO, which branded him as a traitor. He viewed his candidature and election as a possible means of opposition in the Legislative Council—a view which SWAPO did not accept. Consequently DEMCOP ceased to be a member of the NNC. He was duly elected to the Council, which he thought implied recognition for himself and his party.

4. *Ovamboland Independent Party*

The Ovamboland Independent Party (OIP) was founded on 10 May 1973, with the then Chief Minister, Chief F. Elifas, as its leader. The immediate purpose was to enable it to participate in the then imminent election which took place in August 1973. Most of the committee members were members of the first Legislative Council and supported the traditional authority. Having received the required official recognition from the Ovamboland Government, the OIP thereafter became the only party that could lawfully take part in elections. However, it is worth mentioning that no members of the OIP's head committee made themselves eligible as candidates for election by the people. They were all nominated and thus automatically became members of the Second Legislative Council.

The constitution of the OIP states the character and aims of the Party as follows in its preamble:

(i) The Party:
    (*a*) acknowledges the Supremacy of God and liberty of conscience and religion for every individual;
    (*b*) strives for the development of our national life and, by respecting all

beneficial traditional laws and customs, will preserve and extend the democratic system of government;

(c) recognises that undivided loyalty and devotion to Ovamboland, mutual trust, common objectives and unity for the citizens of Ovamboland are essential pre-requisites for development, and proposes to realise these aims with the motto 'OVAMBOLAND FIRST':

(d) guarantees the just and equitable treatment of all sections of Ovamboland and the impartial maintenance of the rights and privileges of every section of the Ovambo population.

(ii) With the above-mentioned aims the Party wishes to unite for political co-operation all those Ovamboland citizens who are prepared to subscribe to its aims and principles and accept in good faith the obligations connected therewith, on the understanding that nobody may become a member of the Party, who is not willing under all circumstances to put the interests of Ovamboland first.[56]

Membership is open to all Ovamboland citizens of 18 years and older. The organizational structure of the OIP consists of a national council, an executive council, regional councils and members, and the duties and composition of each are defined at length. Special provision is made for youth affairs in that national youth societies can be founded, and a youth leader is a member of the executive council of the Party.

In its programme of principles its primary object is stated as political development, in the following terms:

The Party strives to develop a Democratic System of Government with due consideration of the position of the traditional leaders, viz. the Chiefs, Senior-Headmen, Headmen and Sub-Headmen. The traditional system will be retained, but it will be adapted and modified in order to meet the needs of a modern society.[57]

The Party programme guarantees freedom of religion and respect for the conscience of every individual. The party also realizes that Ovamboland must be developed economically so that it can form the basis of economic stability and growing welfare for the Ovamboland nation.

In the field of education, preference is given to the development of a sound, suitable and acceptable system; free and compulsory education is considered essential. Stress is laid on the award of bursaries, decent salaries and better conditions of service for teachers. The Party likewise aims at introducing more teaching and training amenities.

To promote social welfare, the Party promises higher old-age pensions, accommodation for and training of the physically handicapped, the establishment of more clinics and more training facilities for nurses, the training of Ovambo doctors and more social workers, the laying out of sports fields and the building of community halls.

An effort will be made to replace all non-Ovambos in government service by suitable Ovambo citizens as soon as possible, while the general improvement of salaries and employment conditions for state officials is another objective. Housing for these officials will be provided, with due regard to their rank and status.

In another point included in its programme, the Party states that it is aware of the great hardships suffered because of certain restrictive measures. It will do all in its power to facilitate the movement of persons from Ovamboland to the south, eliminate long procedural delays and do away with all unnecessary documents.

Where work opportunities and working conditions are concerned, the Party's goal is to increase the former and to give preference to Ovamboland citizens when providing jobs. The Party will do its best to negotiate with the relevant employers to end discrimination against Ovambos, to increase earnings and improve working conditions, and to create healthy relations between employer and employee. These benefits along with improved housing, are also guaranteed to Ovambo citizens employed outside Ovamboland, existing links with whom will be strengthened.

In the matter of liaison and relations with nations and bodies outside Ovamboland, the Party is determined, where Namibia is concerned, to co-operate and consult with all national groups on matters of common interest. South African assistance will be accepted, and the existing cordial relations further extended. The same attitude will be maintained with regard to the international community and international organizations.

The Party also intends to establish properly planned towns in every tribal area, provide sites for schools, churches, recreational amenities, commercial and industrial centres and plots where individuals can build houses according to their means; and to construct roads, lay on water, improve and expand means of communication and traffic systems and build a rail connection with the south.

Lastly, the Party programme gives the assurance that if any individual or organization should threaten the security of Ovamboland or disturb the peace, appropriate proceedings will be taken. It also contemplates the training of Ovambo police gradually to take over the functions of the South African police.[58]

The OIP was active in nominating candidates for the Ovamboland election in August 1973, as the only party legally empowered to do so. It nominated three candidates in each of the seven tribal areas (equal constituencies). In five of these there was no opposition and the candidates were elected without a contest, but in the Kwambi tribal area the OIP was opposed by an independent who won the seat. In the Kwanyama tribal area the three OIP candidates were opposed by four independents, and all three OIP candidates were defeated. The OIP's efforts to wage an active electoral campaign in the urban areas outside Ovamboland miscarried from the start because of resistance from SWAPO and DEMCOP.[59]

The low percentage poll during the election indicated that the OIP was rejected by most of the population. There were several reasons for this. It was considered a traditional party, working for the continuance of the traditional authority and status structure, an aim largely discredited by the forces of modernization. It was also made clear that the committee members of the party mostly came from the nominated first Legislative Council or from among its sympathizers. Another strong objection was that the OIP championed an exclusive nationalism confined only to Ovamboland, and frowned on the unity concept of a single Namibia. There was dissatisfaction that only this party was allowed, to the exclusion of DEMCOP. It was claimed that the OIP had been founded deliberately with the support of the white authority and had thereby obtained immediate recognition, and it was pointed out too that the last clause in the OIP's programme could result in a perpetual ban on any party which opposed the current power structure. These complaints had more potency than the benefits and promises proposed in the programmes.

Viewed as a whole, the party had not demonstrated its strength in the political development of Ovamboland, neither was it prepared to nominate official candidates for the election of the Third Legislative Council in 1975. Some of its members did stand without the official support of the Party but most were defeated. The OIP showed its awareness of how little popular support it enjoyed by its unwillingness to take part in the election. The risk of total defeat was too great, and this would certainly have happened.

Hostility from the modernizing élites and the great majority of the people has hitherto prevented the OIP from building up a recognized and effective political élite. It clearly has the confidence of only a minority of the inhabitants. While it could seek support on the basis of its programme, which possesses some very real virtues, it meets with opposition because of its insistence on the retention of the traditional system, and its alleged dependence on white protection.

5. Conclusions

The three parties we have discussed all have distinctive traits. The Ovamboland Independent Party represents a solid Ovamboland-oriented point of view. It has a definite programme geared for development and with its ideas clearly expounded. In contrast to the other parties, its programme consists not of a list of complaints and anti-white grievances, but of suggestions for improving an existing states of affairs. Alternatives are propounded which can aid and expedite the modernization process. Because as a party it has not been prepared to adjust itself to the popular antagonism towards the traditional authority, its impact must remain limited, its survival and the implementation of its programme depending on the South African Government.

In the centre stands the Democratic Co-operative Development Party. Although a gradual radicalization is noticeable in its outlook, its recognition in Ovamboland might have made an important contribution to political development and the formation of a political élite. Political frustration might then have been channelled through an essentially Ovamboland-oriented party. If this party had been permitted, other existing non-political institutions which became politically involved would probably not have felt the compulsion to do so. No doubt it was a mistake not to involve DEMCOP as early as 1970 in Ovamboland's political development process. The advantages in allowing it to exist would probably have far out-weighed the disadvantages. Nangutuuala, its leader and founder, was ready for dialogue from the beginning, but no effective use was made of this. Recognition of DEMCOP might well have obliged SWAPO to compete with it and could have caused the latter's influence to decline, as many former SWAPO members would probably have voted for DEMCOP despite its far more moderate programme. A further result might have been that SWAPO abroad would no longer have been able to count on a powerful home front organization.

When SWAPO was discussed as the most radical organization claiming to represent Ovambo interests, the difference between its external and internal wings was clear. The average standard of education is higher among members of SWAPO's external head committee, being part of an Ovambo political élite, than among their counterparts inside Namibia, but more significant is the fact that SWAPO's external members are internationally recognized and move in a quite different milieu. Yet both wings of the party repudiate a Homelands development in the territory and emphasize Namibia's future as a unitary state, and both are opposed to the traditional authority and both agree with the United Nations decision that South Africa must evacuate Namibia which is to achieve immediate independence and be known by its modern name.

A notable distinction between the domestic and foreign wings of SWAPO is the less extreme attitude of the party within Namibia, except for the SWAPO youth movement. The influence upon SWAPO of the churches, most of all in its rejecting of violence in the political struggle, is umistakable. The rarity of violence hitherto is due largely to the discipline exercised by the churches, especially the Ovambokavango Church, over its members, many of whom belong to SWAPO. The ascendancy of religious belief was manifest during the concluding speech of its leader, Toivo, in the Pretoria trial, and in many subsequent speeches, pamphlets and acts. This particular influence is not discernible in SWAPO abroad. The internal and external wings of SWAPO were quick to realize that they could not rival the authority and influence of the churches.

SWAPO has emphasized that it would include religious leaders in its delegation if independence talks on Namibia were held on neutral ground. According to its president, the Black church leaders "are true patriots. Although they are waging the struggle from a different angle, they are not opportunitists". He particularly mentioned Dr. Lukas de Vries and Bishop Leonard Auala, the leaders of the indigenous black Evangelical Lutheran Churches. Sam Nujoma considers them "freedom fighters just like ourselves".

It is reasonable to think that SWAPO would have become less radical and that fewer of its members would have gone into exile had the white authority conducted a dialogue with this mouthpiece of the Ovambo people at an early stage. Under the current circumstances and against the background of SWAPO's recent actions inside and outside Namibia, the South African Government will clearly never recognize it as a political mouthpiece of the Blacks. However, a ban is equally improbable in the light of the Government's promise to the UN to permit political organizations and activities in Namibia.

All the three parties have contributed to the political awareness and mobilization process of Ovamboland. SWAPO and DEMCOP operate within the framework of their resistance to the traditional and South African authorities and policy, whereas OIP is working for the survival of the traditional structure and the South African Government's Homelands policy.

Ovamboland is going through a situation of virtual political stalemate with the possibility of future serious and disruptive tendencies within its political development process. The whole state of affairs discourages, to a great extent, the rise of effective action by a strong functionally orientated modernizing political élite in Ovambo, which could operate as a power group and as such make a constructive contribution to the country's political development. At the same time it has to be remembered that SWAPO, as the strongest political party in Ovamboland, is no longer interested in being a political power group in a possible independent Ovamboland. Its aim is to be the dominant political force in the whole of Namibia. It is clearly aware of the consequences of success for the Turnhalle Constitutional Conference and its successor, the Democratic Turnhalle Alliance. Increased military involvement by SWAPO on the northern border and inside Ovamboland and a government-in-exile would probably follow that eventuality, especially if the South African Government refuses direct consultations with SWAPO on the political future of Namibia, with Ovamboland as an integral part of it.

NOTES

Chapter I—*Introduction*

1. Stals, E., "Die aanraking tussen Blankes en Ovambos in Suidwes–Afrika 1830—1915", unpublished D.Phil. thesis, University of Stellenbosch, 1967, p. 111, as cited from Akten Nr. A.I. b. 5 Bd. 1: Abgrenzung des Schutzgebietes, Specialia, Nordgrenze, 1885–1914: Danckelmann—Auswärtiges Amt, Kolonial-Abteilung, 8 Juli 1885, pp. 19–20.

2. The original German wording of article 1 of the Convention is as follows: "Die Grenzlinie, welche in Südwestafrika die deutsche und portugiesischen Besitzungen scheiden soll, folgt dem Laufe des Kuneneflusses von seiner Mündung bis zudenjenigen Wasserfällen, welche südlich von Humba beim Durchbruch des Kunene durch die Sierra Canna gebildet werden. Von diesem Punkt ab läuft die Linie auf dem Breitenparallel bis zum Kubango [Okavango], dann im Laufe dieses Flusses entlang bis zu dem Orte Andera, welcher der deutschen Interessensphäre überlassen bleibt, und von da in gerader Richtung östlich bis zu den Stromschnellen von Catima am Zambesi." Barnard, W. S., "Staatkundig-Geografiese Aspekte van Suidwes-Afrika", unpublished M.A. thesis, University of Stellenbosch, 1959, p. 226.

3. Union of South Africa, Department of Native Affairs, *Report by the officer-in-charge of Native Affairs on his tour to Ovamboland* (S. Pritchard), Pretoria, 1915. U.S. 38, p. 14.

4. Stals, E., op. cit., p. 112.

5. The total area of Namibia, including the area of Walvis Bay (1,124 sq. km.) is 824,269 sq. km.

6. See Barnard, W. S., "Staatkundig-geografiese aspekte van Suidwes-Afrika", unpublished M.A. thesis, University of Stellenbosch, 1959, p. 85.

6a. *To the Point*, Johannesberg, 14 May 1976.

7. During the period 1941–61 the fluctuation was between 293 and 972 mm. Wellington, J. H., *South West Africa and its human issues*, Oxford, 1967, p. 20.

8. Department van Buitelandse Sake, *Owambo*. Pretoria, 1971, p. 3.

9. Wellington says that in Ovambo "the annually flooded surface soils containing about 95% fine to very coarse sand, overlie an impervious subsoil layer containing rather more than 13% silt and clay with high salt concentrations". Op. cit., p. 67.

10. Arden-Clarke maintains that the Ovambos settled in Ovamboland about 300 years ago, while Tyrrell wrongly maintains that they settled in South West Africa in 1700. Arden-Clarke, C. 1, "South West Africa, the Union and the United Nations", *African Affairs*. Vol. 59, 1960, p. 29; Tyrrell, B., *Tribal Peoples of Southern Africa*, Cape Town, 1968. p. 9.

11. Bruwer, J. P., *South West Africa, the Disputed Land*, Cape Town, 1966, pp. 21–3; the same author in International Court of Justice, *South West Africa Cases*, The Hague, 1966, Vol. IX, p. 248; also Giniewkski, P., *Die Stryd om Suidwes-Afrika*, Johannesburg, 1960, p. 18.

12. Ondonga nach Pettinen: 'Sagen, Mythen der Aandonga' (*Zeitschrift für*

220

Eingeborenensprachen, Band XVII, 1926, Heft 1) in Lebzelter, V., *Eingeborenenkulturen in Südwest- und Süd-Afrika,* Band II, Leipzig, 1934, p. 192.

13. Vedder, H., *Das alte Südwestafrika,* Berlin, 1934, p. 160.

14. Lehmann points out that in the upper reaches of the Zambesi river between 14°S. and 31°E., an ethnicity can be found with the name Ambo. Lehmann, E. R., "Die anthropogeographischen Verhältnisse des Ambolandes", in *Zeitschrift für Ethnologie.* Bd. 79, Heft I, 1954, p. 12.

15. Hahn, L. H. L., "Preliminary Notes on certain customs of the Ovambo", in *South West Africa Scientific Society,* Windhoek, 1927–8, Vol. III, pp. 5–6; Rhoodie, E., *South West Africa: The Last Frontier in Africa,* Johannesburg, 1967, p. 119.

16. Although the Ovambos are part of the Bantu tribes, Green's comments about their being descendants of the Zulus are open to doubt. Similarities in both languages like *hyama* for meat and *umvula* for rain are insufficient proofs for his assertions of blood relationship. Green, L. G., *Lords of the Last Frontier,* Cape Town, 1962, p. 240.

17. Bruwer, J. P., op. cit. p. 23; *Eume,* no. 4, 1972, p. 2.

18. Department of Foreign Affairs, op. cit., pp. 6–7, according to H. Vedder, *South West Africa in Early Times,* 1938.

19. Bruwer, J. P., op. cit., pp. 21–3.

20. Schinz, H., *Deutsch-Südwest-Afrika,* Oldenburg, 1891, p. 271; Lehmann, F. R., op. cit., p. 54.

21. Schinz, op. cit., p. 272.

22. Bruwer, J. P., op. cit., p. 21; Himmelreich, F., *Ovamboland: Land, Leute, Heidentu.* Barmen, 1900, p. 6; Tuupainen, M., *Marriage in a Matrilineal African Tribe,* Helsinki, 1970, p. 12.

23. Andersson, C. J., *Notes of Travel in South Africa,* London, 1875, p. 154; Andersson, C. J., *Lake Ngami or Explorations in South West Africa,* London, 1856, pp. 183, 190.

24. Tönjes, H., *Lehrbuch des Oskuanyama-Dialekts,* Berlin, 1910, p. VI.

25. Andersson, C. J., *Notes of Travel in South Africa,* p. 230.

26. Galloway, A., "The physical Anthropology of the Ovambo", *South African Journal of Science,* Vol. XXXIV, Nov., 1937, p. 363.

27. Schinz, op. cit., p. 274.

28. Green, L. G., op. cit., p. 240.

29. As cited by Bruwer, S. P., "The Kwanyama of South West Africa", unpublished ms., Stellenbosch, 1961, p. 15.

30. International Court of Justice, *South West Africa Cases,* The Hague, 1966, Vol. II, p. 320.

31. Redinha, R., *Distribuicao Etnica Da Provincia De Angola.,* Lisbon, 1960, p. 8; Direccao dos Servicas de Estatisticia, *3° Recenseamento Geval da Populacao 1960,* vol. 3, Luanda, 1968, pp. 84–5.

32. Palgrave, W. C., *Report of his mission to Damara and Great Namaqualand in 1876,* G.50—1877, Cape of Good Hope, 1877, p. 49.

33. Schinz, H., op. cit., p. 273.

34. Brincker, P. H., "Die Eingeborenen von Deutsch-Südwestafrika", *Mitteilungen des Seminars für Orientalische Sprachen,* Bd. II, Berlin, 1899, pp. 135–6.

35. Unie van Suid-Afrika, *Rapport van die Regering van die Unie van Suid-Afrika omtrent Suidwes-Afrika,* U.G. 38/1915, Pretoria.

36. Lebzelter, V., op. cit., p. 190.

37. Unie van Suid-Afrika, *Rapport van die Regering van die Unie van Suid-Afrika omtrent Suidwes-Afrika,* U.G. 17/1932, Pretoria.

38. Unie van Suid-Afrika, *Rapport van die Regering van die Unie van Suid-Afrika omtrent Suidwes-Afrika,* U.G. 25/1938, Pretoria.

39. Bruwer, S. P., "The Kwanyama of South West Africa", Stellenbosch, 1967, p. 11.

40. Report of the Commission of Enquiry into South West Africa Affairs, 1962–3. Pretoria, R.P. 12/1964, p. 35.

41. *Verslag van die Kommissie van Ondersoek na Aangeleenthede in Suidwes-Afrika*, 1962–3. Pretoria, R.P. 12/1964, p. 35.

42. Statistiese Nuusberig No. 64, 23 September 1971. The tribal figures are estimates of Kritzinger, J. J., 'Sending en Kerk in Suidwes-Afrika', unpublished D.Phil. thesis, Pretoria 1972, p. 192, table 17.

43. Official estimate.

44. Andersson, C. J., *Notes of Travel in South Africa*, p. 219.

45. Olivier, M. J., "Inboorlingsbeleid en-administrasie in die Mandaatsgebied van Suidwes-Afrika", unpublished D.Phil. thesis, University of Stellenbosch, 1961, p. 25.

46. *Eume*, no. 4, 1972, p. 2.

47. Andersson made the following remark in the nineteenth century: "The Ovambo are very national and exceedingly proud of their native soil." Andersson, C. J., *Lake Ngami*, p. 198.

48. Van Tonder, L. L., "Leadership, Power and Status stratification with reference to Bushmen, Hottentot and Ovambo Society", unpublished M.A. thesis, University of Stellenbosch, 1963, p. 123; Andersson, C. J., *Notes of Travel in South Africa*, p. 236.

49. Dymond, G. W., "The idea of God in Ovamboland", in Smith, D. W. (ed.): *African Ideas of God*, London, 1966, pp. 143–4.

50. Ibid., p. 149.

51. Van Tonder, op. cit., pp. 77–80; Warneck, J., "Studien zur Religion der Ovambo", *Allgemeine Missionszeitschrift*, Vol. 37, Berlin, 1910, p. 314; Himmelreich, F., op. cit., p. 12; Vedder, H., *Das alte Südwestafrika*, p. 74; Tönjes, H., *Ovamboland: Land, Leute, Mission*, Berlin, 1911, p. 193.

52. Warneck, op. cit., p. 315 and Van Tonder, L. L., op. cit., p. 78.

53. A tribal chief in conversation with Warneck: "You speak about God but I am God." Warneck, op. cit., p. 315.

54. Vedder, op. cit., p. 74.

55. For a full discussion see Dymond, G. W., op. cit., pp. 137–52.

56. Hahn, C. H. L., op. cit., p. 6.

57. Schinz, H., op. cit., p. 319; Brincker, P. H., op. cit., p. 139; Vedder, H., op. cit., p. 71; Tönjes, H., op. cit., p. 111; Estermann, C., "Ethnographische Beobachtungen über die Ovambo", *Zeitschrift für Ethnologie*, Vol. 63, 1931, pp. 41–2; Van Tonder, J. J., op. cit., p. XXXIII; Hahn, C. H. L., *The Native Tribes of South West Africa*, Cape Town, 1928, pp. 8 and 18; Schwabe, K., *Im deutschen Diamentenlande. Deutsch Südwestafrika 1884–1910*. Berlin, 1910, p. 427; Louw, W. "Die sosio-politieke stelsel van die Ngandjera van Ovamboland", M.A. unpublished thesis, University of Port Elizabeth, 1967, p. 120. See also review of C. Estermann, *Etnografie do Sudoeste Angola*, Vol. I: "Os povos nao-Bantos e o grupo etnico dos Ambos" (Lisboa, 1956) in *Africa*, I.A.I., London, Vol. 28, 1958, pp. 288–90.

58. Kotze, J. C., "Die Kuanyama van Ovamboland—'n studie van waarde opvattinge", unpublished M.A. thesis, University of Stellenbosch, 1968, pp. 60–2.

59. Louw, W., op. cit., p. 123.

60. Bruwer, J. P., "Suidwes-Afrika sedert Maharero", *SWA Science Society*, Vol. XVI, Windhoek 1961/62, p. 78.

61. *Windhoek Advertiser*, 25 February 1975.

62. Ibid., p. 107.

63. *Owambo Official Gazette*, Vol. 2, no. 10, 13 Sept. 1974.

64. Krafft, M., "Die Rechtsverhältnisse der Ovakuanjama und der Ovandonga", *Mitteilungen aus den Deutschen Schutzgebieten*, Band XXVII, Berlin, 1914, pp. 20–6; Rautanen, M., "Die Ondonga" in Steinmetz, S. R., *Rechtsverhältnisse von Eingeborenenvölkern in Afrika und Ozeanien*, Berlin, 1903, pp. 327–43; Lebzelter, V.; op. cit., pp. 237–8.

65. Kotzé, J. C., op. cit., p. 133.

66. *Notule van die Gekose Komitee oor Grandbesit en Benutting*, Oshakati (Ovamboland) 4 Dec. 1970.

67. Louw, W., op. cit., p. 99.

68. Bruwer, J. P., op. cit., p. 78.

69. Kotze, J. C., op. cit., p. 99.

70. Loeb, E. M., "The Kuanyama Ambo", *Scientific American*, Vol. 183, no. 4, New York, 1950, p. 53.

71. Galton, F., *Narrative of an Explorer in Tropical Africa*, London, 1889, p. 125; Andersson, C. J., *Lake Ngami*, p. 172.

73. The importance of this staple food is reflected by translating "our daily bread" in the Lord's prayer by "*omahangu*".

73. Barnard, W. S., *Die Struktuurpatrone van Suidwes-Afrika*, p. 304.

74. Galton gives an example of this in one of his travel books after a visit to Ovamboland in 1861: "Two Ovambo caravans, each consisting of from twenty to thirty men on foot, come here with beads, shells, assegaais, wood choppers and such-like things, which they exchange for cattle." Galton, F., op. cit., p. 105.

Chapter II—*Contact with the Whites*

1. Stals, E., "Die aanraking tussen Blankes en Ovambos in Suidwes-Afrika 1830–1915". D.Phil. thesis, unpublished, University of Stellenbosch, 1967, pp. 43–4. For more detailed literature on this period see: Finse Sendingdrukkery, *Die Finse Sendinggenootskap en die Evangelies Lutherse Ovambokavango-Kerk*, Oniipa, 1958, pp. 5–17; Andersson, C. J., *Notes of Travel in South Africa*, p. 250; Schinz, H.: op. cit., pp. 489–97; Thamäki, K., "Finland in Ovamboland", *Suidwes-Afrika Jaarboek*, Windhoek, 1970, pp. 163–7.

2. Stals, E., op. cit., pp. 67, 77.

3. These figures were obtained from Bishop L. Auala and the Rev. Shipena at Oniipa, Ovamboland, in June 1972 and 1973. The Christians of Kavango are included in the total. Of the 213,796 Christians belonging to the Ovambokavango Church in 1972 altogether 10,859 were from the Kavango. Also Auala, J. et al., *The Ovambo-Kavango Church*, Helsinki, 1960, pp. 24–32.

4. Penti writes: "Finnish mission workers who themselves knew little Afrikaans enthusiastically compiled and printed an Afrikaans conversation book at the cost of the mission. They even published an Afrikaans magazine called *Ons Vriend* for a while to acquaint Ovambo-teachers with the new language. As you know there are few foreign mission societies in South and South West Africa which preferred Afrikaans to English. We, however, who did so, feel convinced that ours was the right choice" (translation from Afrikaans). See an address given by Rev. E. J. Penti at Engela, Ovamboland, in 1959 with the title "Die Bykomstige Resultate van die Finse Sendingwerk in Ovamboland" (Additional Results of Finnish Missionary Work in Ovamboland).

5. Strassberger, E., "Women in Church Service. 3", *Pro Veritate*, Johannesburg, Vol. X, 1972, no. 12, p. 7.

6. Smith, E. W., op. cit., pp. 152–5.

7. Ibid., p. 153.

8. Ibid., p. 153.

9. Ibid., p. 153.

10. Tuupainen, M., op. cit., p. 9.

11. Kritzinger, J. J., 'Sending en Kerk in Suidwes-Afrika', unpublished D.Phil. thesis, Pretoria, 1972, p. 385.

12. Many of the facts were obtained during an interview with Father Schneider at Okatana, Ovamboland, in June 1971 and 1972.

13. Wolfe, E. M., *Beyond the Thirst Belt: The Study of the Ovamboland Missions*, London, 1935, pp. 9, 34, 35, 58.

14. Facts obtained during a conversation with the Archdeacon, the Most Rev. Shilongo at Odibo, Ovamboland, in July 1972.

15. According to copied document and personal interview with the Rev. P. Kalangula, at Ondangwa, Ovamboland, in July 1972.

16. Kritzinger, J. J., op. cit., p. 219.

17. Ibid., p. 219.

18. The Triangular Agreement of 1947 states that the Dutch Reformed Church pays the salaries of Ovambo clergymen ministering to the Ovambo workers in the South; that ELOC supplies the clergymen and their theological training, and that the ELC (Rhenish Mission) puts its buildings in non-white areas at the disposal of ELOC.

19. Kritzinger, J. J., op. cit., pp. 152–5.

20. Unie van Suid-Afrika, *Rapport van die Regering van die Unie van Suid-Afrika omtrent die Administrasie van Suidwes-Afrika vir die jaar 1927.* U.G. 31, Pretoria 1928, p. 46 (translation from Afrikaans).

21. Unie van Suid-Afrika, *Verslag van die Unie van Suid-Afrika omtrent die Administrasie van Suidwes-Afrika vir die jaar 1935*, Pretoria, U.G. 26/1936, pp. 21–2 (translation from Afrikaans).

22. Union of South Africa, *Report presented by the Government of the Union of South Africa to the Council of the League of Nations concerning the Administration of South West Africa for the year 1937*, Pretoria, U.G. 25/1938, p. 63.

23. Proclamation no. 31 of 1932, *The Control of Sites—Church Missions and Schools.*

24. *U.G. 25/1938*, p. 64.

25. *U.G. 26/1936*, p. 22.

26. *U.G. 25/1938*, p. 66.

27. Department of Bantu Administration and Development, "Verslag oor Konferensie te Rundu in 1970," unpublished, p. 109 (translation from Afrikaans).

28. For all practical purposes the traditional Ovambo Independent Party, founded in 1973 and suspected of being established with South African Government help but in any case founded by traditional leaders and their supporters, has been excluded.

29. Bishop Auala was born in 1908 and worked in the diamond mines in the South as a young man. He then qualified as a teacher at Oniipa, taught for some time and then became head of the first Teachers' Training College in Ovamboland. After qualifying as a minister as well, he in 1960 became the first African head of the Finnish Mission Church. In 1963 he was elected the first bishop of the independent Ovambokavango Church (former Finnish Mission Church). In 1967 he was awarded an honorary doctorate in theology by the University of Helsinki. He also received honorary doctorates from the University of Pennsylvania (U.S.A.) on 2 June 1974 and from the Lutheran Theological Seminary of Ohio (U.S.A.) on 9 June 1974.

30. Auala, L., *Hoekom die Finse Sendelinge nog nodig is in Ovamboland en Okavango in Suidwes-Afrika.* Copied address, p. 4 (translation from Afrikaans).

31. *Eume*, no. 10, October 1970, p. 3.

32. Open letter to the Prime Minister of the Republic of South Africa, B. J. Vorster, p. 2.

33. Complete text owned by author. Cf. also *Allgemeine Zeitung* (subsequently "*AZ*"), 12 August 1971.

34. Introductory address by Bishop Auala (in private possession), p. 1.

35. Information obtained from tape-recording made during the talks.

36. Ibid.

37. De Vries, L., in *Immanuel*, Windhoek, June 1975, no. 14/9, p. 4.

38. Bishop Auala told the author at a private talk that he considers *Omukwetu* as a general newspaper published by the Church and not as an exclusively religious magazine. (Interview at Oniipa, June 1973.)

39. *Omukwetu*, no. 6, April 1972, p. 1 (translation).

40. *Evangeliese Informasiediens in Suidwes-Afrika*, Karibib, Vol. 11, no. 5, April 1972, p. 3.

41. Report of the Secretary-General of the UN to the Security Council. S/10832, 15 November 1972, p. 12.

42. Ibid., p. 13.

43. *Windhoek Advertiser* (subsequently "*WA*"), 11 April 1973.

44. *Evangeliese Informasiediens in Suidwes-Afrika*. Vol. 12, no. 3, May, 1973, pp. 7–8; Lutheran World Federation News Service, *Information*, 44/73, p. 6.

45. *Suidwes-Afrikaner* (subsequently "*S-A*"), 27 July 1973.

46. Ibid.

47. *AZ*, 11 July 1974.

48. Photocopy of original as translated from Oshidonga.

49. *WA*, 14 May 1976. The Appellate Division of the South African Supreme Court set the sentence aside in March 1977 due to technical irregularities in the conduct of the case.

50. *WA*, 16 July 1976.

51. Stals, E., op. cit., p. 140; Bruwer, J. P., *The Kwanyama of South West Africa*, pp. 21–3; Lehmann, F. R., "Die Politische und soziale Stellung der Häuptlinge im Ovambo-Land während der deutschen Schutzherrschaft in Südwest-Afrika" in *Zeitschrift für Ethnologie—TRIBUS*, Vol. 4/5, Stuttgart, 1956, pp. 269–95.

52. At that stage there were only seven Germans—four soldiers and three farmers—to defend the fortress. During the battle 108 Ovambos were killed, but the seven Germans disappeared overnight and the Ovambos took the fortress the following day.

53. *U.G. 38/1915*, p. 1.

54. Ibid., pp. 14–15.

55. Olivier, M. J., op. cit., p. 152.

56. Cf. Van der Westhuizen, W. M., "Bevoegdhede van die Verenigde Volke om die mandaat vir Suidwes-Afrika te beëindig", *Tydskrif vir Hedendaagse Romeins-Hollandse Reg*, 1968, p. 330.

57. U.G. 38/1915, p. 13.

58. Bruwer, J. P., *The Kwanyama of South West Africa*, p. 27, as quoted from a report by Fairlie on 25 March 1917.

59. For an explanation of the chieftain and headman system see chapter 1.

60. This opinion is expressed in the report of the Administrator to the Union Government, cf. U.G. 37/1917, p. 7; in a report to the Union Government by Major Fairlie, cf. U.G. 33/1925, p. 28, and by the Secretary of South West Africa, cf. Bruwer, J. P., *The Kwanyama of South West Africa*, p. 29.

61. Union of South Africa, *Report presented by the Government of the Union of South Africa to the Council of the League of Nations concerning the Administration of South West Africa for the Year 1931*, Pretoria, U.G. 17/1932, p. 50.

62. Unie van Suid-Afrika, *Verslag van die Unie van Suid-Afrika omtrent die Administrasie van Suidwes-Afrika vir die jaar 1935*, Pretoria, U.G. 26/1936, p. 17.

63. Ibid., pp. 18–20.

64. Ibid., p. 21.

65. Ibid., p. 80.

66. The tribal secretary is now appointed by the Department of Bantu Administration and Development with the consent of the chief or the council of senior headmen. The tribal secretary acts as a link between the central government and the tribe, and obtains considerable influence in tribal affairs. His most important tasks are the registration of births and deaths, the keeping of minutes of tribal meetings and tribal trials, the collection of yearly taxes which are deposited in the tribal fund from which the tribal secretary is paid his salary.

67. Liebenberg, P. W., "Die Inlywing van Suidwes-Afrika by die Unie van Suid-Afrika", M.A. thesis, University of Pretoria, 1970, p. 57.

68. Unie van Suid-Afrika, *Dokumente wat betrekking het op die oorweging wat die Algemene Vergadering van die Verenigde Volke geskenk het aan die verklaring deur die Regering van Suid-Afrika betreffende die resultaat van hul beraadslagings met die bevolkingsgroepe van Suidwes-Afrika in verband met die toekomstige status van die Mandaatsgebied en die uitvoering wat aan die wense wat aldus uitgespreek is, gegee moet word*, Pretoria, 1947, p. 27.

69. Ibid., p. 28.

70. Ibid., p. 33.

71. For detailed objections of some Ovambos see Troup, F., *In Face of Fear, Michael Scott's Challenge to South Africa*, London, 1950, pp. 107–11. Although the factual content of her book is not above criticism, the objections about the "referendum" are convincing and acceptable. A further commentary on this "referendum" is made by one of South Africa's most vehement political opponents, Rev. M. Scott. Cf. Scott, M. "South West Africa and the Union—How the Natives 'Voted for the Union' " in *The British Africa Monthly*, Vol. I(12), August 1948, pp. 13–15.

72. Imishue, R. W., *South West Africa: an International Problem*. London, 1965, pp. 46–7.

73. Goldblatt, I., *The Mandated Territory of South West Africa in Relations to the United Nations*, Cape Town, 1961, p. 60. Ruth First points out that the petition of the Kwanyama tribal authority which was mailed in Angola, requested that South West Africa should be placed under the trusteeship of Canada. First, R., *South West Africa*, Harmondsworth (Penguin Books), 1963, p. 40. For a full report of the oral testimony of the Rev. M. Scott and K. Getzen see *United Nations Review*, Petitioners' Views on conditions in South West Africa. Vol. 4, 1957, pp. 54–5. Both petitioners claimed to be speaking on behalf of Ovamboland as well, since in their opinion the South African Government would not allow any Ovambo to testify before the Committee. Getzen alleged that an Ovambo clergyman, T. H. Hamtambangela, was arrested for sending a petition to the UN. Cf. ibid., p. 54.

74. For background reading Ballinger, R. G., *South West Africa—The Case against the Union*, Johannesburg, SAIRR, 1961, pp. 1–53.

75. Imishue, op. cit., p. 62.

76. Republiek van Suid-Afrika, *Verslag van Kommissie van Ondersoek na Aangeleenthede van Suidwes-Afrika*, Pretoria, R.P. no. 12/1964, p. 2.

77. The chairman of this commission, after whom the report was named, was F. H. Odendaal. The other members were Dr. H. J. van Eck, Prof. H. W. Snyman, Prof. J. P. van S. Bruwer, Dr. P. J. Quin, and the secretary, Dr. O. J. Claassen.

78. *R.P. No. 12/1964*, p. 514.

79. Ibid., p. 80.

80. Ibid., pp. 82–4.

81. For an exposition of the separate development policy and South West Africa

see Mason, P., "Separate Development and South West Africa: Some Aspects of the Odendaal Report", *Race*, Vol. V, no. 4 (April 1964), pp. 83–97.

82. *R.P. No. 12/1964*, pp. 538–42. The number of respondents as stated in the report is incorrect since the first names and surnames of the respondents were counted as separate persons.

Chapter III— *The Implications of Political Development in Ovamboland*

1. Bruwer, J. P., *South West Africa—The Disputed Land*, p. 110; *Rand Daily Mail*, 27 March 1964 as quoted in Horrell, M., *A Survey of Race Relations*, SAIRR, Johannesburg, 1974, pp. 362–7; Dale, R., "Ovamboland: 'Bantustans without Tears?' " in *Africa Report*, Vol. 14, no. 2 (February 1969), p. 18; *Hansard* 15, col. 5458–9, 5484; *Eume*, no. 1, January 1972, p. 10.

2. See M. C. Botha's concluding remarks at conference of the Department of Bantu Administration and Development and Bantu Education at Rundu in 1970. Copied report, p. 131.

3. Ibid., p. 132.

4. Horrell, M., *A Survey of Race Relations*, SAIRR, Johannesburg, 1965, p. 316, as quoted in the *Cape Times* (subsequently "*CT*"), 24 February 1965. In this request to the Prime Minister the wish was also expressed that traditional leaders would be given the opportunity of visiting the Republic. In February 1965, 62 Ovambos were taken on a tour of homelands in the Republic and they also visited mines and factories in Johannesburg.

5. Department of Information, *Ovamboland*. Fact Paper Series. Johannesburg, 1967, pp. 7–8.

6. For full details *U.P. 3/1968*, pp. 2–8.

7. *Official Gazette of the Republic of South Africa*, vol. 40, no. 2177, p. 2.

8. This statement by M. C. Botha was made during a conference of the Department of Bantu Administration and Development and Bantu Education at Rundu in 1970. Copied Report.

9. The following abbreviations are used: T. (Teachers), R./L. (Religious Leaders), O./C. (Official/Clerks), Comm. (Traders), N. (Nurses), Trad. (Traditional Leaders), Ov./Av. (Ovamboland Average), Kat./Av. (Katutura Average). The percentage is brought to the nearest decimal and can vary from 99.9% to 100.1%.

In the table, each élite group in Ovamboland is represented by the following number of respondents: Teachers, 46; Religious leaders, 26; Officials and Clerks, 28; Nurses, 20; Traditional leaders, 24; Traders, 11. Total, 155. In Katutura the following numbers and types of respondents are represented in the table: Teachers, 9; Religious leaders, 1; Officials and Clerks, 6; Nurses, 18; Traditional Leaders, nil (none live in Katutura); Traders, 1; students, 23. Five labourers, one farmer and two without occupation were also questioned. Total: 66. Ovamboland and Katutura together represent a total of 221 respondents. In the tables, only the average percentages are given for Katutura to compare them with the average percentages for Ovamboland.

10. Republiek van Suid-Afrika, *Verbatimverslag van die Ovambolandse Wetgewende Raad*. 1st session, 1st Legislative Council: 14–17 October 1968 te Oshakati, p. 14.

11. *Eume*, no. 6, June, 1968, pp. 4, 12 (translation).

12. *Medu Letu*, Vol. V, no. 4, October 1968, pp. 2–5 (translation).

13. Republiek van Suid-Afrika, *Verbatimverslag van die Ovambolandse*

Wetgewende Raad. 2nd Session–1st Legislative Council, 10 February 1969 te Oshakati, p. 4.

14. Ibid., p. 6.

15. For example, the senior headmen of the Kwanyama tribe received from 1967 a yearly renumeration of R300 plus a bonus each. A certain percentage of fines for some crimes was another source of income.

16. *Verslag van Gekose Komitee insake Pligte, Bevoegdhede en Diensvoorwaardes vir Hoofmanne en Onder-Hoofmanne.* Copy.

17. Republiek van Suid-Afrika, *Verbatimverslag van die Ovambolandse Wetgewende Raad.* 2nd Session, 1st Legislative Council, 10 February 1969, p. 16; Republiek van Suid-Afrika, *Verbatimverslag van die Ovambolandse Wetgewende Raad.* 3rd session, 1st Legislative Council, 16–25 March 1970, p. 14.

18. Republic of South Africa, *Verbatim Report of the Ovambo Legislative Council.* Fifth Session First Legislative Council, 28 March–18 April 1972, p. 19.

19. Cf. Senior Headman A. Shilongo's significant remark concerning this. Republiek van Suid-Afrika, *Verbatimverslag van die Ovambolandse Wetgewende Raad.* 2nd session 1st Legislative Council, pp. 40–4.

20. *Eume,* no. 3, March 1970, p. 3 (translation).

21. E.g. Republic of South Africa, *Verbatim Report of the Ovambo Legislative Council.* Fifth Session First Legislative Council, 28 March–18 April 1972, pp. 58, 60.

22. The following remark by a member of the House, the Rev. T. Heita, can be interpreted as an oblique reference to the illiteracy of the Chief Councillor: "We do not want to accuse the Chief Councillor but we have sympathy for the fact that his eyes are growing weak. And I therefore now request that in future somebody else who can read well must read in his stead" (translation)—Republiek van Suid-Afrika, *Verbatimverslag van die Ovambolandse Wetgewende Raad.* 3rd Session–1st Legislative Council, 16–25 March 1970, p. 14.

23. *Eume,* no. 6, June 1972, pp. 13–14 (translation).

24. Ovamboland Legislative Council, Verbatim Report of Special Sessions, 14 Jan. 1972, 28 July 1972, p. 9.

25. Ibid., pp. 9–10.

26. Ibid., p. 11.

27. *Eume,* no. 6 June 1972, p. 13 (translation).

28. *WA,* 22 June 1973.

29. Article 5A of the mentioned law.

30. Article 5A, c-j, of this law.

31. *Ovambo Official Gazette,* Vol. 2, no. 2, 15 June 1973, pp. 5–6.

32. *Rapport,* 29 July 1973.

33. *WA,* 3 August 1973.

34. *Cape Times,* 3 August 1973.

35. *WA,* 3 August 1973.

36. *WA,* 27 July 1973.

37. *WA,* 3 August 1973.

38. *Sunday Times,* 5 August 1973.

39. *WA,* 3 August 1973.

40. *Ovambo Amptelike Koerant,* Vol. 2, no. 3, 28 March 1974.

41. *Ovambo Amptelike Koerant,* Vol. 2, no. 4, 3 May 1974.

42. *Ovambo Wetgewende Raad: Verrigtinge van die Tweede Sessie van die Tweede Wetgewende Raad,* Vol. I, 14 May–6 June 1974, Ongwediva.

43. Ibid., Vol. I.

44. Ibid., Vol. I and II.

45. Ibid., Vol. II, p. 614.

46. Ibid., Vol. II, p. 618.

47. *Ovambo Legislative Council: Proceedings of the Special Session of the Second Ovambo Legislative Council*, 8 Oct. 1974, Ongwediva, p. 12.

48. *WA*, 22 April 1975.

49. International Commission of Jurists, *Press Release*. Geneva, 13 April 1975.

50. *WA*, 7 April 1975.

51. *WA*, 15 April 1975.

52. Ovambo Legislative Council: *Proceedings of the First Session of the Third Legislative Council*, 13 May–9 June 1975. Ongwediva, pp. 129, 131–5, 150.

53. Ovambo Legislative Council: *Proceedings of the Second Session of the Third Legislative Council*, 20 April–18 May 1976. Ongwediva, pp. 103, 105–6.

54. Ibid., p. 21.

55. Ibid., p. 307.

56. Ibid., p. 362.

57. Ibid., p. 328.

58. Ovambo Legislative Council: *Proceedings of the First Session of the Third Legislative Council*, 13 May–9 June 1975. Ongwediva, p. 145.

59. Ovambo Legislative Council: *Proceedings of the Second Session of the Third Ovambo Legislative Council*, 20 April–18 May 1976. Ongwediva, p. 202.

60. Ovambo Legislative Council: *Proceedings of the First Session of the Third Ovambo Legislative Council*, 13 May–9 June 1975. Ongwediva, p. 265.

61. Ibid., p. 138.

62. Ibid., p. 139.

63. Ibid., p. 369–71.

64. *Die Burger*, 7 August 1975.

65. Department of Bantu Administration and Development, *Staatkundige en ekonomiese ontwikkeling van die tuislande in Suidwes-Afrika*. Conference at Rundu, 22/23 October 1970, p. 10. Here translated from Afrikaans.

66. Ibid., p. 18.

67. Ibid., p. 20.

68. Ibid., pp. 28–9.

69. *Eume*, Sept./Oct. 1970, p. 1 (translation).

70. *Eume*, no. 7, July 1971, p. 1 (translation).

71. Ibid., p. 1 (translation).

72. Author's notes during the meeting referred to.

73. At this stage the Peoples' Republic of China was not yet a member of the UN.

74. *WA*, 11 Nov. 1974.

75. *WA*, 16 January 1975.

76. *WA*, 8 January 1975.

77. *Die Suidwester*, 30 June 1975.

78. *Eume*, no. 1, January 1975 (translation).

79. *WA*, 10 May 1975.

80. Ovamboland Legislative Council, *Proceedings of the First Session of the Third Ovambo Legislative Council*, 13 May–9 June 1975, Ongwediva, p. 35.

81. *Die Suidwester*, 30 June 1975.

82. WA, 14 May 1975; 9 Nov. 1973.

83. *Eume*, No. 1, January 1975 (translation).

84. *Die Burger*, 15 May 1975.

85. *WA*, 21 Jan. 1975; 26 Feb. 1975; 26 May 1975.

86. Ovamboland Legislative Council, *Proceedings of the First Session of the Third Ovambo Legislative Council*, 13 May–9 June 1975, Ongwediva, pp. 18–19.

87. Ibid., pp. 108–9.

88. Ibid., p. 222.

88a. Ovamboland Legislative Council, *Proceedings of the Second Session of the Third Ovambo Legislative Council*, 20 April–18 May 1976, Ongwediva, pp. 14–15.

89. *Windhoek Advertiser*, 11 January 1977.

90. *Windhoek Advertiser*, 8 November 1976.

91. *Eume*, no. 10, October 1976, p. 3.

92. *Windhoek Advertiser*, 10 March 1977.

93. Only the first five alternatives were given in the original question, but during the interviews it transpired that a wider choice should have been offered.

94. *WA*, 19 December 1975.

95. *Rand Daily Mail*, 19 May 1976; *WA*, 4 October 1976 and 26 January 1977.

96. *WA*, 29 October 1973; 3 Dec. 1973; 25 Feb. 1974; 13 March 1974; 23 April 1974; 19 June 1974. *Weekend Argus*, 10 Nov. 1973; *Argus*, 4 April 1974; *Sunday Times*, 28 Oct. 1973; *Evangeliese Informasiediens in Suidwes-Afrika*, December 1973, pp. 6–7; *Lutheran World Federation News Service*, 28 Nov. 1973, pp. 9–10.

97. Ovambo Legislative Council: *Proceedings of the Second Session of the Third Ovambo Legislative Council*, 29 April–18 May 1976. Ondangwa, pp. 263–4.

98. For a detailed acount of the 1971 advisory opinion of the International Court of Justice see Lejeune, A., *The Case for South West Africa*, London, 1971, pp. 13–185.

99. International Court of Justice, *Legal Consequences for States of the Continued Presence of South Africa in Namibia (South West Africa) notwithstanding Security Council Resolution 276 (1970)*, The Hague, 1971, p. 16.

100. Dugard, J., *South West Africa/Namibia*. *Review of the International Dispute*, Paper, SAIRR, Johannesburg, 1973, pp. 10–11.

101. SWAPO, which is responsible for the name Namibia, explains it as follows: "The choice of the name Namibia is not necessarily governed by historical nostalgia. Rather it is predicated on some essential features of the geographical nature of our national homeland. This name is derived from the 'Namib' on the coastal desert of 'South West Africa'. *Namib* is a Nama/Damara word, literally meaning the shield or enclosure. ... The natural defense shield, the rich fishing ground, and the diamond fields, of the Namib are valuable attributes of our national territory. This is the reason why we have chosen to call our country Namibia—the land of the Namib." SWAPO, *The Namibian Documentation*. Printed in the German Democratic Republic, probably published 1970. pp. 33–4.

102. *AZ*, 8 March 1973.

103. *Daily Despatch*, 9 March 1973; *Argus*, 9 March 1973.

104. *AZ*, 8 and 10 August 1972.

105. *Report by the Secretary-General on the Implementation of Security Council Resolution 319 (1972) concerning the question of Namibia*. S/10832, 15 November 1972, p. 10.

106. Ibid., pp. 10–11.

107. Ibid., pp. 8–9.

108. Ibid., p. 4.

109. Ibid., p. 6.

110. Ibid., p. 6.

111. Ibid., pp. 22–3.

112. *WA*, 21 Nov. 1972.

113. *WA*, 2 May 1973.

114. South African Institute of International Affairs, *Southern Africa Record*. No. 2, June 1975, pp. 44–52.

115. *WA*, 4 Sept. 1975.

116. *WA*, 8 Sept. 1975.

117. Constitutional Conference of South West Africa, *Report*, 1976, pp. 9–10.

118. *WA*, 23 Aug. 1976.

119. *The Argus*, 11 Aug. 1976.
120. *WA*, 21 Dec. 1976.
121. Huntington, S. P., *Political Order in Changing Societies*, p. 5.

Chapter IV—*Socio-Economic Development*

1. With the opening in 1973 only seven students, including two Hereros, enrolled, although the College has a capacity for ninety-six students.

2. In 1971 Ovamboland had a livestock of 520,094 cattle, 7,363 sheep, 294,469 goats, 1,244 horses and 49,367 mules and donkeys. Cf. Regering van Ovambo: *Jaarverslag van Departement Landbou vir 1917.* p. 2.

3. Departmen't Bantoe-administrasie en -ontwikkeling, op. cit., p. 62.

4. According to information given by J. Hopkirk, director of Economic Affairs, Government of Ovamboland, in July 1972.

5. Ovambo Wetgewende Raad, *Verrigtinge van die Tweede Sessie van die Tweede Wetgewende Raad*, Vol. II, Ongwediva 1974, p. 565.

6. Stals, E., 'Die aanraking tussen Blankes en Ovambos in Suidwes-Afrika 1830–1915'. Ph.D. thesis (unpublished), University of Stellenbosch, 1967, p. 190.

7. Andrew, V., *Ovamboland*. London, 1953, p. 9.

8. *U.G. 38/1915*, pp. 13–14.

9. International Court of Justice, *South West Africa Cases, Counter Memorial of South Africa*. The Hague, 1966, Vol. III, p. 71.

10. Kritzinger, J. J., "Sending en Kerk in Suidwes-Afrika". Ph.D. thesis (unpublished), Pretoria, 1972, p. b373; Banghart, P. D., 'Migrant Labour in South West Africa and its effects on Ovambo Tribal Life'. M.A. thesis (unpublished), University of Stellenbosch, 1969, p. 49.

11. *Financial Mail*, "South West Africa: Desert Deadlock", 2 March 1973, p. 50.

12. *Eume*, no. 10, October 1974, p. 10.

13. The divisional inspector of the Department of Labour in Windhoek supplied the following information at the request of Eume: "In the Republic of South Africa job reservation is applied according to the authorizing regulatiops of the Industrial Conciliation Act. This act is not valid for South West Africa and the local ordinance on wages and industrial conciliation does not have corresponding stipulations. In South West Africa there is therefore no machinery of the law according to which job reservation could be promulgated in the Territory" (translation from Afrikaans). *Eume*, no. 6, June 1973, p. 5.

14. Kane-Berman, J., *Contract Labour in South West Africa*. SAIRR, Johannesburg, 1972, pp. xi–xiv.

15. *United Nations Monthly Chronicle*, Vol. IX, no. 2, February 1972, pp. 21–2.

16. See *Eume*, no. 1, January 1972, p. 1.

17. Republiek van Suid-Afrika: *Proklamasie R. 83. Regulasie vir Werkverskaffingsburo's.* 30 March 1972, art. 4, sub-art. 2–6.

18. *Eume*, no. 2, February 1974.

19. Copy in author's possession.

20. Kane-Berman, J., op. cit., pp. 18–21.

21. *Financial Mail*, op. cit., p. 49.

22. *Die Burger*, 10 Jan. 1972.

23. *Die Burger*, 13 Jan. 1972.

24. *CT*, 18 Jan. 1972.

25. *AZ*, 27 Jan. 1972.

26. *Omukwetu*, no. 3, February 1972, p. 7 (translation).

27. *CT* and *Die Burger*, 29 Jan. 1972; Republiek van Suid-Afrika, *Volksraad-Debatte* (Hansard). Derde Sessie—Vierde Parlement, 31 Januarie 1972, Cols. 113–114.

28. AZ, 1 Feb. 1972.

29. Republiek van Suid-Afrika, *Volksraad-Debatte* (Hansard). Derde Sessie—Vierde Parlement, 31 January 1972, Cols. 113–114.

30. S.A.U.K., *Nuus om Nege*, 6 Feb. 1972.

31. *Eume*, no. 1 January 1972, pp. 13–14; *Rapport*, 16 Jan. 1972. A Finnish woman missionary is also vaguely referred to, possibly Miss R. Voipio, author of a book on the contract labour system. Personal interviews with Miss Voipio left no impression whatsoever that she had anything to do with the strikes.

32. Voipio, R., *Kontrak—soos die Ovambo dit sien.* Karibib, SWA, 1972, p. 33 (translation).

33. Ibid., p. 34.

34. From 25 January to 11 April 1972 (Proclamation R17 was made retroactive), 213 persons were arrested and imprisoned according to the emergency regulation. The Minister for Police, S. L. Muller, announced that 130 persons were detained from one to 53 days. A total of 83 persons were at that stage under arrest for periods varying from five to 62 days. (Cf. *Argus*, 12 April 1972). At the end of May, Muller declared that fifteen of the 83 persons under arrest on 11 April were still in prison. The terms of imprisonment of these detainees were as follows: one for 115 days, three for 107 days, one for 87 days, three for 80 days and the rest for 50 to 69 days. Up to the end of May 1972, a total of 88 persons were tried and convicted on charges of several transgressions according to Proclamation R17. These persons were detained between five and seventy days before they were tried (*Argus*, 29 May 72 and *AZ*, 13 June 72.)—A trial in Windhoek revealed that the majority of the detainees were kept in a special fenced camp of 500 × 500 m. in the Kwanyama tribal area (*WA*, 29 Sept. 1972.)

Accusations of maltreatment and torture of Ovambos were made by several sources, especially the churches. These accusations have been made regularly since 1967. Although the true facts are difficult to ascertain, it seems that the South African police, because of the growing tension and the antagonism with which they were confronted, sometimes went too far in the exercising of their powers. This conduct worsened relations, although both sides were probably at fault. During his research the author often experienced mistrust and had to identify himself as not being a member either of the South African Security Police or the Bureau of State Security. As a result of complaints by black Lutheran Church leaders in Namibia of maltreatment, including torture by electric shock, made to the South African Prime Minister, B. J. Vorster, on 18 August 1971, he promised on receiving proof of these accusations to act strongly against misuse of authority. Strict orders were given to the white protecting forces (police, army) to improve relations between the Ovambos and the Whites. The complaints were rejected by the Prime Minister as unfounded.

35. *Argus*, 25 May 1973, and personal information by witnesses. The text of the song "Namibia" is translated as follows:

Hail Namibia—Hail Namibia
Namibia our land
Our own country: Namibia
Robbed from us by the Boers
The Boers must keep back
So that we can get independence.

36. Voipio, R., op. cit., pp. 6–20.

37. As made known to the author by clergymen of the Ovambokavango Church.

38. Copied letter in author's possession.

39. Lyon, A., "The Trial at Windhoek", in *South African Outlook*. Vol. 102, no. 1209, February 1972, p. 28.

40. See remarks made by the Rev. P. D. Strauss, mission secretary of the Dutch Reformed Church in Namibia during a SABRA conference in June 1973 at

Swakopmund; *Die Suidwester,* 29 June 1973; also remarks made by Mr. D. Mudge, M.E.C. in *S-A,* 29 Feb. 1972.

41. Voipio, R., op. cit., p. 13.

42. See also the requests made to the South African Prime Minister during the second session of the Advisory Council of South West Africa on 16 August 1973.

43. Testimony by Prof. J. Bruwer in the International Court: International Court of Justice, *South West Africa Cases,* 1966, vol. IX, p. 304.

44. Regering van Ovambo, Departement van Onderwys, *Jaarverslag 1972.*

45. International Court of Justice: *South West Africa: Pleadings, Oral Arguments, Documents.* Vol. I, The Hague, 1971, p. 801; Regering van Ovambo, Departement van Onderwys, *Jaarverslae 1970, 1971, 1972.* Also written information by the Inspector of Education, Ondangwa, Ovambo.

46. Regering van Ovambo, Departement van Onderwys, *Jaarverslag 1970.*

47. Ibid.

48. Information from the Director of Education, Mr. Gouws, Ondangwa, July 1971.

49. The Commissioner-General for South West Africa, J. de Wet, states that 75% of children of school age attend school. Cf. *South West Africa Yearbook 1972,* Windhoek. Other official sources, such as the Department of Information at Oshakati in Ovamboland, put it as high as 80%.

50. Regering van Ovambo, Departement van Onderwys, *Jaarverslag 1972.*

51. Ibid.

52. Ovambo Wetgewende Raad, *Verrigtinge van die Tweede Sessie van die Tweede Wetgewende Raad,* Vol. I, 14 May–6 June 1974, Ongwediva, 1974, p. 266.

53. Ibid., p. 276.

54. Ibid., p. 284.

55. This letter was written in June 1971. Typed copy in author's possession.

56. According to a report of a meeting of parents and teachers on 4 September 1971 at Old Ongwediva. Copy of report in author's possession.

57. Typed copy in author's possession.

58. *The Argus,* 16 August 1973; *AZ,* 10 Aug. 1973. Apart from protest marches the official opening of the Ongwediva Training Centre on 5 August 1971 by the South African Minister M. C. Botha, was also boycotted by nearly 90% of its pupils and students.

59. Report by the UN Secretary-General to the Security Council, S/10832, 15 Nov. 1972, p. 13.

60. *WA,* 22 May 1973. Nearly 800 pupils and their teachers took part in a protest meeting to demonstrate against the trial of four political leaders, including J. Nangutuuala and J. Otto, in May 1973 at Ondangwa.

61. *WA,* 23 May 1973 and 13 Aug. 1973; CT, 8 Aug. 1973.

62. Ovambo Wetgewende Raad, Verrigtinge van die Tweede Sessie van die Tweede Wetgewende Raad, Vol. I, p. 311; Vol. II, p. 529.

63. Radio Ovamboland was inaugurated in 1969, and broadcasts daily on FM in both official Ovambo languages. The programmes are relayed to Windhoek, Walvis Bay and Tsumeb, where large numbers of Ovambos live. Radio Ovamboland is controlled by the South African Broadcasting Corporation and compiled and broadcasted by whites and Ovambos.

64. *WA,* 12 Feb. 1975.

65. As stated by Mr. Vorster, Radio Ovamboland, to author on 30 June 1971.

Chapter V—*Political Parties*

1. Hamutenya, H. L., and Geingob, G. H., "African Nationalism in Namibia",

in Potholm, C. P., and Dale, R., *Southern Africa in Perspective*. New York, 1972, p. 89.

2. Giniewski, P., op. cit., p. 154.

3. Jenny, H., *Südwestafrika—Land zwischen den Extremen*. Stuttgart, 1968, p. 285.

4. International Court of Justice, *South West Africa Cases*. The Hague, 1966, Vol. XI, p. 265.

5. Horrell, M., *A Survey of Race Relations, 1967*. SAIRR, Johannesburg, p. 59.

6. Ibid., p. 59.

7. Horrell, M., *A Survey of Race Relations, 1964*. SAIRR, Johannesburg, p. 361.

8. Oelkumenischer Rat der Kirchen, *Namibia, Der Kampf um die Freiheit*, Geneva, 1971, p. 8.

9. For full text see International Commission of Jurists, *Erosion of Law in South Africa. Observer's Report on the State v. Tuhadeleni and Others*. Geneva, 1968, pp. 55–60.

10. Ibid., p. 57.

11. Ibid., p. 58.

12. It appears from his statement that they were merely instruments for obtaining freedom without any obligation to any ideology or country.

13. Originally nineteen of the accused were convicted to life imprisonment, ten to twenty years and five to five years. Three of the last-mentioned were accused solely under the Suppression of Communism Act. Their penalty was suspended except for one month. After a successful appeal the sentences of five of those given life imprisonment was shortened to twenty years. For a detailed discussion of the case of appeal see: South African Law Reports, *Case State versus Tuhadeleni and Others*. Feb. 1969 (1), pp. 153–90. For a commentary see also Dugard, J., "South West Africa and the 'Terrorist Trial' ", *American Journal of International Law*, Vol. 64, January 1970, pp. 19–41.

14. SWAPO, *The Namibian Documentation 1*. Published in East Germany, n.d. (possibly 1970), p. 9. The reference to tribal attachment is made by the author.

15. Ibid., p. 12.

16. Hall, R., and Scott, M., "New Initiatives for the 1970's: Proposals for Action", *South West Africa (Namibia): Proposals for Action*. The Africa Bureau, London, 1970, p. 23. See also *WA*, 7 Dec. 1972.

17. Hamutenya, H. L., and Geingob, G. H., op. cit., p. 92.

18. Ibid., p. 93.

19. *The Argus*, 5 May 1973.

20. *WA*, 6 Jan. 1975.

21. *WA*, 25 July 1973.

22. *WA*, 13 Aug. 1973.

23. *WA*, 26 Nov. 1973; 25 Feb. 1974.

24. *WA*, 25 July 1973.

25. *WA*, 20 Aug. 1973; *AZ*, 20 Aug. 1973.

26. *WA*, 5 June 1975; *Suidwes-Afrikaner*, 25 July 1975.

27. *The Argus*, 7 Aug. 1973; *WA*, 14 Aug. 1973; 21 Jan. 1974; *CT*, 16 Aug. 1973.

28. *Sake van die Dag*, 6 Aug. 1973. SAUK, Johannesburg.

29. SWAPO of Namibia 1, Discussion Paper on the Constitution of Independent Namibia, Windhoek, September 1975.

30. *WA*, 22 Sept. 1976.

31. *WA*, 12 Apr. 1977.

32. *WA*, 28 Mar. 1977.

33. *WA*, 12 Apr. 1977.

34. *WA*, 17 Sept. 1976.

35. *WA*, 23 Sept. 1976; 7 Oct. 1976.
36. *WA*, 8 Feb. 1977.
37. Ibid.
38. Copied programme of DEMCOP. In private possession, p. 1.
39. Ibid., p. 3.
40. Ibid., p. 4.
41. Ibid., p. 5.
42. Ibid., p. 6.
43. Ibid., p. 8.
44. Ibid., p. 9.
45. Ibid., p. 10.
46. Ibid., p. 10.
47. Ibid., p. 10–11.
48. Ibid., p. 11.
49. Ibid., p. 12.
50. *WA*, 7 July 1972.
51. Personal statement to author, June 1972.
52. *S-A*, 7 July 1972.
53. *WA*, 7 July 1972.
54. *S-A*, 7 July 1972.
56. Constitution of Ovamboland Independence Party. Copy in author's possession, p. 1.
57. Ibid., p. 6.
58. Ibid., pp. 7–11.
59. *WA*, 18 July 1973.
60. *WA*, 8 Feb. 1977.
61. *Ekumeniese Informasie*, Windhoek, Vol. 16, nos. 2/3, Dec. 1976/Jan. 1977, p. 1.

BIBLIOGRAPHY

Books

Afrikaanse Handelsinstituut, *This is South West Africa*. ABC Press, Cape Town, 1974.

Andersson, C. J., *Lake Ngami, or Explorations and Discoveries in the Wilds of South Western Africa*. Hurst and Blackett, London, 1856.

——, *Notes of Travel in South Africa*. Hurst and Blackett, London, 1875.

Andrew, V., *Ovamboland*. S.P.G., London, 1953.

Angebauer, K., *Ovambo*. A. Scherl, Berlin, 1927.

Auala, J. (ed.), *The Ovambo-Kavango Church*. Suomen Lähetyssenra, Helsinki, 1970.

Ballinger, R. B., *South West Africa—The Case against the Union*. South African Institute of Race relations (SAIRR), Johannesburg, 1961.

Baumann, J., *Van Sending tot Kerk; 125 jaar Rynse Sendingarbeid in Suidwes-Afrika*. Evangeliese Lutherse Kerk in S.W.A., Karibib, 1967.

Bley, H., *South West Africa under German Rule, 1894–1914*. Heinemann, London, 1971.

Brincker, P. H., *Unsere Ovambo-Mission sowie Land, Leute, Religion, Sitten. Gebräuche, Sprache, u.s.w. der Ovankwanjama-Ovambo*. Rheinische Mission, Barmen, 1900.

Bruwer, J. P. van S., *South West Africa—The Disputed Land*. Nasionale Boekhandel, Cape Town, 1966.

——, "The Kwanyama of South West Africa". Unpublished manuscript, Stellenbosch, 1961.

Calvert, A. F., *South West Africa during the German Occupation, 1884–1914*. Laurie, London, 1916.

Carroll, F., *South West Africa and the United Nations*. University of Kentucky Press, Lexington, 1967.

Dale, R., *Divergent Political Futures for South West Africa (Namibia)—Separate Development and African Nationalism*. Paper, African Studies Association, Denver, 1971.

Dammann, E. and Terronen, T. E., *Ndonga Anthologie*. Dietrich Reimer, Berlin, 1975.

Department of Foreign Affairs, *Ovambo*. Cape and Transvaal Printers, Pretoria, 1971.

——, *South West Africa Survey, 1967*. Cape and Transvaal Printers, Pretoria, 1967.

——, *South West Africa Survey, 1974*. Govt. Printer, Pretoria, 1975.

Department of Information, *Ovamboland*. Government Printer, Pretoria, 1967.

——, *Ethiopia and Liberia versus South Africa*. Dagbreek, Johannesburg, 1966 (2nd ed.).

——, *South West Africa: the Land, its peoples and their future*. Pretoria, 1964.

Departement van Bantoe-Administrasie en -Ontwikkeling, *Staatkundige en*

236

ekonomiese ontwikkeling van die tuislande in Suidwes-Afrika (Conference at Rundu, 22–23 October 1970).

Departement van Inligting, *Gesondheid en Genesing. Hospitaal-en mediese dienste vir die ontwikkelende volke van Suid-Afrika.* Pretoria, 1969.

Drascher, W., *Ein Leben für Südwestafrika: Festschrift Dr. H. C. Vedder.* S.W.A. Wissenschaftliche Gesellschaft, Windhoek, 1961.

Dugard, J., *South West Africa/Namibia: Review of the International Dispute.* SAIRR, Johannesburg, 1973.

———, (ed.), *The South West Africa/Namibia Dispute: Documents and Scholarly Writings on the Controversy Between South Africa and the United Nations.* University of California Press, Berkeley, 1973.

Dugard, J., and Grosskopf, E. M., *South West Africa and the International Court: Two viewpoints on the 1971 Advisory Opinion.* South African Institute of International Affairs (SAIIA), Johannesburg, 1974.

Dundas, Sir Ch. C. F., *South West Africa: The Factual Background.* SAIIA, Johannesburg, 1946.

Eiselen, W., *Stamskole in Suid-Afrika.* Van Schaik, Pretoria, 1929.

Ellertson, C. F., *The Lutheran Almanac 1973.* Lutheran Publishing House, Durban, 1973.

Estermann, C., *Etnografia do Sudoeste Angola.* Vol. I: *Os povos nao.-Bantos e o grupo etnico dos Ambós.* Lisbon, 1956.

Fehr, E., *Namibia. Befreiungskampf in Südwestafrika,* Imba, Freiburg, 1973.

Finse Sending (Finnish Mission), *Die Finse Sendinggenootskap en die Evangelies Lutherse Ovambokavango Kerk.* Oniipa, 1958.

Finse Sendinggenootskap en die Evangelies Lutherse Ovambokavango-kerk, *'n Eeu van Genade, 1859–1959.* Kerkdrukkery Oniipa, Ovambo, 1959.

Finnish Missionary Society, *Sixty Years of Finnish Medical Mission.* Church Printing Works, Oniipa, Ovamboland, 1968.

First, R., *South West Africa.* Penguin, Harmondsworth, 1963.

Galton, F., *Narrative of an Explorer in Tropical South Africa.* Ward, Lock & Co., London, 1889.

Gey van Pittius, E. F. W., *Plaaslike en Sentrale Bestuur in Suid-Afrika in teorie en praktyk.* De Bussy, Pretoria, 1937.

Giniewski, P., *Die Stryd om Suidwes-Afrika.* Nasionale Boekhandel, Johannesburg, 1960.

Goldblatt, I., *History of South West Africa.* Juta, Cape Town, 1971.

———, *The Conflict between the United Nations and the Union of South Africa in regard to South West Africa.* Published by the Author, Windhoek, 1960.

———, *The Mandated territory of South West Africa in relation to the United Nations.* Struik, Cape Town, 1961.

Green, L. G., *Lords of the Last Frontier, The Story of South West Africa and its people of all Races.* Timmins, Cape Town, 1952.

Hahn, C. H. L., *The Native Tribes of South West Africa.* Cass, London, 1928.

Hailey, Lord, *An African Survey,* Oxford University Press, London, 1957.

Halbach, A. J., *Die Wirtschaft Südwestafrikas.* IFO-Institut, München, 1967.

Himmelreich, F., *Ovamboland.* Heft 1: *Land, Leute, Heidentum der Ovambo.* Heft 2: *Geschichte der Mission unter den Ovambo.* Rheinische Mission, Barmen, 1900.

Hintrager, O., *Südwestafrika in der deutschen Zeit.* Oldenbourg, München, 1955.

Horrell, M. (ed.), *A Survey of Race Relations in South Africa.* Vol. V–XXVIII, SAIRR, Jonahnnesburg, 1950–1974.

Horrell, M., *South West Africa.* SAIRR, Johannesburg, 1967.

Idenburg, P. J., *Zuid-West Afrika als Internationaal Staatkundig Probleem.* Afrika-Instituut, Leiden, 1950.

Imishue, R. W., *South West Africa—an International Problem*. Institute of Race Relations, London, 1965.

International Court of Justice, *International Status of South West Africa: Advisory Opinion of July 11th 1950*. The Hague, 1950.

——, *South West Africa Case (Ethiopia vs. the Union of South Africa). Memorial submitted by the Government of Ethiopia*. The Hague, 1961.

——, *South West Africa Cases; Counter Memorial filed by the Government of the Republic of South Africa*. Vol. III. The Hague, 1963.

——, *South West Africa Cases (Ethiopia and Liberia versus the Republic of South Africa). Reply of the Government of Ethiopia and Liberia*. The Hague, 1964.

——, *Pleadings, Oral Arguments, Documents: South West Africa Cases (Ethiopia and Liberia versus the Republic of South Africa)*. Vol. I–XI. The Hague, 1971.

——, *Namibia (South West Africa). Written Statement of South Africa (I)*. The Hague, 1971.

——, *Legal Consequences for States of the Continued Presence of South Africa in Namibia (South West Africa) notwithstanding Security Council Resolutions 276 (1970)*. Vol. I. The Hague, 1971.

Jenny, H., *Südwestafrika—Land zwischen den Extremen*. Kohlhammer, Stuttgart, 3. Auflage, 1968.

Kane-Berman, J., *Contract Labour in South West Africa*. SAIRR, Johannesburg, 1972.

Kapuuo, C., *The Internal Situation in South West Africa*. Paper. SAIRR, Johannesburg, 1973.

Lawrie, G., *New Light on South West Africa: some extracts from and comments on the Odendaal report*. Witwatersrand University Press, Johannesburg, 1964.

Lebzelter, V., *Eingeborenenkulturen in Südwest und Süd-Afrika: wissenschaftliche Ergebnisse einer Forschungsreise nach Süd- und Südwest-Afrika in den Jahren 1926–1928*. Hiersemann, Leipzig, 1934.

Lee, F. J. T., *Südafrika vor der Revolution?* Fischer, Frankfurt, 1973.

Lejeune, A., *The Case for South West Africa*. Tom Stacey, London, 1971.

Loth, H., *Die Christliche Mission in Südwestafrika. Zur destruktiven Rolle der Rheinischen Missionsgesellschaft beim Prozess der Staatenbildung in Südwestafrika, 1842–1893*. Akademie-Verlag, Berlin (DDR), 1963.

Lowenstein, A. K., *Brutal Mandate: a Journey to South West Africa*. Macmillan, New York, 1962.

Mittlebeeler, E. V., *South Africa and South West Africa—Process of Integration*. Paper. African Studies Association, Denver, 1971.

Molnar, T., *South West Africa: The last Pioneer Country*. Fleet Publishing Co., New York, 1966.

Moritz, E., *Die ältesten Reiseberichte über Deutsch-Südwestafrika*. Mittler, Berlin, 1915.

Ökumenischer Rat der Kirchen, *Namibia—der Kampf um Freiheit*. Geneva, 1971.

O'Linn, B., *The Internal Situation in South West Africa*. Paper. SAIIR, Johannesburg, 1973.

——, *Die Toekoms van Suidwes-Afrika gebou op die Werklikheid*. Verenigde Pers, Windhoek, 1974.

Ovamboland Girl Guides, *Girl Guiding in Ovamboland. The First Five Years*. Church Press, Oniipa, Ovamboland, 1971.

Pendleton, W. C., "The Economic Differentiation of the Windhoek Population." Seminar of the Abe Bailey Institute of Interracial Studies, Cape Town, 11 May 1972.

——, *Katutura: A Place where we do not Stay*. San Diego State University Press, 1974.

Potholm, C. P., and Dale, R., *Southern Africa in Perspective*. Macmillan, New York, 1972.

Raunard, A. V., *The Alternative*. Raunard, Windhoek, 1975.

Redinke, R., *Distribuicao Etnica da Provincia de Angola*. Lisbon, 1960.

Rhoodie, E., *South West Africa—The Last Frontier in Africa*. Voortrekkerpers, Pretoria, 1967.

Roman Catholic Mission, *Zwischen Namib und Kalahari*. Döbra, Windhoek, 1971.

St. Mary's Mission, *Ovamboland: Report, covering Evangelization, Education and Medical Department*. Odibo, no date.

Schinz, H. *Deutsch-Südwest-Afrika*. *Forschungsreisen durch die deutschen Schutzgebiete Gross-Nama- und Hereroland nach dem Kunene, dem Ngami-See und der Kalahari 1884–1887*. Schulze, Oldenburg, 1891.

Schlosser, K., *Eingeborenenkirchen in Süd- und Südwest Afrika—Ihre Geschichte und Sozialstruktur*. Mühlau, Kiel, 1958.

Schwabe, K., *Im deutschen Diamantenlande*. *Deutsch Südwestafrika*. Mittler, Berlin, 1910.

Segal, R., and First, R. (*ed.*), *South West Africa: Travesty of Trust*. Steering Committee of the International Conference on Economic Sanctions against South Africa, London, 1967.

Slonim, S., *South West Africa and the United Nations: an International Mandate in Dispute*. John Hopkins Press, Baltimore, 1973.

South African Society, *Collective Selfhoods—an element in the South West African Case*. London, 1965.

SAIIA, *Questions affecting South Africa at the United Nations. Resolutions of the Security Council and General Assembly (25th Session)*. Johannesburg, 1970.

SWAPO, *The Namibian Documentation, 1*. Printed in German Democratic Republic, no date.

Südwestafrika Wissenschaftliche Gesellschaft, *Die Ethnischen Gruppen in Südwestafrika*. 3. Folge. Windhoek, 1965.

Stow, G. W., *The Native Races of South Africa*. Swan Sonnenschein, London, 1965.

Sundermeier, T., *Wir aber suchten Gemeinschaft, Kirchwerdung und Kirchentrennung in Südwestafrika*. Luther Verlag, Witten, 1973.

Sundkler, B. G. M., *Bantu Prophets in South Africa* (2nd ed.), Oxford University Press, London, 1961.

Tuupainen, M., *Marriage in a Matrilineal African Tribe: a Social Anthropological Study of Marriage in die Ondonga Tribe in Ovamboland*. Helsinki, 1970.

Tönjes, H., *Ovamboland, Land, Leute, Mission: mit besonderer Berücksichtigung seines grössten Stammes Oukuanyama*. Reimer, Berlin, 1911.

Troup, F. *In Face of Fear: Michael Scott's challenge to South Africa*. Faber, London, 1950.

Tyrrell, B. *Tribal Peoples of Southern Africa*. Books of Africa, Cape Town, 1968.

United Nations, *A Trust Betrayed: Namibia*. UNO. New York, 1974.

——, *Report by the Secretary-General on the Implementation of Security Council Resolution 319 (1972) concerning the question of Namibia*. S/10832. New York, 15/11/1972.

Van Warmelo, N. J., "Memo oor Ovamboland". Unpublished, Pretoria, 1956.

Vedder, H., *Das alte Südwestafrika*. Warneck, Berlin, 1934.

Voipio, R., *Kontrak—Soos die Ovambo dit sien*, Evangeliese Lutherse Ovambokavango-Kerk, Karibib, 1972.

Weidner, C., *In re South West Africa 1914–1938*. Published by the Author, Goodhouse, 1939.

Wellington, J. H., *South West Africa and its Human Issues*. Clarendon Press, Oxford, 1967.

Wessels, L. H., *Die Mandaat vir Suidwes-Afrika*. Nijhoff, The Hague, 1937.

Westermann, D., *Geschichte Afrikas: Staatenbildung südlich der Sahara.* Greven, Köln, 1952.

Wiechers, M., *South West Africa/Namibia: Review of the International Dispute.* Paper. SAIRR, Johannesburg, 1973.

Wolfe, E. M., *Beyond the Thirst Belt: the Study of the Ovamboland Missions.* London, 1935.

Wulfhorst, A., *Aus den Anfangstagen der Ovambomission.* Rheinische Missions verlag, Barmen, 1904.

——, *Von Hexen und Zauberern: Bilder aus dem Leben der heidnischen Amboleute in Südwestafrika.* Rheinische Missionsverlag, Wuppertal-Barmen, 1935.

Articles

Abel, H., "Völkerkundlich-kulturgeographische Beobachtungen in Südwestafrika und Angola." *Übersee-Museum,* Vol. I, no. 3, 1959, pp. 165–87.

Ardon-Clarke, C., "South West Africa, the Union and the United Nations." *African Affairs,* Vol. 59, 1960, pp. 26–35.

Ballinger, R. B., "South West Africa after the judgement." *Optima,* Vol. 14, 1964, pp. 142–54.

Basson, J. D. du P., "Homelands—historical and mythical." *Forum,* March 1964, pp. 10–13.

Beichmann, A., "The South West Time Bomb." *Spectator,* 19 Nov. 1965, pp. 653–4.

Brincker, P. H., "Die Eingeborenen Deutsch-Südwestafrikas nach Geschichte, Charakter, Sitten, Gebräuchen und Sprachen." *Mitteilungen des Seminars für Orientalische Sprachen,* Band 11, 1899. *Die Ovambo,* pp. 135–9.

——, "Zur Sprachen- und Völkerkunde der Bantuneger und verwandter Stämme Südwestafrikas." *Internationale Zeitschrift für allgemeine Sprachwissenschaft,* Band 5, no. 1, pp. 19–46.

——, "Character, Sitten und Gebräuche speciell der Bantu Deutsch-Südwestafrikas." *Mitteilungen des Seminars für Orientalische Sprachen,* Band III, 1900, pp. 66–92.

Bruwer, J. P. van S., "Ovamboland vandag." *Die Huisgenoot,* No. 42, 30 Aug. 1963, p. 56.

——, "Groot volk by 'n kruispad." *Die Huisgenoot,* No. 43, 6 Sept. 1963, pp. 52–5.

——, "Suidwes-Afrika sedert Maharero." *Journal of the South West Africa Scientific Society,* Vol. XVI. 1961/2, pp. 73–9.

Calvocoressi, P., "South West Africa." *African Affairs,* Vol. 65, 1966, pp. 223–44.

Crosby, O. T., "Notes on Bushmen and Ovambo in South West Africa." *Journal of the African Society,* Oct. 1931, pp. 344–60.

Dale, R., "Ovamboland: Bantustans without tears?" *Africa Report,* Feb. 1969, p. 16.

——, "The Political Futures of South West Africa and Namibia." *World Affairs,* Vol. 134, no. 4, 1972, pp. 325–43.

——, "The Road from the United Nations: The Struggle over South West Africa." *The New Leader,* 16 Oct. 1972, pp. 10–12.

D'Amato, A., "The Bantustan Proposals for South West Africa". *Journal of Modern African Studies.* No. 4, 1966, pp. 177–92.

De Beer, D., "The Ovambo Strike." *South African Outlook,* Feb. 1972, pp. 25–7.

De Villiers, D. P., "Huidige tendensies in die beleid van Afsonderlike Ontwikkeling in die lig van die Suidwes-Afrika-saak voor die Internasionale Hof." *Instituut van Administrateurs van Nie-blanke Aangeleenthede (Suidelike Africa),* Vol. 15, 1967, pp. 85–107.

Dugard, C. J. R., "South West Africa and the supremacy of the South African parliament." *South African Law Journal.* March 1969, pp. 194–204.

——, "South West Africa and the terrorist trial." *American Journal of International Law,* Jan. 1970, pp. 19–41.

——, "South West Africa returns to the International Court." *New Nation,* Feb. 1971, pp. 6–7.

——, "The Opinion on South West Africa (Namibia): The teleologist triumph." *South African Law Journal.* Nov. 1971, pp. 460–77.

——, "The South West Africa Case. Second Phase, 1966." *South African Law Journal.* Nov., pp. 429–60.

Duncan, P., "South West Africa: timetable for freedom." *The Nation,* 16 March 1964, pp. 265–7.

Dymond, G. W., "The Idea of God in Ovamboland." In: Smith, E. W. (ed.): *African Ideas of God.* Edinburgh House Press, London, 1966, pp. 135–55.

Eggers, H., "Das Ovamboland in Südwestafrika." *Geographische Rundschau,* 18. Jahrgang, no. 12, 1966, pp. 459–68.

Enahoro, P., "Namibia: Issues at Stake." *Africa,* April 1972, pp. 21–5.

Engers, J. F., "United Nations travel and identity document for Namibians." *American Journal of International Law,* July 1971, pp. 571–8.

Estermann, C., "Ethnographische Beobachtungen über die Ovambo." *Zeitschrift für Ethnologie,* Vol. 63, 1931, pp. 40–5.

Falk, R. A., "Observer's Report on The State versus Tuhadeleni and others." International Commission of Jurists: *Erosion of the Rule of Law.* Geneva, 1968, pp. 40–54.

Financial Mail, "Learning to live with Ovambo." 24 Dec. 1971, p. 1093.

Financial Mail, "Desert Deadlock. South West Africa." (Special Survey), 2 March 1973, pp. 1–68.

First, R., "Namibia—Africa's Move." *Africa,* Jan. 1973, pp. 17–18.

Frey, K., "Odendaalplan und die Südwester Eingeborenen." *Afrika Post,* April 1965, pp. 47–9.

Galloway, A., "A Contribution to the physical Anthropology of the Ovambo." *South African Journal of Science,* Nov. 1937, pp. 351–64.

Gibbs, H., "South West Africa". *New Statesman,* 5 Aug. 1950, pp. 148–9.

Hahn, C. H. L., "Preliminary Notes on certain customs of the Ovambo." *Journal of the South West Africa Scientific Society,* Vol. III, 1927/28, pp. 5–33.

Hailey, Lord, "South West Africa." *African Affairs.* April 1947, pp. 77–86.

Hall, R., and Scott, M., "New Initiatives for the 1970's: Proposals for Action" in *South West Africa (Namibia): Proposals for Action.* The Africa Bureau, London, 1970, pp. 27–45.

Hayes, S., "The Ovambo Strike." *Pro Veritate.* 15 Feb. 1972, pp. 12–14, 17.

Heese, N., "Ongwediva: 'n jong volk help homself op." *Die Huisgenoot.* 10 Sept. 1971, pp. 78–81.

Hesselberger, K., "Mandatsgebiet Südwestafrika und die Vereinten Nationen." *Afrika Post.* März 1971, pp. 139–45.

Holder, William E., "1971 Advisory Opinion of the International Court of Justice on Namibia (South West Africa)." *Federal Law Review,* Vol. 5, 1972, pp. 115–24.

Hynning, C. J., Gross, E. A., and Eksteen, J. A., "Future of South Africa: A Plebiscite?" *American Journal of International Law,* September 1971, pp. 144–68.

Ihamäki, K., "Finland in Ovamboland." *Suidwes-Afrika Jaarboek,* Windhoek, 1970, pp. 163–7.

International Commission of Jurists, "Apartheid in South West Africa." *International Commission of Jurists Bulletin.* June 1967, pp. 26–37.

Jones, J. D. R., "Administration of South West Africa: welfare of the indigenous population." *Race Relation Journal*, No. 19, 1952, pp. 3–21.

Joubert, P. A., "Suidwes: speelbal van groot politiek." *Die Huisgenoot*, 21 April, 1967, pp. 16–19, 23.

Kahn, E. J., Jr., "Reporter at large: Apartheid." *Newsweek. 3 Feb. 1968, pp. 32–8.*

Köhler, O., "The Stages of Acculturation in South West Africa." *Sociologus.* Vol. VI, no. 2, 1956, pp. 138–53.

Koll, A., "Mangel an eingeborenen Arbeitskräften in Südwestafrika." *Afrika Post.* Vol. 1, no. 6, 1954, pp. 10–11.

Komati, T. N., "Solitary Confinement." *South African Outlook*, January 1975, pp. 6–7.

Kozonguizi, J., "South West Africa." *Africa South*, Oct./Dec. 1957, pp. 64–72.

Krafft, M., "Aus dem deutsch-südwestafrikanischen Schutzgebiete. Die Rechtsverhältnisse der Ovakuanjama und der Ovandonga." *Mitteilungen aus den deutschen Schutzgebieten.* Band 27, Heft 1, 1914, pp. 17–35.

Landis, E. S., "Namibia: The Beginning of Disengagement." *Studies in Race and Nations*, Vol. 2, no. 1, 1970/71, pp. 17–34.

——, "American Responsibilities toward Namibia: Law and Policy." *Africa Today*, October 1971, pp. 38–49.

Lebzelter, V., "Die religiösen Vorstellungen der Khun-Buschmänner, der Buschmänner der Etoschapfanne und des Ovambolands und der Ovambo-Bantu." *Festschrift P. W. Schmidt.* Anthropologischer Verlag, Wien, 1928, pp. 407–15.

Lehmann, F. R., "Die Anthropogeographischen Verhältnisse des Ambolandes im nördlichen Südwestafrika. Grundsätzliche Erwägung zur anthropogeographischen Grundlegung völkerkundlicher Untersuchungen." *Zeitschrift für Ethnologie.* Band 79, Heft 1, 1954, pp. 8–58.

Lehmann, R., "Die politische und soziale Stellung der Häuptlinge im Ovamboland." *Tribus.* Vol. 4/5, 1956, pp. 265–328.

Lissitzyn, O. J., "International Law and the Advisory Opinion on Namibia." *Columbia Journal of Transnational Law*, Vol. II, 1972, pp. 50–73.

Loeb, E. M., "The Kuanyama Ambo." *Scientific American*, Vol. 183, no. 4, 1950, pp. 52–5.

——, "Transition Rites of the Kuanyama Ambo" (Parts I and II). *African Studies*, June/Sept. 1948, pp. 16–28, 71–83.

Logan, R. F., "South West Africa". *Collier's Encyclopedia*, Vol. 21, p. 340.

Lyon, A., "The trial at Windhoek". *South African Outlook*, Feb. 1972. pp. 28–9.

Manning, C. A. W., "Political Justice at the Hague." *Cambrian Law Review*, 1972, p. 64.

Mason, Philip, "Separate Development and South West Africa: Some aspects of the Odendaal Report." *Race*, April 1964, pp. 83–97.

Penti, E. J., "Die bykomstige resultate van die Finse Sendingwerk in Ovamboland." *Afgerolde Lesing*, Engela, Ovamboland, 1959.

Phillips, H. A., "South West Africa, stepchild of the United Nations." *Travel*, September 1948, pp. 9–13.

Pincus, D., "South West Africa needs an answer from within." *New Commonwealth.* March 1961, pp. 151–4.

Rautanen, M., "Die Ondonga", in Steinmetz, S. R., *Rechtsverhältnisse von Eingeborenenvölkern in Afrika und Ozeanien.* Julius Springer, Berlin, 1903.

Roger, L., "The South West African Origins of the 'Sacred Trust', 1914–1919." *African Affairs.* Vol. 66, 1967, pp. 20–39.

Rogers, B. L., "Freedom demand is spreading." *Africa Report*, Feb. 1972, pp. 30–2.

Rovine, A. W., "The World Court Opinion on Namibia." *Columbia Journal of Transitional Law*, Vol. 11, 1972, p. 203.

Schneider, A. R. H., "Die Südwestafrikafrage 1971 wieder vor dem Internationalen Gerichtshof in Den Haag." *Afrika Post.* April 1971, pp. 91–5.

Schwelb, E., "International Court of Justice and the human rights clauses of the Charter." *American Journal of International Law.* April 1972, pp. 337–51.

Scott, M., "South West Africa and the Union: how the Natives voted for the Union." *British Africa Monthly,* August 1948, pp. 13–15.

Slonim, S., "The Origins of the South West Africa Dispute: The Versailles Peace Conference and the Creation of the Mandates System." *The Canadian Yearbook of International Law.* Vol. 6, 1968, p. 142.

South African Law Reports, "Case: State versus Tuhadeleni and others." (Transvaal Provincial Division) *South African Law Reports.* Part IV, 1967. pp. 511–20.

——, "Case: State versus Tuhadeleni and others" (Appellate Division of the Supreme Court of South Africa). *South African Law Reports.* Part I, 1969, 153–90.

South African Outlook, "Finnish Mission, Ovamboland Appeal Fund." Aug. 1940, p. 143.

Stone, J., "Reflections on Apartheid after the South West Africa Cases." *Washington Law Review.* Vol. 42, no. 1065, 1967, pp. 1069–82.

Strassberger, E., "Women in Church Service (3)". *Pro Veritate.* Vol. X, no. 12, 1972, pp. 6–8.

Strating, A., "Indrukke van Ovamboland". *Geneeskunde.* December 1963, pp. 330–6.

The Economist "Plan for Namibia?" 18 March 1972, p. 38.

Tötemeyer, G. K. H., "Ovamboland im Übergang." *Heimatkalender,* Windhoek, 1971, pp. 123–55.

Umozurike, K. O., "International Law and self determination in Namibia." *Journal of Modern African Studies.* December 1970, pp. 585–603.

United Nations—Council for Namibia, "Miners attempt to liberate themselves from South African Control." In: *UNO Monthly Chronicle.* Vol. 9, April 1972, pp. 33–5.

——, "Statement by the president on the labour strike." *UNO Monthly Chronicle.* February 1972, pp. 21–2.

——, "Statement by Bishop C. O. Winter to the U.N. Council of Namibia." *UNO Monthly Chronicle,* April 1972, p. 35.

United Nations, "Petitioners' Views on conditions in South West Africa." *United Nations Review.* December 1957, pp. 54–5.

Uys, S., "Ovambos' 'no'" *New Statesman,* 4 February 1972, pp. 138–90.

Van der Westhuizen, W. M., "Bevoegdheid van die Verenigde Volke om die mandaat van Suidwes–Afrika to beëindig." *Tydskrif vir Hedendaagse Romeins–Hollandse Reg.* November 1968. pp. 330–45.

Van Wyk, J. T., "The Request for an advisory opinion on South West Africa." *Acta Juridica,* 1970. pp. 219–29.

——, "The International Court at the Cross Roads." *Acta Juridica.* 1967. pp. 201–13.

——, "United Nations, South West Africa and the law." *Comparative International Law Journal of South Africa.* March 1969, pp. 48–72.

Von Lucius, R., "Die verfassungs- und völkerrechtliche Entwicklung Süd-westafrikas." *Journal XXIX SWA Wissenschaftliche Gesellschaft,* Windhoek, 1974/5, pp. 78–93.

Warneck, J., "Studien zur Religion der Ovambo." In: *Allgemeine Missions Zeitschrift.* Vol. 37, 1910, pp. 313–30.

Wellington, J. H., "South West Africa: The facts about the disputed territory." *Optima.* Vol 15, No. 1, March 1965, pp. 40–54.

Wiechers, M., "Suidwes-Afrika-saak: enkele aspekte van die uitspraak van die Internasionale Geregshof van 18 Julie 1966." *Tydstrif vir Hedendaagse Romeins-Hollandse Res.* November 1966, pp. 297–319.

——, "South West Africa and the International Court of Justice." *Codicillus.* October 1971, pp. 46–50.

——, "South West Africa: The Background, Content and Significance of the Opinion of the World Court of 21 June." *Comparative and International Law Journal of Southern Africa.* Vol. 5, 1972, pp. 123–70.

Winter, C., " 'Justice and S.W.A.' Cracks in the Granite Wall ...? ... a consideration of Church/State relations in South West Africa." *Pro Veritate.* 15 December 1971, pp. 10–12.

Unpublished Dissertations

Banghart, P. D., "Migrant Labour in South West Africa and its effects on Ovambo Tribal Life" (M.A.) Stellenbosch, 1969.

Barnard, W. S., "Staatkundig-geografiese aspekte van Suidwes-Afrika" (M.A.) Stellenbosch, 1959.

Barnard, W. S., "Die Streekpatrone van Suidwes-Afrika" (Ph.D.) Stellenbosch, 1964.

Dale, R., "The Evolution of the South West African Dispute before the United Nations, 1945–1950." (Ph.D.) Princeton, 1962.

De Vries, "Sending en Kolonialisme in Suidwes-Afrika." (Ph.D) Brussels, 1971.

Jooste, G. P., "Die Administrasie van die Mandaat vir Suidwes-Afrika." (M.A.) Pretoria, 1942.

Kotzé, D. A., "Duits–Inboorlingsverhoudinge in Suidwes-Africa, 1880–1914." (Ph.D.) Pretoria, 1969.

Kotzé, J. C., "Die Kuanyama van Ovamboland—'n studie van waardeopvattinge." (M.A.) Stellenbosch, 1968.

Kritzinger, J. J., "Sending en Kerk in Suidwes-Africa." (Ph.D.) Pretoria, 1972.

Liebenberg, P. W., "Die Inlywing van Suidwes-Afrika by die Unie van Suid-Afrika. 'n Ontleding van die Geskil met die Vernigde Nasies tydens die 1946–sitting." (M.A.) Pretoria, 1970.

Louw, W., "Die sosio-politieke stelsel van die Ngandjera van Ovamboland." (M.A.) Port Elizabeth, 1967.

Nitsche, G. J. K., "Ovamboland: Versuch einer landschaftlichen Darstellung nach dem gegenwärtigen Stand unserer geographischen Kenntnis." (Dr.Phil.) Kiel, 1913.

Olivier, M. J., "Inboorling beleid en -administrasie in die Mandaat gebied van Suidwes–Afrika." (Ph.D.) Stellenbosch, 1961.

Pretorius, J. W. C., "Die Staatkundige Ontwikkeling van Suidwes-Afrika." (M.A.) University of the Orange Free State, 1959.

Stals, E., "Die Aanraking tussen Blankes en Ovambos in Suidwes-Afrika, 1830–1915." (Ph.D.) Stellenbosch, 1967.

Taylor, P. R., "The Union Governments' Treatment of the South West Africa Mandat, 1920–1944." (M.A.) Cape Town, 1944.

Van der Merwe, P. S., "Die Ontwikkeling van Selfbestuur in Suidwes-Afrika, 1919–1960." (M.A.) University of South Africa, 1963.

Van Rensburg, H. M. J., "Die Internasionale Status van Suidwes-Africa." (Ph.D.) Leiden, 1953.

Van Tonder, L. L., "Leadership, Power and Status Stratification with Reference to Bushmen, Hottentot, and Ovambo society." (M.A.) Stellenbosch, 1963.

Government Publications

Cape of Good Hope, "Report of W. Coates Palgrave, Esq., Special Commissioner to the tribes North of the Orange River, of his Mission to Damaraland and Great Namaqualand in 1876." Ministerial Department of Native Affairs. Cape Town, 1877. G.50.

Ovamboland–Wetgewende Raad, "Begroting van die Uitgawes wat uit die Inkomstefonds gedurende die boekjaar wat op 31 Maart 1970 cindig bestry moet word." Oshakati, 1969.

Ovambo Legislative Council, " Proceedings of the Special Session of the Second Ovambo Legislative Council, 8 October 1974." Ongwediva 1974.

Ovambo–Wetgewende Raad, "Begroting van die Uitgawes wat uit die Inkomstefonds gedurende die boekjaar wat op 31 Maart 1971 cindig bestry moet word." Oshakati, 1970.

——, "Notule van die Gekose Komitee oor Grondbesit en -benutting." Oshakati, 4.12.1970.

——, "Opsommings en aanbevelings van die Gekose Komitee insake ondersoek na die pligte, bevoegdhede, voorregte, en diensvoorwaardes vir hoofmanne en onder-hoofmanne." Oshakati, 1971.

——, "Begroting van die Uitgawes wat uit die Inkomstefonds gedurende die boekjaar wat op 31 Maart 1971 eindig bestry moet word." Oshakati, 1971.

——, "Begroting van die Uitgawes wat uit die Inkomstefonds gedurende die boekjaar wat op 31 Maart 1973 eindig bestry moet word." Ongwediva, 1972.

——, "Verbatimverslag van die Ovambo Westgewende Raad." Vyfde Sessie—Eerste Wetgewende Raad. 28.9.1972–18.4.1972. Ongwediva.

——, "Ovambo Wetgewende Raad. Verbatimverslag van Spesiale Sessies." 14.1.1972 en 28.7.1972. Ongwediva.

——, "Verbatimverslag van die Ovambo Wetgewende Raad." Sesde Sesse—Eerste Wetgewende Raad. 9.4.1973–26.4.1973. Ongwediva.

——, "Verrigtinge van die Buitengewonne Sessie van die Tweede Ovambo Wetgewende Raad." 19.2.1974. Ongwediva.

——, "Verrigtinge van die Tweede Sessie van die Tweede Ovambo Wetgewende Raad." Vols. I and II, 14.5.–25.6.1974, Ongwediva.

——, "Verrigtinge van die Spesiale Sessie van die Tweede Ovambo Wetgewende Raad." 8.10.1974. Ongwediva.

——, "Verrigtinge van die Eerste Sessie van die Derde Ovambo Wetgewende Raad." 25.2.1974–28.2.1974. Ongwediva.

——, "Verrigtinge van die Tweede Sessie van die Derde Ovambo Wetgewende Raad." 13.5.1975–9.6.1975. Ongwediva.

——, "Verrigtinge van die Spesiale Sessie van die Derde Ovambo Wetgewende Raad." 26.8.1975. Ongwediva.

——, "Begroting van die Uitgawes wat uit die Inkomstefonds gedurende die boekjaar wat op 31 Maart 1974 eindig bestry moet word." Ongwediva, 1973.

——, "Jaarverslag van die Department van Ekonomiese Sake vir die kalender jaar 1971." Ondangwa.

——, "Verslag van die Departement van Werke vir die tydperk 1.1.1971–31.1.1971." Ondangwa.

——, "Jaarverslag van die Departement van Onderwys en Kultuur vir 1970." Ondangwa.

——, "Departement van Onderwys en Kultuur. Jaarverslag 1971." Ondangwa.

——, "Departement van Onderwys en Kultuur. Jaarverslag 1972." Ondangwa.

——, "Verslag van die Departement van Owerheidsake en Finansies vir die tydperk 1.1.1971–31.1.1971." Ondangwa.

——, "Verslag van die Departement van Landbou vir die tydperk 1.12.1971." Ondangwa.

——, "Verslag van die Departement van Owerheidsake en Finansies vir die tydperk 1.1.72–31.12.72." Ondangwa.

——, "Konsep-Verslag oor die Opknapping van die afdeling Plaaslike Bestuur (Ovambo Dorpe) Departemente Justisie en Gemeenskapsbou, ten einde doeltreffende beheermaatreëls vir Ovambo-dorpe daar te stel." Ondangwa. 9.2.1972.

Ovambo Regering—Republiek van Suid–Afrika, "Hou van verkiesings van die verkose lede van die Ovambo-Wetgewende Raad.1" Amptelike Kennisgewing no. 1 van 1973. Ovambo Amptelike Koerant, Vol. 1, no. 1, Ondangwa, 4.5.1973.

——, "Hou van verkiesing van verkose lede van die Ovambo-Wetgewende Raad. Nominasie van. kandidate." Algemene Kennisgewing no. 2 van 1973. Ovambo Amptelike Koerant. Vol. I, no. 2. Ondangwa, 15.6.1973.

——, "Aanwysing van lede van Wetgewende Raad." Algemene Kennisgewing no. 3 van 1973. Ovambo Amptelike Koerant. Vol. 1, no. 3, Ondengwa, 31.8.1973.

——, "Amptelike Koerant/Official Gazette." Vol. I–III (1973–75), Ongwadiva.

Republiek van Suid-Afrika, "Verslag van die Kommissie van Ondersock na Aangeleenthede van Suidwes–Afrika, 1962–1963." R.P. No. 12/1964. Staatsdrukker, Pretoria, 1964.

——, "Wet op die Ontwikkeling van Selfbestuur vir Naturellevolke in Suidwes–Afrika, 1968." Staatsdrukkor, Pretoria, 1968.

——, "Verklarénde Memorandum ter verduideliking van die agtergrond en doelstellinge van die Wetsontwerp op die Ontwikkeling van Selfbestuur vir Naturellevolke in Suidwes–Afrika, 1968." W.P. 3/1968. Staatsdrukker, Pretoria, 1968.

——, "Erkenning van Stamowerhede in Ovamboland. Proklamasie op die Ovambolandse Wetgewende Raad. 1968." Proklamasies R 290 en R 291 in Staatskoerant van 2.10.1968, Vol. 40, no. 2177. Staatsdrukker, Pretoria, 1968.

——, "Reglement van Orde vir die Ovambolandse Wetgewende Raad." Proklamasie R 294 in Staatskoerant van 11.10.1968, Vol. 40, no. 2189. Staatsdrukker, Pretoria, 1968.

——, "Ovambolandse Wetgewende Raad: Salarisse en toelaes van lede." Proklamsic R 295 in Staatskoerant van 11.10.1968. Vol. 40, no. 2189. Staatsdrukker Pretoria, 1968.

——, "Ovambolandse Wetgewende Raad: 1. Instelling van Departemente. 2. Finansiële Regulasies vir die Ovambolandse Wetgewende Raad en Stamowerhede in sy gebied." Proklamasie 298 in Staatskoerant van 11.10.1968. Vol. 40, no. 2189. Staatsdrukker, Pretoria, 1968.

——, "Toespraak van Sy Edele M.C. Botha, L.V., Minister van Bantoe-Administrasie en -Ontwikkeling en van Bantoe-Onderwys, tydens die amptelike opening van die Eerste Sessie van die Ovambolandse Wetgewende Raad op Donderdag, 17 Oktober 1968 te Oshakati." Staatsdrukker, Pretoria, 1968.

———, "Verbatimverslag van die Ovambolandse Wetgewende Raad." Eerste Sessie—Eerste Wetgewende Raad. 14.10.1968–17.10.1968. Eerste Druk.

——, "Verbatimverslag van die Ovambolandse Wetgewende Raad." Tweede Sessie—Eerste Wetgewende Raad. 10.2.1969–19.2.1969. Eerste druk.

——, "Ovambolandse Wetgewende Raad. Maatreël 2 van 1969. Maatreël tot Wysiging van die Reglement van Orde vir die Wetgewende Raad." Proklamasie R 3126 in Staatskoerant van 15.8.1969, vol. 50, no. 2504. Staatsdrukker, Pretoria, 1969.

——, "Ovambolandse Wetgewende Raad. Maatreël 4 van 1970. (Wysigingsmaatreëls op die Besoldiging van Raadslede)." Proklamasie R 1931 in Staatskoerant van 6.11.1970, no. 2916, Staatsdrukker, Pretoria, 1970.

——, "Verslag van die Kontroleur en Ouditeur-Generaal oor die Rekenings van die Ovambolandse Uitvoerende Raad en van die Stamowerhede in sy gebied." (i) 1968–70; (ii) 1970–1; (iii) 1971–2. Staatsdrukker, Pretoria.

——, "Verbatimverslag van die Wetgewende Raad." Derde Sessie—Eerste Wetgewende Raad. 16.3.1970–25.3.1970.

——, "Erkenning van Stamowerhede in Ovamboland, Wysiging van Proklamasie R 290 van 1968." Proklamasie R 72 van 1971 in Staatskoerant van 16.4.1971, Vol. 70, no. 3071. Staatsdrukker. Pretoria, 1971.

——, "Ovambolandse Wetgewende Raad. Wysiging van Proklamasie R 291 van 1968." Proklamasie R 73 van 1971 in Staatskoorant van 16.4.1971. Vol. 70, no. 3071. Staatsdrukker. Pretoria, 1971.

——, "Debatte van die Volksraad (Handsard)." Derde Sessie—Vierde Parlement. 28.1.-42. 1972. Weeklikse Uitgawe no. 1. Staatsdrukker. Pretoria, 1972.

——, "Regulasies vir die Administrasie van die Distrik Ovamboland." Proklamasie R 17 in Staatskoerant van 4.2.1972. Vol. 80, no. 3377. Staatsdrukker. Pretoria, 1972.

——, "Regulasies vir die Instelling van Werkverskaffingburo's in die Gebied Suidwes–Afrika." Proklamasie R 83 in Staatskoerant van 30.3.1972, Vol. 81, no. 3442. Staatsdrukker. Pretoria, 1972.

——, "Wysigingswet op die Ontwikkeling van Selfbestuur vir Naturellevolke in Suidwes–Afrika, 1973. Wet no. 20 van 1973." Proklamasie no. 566 in Staatskoerant van 5.4.1973. Vol. 94, no. 3845. Staatsdrukker. Pretoria, 1973.

——, "Ovambo.—Verklaring tot Selfregerende Gebied en Samestelling van Wetgewende Raad." Proklamasie R 104 in Staatskoerant van 27.4.1973. Vol. 94, no. 3876. Staatsdrukker. Pretoria, 1973.

——, "Hou van Verkiesings van die Verkose Lede van die Ovambo—Wetgewende Raad." Proklamasie R 105 in Staatskoerant van 27.4.1973. Vol. 94, no. 3876. Staatsdrukker. Pretoria, 1973.

——, "Ovambo. Ontbinding van die Wetgewende Raad, bepaling van datum vir die aanwysing van die lede van die Wetgewende Raad en bepaling van die datum van 'n algemene verkiesing." Proklamasie No. 117 in Staatskoerant van 4.5.1973, Vol. 95, no. 3878. Staatsdrukker, Pretoria, 1973.

Unie van Suid-Afrika, "Rapport van die Regering van die Unie van Suid-Afrika omtrent Suidwes-Afrika vir die jaar 1927." U.G. 31/1928. Cape Times Bpk., Kaapstad, 1928.

——, "Rapport aangebied deur die Regering van die Unie van Suid-Afrika aan die Raad van die Volkebond omtrent die Administrasie van Suidwes-Afrika vir die jaar 1935." U.G. 25/1936. Staatsdrukker, Pretoria, 1936.

——, "Verslag van die Suidwes-Afrika Kommissie" U.G. 26/1936. Staatsdrukker, Pretoria, 1936.

——, "Dokumente wat betrekking het op die oorweging wat die Algemene Vergadering van die Verenigde Volke geskenk het aan die verklaring deur die Regering van Suid-Afrika betreffende die resultaat van hulle beraadslagings met die bevolkingsgroepe van Suidwes-Afrika in verband met die toekomstige status van die Mandaatsgebied en uitgespreek is, gegee moet word." Staatsdrukker, Pretoria, 1947.

——, "Rapport over het gedrag van het Ovakuanyama-opperhoofd Mandume en over de militaire operaties tegen hem gevoerd in Ovamboland." U.G. 37/1917. Kaapstad, 1917.

Union of South Africa, "Report by the Officer-in-charge of native affairs on his tour to Ovamboland. By S. M. Pritchard." Department of Native Affairs. Government Printer, Pretoria, 1915. UG 38/1915.

——, "Report of the Conduct of the Ovakuanyama Chief Mandume and on the Military Operations conducted against him in Ovamboland." U.G. 37/1917. Government Printer, Pretoria, 1917.

——, "Territory of South West Africa. Report of the Administrator for the year 1921." U.G. 32/1922. Government Printer, Pretoria, 1922.

——, "Report of the Administrator of South West Africa for the year 1922." U.G. 21/1923. Government Printer. Pretoria, 1923.

——, "Report presented by the Government of the Union of South Africa to the Council of the League of Nations concerning the Administration of South West Africa for the year 1931." U.G. 17/1932. Government Printer. Pretoria, 1932.

——, "Report presented by the Government of the Union of South Africa to the Council of the League of Nations concerning the Administration of South West Africa for the year 1937." U.G. 25/1938. Government Printers, Pretoria, 1938.

——, "Report presented by the Government of the Union of South Africa to the Council of the League of Nations concerning the Administration of South West Africa for the year 1938." U.G. 20/1939. Government Printers, Pretoria, 1939.

Bibliographies

Both, E. L., *Books and pamphlets published in German relating to South and South West Africa. 1950–1964.* University of Cape Town, 1969.

De Jager, T., and Klaas, B., *South West Africa—Suidwes-Afrika.* Bibliography no., 7. Staatsbiblioteek Pretoria, 1964.

Loening, L. S. E., *A Bibliography of the Status of South West Africa up to June 30th, 1951.* University of Cape Town, 1961.

Tötemeyer, G. K. H., *South Africa—South West Africa: a Bibliography. 1945–1963.* Arnold-Bergstraaser-Institut, Freiburg, 1963.

Welch, F. J., *South West Africa: a Bibliography.* University of Cape Town, 1967.

Newspapers and Periodicals

NEWSPAPERS
Allgemeine Zeitung ("*AZ*"), Windhoek.
Cape Times, Cape Town.
Die Burger, Cape Town.
Die Suidwes-Afrikaner, Windhoek.
Die Suidwester, Windhoek.
Rapport, Johannesburg.
Sunday Times, Johannesburg.
The Argus, Cape Town.
Windhoek Advertiser ("*WA*"), Windhoek.

PERIODICALS
African Studies, Johannesburg.
Afrika Post, Pretoria.
Deurbraak, Cape Town.
Eume, Oshakati/Ovamboland.
Evangeliese Informasiediens in Suidwes-Afrika, Karibib/Windhoek.
Heimatkalender, Windhoek.
Immanuel, Windhoek.

Journal of the South West African Scientific Society, Windhoek.
Medu Letu, Oshakati/Ovamboland.
Omukwetu, Oniipa/Ovamboland.
Optima, Johannesburg.
PRO (Pro Nat), Cape Town.
Pro Veritate, Johannesburg.
SABRA—Tydskrif vir Rasse-aangeleenthede, Pretoria.
South African Outlook, Mowbray/Cape.
Southern Africa Record, SAIIA, Johannesburg.
South West Africa Yearbook, Windhoek.
To the Point, Johannesburg.

INDEX

Act on "the Development of Self-Government for Native Nations in South West Africa" (1968), 56-7, 102; Amendment Act (1973) No. 20 to the, 87-8
Afrikaans Churches, 26, 30
Afrikaans: language, 20, 88, 177, 184, 206; literature, 183
agriculture, 143-9
Ajamba, 5
Amangundu, 3
Amathila, Ben, 198
Amukwa, F., 86
Amupolo, Rev. G., 86
Andara, 1
Andersson, Charles John, 5, 6, 17, 19
Andjamba, Johannes, 100
Anglican Church, 32, 36, 37, 38, 39, 140, 167, 171, 201
Anglican Mission, 23, 24, 25
Angola, ix, 1, 2, 4, 19, 23, 35, 42, 97, 99-100, 108, 110, 124, 156, 207, 212; Ovambos' military training in, 193; Portuguese coup (1974) in, 127
apartheid legislation, 35, 138, 196, 213
Apostolic Faith Mission, 25
Appolus, Dr. Libertine, 199
Arden-Clarke, Sir C., 3
Ashikoto, Chief Martin, 12
Ashimbanga, Senior-Headman, 63
Ashipala, J., 66
Auala, Bishop L.: appeal for peace, 38; attitude towards Ovambos' exodus, 35; as head of Ovambo-kavango Church, 21, 31, 33, 34, 121, 122; and labour unrest, 167; as member of Legislative Assembly, 86; and Open Letter to Mr. Vorster, 190; and Ovamboland election, 97; SWAPO and, 218; teachers' support to, 180

baasskap policy, 32
Bantu: education system, 172, 177; groups, 3, 5, 8; homelands, 90
Bantu Administration and Development: Department of, 12, 50, 153; 1970 conference at Rundu, 101; Minister of, 54, 88
Bantu Development Corporation, 119
Bantu Investment Corporation (BIC), 119, 126, 151, 152, 153, 159, 177
Basters, 123, 138
BIC, *see* Bantu Investment Corporation
"Black Boers", 201
Black Evangelical Lutheran Churches, 38, 39, 218
Black Power, 35
Black Theology, 35
Bloemfontein, South African Appeal Court in, 14, 15, 38
"Boer Government", 180, 201
Boesmanland, 90
Botha, M. C., 54, 57, 101-2
Botswana, 205, 207
Brandberg West mine, 157
British Broadcasting Corporation, 184
Bruwer, J. P., 3, 5
Bushmen, 7, 123, 138

Calvinist Afrikaners, 29
Canada, 139
Cape Town, 83, 192, 195
Caprivi Strip, 90, 193